Private Domain

Private

PAUL TAYLOR

Domain

ALFRED A. KNOPF   NEW YORK   1987

THIS IS A BORZOI BOOK
PUBLISHED BY ALFRED A. KNOPF, INC.

Copyright © 1987 by Paul Taylor
All rights reserved under International
and Pan-American Copyright Conventions.
Published in the United States by Alfred A. Knopf, Inc., New York,
and simultaneously in Canada by Random House of Canada Limited, Toronto.
Distributed by Random House, Inc., New York.
Photographic Credits are on page 373.

Library of Congress Cataloguing-in-Publication Data

Taylor, Paul, [date]
Private domain.

1. Taylor, Paul   2. Dancers—United
States—Biography.   3. Choreographers—United States—
Biography.   4. Modern dance.   I. Title.
GV1785.T39A3   1987   793.3'2'0924   [B]   86-45366
ISBN 0-394-51683-4

Manufactured in the United States of America
FIRST EDITION

Contents

Private Domain

Beginnings

Full name: Paul Belville Taylor, Jr.; as a tot called Pete after Peter Rabbit (we both liked carrots); called Darlin' when in my mother's lap; in boyhood was Paulie to the Buttses—unofficial foster parents, whom I lived with for a while; was Pedah to a college sweetheart; a sign-language P to deaf-mute friend Babe; Peter Paul's Mounds to several dancers in New York; Pablo to Martha Graham; Geek to Lincoln Kirstein; lately known as Boss or PT to my troupe.

Put chronologically, these names chart a zigzag course that begins in cuteness, climbs to various levels of endearment, takes a dip on reaching geekhood, then reaches solid respectability. Ahem. Am proud to be a plurality—ambivalent and inexplicable maybe, yet definitely a group—a whole band of crisscrossing travelers unto myself. There have been other, less loving names, of course, ones flung hotly when the perpetrators were out of sorts, confused, or envious. But me, I'm adaptable. Trouping builds your endurance; bumpy dance roads lead to thick soles and an unnatural kind of tolerance. It's like turning to the left.

Basic rule of life: Never be seen in the same room with more than three of myselves at the same time.

Vital statistic: insatiable itch to communicate to the world at large.

All told, I'm a very nice people.

Mother's maiden name: Elizabeth Rose Pendleton; first married name, Knox; second, Taylor. I called her Mammy. One of her ancestors, William Rust, came to this country from Suffolk County, England, around 1650, and settled in Westmoreland in the colony of Virginia. Though some of Mother's ancestors had been wealthy landowners, her parents were anything but. Nevertheless, she was brought up to consider herself part of Virginia's elite and was to pass on this tradition when raising her own children, including me, although in my case less Southern gentility seems to have taken than with the others. I have, however, always been fond of magnolias and grits.

When she was eighteen, Mother left the village of Oak Grove, Virginia, to attend a business school in Washington, D.C., at the same time working as a secretary to her uncle Harry Rust, a realtor, and in the kitchen of a hotel dining room run by that uncle's sister. In Washington she was active in women's rights, was a suffragette and one of the first women to vote. She soon married Thomas Knox (Dear Daddy), whom she'd previously met in his hometown, Fredericksburg, and who was now working as a draftsman for the Navy Department. During the five years that they were married they had three children—Sophie, Tom, and Bettie. On New Year's Day, 1919, soon after World War I ended, an influenza epidemic took the life of Dear Daddy. My mother's love for him remained undiminished, if not increasing, throughout the rest of her days.

Left to raise the three children by herself, she found work as a playground supervisor in Georgetown and supplemented her income by renting out two rooms of her home in Clarendon, another suburb of Washington. Even so, the income was barely adequate, and raising the children was difficult. During this time my father and his mother were her roomers.

My father, Paul Belville Taylor, Ph.D., was descended from Huguenots—French Protestants who came to this country from the small island of Ré around 1670 and settled on Staten Island, which was then under Dutch rule. Born in 1891 in Pasadena, California, my father graduated from the University of Southern California, then came to Washington, where he worked toward his doctorate in physics while holding a job with the War Department. The Government then relocated him in Philadelphia, where he stayed for two years and then returned to Washington. At this time,

1928, he and my mother were married. The family, including my father's mother, then moved to Morristown, New Jersey, and then to Edgewood, Pennsylvania, just outside Pittsburgh, where he took a job with Westinghouse.

Two years later, in 1930 during the Great Depression, I was born. Mother was then forty; my father, a year younger. (Between Sophie, my eldest half-sister, and myself there is a difference of sixteen years.) When the Depression drastically reduced my father's income, he left his job and the family returned to Washington, where Mother once again became breadwinner, this time operating a dining room at the Brighton Hotel on California Street, which she took over from her sister, Emily.

Like many others hit by the Depression, the family did not draw together. I wouldn't say that the hard times were to blame, but they certainly didn't help. My father had been unacceptable to his three stepchildren. To them he seemed an overly strict disciplinarian, peculiar and a typical absentminded professor. He insisted on having Mother and her children address him as "Dr. Taylor," which they did, although thinking it a bit odd to be calling a physicist a doctor—not to mention the distancing effect that it had. The children, unable to transfer to him any of the love that they still held for their real father, considered him an intruder. My mother, too, soon regretted the marriage. She found her mother-in-law domineering and difficult to live with; she was exhausted by the restaurant work; and when it became clear that my father had become overly attracted to her elder son, she eased the situation by sending Tom off to a military academy. Sophie was enrolled at William and Mary College, and fifteen-year-old Bettie was kept at home to look after me, the hotel dining room taking most of Mother's time. My father then moved to Ohio and, after the legally required five-year separation, was divorced by Mother.

Other than these things, I had not known very much about my father. I once asked if what I'd heard about his attraction to Tom was true, to which he replied, "Yes, I was fond of Tom"—a reasonable enough reply, I thought, although not quite as enlightening as I'd hoped. He then added hesitantly, "We do only what we can do." Afterwards, thinking it over, I was unable to determine whether by the "we" he had meant himself, both of us, or all males everywhere. It had bothered me that a disruptive gene might have been passed on to me, but later on I read somewhere a scientist's announcement that there is no such thing as one hundred percent male or one hundred percent female, and so I began to view varying degrees of attraction between like genders as being a trait common not only to all humans but to all life forms.

When my parents separated, my father left Washington to go to Ohio, where he worked at Wright-Patterson Air Force Base as a civilian radio engineer and, while there for the next twenty-five years or so, taught classes and made important contributions to the early development of radar. He remarried—again to a widow—and then, after being divorced a second time, arranged for a third widow to be his live-in cook and housekeeper. She already had two sons of her own, whom he sent through college.

When I was three or four, from fragments of overheard conversation, I was able to piece together most of the facts surrounding the absence of my father. Although I was unable to understand the main reason for the divorce, it was clear to me that my mother and her three other children held little affection for him. I had no memories of the family's dispersal or the divorce proceedings. Whenever his name was mentioned—which, believe me, wasn't often—it was a relief for me to hear him referred to as "Dr. Taylor" instead of "your father." I soon figured out that I was called Pete not so much because I shared a liking for carrots with Peter Rabbit but more because the name Paul had an unwelcome ring to it.

By court ruling, my father was allowed to visit me once or twice a year. I both dreaded and looked forward to his day-long visits. Allegiance to my mother vied with excitement over the gifts of toys that he'd be bringing me, gifts that I wasn't sure would be proper to accept; but, though feeling somewhat compromised, I always did. It seemed to me that my father was visiting as a duty more than for any other reason. It never occurred to me that his air of detachment might have been due to an undemonstrative nature or a decision on his part not to compete with my mother for my affections. Shyly, in an embarrassingly befuddled way, he would take me to the zoo or Glen Echo amusement park or the Smithsonian. Before each visit I was left by Bettie to wait for him in the Brighton Hotel's lobby and, while there, often fantasized about what it might be like to have a regular father. During the visits there was little communication between us. By nature I was quiet and rarely asked questions or spoke unless spoken to. When the visits were over, I felt relieved, then played surreptitiously with the gifts, always being careful to hide them away afterwards.

The Brighton's halls were largely unexplored. There was no telling who lived behind the long rows of closed doors. My impression was that nearly everyone was old at the old Brighton. Soph and Tom were away, Mammy nearly always at work, and only teen-age Bettie around. Naturally, she tended to be more involved with her own affairs. Friend Jackie Willett was the only one of my own age at the Brighton. He had a pale complexion, asthma, a whine, and a mother who sang in amateur Gilbert and Sullivan operettas. I would have considered him better company if he hadn't carried on so much every time I bit him.

A lot of time was spent amusing myself with made-up games and imaginary playmates. I don't remember ever being lonely—I had health, privacy, and a mother whom I was wild about. Though more of a figure to love than an actual presence, she made me feel special. Noticing that I liked to draw, she arranged art lessons for me on Saturdays at the Corcoran Gallery. While other kids there painted stick-limbed potato people, I turned out realistic figures with foreshortened limbs, portraits that resembled the models, and buildings done in perspective. When my teacher deemed me a child prodigy, the classes were discontinued, my mother explaining that she had once been married to someone who was considered a genius in his field and that she didn't intend to have another in the family.

She liked her Darlin' the way he was—wholesome and sensible. She saw me as being a good little boy who never cried and hardly ever sucked his thumb; I saw my Mammy as being the best ever.

But I was worried about her having to work so hard and, prematurely poetic at about age six, before going to bed every night, left verses for her to find tucked under her pillow. They were there to let her know that I loved and was proud of her. Dozens of them, lettered on small pieces of colored construction paper, were stuffed into a large envelope by her, tied with darning yarn and saved.

One of them illustrated an overly strict sense of rhyme:

> IF I ARCHED OVER
> ALL THE WORLD
> I COULD NEVER FIND
> A BETTER MOTHER IN THE WORLD.

In time the rhyming loosened up:

> MY DARLING PRISHUS
> MOTHER
> I WILL NEVER LOVE
> ANOTHER.

Rhyme schemes having become old hat, I then tackled free verse:

> YOUR PEARTER THAN A BIRD IN THE SKY
> HOW I DON'T KNOW SO DON'T ASK.

To Mammy, well into middle age, this one was probably flattering:

> WHEN YOUR OLD AND GET TO BE
> THIRTY FOUR OR FOURTY THREE

DON'T YOU HOPE THAT YOU WILL SEE
LOTS OF FLOWERS AND A BEE.

These represented an "unferld" period:

YOUR THE
PERTIST THING
IN THE HOLE
WORLD
PERTIER THAN
ALL THE FLOWERS
UNFERLD.

YOU ARE THE MOST
WONDUFUL MOTHER IN THE WORLD
MORE PREASUS TO ME
THAN AMERICA UNFERLD.

IF I HAD MY
CHOICE BETWEEN
YOU AND THE WORLD
ID PICK YOU OUT
FIRST BEFORE A
SNAKE COULD UNFERLD.

I felt loved at the Brighton—most times, but at other times not quite enough, and it then seemed sensible to leave. The first runaway occurred just after Bettie had declared my beloved pillow, Pody, unsanitary. She'd taken me down to an incinerator in the basement, where she had me watch while she removed the pillowcase and tossed Pody into the flames. We returned upstairs, I packed a few duds in Pody's leftover case, gave Bettie a peck on the cheek, and said, "That's the last one," then got as far as Rock Creek Park before being brought back by a policeman.

The second runaway was really more of an elopement. Alicia, a fellow inmate at the Kalorama Day School (which, by the way, was mostly unsuccessful at teaching French to five-year-olds), had pretty curls that reached her waist. Reason enough to propose. We then went off on our honeymoon, but, again, the police intervened.

It was always good to get back to Mammy. I'd wait till she'd come from work and settle into her rocking chair. I'd then climb onto her lap, and we'd navigate gentle waters while she softly sang "Go Tell Aunt Nancy the Old Gray Goose is Dead," her voice wonderfully off-key. The song sounded sadly nostalgic, as were the outer edges of her downward-sloping eyes, which, when tired, sometimes brimmed at memories of her first husband. Lulled by her rocker's rhythmic tick, and intoxicated by the scent of her sachet, I'd relax my grip from around her neck, drift off, and be carried to my bed.

Having spent much time in the bed—it doubled as a playpen—I remember it well. It was a blue haven, wheeled, with decal ducks and bubbles; one of its barred sides was lowerable. The rectangular world within was one to pretend in. Pody was its flora; Teddy Bear its fauna.

A good two feet tall, President Roosevelt's namesake had a threadbare nose continually damp from kisses. His nutmeg-brown eyes, each backed with a wire, whenever lost were always found and stuck back in, but carefully—a sharp wire could smart. Not up to Victorian standards, he'd been rescued from impropriety by grandmother Mocky, who had sewn him some green pants and striped jacket firmly secured with unbuttonable mother-of-pearl buttons.

Friend bear was well-spoken and an authority on dinosaurs (we'd seen them in books). He traveled far and wide, bringing back lots of fanciful stories. He also listened well, even though both ears had been singed during an adventure at the edge of a volcanic crater with a piranha and a pterodactyl.

He realized that the rules of conversation required us to take turns, and so I got to tell him some of my own stories. One of these, a true one, was about a walk through woods that I'd taken with Mammy, how she'd removed her bloomers so as to catch an owl in them, and how we'd had to let it go again because it had cried. "Owls don't cry," countered Teddy Bear. "Everybody knows that that wet stuff around their eyes is from owl disease."

He sometimes advised me not to be such a sissy over things that bothered me, such as when Soph and Tom came home from school on holidays. They and their dates would tiptoe to my bed, lift me out, and place me, still sleeping, on the center of the living room rug, where I'd wake to the sounds of their laughter. These were the first times that I remember entertaining an audience, something that I didn't much enjoy. The feeling of being watched was bad enough, but to be seen while in the most vulnerable state—with eyes closed—was mortifying. Carried back to bed, indignant and burning with shame, I was required to finish off the entertainment with a baby's prayer, usually "Now I Lay Me Down to Sleep." My preferred prayer, one that Teddy Bear and I murmured in private, was a plea that Mammy not have to work so hard. Inside our barred blue haven, pillow Pody, before cremation, wasn't big enough for two, so friend bear laid his head on it while I used my elbow.

Another friend, thin and elderly George H. Tacet, Ph.D., the most memorable of all my imaginary ones, lived at the end of one of the many doored halls at the Brighton. Naturally, I was the only one who ever saw or spoke to him. Everyone else disapproved of his calling himself a Ph.D., because, as gathered from inside sources, he was only a doctor of phrenology (I'd been fascinated by drawings of sectioned-off brains, each section numbered and categorized as to exact function). He sometimes materialized in the lobby, where he could be seen sitting in one of the art deco chairs and admiring a reflection that came across the room from a large rococo mirror. His head looked like a misshapen light bulb, smelled of pomade, and his elegant long trousers were made of the same navy blue serge as my short ones. If asked, he'd lift me up onto his bony knee, warn me not to interrupt, and become extremely talkative. Not even the song of a locust enchanted me the way his raspy voice did. His dissertations and grandiose airs were delightful, and it was a special treat to be permitted to finger the odd bumps on his head. I always eagerly anticipated these times with him, which, unlike Dr. Taylor's visits, came often and were without embarrassment.

In those days he seemed to be a nice old gentleman, and his existence always served practical purposes, such as when I was accused of misconduct, for then I could shift the blame to him by saying, "Old Tacet did it." Naturally, no one ever believed me, this being a last-ditch effort to avoid the hairbrush. If my mother were alive today, she'd laugh at me for still fantasizing—yet it's the truth.

Even now, whenever necessary, I still summon forth the old geezer—in theater programs, for example, to credit him for costumes that I've designed, ones for which I prefer not getting the hook. Yes, he's another of my names: the unlikely but lovely and perfectly logical Tacet/Taylor. As to my other names, the ones hotly flung as well as those kindly intended, I do my best to live up to all of them. What's in a name? Say my name—no numbers, please. Say my name, any of them, and for you, from your point of view, that's who I'm likely to be.

Sunnyside

Edgewater Beach, a small community on the South River in Maryland about fifteen miles from where the river joins Chesapeake Bay, is divided by an inlet into two sections, Sunnyside and Shadyside. Like an area of opposites, like certain people, the place is pluralistic.

In Sunnyside a long, steep flight of wooden steps leads directly from the shore to Mammy's summer cottage. In July I could sit on the top step and watch the sun sink behind the exact center of a distant bridge or, better yet, lie upside down there and watch sunsets in reverse. A wash of pink twilight turns cattails greener and shoulders of red-winged blackbirds brighter; the river darkens; a cove on the far side melts away; and when the last tiny edge of the sun blinks out, all Sunnyside seems to sigh.

I was sighing, too, but not about the sunset. A long-hoped-for playmate of my own age had arrived only to be taken away. It was to be another summer of solitary games. Mammy arranged with an orphanage to borrow one of its boys for me to spend the summer with, but, uninterested in any of the activities I could suggest, he'd become listless and homesick and had to be returned.

That would've left the three neighborhood kids, if they'd been more approachable—they say I'm too young for them. Their boat trips, cookouts, and birthday parties are to be envied; but mostly I envy them for their father, who shows cartoon movies at dusk. Uninvited, I sometimes sneak over to watch Betty Boop from outside their rec room window. At other times I catch lightning bugs, store them in a mayonnaise jar with icepicked top, and save them for half-sister Bettie in case she comes to the cottage. Bettie is real old—eighteen—has personality, goes dancing at Annapolis, and sometimes stops off here between proms. Wearing a net filled with lightning bugs in your hair is glamorous, she says; and though they smell funny, the flashing effect is just wonderful. Now that I'm six, she's stopped telling everybody that she's my mother. Seems more distant. It's maybe because I try to tag along on her dates. On the last one I heard her whisper to her newest beau, "Jeepers, here he comes again. Quick, let's scram!"

But even without pals Sunnyside is swell. There's lots of nature, and I'm crazy about anything that flies, crawls, or slithers. The backyard mimosa is usually good for a locust or two, even a flying squirrel, and hollyhock blossoms are good for closing around the bumblebees that feed inside. It's exciting to hear their angry buzzing, then release the petals and run.

The best time for wading in the river is at low tide, when it's easy to imagine the tide being in and that you're strolling underwater through the giant eel grass. There on the bottom everything looks larger and more colorful. Minnows are monsters gliding silently. The striped ones I call tigers; the stubby, toe-nibbling kind, pigs. The needle-nose ones are streaks; and the fatties with blue-bordered gills, sunnies. When taken out of their salt-water home and put into a pail of fresh water, they soon float to the surface, tummies first. It's very interesting, how fast their colors fade.

And you can grab the heads of pulsing pink jellyfish without getting stung and fling them up onto the beach where they dry into nothing.

Finger-nipping blue-clawed crabs can be lifted by their back flippers and flopped over on their backs to see if they are boys or girls. The soft-shelled kind can't bite and are Mammy's favorite dish, so whenever she leaves her work at the Brighton and comes to visit I always have some waiting. I stuff them live into my pockets until the right moment and then, since they're tightly packed, have to present them piece by piece. "Mercy, Darlin'!" she always says.

And along the strip of motor-oil-dotted wildflowers that marches between two sandy ruts of the road that leads to the highway flit my chums, the monarchs, swallowtails, and small grays who are bewitched by rainbow-colored meat and mud puddles. I want to do my share by helping Mammy earn our living, so sometimes I wait at the side of the road with locust clusters in one hand and a For Sale sign in the other. But approaching cars make me shy, and, hiding the flowers and sign behind my back, I usually pretend to be only out for a walk.

The next summer, since the family is staying in Washington, the cottage is locked up and I'm room-and-boarded with Mrs. Wilson, a Sunnyside neighbor. She teaches me to swim, lets me listen to "I Love a Mystery" and the abdication of Edward on her domed wooden radio, and doesn't seem to mind that I spend a lot of time sitting at the top of the sunset steps.

I go there to remember, to pretend that Mammy's still standing in front of a Frans Hals *Laughing Cavalier* that hangs over the mantel inside, also to picture the attic where I slept, its trap door and the secret place under a loose floorboard where treasures are hidden—my Indian-head pennies and collections of locusts and dried mice—the attic where I'd been sent on the day that Dr. Taylor had come to see me and Mammy had not wanted him here. Afterwards she'd told me that when he wouldn't leave, force had been administered. With Sunnyside cheer and Shadyside gloom, I'm still trying to imagine what type of punch brother Tom used to knock him down.

But until I can go back to the Brighton, there are better things to do than sit around in the past. There's blue clay and red to be dug from under the sand, both needed for The Secret Sinking of the Seven. First the heads of seven minnows, no more, no less, have to be encased in clay. Red for boys, blue for girls, and then you toss the victims into the river, where, tails thrashing uselessly, they plummet to the bottom.

Though the ritual gives my spine a lovely tingle of evil, I prefer the other one—The Sacrificial Punishment of the Ogre. For this you make little nude men out of the soft clay and hurl them hard against the cement sea wall. The

thrill comes afterwards while inspecting their parts to see which have gotten squashed flat. And all the time I'm thinking of Dr. Taylor, my no-good
absent father.

The Buttses

When I was nearing ten, my mother sent me to a boy's camp in Vermont.
After buying me a metal trunk, she packed it with clothes and camping
gear—a canteen and a cooking kit, in thrilling olive-drab jackets—and then
she kissed me and put me on a train that was to take me on my first real trip.

Like many others to follow, it was to be a leg of a long tour, each segment
to bring discoveries, premonitions, promises. Looking back now, I see each
relocation—by bus, train, plane, or thumb—as being a part of a whole.
Each leg changed something in my life, each had its own revelation, though
I couldn't have put what it was in so many words. Like a dance they showed
me another world, and they each took on their own identity of direction,
movement, development, change. And though they happened in sequential order, in meaning they had a different chronology, were an itinerary
with a backwards or sideways logic. As experienced by a troupe of dancers,
trips stayed very much in the present, and it was only later that something
subjective in me sometimes explained the continuous thread of the perpetual journey's meanings.

All the way to camp I sat with my nose glued to the window. Being inside
the train was like being wrapped in a protective cocoon; outside, landscapes
were passing. I saw myself as passing them; but later, with an older, more
practiced and self-centered eye, I learned to see them as passing me. And
later I remembered the window frame as being a wonderful, practically
holy window frame, not one of those inadequate small prosceniums that
crowded and forced me into the wings.

Soon after arriving at camp, splendiferous old Tacet was put on hold,
immediately having been replaced by a sturdier model—Mr. Butts, the
camp's director. Because of his brawny build, the rolling lope to his walk,
and prehensile toes that looked as if able to get a good grip on branches and
vines, to me he was Tarzan. I was sure that he was out of Africa, and not,
as everyone else believed, from Oklahoma. According to his wife, Miz

Butts, the "R." in his name, R. Beecher Butts, didn't stand for anything. (Likely, the whole name was an alias.) She says that when he himself was a boy, the other kids called him "our beat-chur Butts," and with a name like that he'd grown up with hard fists.

I've been studying his manly movements from a distance, and timid about giving away strong admiration for him, I'm reluctant to speak. He doesn't know that I've adopted him as my father, or that I've been trying to copy the Western way he walks, and pulling at my nose daily so it will grow long like his, and pushing on my uppers so as to have the same buck teeth.

When left to our own devices, the other campers and I do what most campers do—place frogs, spiders, and phosphorescent wood into each other's short-sheeted beds, spit into each other's soup, and play Dodge the Yellow Stream (fresh urine aimed straight from the source).

By midsummer Mr. Butts still seems not to have noticed me, perhaps because of being too busy making a new tennis court and rolling it smooth, and so one day, after a heavy rain which has turned the new tennis court to mud, I decide to catch his eye. I wait there until he comes and then wade back and forth in the court, forming deep ruts. It works. He notices me, lifts me out by one ear, and says, "Paulie, by gum, you sure are a disappointment." He's known my name and given me a pet one! Even hinted that he's had expectations! My ear throbs with joy.

The summer ends too soon, but my heavy sighs at leaving camp are lightened by being given the honor of riding back to Washington with the Buttses in their wooden station wagon, one featuring the latest in wood paneling. And I'd be able to hear how married people converse with each other.

On the way we stop in New York to see the World's Fair with its Trylon and Perisphere. Although I drop hints that I'd like to see Sally Rand's fan dance, Mr. Butts takes us to see the General Electric display instead. We also visit GE's talking robot, which, supposedly, is able to repeat anything it's been told and which, to my delight, breaks down while trying to say Camp Winnipesaukee. To me this proves that, as I've often been told, silence is golden, and taking things one step further, I conclude that any sort of verbal communication is risky at best.

Much later, when looking back on the summer's benefits, I could see that even then I was learning the basic premise of a dancer's profession—that speaking with movement is best, and that most sorts of verbal communication were risky, as proved by the robot's breakdown and my silent plowing of the tennis court.

Mother now moves Tom, Bettie, and me to 2929 Connecticut Avenue, a new ten-story skyscraper apartment house next door to the Washington zoo. She's left the dining room at the Brighton to start a new one here. Tom is working for Bell Telephone Company as a pay-phone "nickle snatcher" and has his own apartment in the same building; Sophie has married a lawyer and is living in nearby College Park, Maryland; Bettie, personality cresting all over the place, has just returned from a grand tour of Europe, where she was taken around by her aunt and uncle, and is now sporting Paris hats—one with a hammock attached, or, as she calls it, an "utterly tray tray bone snood." Padded shoulders, long red fingernails, and an off-putting continental air complete her wacky new exterior.

But nothing much has really changed. She's still oozing vivaciousness, still being overly fastidious about certain belongings of mine. When a pet duck that I've won at a grade-school raffle sprouts its first feathers, she gets Tom to throttle it and tell me that it's had a conniption from paddling around in the contaminated waters of Rock Creek. Other dooms are devised for my alley cat, an Easter rabbit that has been dyed fuchsia, and my home-hatched tadpoles. Nevertheless, Bettie is beautiful and easy to forgive. Although I see little of Tom, he sometimes makes brotherly gestures and is generous at Christmas time. An Erector Set and a microscope indicate his sympathy. He knows about fatherlessness, and it's as if he's trying to apologize for not being able to be more of a stand-in.

I attend James F. Oyster Elementary School, deliver the *Washington Star,* and do homework in the evening. Weekends I spend at the zoo, the reptile and ape houses being my favorites.

For the next two summers I return to the Buttses' camp, which is now at a two-hundred-fifty-acre farm in Bethesda, Maryland, and where on a third summer I become a junior counselor. Mother then suggests that living in the country could be an improvement over living in Washington, to which I agree, and so an arrangement is made for me to move in with the Buttses. When not at a nearby Chevy Chase grade school that I've switched to, I'm working at the Buttses' farm. Mr. Butts shows me how to herd his four cows into a milk shed by twisting their tails, de-dung and then milk them, how to drive and plow with a tractor, curry horses, and build electric fences. I also feed the chickens and do other chores. When I ask, he lets me paint one of the camp station wagons with pictures of boys riding horses, cows, pigs, and each other, but when I add one of a cow mounting another cow, he has me paint it out, saying, "Come on, Paulie, even a mounting bull would be off limits."

Living with the Buttses is great. Being a teenager, however, is making me feel a little restless, rebellious, and out of sorts with the older generation. I'm even critical of Mr. Butts. I'd hoped to earn his and Miz Butts's affection by taking my chores seriously, but things aren't working out. Tacet or somebody has given me the idea that old Buttsy is only interested in having me there to help earn himself a good living, and when I get careless with my chores, he brings in an additional hand, Johnny, who is better and quicker with the work and is getting paid weekly wages. Jealous, I give him the cold shoulder, and Mr. Butts has to give me a talk. "Boy howdy," he says, "if you two can't get along, one of you is gonna have to git." I'm startled by the possibility of having to move again, but never need to mend my ways, as I soon come down with scarlet fever.

I'm delirious, and deliriously happy. Before driving me to D.C. General Hospital, it being the only hospital in the area with an isolation ward, Mr. Butts has leaned over and pressed his lips to my hot forehead. A symbol of affection, the kiss was one given at risk. My disease was highly contagious and one that could have had fatal complications if not quickly treated.

The ward is filthy and the food all but inedible. The other patients and I are tormented by noisy rats that run across our beds at night and keep us awake. Daily, nurses add to the discomfort by taking blood tests by means of a springed gismo that fits over the fingertip and whose dull point makes many painful polka-dot punctures before producing enough blood for a sample. The following three months are spent crossing off days on a calendar that the Buttses have sent, and nervously awaiting the next blood test or rat.

Soon after my release, the hospital is condemned. I'm then sent to spend another season at the cottage, where hair that's fallen out grows back and about thirty pounds of lost weight are regained.

Mother's restaurant still taking most of her time, she now decides to let Sophie have a turn with me. I move in with her, her husband, John Clagett, and their three boys, Jock, George, and Tommy. My half-nephews are closer to my age than Soph is, but not old enough to pal around with much. Everything possible is done to make me feel welcome. Of my mother's children, Sophie has always been the most attentive to me. She doesn't have Bettie's oomph or Tom's knack for telling a joke, but with her I can get a word in edgewise. John is a nature enthusiast and sometimes takes me with him to fish. The boys make a good audience whenever I tell them the ghost stories that I've heard from Mr. Butts or the Jules Verne ones that I've read. I sometimes illustrate them with crayon drawings done on brown grocery-bag paper.

Although missing the Buttses, I make no effort to stay in touch. I've found out that Mother was paying them to have me live at their farm, and since I'd thought they had taken me in to help with the chores, maybe even because they had become fond of me, I'm too disappointed and embarrassed to visit. It isn't easy to accept the fact that affection sometimes needs to be arranged for with hard cash.

Moving from school to school has been pesty, if not downright dangerous. Always being the new boy in class makes it necessary to prove myself by taking on all comers. After losing a fist fight with the latest class bully, I return home banged up and with a shiner. Soph bandages me, gives a pep talk, and John sets up a punching bag in the basement. From then on I usually give about as much as I get; but just as a new schoolyard pecking order has been established and I'm beginning to make friends, Mother gives up the dining room to become the manager of a housing development in Arlington, where her working hours are fewer, and she's able to have me back.

By this time Tom has married Louise Bachus, the daughter of a prominent Alexandria family, and is now a soldier in the South Pacific, seeing World War II from up close. Bettie, always swamped with beaus (a couple had been stolen from Soph), has finally married one—Jack Gray, a pilot with American Airlines.

In Arlington I attend Thomas Jefferson Junior High, where my homeroom teacher, Miss Gee, teaches math. Though not particularly interested in math, I gain an appreciation for logic and order, things that have seemed somewhat lacking outside her classroom. The way she covers a blackboard with precise and beautifully formed numbers, then erases them with equally precise finesse, is impressive and something I'm not soon to forget.

Though I still enjoy drawing and painting, I'm getting the idea that they are an unlikely way to earn a living. Tom recommends commercial art, so I take a course in mechanical drawing and ad design, but find them tedious.

None of my family are what you might call artistic except Bettie, who can design and sew hats and is excellent at gluing feathers to place cards in a way that looks like the zoo birds that I'd plucked them from; nor does the family have any special interest in literature, music, or the other arts. Mother has told me that Dr. Taylor was a sometime organ player, but since the family has always said that he was "peculiar," I'd misunderstood "organ playing" as meaning something else. My general impression is that art of all kinds has a taint to it. Nice people worked for a living, and good boys played football. Everyone has been very definite about that. Even so, old Tacet and I agree that football is ridiculous and work something to avoid.

Increasingly, I'm aware that I possess traits that make me somehow different from the others—a sensitivity to slights, an anger maybe. And I sense continued isolation, and have a strong urge to stop being shifted from home to home, from isle to isle.

Looking back, I see that a pattern had already formed. Childhood stamps you with its learnings, marks you with its pulse. Early on, bloodhoundlike sensors had tuned in to smells, tastes, sounds that spoke of a trail to be taken. When we're young, all of our senses may be more acute; later on, some of us discover these sensations all over again and are able to recreate them. Now and again our manufactured worlds relate to the real one, and sometimes we hear from an artist who has never lost the magical moments of his childhood.

My earliest recognized pattern was a two-edged semaphore of solitude— a beautiful curse, and the one without which I doubt all other patterns would have grown. I still smell the nights at the hospital ward; I can hear the quietness of days at the Brighton; I can still lie upside down at the top of the steps at Sunnyside, can watch the sunsets in reverse, can see Mammy through the bars of Pete's bed, taste her words that first gave me a feeling of being special; and with a stretch of imagination I can even taste isolation reaching all the way back to my ancestors' small island of Ré.

I always trust my imagination. This trust I have never lost. Over and over it keeps bringing me to a place of independence—not total, of course, but always there like a safety net to fall on. After dance had placed me within a strictly controlled discipline—dancing is a gambler's game that's fraught with rules—I found that my lot was drawn from the early patterns of solitude. And then, after a career had tightened around me, I scented the toughest, most isolating thing of all. Success.

Lynchburg and Mexico

The next thing I know I'm on a train bound for Lynchburg. A conductor tells me to remove my feet from the seats and punches my one-way ticket. I flip the ticket at his receding back and am thinking of doing the same with my old camp trunk. The sniffy old SOB. I remove the feet, but only because the sooty seats are smudging up my new saddle shoes.

I'm about to have my longest stay in any one place yet. After living in Arlington for a year and a half, I'm to serve a three-year sentence at Virginia Episcopal School, a boys' prep school in Lynchburg. Unable to squelch strong urges to rebel against nearly everything, I've had a run-in with the Arlington police, and so Mother has arranged for me to be placed in stricter surroundings.

Now sorting out what's led up to my latest change of address, I'm hearing her say, "Darlin', this is the last straw." She'd meant my latest caper, one carried out in cahoots with a junior-high-school chum. Perhaps we'd hoped to make a great big antiauthoritarian statement, or maybe we did it just for the heck of it. Who knows. Anyway, we'd dared each other to heist the local variety store's largest item, a baby stroller. While he was wheeling it away with me stuffed into it, a floorwalker spotted us. My friend was able to beat it, but my own getaway had been delayed due to my inability to squeeze free. I was then collared and Mother notified. We'd both been upset—she said I'd been a disappointment. Anxious to make it up to her, I've promised to improve. Am very repentant, so much so that I've been fairly unintimidated by the motto that she's underlined in a VES brochure: *The Full Stature of Manhood.* I'll miss a girlfriend I've been dating, but at the same time am looking forward to being at a place that will offer fewer temptations to pet, filch, and rebel. Am thinking that maybe life at a boys' school will be sort of monastic and good for me.

VES turns out to have a rigidly maintained schedule. Someone's carefully organized each hour, day and night, seven days a week, to prepare us for our Full Stature of Manhood. The place is like a military school except that jackets and ties are worn instead of uniforms, a big bell on a tower replaces a bugle, and there aren't any rifle drills. But many of us are forever marching around a well-worn demerit track.

The headmaster is Dr. Barton, a thin, bony type, better known as Barbells. An avid scholar of Latin and Greek, he's a dead ringer for old Dr. Tacet, only his skull has no lumps and I doubt he'll be taking me up on his knee. Though his credentials are probably impressive to the trustees, and though he's nice to us boys—sympathetic to puberty and all—the snatches of Greek that he dumps into his chapel sermons and weekly dissertations are pretty hard to bear. He's all right, though, and he has a rangy setter, Chief, that he's also sympathetic to. The older boys say that every year Chief gets seriously hung up on "thermae caniae"—hot bitches—and that come spring, we should leave our desks and rush to the windows so as not to miss Barbells's famous unhitching routine.

As nice as Dr. Barton is, my favorite master is Kookoo Follette, a master less likely to be clever with dogs in tandem, and rounder. Since at least half of us students have been sent here because of being troublesome at home, and since Kookoo is myopic, has a twitchy nose, a lisp, and other peculiarities, he's victimized by continual and diabolic harassment. Yet he flashes forth English literature and correct usage like a little spectacled thunderbolt, and he does this in spite of classroom bedlams of spitballs and raucous laughter.

Lynchburg girls are more or less catch as catch can. The catching isn't easy because of the tight schedule, and because the school's two proms per year are well chaperoned. Even so, some of us make out, or brag that we do. According to most of us, our Manhoods couldn't be more staturesque. In reality we're not all that active, thanks to the school dietician, who sees to it that all the milk is saltpetered. ("Naturally," adds old geezer Tacet, "and also *au contraire,* but that does not prevent many of you young tads' mattresses from having surreptitious holes hollowed out in them.")

Punctual attendance at classes, chapel, and gym is stressed. As a reward, we're allowed a few hours of free time on Saturdays. The most gratifying way to spend this is to go to a prearranged trysting place, a spot under a nearby bridge that's been traditionally used by past generations of VES boys. It's where we meet our rivals, the hated townies, who we always do our best to beat up.

And there are other ways to ease the rigid schedule. We can join the chapel choir, which means avoiding one study hall a week and not having to wear a tie and jacket, since nobody cares what you wear under your cassock. And the graffiti left in hymnals by past students—lots of traditions here—makes nifty reading during sermons. And if it's your turn to set up the altar, you can snitch gulps of communion wine, which can then be replaced by adding holy water to the bottle. Personally, I don't care for wine, prefer boilermakers, and am bored by and totally foolproof to Episcopalian rituals or any other kind. (In fact, it isn't until much later, when dancing in Bethlehem, that I got around to even considering the existence of Christ.)

Am also doubting the existence of spooks, but not one hundred percent sure, on Halloween I invite some of my dorm to visit a nearby abandoned graveyard at midnight. "Hey, guys," I suggest, "tonight you all are coming with me to dig up an abandoned grave!" Using some picks and oil lamps found at a roadside repair site along the way, we excavate a coffin and, on prying it open, are hit by fumes of formaldehyde (which, by the way, is a smell I'd experienced when double-dating at a Lynchburg mortuary). After studying a decomposed dress and mummified face, we let the coffin crash back into place, then replace the earth and reverently tidy up the signs of our visit—chewing-tobacco wrappers, empty beer bottles, a piss-moistened spot on the fresh earth. Somehow, one of the lamps has gotten left inside the coffin. "Baxter, you little jerk!" I remark. (Baxter has unlimited gullibility, as yet no peach fuzz, and less Full Stature than anybody.) "Baxter, how could you *do* that? And stop that awful puking. The only spook around here is you!"

Every fall I make a swell show of playing football. Though never caring enough about the game to learn its exact rules, I've earned my letter here as a right tackle. It's been easy. All you have to do is push on whoever's in front of you. And in the winter there's ice skating, a sport preferable to others because it isn't required, or even offered. Some of us sneak out of our dorm before daybreak and go down to the James River, usually taking Baxter so we can deposit him on the ice to see if he'll go through. If he doesn't, it probably means that the ice is thick enough to skate on.

Though Baxter is handy, my best pal is Scott Taylor. Since the double seating in classrooms and study halls is alphabetical, we've spent a lot of time together. He's less eager to ramble off limits than I, but sometimes lets himself be talked into it. Once, after crossing the James in a "borrowed" rowboat, we scaled a cliff on the other side, where, while rolling boulders off the top, he lost his balance and fell, bumped all the way down, landed on the boat, crushed it to smithereens, and, as if that wasn't enough, got himself all wet. Supporting him under the arms, I helped him back to school by way of a high railroad trestle, one that's near the place where we sometimes play Chicken—when trains come, whichever one of us gets off the track first loses. Anyway, when we're halfway across, a train comes, and since there's no room for both Scott and me at a small safety platform that's sticking out over the river, I have to let him get wet again.

After the first year at VES, I find summer jobs as a lifeguard, waiter, and short-order cook at Virginia Beach, where Scott's parents run a hotel. On returning to school in the fall, we are made student proctors—keep dorms and study halls quiet, start giving as well as getting demerits, stuff like that. And then I'm voted to head the hop committee. Held in the gym, each of the proms needs a different set of decorations. I transform the gym into a Greek atrium with a fountain that squirts perfumed water (recommended by Barbells), a zoo with caricatures of all the masters behind bars (unrecommended), and then, my coop of grace, the Garden of Eden, complete with larger-than-life Adam and Eve—bare-ass but, sorry to say, fig-leafed in the nick of time. Distrustful about what I might try to pull next, Barbells requests less biblical subjects and recommends Alice in Wonderland.

One of the best decorations has been a large reflecting globe that I've made by gluing thick slivers of broken mirror onto a flimsy paper-covered frame of balsa wood strips. The contraption weighed over sixty pounds, was hung directly over the middle of the basketball court, and revolved by a motor. By some miracle the globe never came crashing down, but during the prom the motor gave out. Although dateless and free to climb up to crank it by hand, I'm able to talk Scottie into doing it and then, for the rest of the evening, jitterbuged with his date.

In my junior year a four-lesson course in the fox-trot and waltz with etiquette thrown in is taught in the gym by two elderly Lynchburg maidens, the Withers sisters—or as Kookoo Follette calls them, "the Withers thisters." At the first lesson I somehow end up with Baxter as my dancing partner, and, no matter what I threaten him with, he refuses to let me lead, so the whole thing is humiliating and I never go back.

One day in the school's library, while leafing through atlases and daydreaming instead of cataloguing books as is expected, I'm bitten by wanderlust. I send off for information on Mexico and make plans to spend the summer bicycling there for next to nothing by joining a group of American Youth Hostelers. Scott agrees to go, too, but at the last minute his parents won't let him. "Gee, Scottie," I say, "that's tough. Never mind, I'll come back and tell you about it."

"You lucky stiff," he answers, "bring me one of those hot tamales in a mantilla?"

"You bet, and I'll bring you a live scorpion, too."

Right before leaving, while I'm trying to open a Coke without using an opener, the bottle breaks and nearly slices my thumb off. Holding a bike's handlebar will be tricky, but even so, I crate my bike and send it ahead, then board a Greyhound bus to Laredo.

Three days and nights later, not having washed or slept, I get off the bus and meet the group of AYHers. Among them are three bohemian types from the Bronx; a pair of middle-aged lady schoolteachers; a girl and her boyfriend, who's just graduated from Syracuse University; a beautiful blonde from Milwaukee; and our group leader, who, as things develop, has a bad habit of guiding us to every church he can find. These folks are the first Northerners I can remember meeting; they're all much older than I'd expected (except for the blonde from Milwaukee) and, like me, have arrived in Laredo bag-eyed, crumpled, and gamy.

From there we peddle for two laborious days across an unpicturesque desert, soon develop sun sores, strong cases of dysentery, and really strong aversions to the seats of our bikes. At night we sleep in sleeping bags by the side of the road, and in the morning, shake a scorpion or two from our shoes. Then we come to steep mountains, have to dismount and push our bikes up them, and on arriving in Mexico City, collapse by an equally aromatic sewer, where we spend several days resting up.

Heading toward Taxco, we again push our bikes up mountains. During a breakneck coast down one, my brakes give out. Since I have to walk the bike the rest of the way down, I get left behind. Nevertheless, after taking a few wrong turns, I at last catch up with the others in Taxco. Relieved at finding them, I learn that the blond girl has been hit and killed by a truck. In shock, the group splits up, most returning to the States.

The remaining six of us pedal on to Guadalajara and Oaxaca. Somewhere along the way we meet the Indian farmer whose corn field has sprouted a volcano, Parícutin. Taking a good close look at it, we get sprinkled with hot ash, and the soles of our shoes are nearly singed off while crossing crusts of molten lava.

Due to the Mexican trots, our progress is often delayed by emergency stops. At one of these, while being pricked by a lacy thorn bush that isn't offering much in the way of privacy, I spot a baby iguana and, after catching it by its leg, bring it back to show the others. "Just keep it to yourself," someone says. "We're all tired of these terrible snakes or insects or whatever they are that you're forever coming up with!" Besides bugs, lizards, bikes, dysentery, and sun sores, some of us have been developing an aversion to each other.

Our next stop is to be Acapulco, where I'm eager to see the Pacific for the first time. I haven't been able to fix my brakes, so I tell the group that I'm taking a bus and will meet them there. With the bike roped securely on top, the bus passes through several low tunnels, and on arrival in Acapulco I'm happy to find that there remains on top nothing but a pretzel.

While waiting for the others to arrive, and nearly out of cash, I spend the night in an outdoor motor court where hammocks can be rented at twenty-five centavos each. During the night a peon is knifed in his hammock. I don't see it happen, but catch a glimpse of someone running away with a knife. The next day, while the other AYHers are sightseeing and swimming, I'm being questioned by the police. This goes on for a day or so, and when they tell me it's okay to leave, I have just time enough to catch up with the others in Mexico City where the trip ends.

Early on, a flea-market gypsy had read my palm and foreseen a totally travel-free life, which came as a great relief, my wanderlust having begun to fade the minute I crossed the border. Long before the trip was over, I had sworn never to put myself through that kind of thing again.

Back at VES, I don't tell Scott much about the trip, and, in Kookoo's class, pass up a chance to write an essay titled "How I Spent My Summer Vacation." Foreign sights and experiences have turned out dismally, as has the experience of traveling with a group. (There was, of course, no way of knowing that I'd be spending more than two decades on the road, constantly circling the globe with a group.)

Graduating cum nada at the end of my senior year—that I've passed my final exams has been due more to my teachers' generosity than to any scholastic ability of mine—I'm faced with the question of which college to attend. VES graduates usually go on to the universities of Virginia or North Carolina, but since the Syracuse graduate I met on the trip has told me that Syracuse has an art department, without investigating other colleges, I apply for an art scholarship there and am given a partial one. It'll be necessary to earn the rest of my tuition and living expenses.

The decision to study painting in Yankeeland doesn't cause Mother to object. She neither encourages nor discourages me, nor tries to steer me toward a more traditional profession. She says, "My darlin', no matter what you do, I'll be content, even if it's art, even in New York—provided you do it well. I'm sure you'll make your Mammy proud."

But almost from the start I've had doubts about becoming a painter. For now, painting might be okay, but my main reason for going to college is to delay the day of having to rise to the Full Stature of, ho hum, Manhood. To prolong salad days seems a better idea—am intending to be a late bloomer, and need to figure out some way of not having to work for a living. Nine-to-five office routines are to be avoided, or any job that requires jackets and ties. And definitely not a profession that involved travel. What I'd be well suited to—I mean, besides crime—was anybody's guess.

Syracuse and Bar Harbor

At Syracuse, most of the other freshmen art students have strong preferences for certain painters of the recent past whom they want to emulate, and so campus cliques have been formed according to whoever's style they favor. Largest by far is the Matisse clique. I know little about modern art or any other kind, have formed no preferences at all; but I have seen *Saturday Evening Post* covers and would choose to copy Norman Rockwell except for realizing that this would put me in a nonexistent clique. For the time being I decide to go along with the Matissites, though not really seeing what all the hullabaloo over him is about. It soon becomes clear, however, that no matter how I try, I'm not going to be able to paint like Matisse. In fact, it's even difficult to absorb my teacher's most basic concepts—that cool colors recede and warm ones come forward, that movement exists within a frame according to compositional placement of shapes, and so forth. To me, a canvas is flat, and nothing painted on it will ever make it three-dimensional.

If your aim in painting is to create space, movement, and light, it seems more sensible to make moving sculptures. Besides having doubts about the basics, I've become impatient with the long delays caused by having to wait for one color of oil paint to dry before being able to apply another, and the relatively static act of painting doesn't answer a strong physical urge to work off energy.

One afternoon I decide to cut classes and go over to the gym to see about joining the swimming team. The idea has come to me while waiting on the football team's training table (the players eat large amounts rapidly, and it takes strength and agility to place their heavy bowls of food before them, then jump backwards quickly), where I've overheard some of them comparing the merits of their sports cars. They've also been given scholarships and living expenses. Since all this is enviable, and since I have energy to burn and think that swimming might be a suitable sport, I'm hoping for an athletic scholarship.

At the pool Coach Webster watches me swim a couple of laps, then says that I can join his team, and that if after my freshman year I've proven myself valuable, he will see what can be done about a scholarship. Like Barbells had, he reminds me a good deal of old geezer Tacet. Both Webster and Tacet are very fond of women, but whereas Tacet dreams of the "aromatic delectations of womanly deltas," the coach, a more down-to-earth type who seems to relate everything to water, says that they all "smell just plain fishy."

The swimming turns out to be more demanding than I'd expected. I'm being trained for freestyle sprints as well as the longer distances; and to build strength and endurance, laps, starts, and flip turns are practiced for four or more hours a day. The training lengthens muscles but makes them lose the kind of snap and resiliency needed for dry-land sports. As a species of athlete, swimmers are recognizable on campus by the way we plop off curbs and other low heights (muscles lose snap), by our enlarged pectorals and thighs, our shriveled fingertips, and our chlorined pink eyes. Water-clogged ears cause us to be yelled at, the most common word in our vocabulary being "what?" We become familiar with the dynamics of water and make its natural laws work for us, resulting not only in speed but in an almost spiritual state of being at one with the water.

I didn't know it then, but the swimming made a good introduction to the equally, if not more, demanding discipline of a dancer's never-ending training. The meets weren't unlike stage performances in that they called for delivery of goods at set and unavoidable times, and they also caused opening-night jitters. Coach Webster was a master of the psychological ruse and before a meet often closed us up in a dark room, supposedly to rest, but in fact to cause our nerves to build until, properly frayed, we'd be turned loose to explode off our starting blocks.

Besides the college meets, I'm entered in races at amateur swimming clubs around the state. I do well and after my freshman year am given a scholarship, meal tickets, and a room in the swimmers' dorm.

Syracuse is a large university, and I at first felt lost among its many students. To find friends, I joined Phi Gamma Delta, lived briefly at their fraternity house, but soon found the living too festive and so moved into the swimmers' dorm, which was quieter, although not much.

At some point during my sophomore year I'm attacked by something much stronger than an itch. Never having experienced anything like it, I don't know what else to call it—a flash of recognition maybe, or necessity, or vertigo, or an unignorable hunch. All at once and seemingly without warning, my future becomes clear. The flash, or whatever it is, is telling me that I'm to become a dancer—not any old dancer, but one of the best.

I don't try to analyze this and accept it as a simple fact. Later on I ponder it, trying to find a logical explanation for my certainty. I ask myself if it was because dance is a form of nonverbal communication, and more physical than painting. Maybe so, I'm not sure. Was it because dancing would be a way of not having to work for a living? Probably. (Wrong! But even if I'd known of the dancer's strict militaristic training, which demands giving up many youthful pleasures, I wouldn't have thought twice.) Was it because of the glamour? Perhaps, but I strongly doubt it. Or because of the chance to please vast numbers of people, get a lot of attention, and be somebody? Maybe so, maybe no. Or was it because I thought that somewhere along the way I might run across a real Dr. Tacet to train and guide me—someone who, if not a true father, might at least be a professional one? ("The more thou diggest, my boy, the emptier thine hole," to quote that gold mine of questionable adages, the silver-throated Dr. T.) And there were dozens of other reasons for the flash, each plausible, yet none that fully explained my sudden and intense sense of mission.

And anyway, no matter what its source, there seems to be no way to scratch my itch, nothing to do but continue with the increasingly lackadaisical laps and art classes. It seems best not to mention the hot flash to Coach Webster or anyone else, and until a plan can be formed, I'll have to make the most of whatever Syracuse might offer in the way of dance-related opportunities.

Then one day, while roaming around in the women's gym, I find a modern-dance class in progress. Its teacher, Miss Nash, looks like she might be able to give better steps if her students were more coordinated. I toy with the idea of joining her classes, but soon decide against it. The steps weren't interesting, and even if they were, being the only male in class would be too intimidating for me to handle.

Anita Dencks, stunning and statuesque, is a classmate and president of the Modern Dance Club. When she asks me to partner her at the club's annual spring concert, to be held on the grass of a nearby park, it sounds like small potatoes. Even so, I agree, and we make up a dancelike duet, a sort of pseudoprimitive thing. A spectacular entrance is needed, so I suggest leaping out onto the grass from over some of the bushes that surround the performing area. Although Anita likes the notion, she is doubtful about being able to clear the bushes, but I assure her that there will be no problem—I know an easy way to get over, so easy that we won't even need to rehearse it. Hesitantly she agrees, and at the performance we crouch down behind some thorny bayberry bushes, she places her foot in my cupped hands, and I shoot her straight up. She then comes straight down and lands in the bush, crushing it and seriously scratching herself. As I help untangle her, she shoots me a killing look, and we then go on with our dancelike duet, one that contains a few other innovations but nothing as spectacular.

My next dance-related experience occurs on top of a large fake drum in the middle of the football field. Not having heard of Anita's mishap, Patty Steele, a carrot-topped drama student who has learned ballet, tap, jazz, and acrobatics at her mother's dance school in her attic, invites me to partner her in *Slaughter on Tenth Avenue* at halftime during homecoming weekend. Patty, by the way, is one of those extraordinary people who can touch the tip of their noses with their tongues. Though versatile, she is like Anita in that she is not a particularly good jumper, but for different reasons—her attic has a low ceiling and shaky floor. After giving me a couple of quick lessons, her mother makes up a number that utilizes all of the abovementioned dance styles. The performance comes off okay except for some minor flaws. The drum turns out to have a large crack down the middle which swallows up one of Patty's new ballet slippers; a follow spot misses us most of the time and leaves us stumbling around in the dark; the marching band plays badly, since their sheet music hasn't arrived as expected; and halfway through there's a torrential downpour which forces everyone in the grandstands to leave, and also the band—which is just as well, it having played several wrong tempos at once. Patty and I go on for a while without the band and are able to ignore the hooting from a few impolite football fans on their way out. Even so, I'm heartened by our performance and think that we've done pretty well under the circumstances. Back at the dorm the swimmers agree, and one of them says that I can count on him as being my strongest athletic supporter.

And there have been other dance-related experiences. When waiting on the training table I met Sally Jewell, a student waitress with ballet training. At the concert on the grass, while dancing *The Sleeping Beauty*, she took advantage of the environment by digging her pointe shoe down into the turf and holding a one-legged pose for an unbelievably long time. It was the first ballet I'd seen. I'd seen dancing in movies by Gene Kelly and Fred Astaire, but somehow couldn't picture myself doing their kind of dance.

And sometime during my junior year the Ballet Russe comes through town. I see a program featuring Alexandra Danilova and Leon Danielian in *Gaîté Parisienne* and am impressed by his energy—he's like a horse on uppers—and enjoy the way she carries on and the way she arches her neck way back, even though seeming to have none. Nevertheless, I find the dated manners and daintiness of ballet hard to relate to.

As yet, none of the types of dance I've seen seem to be my cup of tea, so I visit the university library and withdraw some dance books. The biography of Nijinsky by his wife (ghost-written by Lincoln Kirstein), Isadora's autobiography, and histories of other modern-dance pioneers are fascinating, and the book with Barbara Morgan photos of Martha Graham bowls me over. I also read some dance periodicals, and in one I run across an ad that offers a job as a chauffeur at a summer dance school in Bar Harbor, Maine. I apply and in a few weeks receive a letter telling me that I have the job. It's from Angiola Sartorio, the school's director, an ex-dancer with the Kurt Jooss Ballet and authority on von Laban theories and practice. Other teachers at her school are to be Felia Doubrovska and Pierre Vladimiroff, once stars of the Diaghilev ballet. I'm to drive them all anywhere they want in a white 1930 touring Chrysler. Incidentally, the car and I are the same age; but though it's a little whiter, I'm more convertible. Soon after I've driven Madam Sartorio from Manhattan to Bar Harbor the car breaks down, leaving me with nothing to do. I ask and am permitted to take beginners' classes in modern dance and ballet and to watch the more advanced ones. To make up for the salary that I'm not being paid, and never had reason to expect in the first place, I answer an ad that's been posted on the school's bulletin board and model for the artist Walter Stumpfig from Philly, who paints a large portrait of me.

Turning twenty-one and sensing that it's about time, I fall for one of the younger teachers, who has just graduated from Sarah Lawrence. As if I needed it, she encourages me to dance, and tells me that if I want career advice, to ask the head of the Sarah Lawrence dance department, Bessie Schönberg. At the end of the summer I go to Bessie and find her to be a Rosetta Stone, as she's been to many other hopefuls who have consulted her. Since I'm starting my training late, she advises me not to attend her school, where the stress is on choreography, but to enroll in the new Juilliard dance department, where more technique classes are offered. While waiting for the next Juilliard entrance exam, I return for a third year at Syracuse, intending to pile up enough college credits that, transferred to Juilliard, would make me eligible for a degree in dance, a degree that would mean little to me but would please Mother, it being the first degree to be earned by any of her children.

And so at the end of my junior year, after throwing out my oil paints and student canvases, and very excited about moving to Manhattan, I screw up my courage and go over to the pool. Coach Webster has been a great trainer, has made two of my three years at Syracuse possible, and is expecting me in my senior year to win more medals. I'm not anxious to disappoint him, but an itch is an itch. In his office I tell him that I'm leaving and won't be back.

"What? Why not?" he says, slapping his desk.

"Well you see, Coach, it's like this. . . . I—uh—you see, I've got to leave because I'm gonna go live in New York."

"You're switching to another college? You've been offered a bigger scholarship at Columbia? Maybe your girlfriend's transferring there? Son of a gun, what did I tell you about fishy . . . !"

"Naw, Coach, it isn't anything like that. I'm going to be a—well, I'm going there to be a dancer."

"A WHAT? What's brought on such a nutty notion?" Then, after toying awhile with his whistle, he says, "Don't tell me you're any good at it."

"No, I haven't had much training, hardly any—no real reason to think so. But something's happened—I mean, I've had a terrific kind of flash, and it's made everything crystal clear, it's told me that . . . I mean, it's been a kind of—well, this is just a hunch."

"Kiddo, you sound like you've gone bonkers, but I guess there's no stopping you." And then, rising to offer his hand, he says, "I don't get it, but good luck to you anyways."

The flash of recognition, the itch, the so-called hunch, had no discernible source, nor would it have one for a long time to come. The future having been sealed and settled, there seemed no point to stumbling through the past looking for the beginnings of something that I felt was unnecessary to understand. The past was for backtrackers; only forward momentum mattered. But now, as I write this, it seems necessary to explain the strange-sounding thing that possessed me. I mean, other people are able to pinpoint their exact moment of flash, so why shouldn't I? One likes to be in on such things, especially if they are searing. But whatever set off my particular flash was not painful, discounting the awful little tap dance that my sister Bettie once tried her best to teach me, and the Cleopatra-type number that I got pal Scott to dance with me as entertainment at a VES prom (we dressed up in mop wigs and red long johns, and nobody ever found out who unbuttoned his back flap); and I certainly wouldn't want to count the childhood dewinging of a house fly—an act that might be misconstrued as a sadistic forerunner to future concerts. Although these activities and a couple of similar ones may have hinted of days to come, it seems doubtful that they could have caused my flash.

But now, after a fairly careful sifting of the past, I believe that the flash grew from the moment when, as a child of four or five on Christmas morning, I was led into our tree-lit living room at the Brighton. There was something large and dark leaning in the shadows, so large that I knew it must be for me from dear Mammy. Santa couldn't have gotten it down the chimney, even if we'd had one. It was folded up flat and made of corrugated cardboard with blue letters across the front—or red or yellow or whatever color my chameleon memory happens to bring back—which I soon learned spelled "Tony Sarge." There is no way for me to know if other kids have exactly the same palpitations that I had then, the same giddy waves that mixed joy with nausea. I'd never seen a marionette stage before and, until it was explained to me, had no idea what it was; but it was enough to know that such a large mysterious gift was mine.

I unfolded and set it together with its two-pronged copper coupling pins. The rectangular space that the proscenium framed looked very much like the space within my barred bed, a frame that defined the borders of a fantasy world. While standing on a chair in back I could raise a cardboard curtain. The moment before its rising was, and still remains, the most thrilling part of all that followed. The expectance was like that felt on picturing the future of some exotic flower's bud before full bloom exposes it to the realities of aphids.

There was scenery to be made and plots to invent. Three marionettes came with the stage. At my request Bettie recostumed them as prince, princess, and ogre. An extra costume could convert the ogre into a witch. My dialogues for them were rarely vocal. They communicated with each other via mental telepathy or by body language. Once in a while they were unsuccessful in their attempts to converse, at which times their strings would be jiggled to produce an acute disturbance of their central nervous systems (probably paving the way for *Last Look*, a dance of alienation I choreographed in 1985).

The plots always involved a journey, more often than not the following of some sort of trail—sniffing out a dragon's spoor, speeding after bread crumbs before forest birds could swoop them up, climbing a damsel's long tresses—the usual story-book things. The journey's endings were usually catastrophic, as were those of my favorite nursery tales. They always had to do with variations on stillness—the hero would be frozen solid, the princess turned to stone, the ogres immobilized by cardboard volcanics. The end of one particularly scary plot, one that had come from a recurrent dream, left the traveler waiting in a dark tunnel, where the loud humming of some unde-fined but unavoidably approaching event signaled its arrival. And then, just before the instant of arrival, the hero would realize that he was to be whisked away to an even darker tunnel where he would be restarting his journey as a leap frog. My God, what a spooky kid I was to have used a plot fraught with the mysteries of reincarnation! But even spookier is the thought that the hero would restart his life, not as a frog, but as another kind of leaper.

There was seldom anyone to watch the shows, so with a few trips from backstage to out front, I played the dual role of audience and puppeteer, which is something that any producer, pastor, dictator—any kind of leader, even anyone who's not a total sheep—needs to learn sooner or later. Per-spective, framing, qualities of light and shade, all are dependent on and determined by the distance of the observing eye. I controlled the visual and emotional shapes of the presentations, and if they seemed wrong to me, I returned to make my changes, the same as I do now.

I grew up watching for the telling movement, both animals' and humans', as I suppose, but have never known for sure, all children do. To see a truth, you also have to spot a lie. I eventually appreciated the artistry of a move-ment lie—the guilty tail wagging, the overly steady gaze, the phony hu-mility of drooping shoulders and caved-in chest, the decorative-looking little shuffles of pretended pain, the heavy, monumental dances of mock happiness. It is said that the body doesn't lie, but this is wishful thinking. All earthly creatures do it, only some more artfully than others. It's just a matter of degree. And although there is much to admire in the beauty of natural movement, much to derive from a pedestrian's smallest gesture, the most communicative dances, in my opinion, are those based on physical truths that in the making have been transformed for the stage into believ-ability by the artistry of calculated lies.

It seems likely to me now that what possessed me at Syracuse was a continuation of what I felt on that Christmas morning when I was bedeviled by the cardboard stage. A proscenium had been stamped in me, a frame, a door that was to swing back and forth between a private and public domain.

That door is still opening to an outwardly spiraling path which, as long as I can produce any good lies, and have a troupe to boss, will keep taking me to each new dance.

New London

After my third year at Syracuse, until I can switch to Juilliard in the fall, I plan to spend the summer at Connecticut College in New London. The American Dance Festival there is one of two or three such places in this country where you can spend July and August studying modern dance. I've applied for a work scholarship, have been given one, and am to get free classes in return for working backstage under the supervision of Thomas Skelton, who's the Festival's teacher of stagecraft and lighting design.

There's no time to lose, twenty-two being a late age to begin dancing. I've read somewhere that, like athletes, dancers are practically over the hump by then. Besides, as if a fire hasn't already been lit under me, the draft board is breathing down my neck. Something stupid is going on in Korea.

To get a head start on the summer course, while paying Mother an overdue visit in Arlington, I take several classes from Ethel Butler. An ex–Graham dancer of the early rugged vintage, she's as strong as an ox— when she contracts, you know it—and she's also a superb teacher. After one of her classes, she takes me aside to give me a rundown on the Graham theory of movement. It sounds sort of psychological but not all that intimidating. Much more interesting to me are the actual steps. They are very rewarding to do, and I'm expecting them, in time, to fit me like a second skin. The sitting-on-the-floor steps don't seem to fit as well—they have been designed specifically for a woman's pelvis, namely Martha's, and require more spread than I ever expect to have. Encouraged by Ethel and equipped with this crash course, I'm hoping to soon impress everyone at the festival.

After tossing a few duds into a bag and giving Mother a goodbye hug, I hitchhike eagerly to New London, only to find that I've arrived two days early. Nobody yet being around to enroll me, I sleep out on the grass until the other, less eager students arrive.

Then, still damp from the New London dew, I sign up for as many advanced technique classes as possible. Naturally, someone—a teacher, or maybe the director, Rusty Bloomer (some name for an ex-dancer!)—decides that I'll be better off at the intermediate level, and so I'm to have three of those a day. Besides technique, I'm taking a composition course from Louis Horst, who was once Graham's musical director and is said to have been her Svengali. Am also taking a composition course from Doris Humphrey. Traditionally, in modern dance, it is more or less taken for granted that at some point dancers will be making up their own dances. However, I'm thinking of the two courses as being mere resting spells between my technique classes, having assumed that once I've learned how to dance, somebody else will be making up dances for me.

My technique classes are taught by Helen McGehee, Bob Cohan, and other dancers from the Graham company.

By the end of the first week I can hardly move. My body, or "instrument," as everybody's been saying, has become wall-to-wall deceleration. The excitement over being able to start training has made sleep brief and fitful, and dragging myself across studio floors is a major effort. My feet, as yet uncallused, have formed huge blisters; I have bruises and floor burns; and, even more annoying, I'm having to take classes in blue jeans, since my mail-order tights haven't come.

Even so, none of this is discouraging, because while watching a class, the mighty Martha has pointed at me and said, "I want him." Later on, when a fellow student tells me about it, he says that she looked just like Uncle Sam in the recruiting poster.

She's come to New London for a brief visit, and I first catch sight of her as she crosses the huge lawn in the center of the campus. A small dot in the distance, she's dressed in red and is carrying her own lighting equipment—a red parasol that filters the bright day, casting down a flattering shade of pink. I change direction to get a better look. Closer up, what has seemed like a smooth regal glide turns out to be a sort of lurching swagger. Her face features a crimsoned mouth artfully enlarged, and she's wearing sun glasses. Behind them the eyes—the eyes!—the eyes are dark and deep-lidded, and there's something very wise and undomesticated in them, like the eyes of an oracle or an orangutan. That is, they look as if they've seen everything that's to be seen in this world. Maybe even more. They give the impression of being placid yet at the same time seem to be spinning around like pinwheels. After the mouth and the eyes there's this more or less unimportant nose. And, as seen from up close, her grooming is telling me that everything possible has been done to prevent nature from taking its course.

Just as our paths are about to cross, she stops, dips her chin down, and looks up at me. I've never heard Martha Graham described as "cute"; nevertheless, that's how she looks as she waits for me to say something. I become confused. Other than throwing myself at her feet, what would be acceptable? Forgetting to disguise my Southern accent, I say that all us students sure are thrilled that she's finally come. (Theatrically speaking, her two-day-late entrance has been an effective buildup.) Lowering her huge lashes, she whispers that being there is, for her, like atoning for all past sins. Immediately I'm dying to know exactly what all her past sins have been, but it seems best not to ask. There have been rumors that she isn't above laying out a student or two, and that she once kicked Antony Tudor in the shins for accusing her of choreographic compromise. Apocryphal or not, these kinds of incidents only add spice to her ongoing legend.

Facing a legend is a blast, but making me jittery. The mouth is uttering oracular things—something about the "little flags of celebration which fluttah all over one's bodaah" (deepest tone on the "bodaah"), and about the "miraculous little bones of the foot," and she's seeming practically gaga. Then she's telling me that she believes I can be a very great dancer if my imagination holds. (Does she mean that it would take imagination to think of myself as being great, or what?) She's also saying that I'm one of only two people whom she's ever said this to. (Who's the other? I'll kill him.) Then she produces a slip of fortune cookie-sized paper and writes down the phone number of her school, saying that she wants me to join her company before the year is out, and that when I get to New York I should call.

Her exit is preceded by an authentic-looking Oriental bow, with flowery wrist gesture thrown in for good measure. I stand transfixed as she diminishes into a floating red dot against the wide green lawn. The lurching swagger had been pretty nice, and saying "bodaah" a big improvement over "instrument," but what I'd loved best were the oracular eyes.

It seems to me that chances for most of the other students, however talented, however determined, to become full-time dancers are practically nil. After a few years of study, most plan to pursue more likely professions. At best, most might expect a teaching position in a college phys-ed department, where their ability to dance would count for little when teaching new generations of dance students, who, in turn, might or might not be receiving diplomas, only to drop dance altogether or become college dance teachers themselves, thereby continuing a pointless cycle that has little to do with being a performer.

At the festival guest artists are scheduled to give weekend performances. This summer the visiting pros include soloists Irving Burton and Ronald Awl. The Humphrey-Limón Company and the New Dance Group are the resident companies. All of them are to be victimized by backstage slip-ups

unintentionally heaped by me under the demanding, but in my case ineffective, direction of Thomas Skelton.

Right from the start Skelton and I haven't hit it off, perhaps due to the
New Englandy snap and bite of his commands, but more likely because of
my continual daydreaming. I'm picturing myself dancing on the stage instead of having to spend a lot of valuable class time mopping it. He prefers
that I take my duties seriously, and often says so. That he's turned out to be
touchy about being skinny, and that I like to call him Mr. Skeleton, is also
something that doesn't exactly ease our relationship. When I prove myself
a flop at the mop, he kicks me upstairs to the lighting board, which brings
worse results, so then I'm transferred to the front curtain, which, as he says,
is "a job simple enough for any halfwit to handle." When explaining its
mysteries to me, he twangs, "You pull this rope for up, and this one for
down. Is that a concept you think you can handle?"

"Yowsa, boss Skeleton," I say, weighing the possibilities of taking my
thumb and squashing this fly in my ointment.

"You got that? This one is *up*, and this one *down*. You sure you've got
that? Absolutely sure?"

"Sho 'nuff," I reply, and at the end of the festival's first concert, not only
bring in the curtain but lower it so far down that everything—it, the pipe
it hangs on, its supporting cables, everything—ends up in a pile on the
floor.

The only thing left to move me to is the victrola or, as he calls it, "the
latest development in sound systems."

"I know I'm taking a terrible risk," he says, "but anyone ought to be able
to lift a needle and put it down on a record without ruining the whole show.
Surely *that* shouldn't confuse or tire you too much." Somehow I can tell
he's less than a hundred percent sure.

That night the guest artist is Irving Burton. He seems like a good guy, so,
mildly determined to get things right, I ease the needle down at the proper
moment, sit back, and am relieved not to see Skelton's usual signs of
asphyxiation. When the dance is over, I carefully remove the needle without scratching the record, but Irving Burton comes off stuttering. It isn't
that he's upset—he always stuttered. He just seems puzzled that the wrong
side of his record has been played.

As with the backstage chores, I have little interest in my composition
classes. While other students are slaving away at their assignments, I'm
usually resting up for the technique classes. If pressed to pick one over the
other, I'd prefer Doris Humphrey's composition course to Louis Horst's.
His have to do with the translation of musical forms into dance terms. Hers
aren't as specific and stress the expression of ideas or emotional states

through gesture-type movement and something or other she calls "body rhythm." The combination of the two different approaches might be a good introduction for a dance maker, but that's not where my mind is. I'm obsessed by a clock that's ticking a race between learning to dance and the draft board. Only one composition assignment sticks with me—a floor study for Miss Humphrey for which I figure out a way of slithering along on the top of my head. It's supposed to express sloth, I think. The floor is splintery and a sliver got stuck in my mind, as it were.

As another kind of resting spell, I take a course in Laban dance notation. It's slightly disappointing to find out that there are no symbols for male and female reproductive organs, or if there are, they're not being taught. It might've been interesting to research and record the campus's nighttime activities. I have the distinct impression that somewhere there's some fooling around going on. But I'm unsure and not wild to find out. Whenever girls flirt with me it makes me nervous, and when a few of the guys do likewise, even more so. It isn't that I think being a loner is all that great, or that I don't want to be friendly; it's just that these dance classes are sapping all my energy. At least that's the excuse. Actually, ever since puberty I've been slightly mixed up about sexual preferences. So far, I've always led a straight life. Well, maybe not *absolutely* always—let's just say that I've preferred to be on top. Anyway, the flirting is beginning to bother me, so much that I feel a need for advice. There's never been anyone with whom I've wanted to discuss these things. In my family the subject has always been taboo, even the words "pregnancy" and "bra" were never to be said out loud—Lord forbid the word "sex" should come up. And there isn't anyone here to ask, no campus counselor or anyone; and since the only person I've met who seems worldly wise is Martha, I'm wondering if I shouldn't go to her for advice. She's supposed to be an authority on caves and columns. I don't know how often she gets this kind of request, and for a while I debate about asking, but finally a hunch tells me she won't mind. I get up my courage and corner her.

Trying to find the right words is harder than I expected. It would be easier if I knew precisely what it is I want to know. I sputter and blush and the question won't come out. Somewhere along the line I've forgotten what the problem is and am hard put to form just the right words, in just the right way, to express my nonthought. I stand there getting redder and redder. Mercifully, she interrupts, says that she understands—that I have hot pants and don't know what street I'm on. (Not her actual words, but this is the gist.) Then she recommends making no choices of gender, to save that for later, just do nothing for the time being.

It's a relief to learn that a person can just shelve his urges. I was worried that she might say that to Dance is to Live, and for me to go get laid, and call me sweetie pie or something.

A Humphrey-Limón repertoire class takes place in a dining room that has been emptied of its furniture, everything except a single chair. Beside the chair lies a cane, and in the chair sits the crippled Doris Humphrey. Three afternoons a week, from two to four, she holds herself as staunchly as a nesting eagle whose chicks are about to flop out from underneath. For some time she's been unable to dance. She has a certain stoic detachment, yet she's kind and patient as she attempts to pass on to her galumphing students not only the experience of performing her works but her belief in the magical power of dance and some of the knowledge she's gained from a lifetime of rich exploration. She doesn't have, or no longer has, as vivid a personality as Martha, but both are dance pioneers, and so, like it or not, they are forced to share the same spotlight. My impression is that the relationship between these two matriarchs and their respective companies is somewhat like an enforced truce between the Hatfields and the McCoys.

Having to use a cane makes it hard for Doris to get around the campus. Though handicapped, she seems well enough, and it never occurs to us students that—unlike Martha, who everybody knows will outlive every-body—Doris won't be with us much longer.

She hasn't picked me for her repertoire class, maybe because I'm not taking her technique classes. During the second week José Limón has taken me aside, asked my age, and mentioned that he began his career the same year I was born. He then tells me that he is planning to retire soon, that he would like me to take over his parts. This second offer in one week doesn't much surprise me. I believe in miracles. But my heart is already set on Martha's company, so I turn his offer down.

After the repertoire class has been going on for three or four weeks, Miss Humphrey invites me to take it because of a casting problem. Someone large enough to carry an Indian goddess around is needed. The name of the student revival is *Song of the West*, to be performed in a concert at the end of the summer. I've heard of another Humphrey work, *The Life of the Bee*, have gotten the two mixed up, and so think I'm about to learn something called *The Song of the Wasp*. Since I've always related well to all types of insects, I anticipate being able to fit right in.

One afternoon Miss Humphrey is explaining that the movements we'll learn next are derived from her impressions of the Southwest—the distant shimmer of heat waves bouncing off the desert, the ritual processions of

Indians, and such. She then goes on to name other images, which I miss since I'm still back at the shimmering heat waves. How on earth can we portray those? Scorpions would be a much better idea. As it turns out, we imitate heat waves by holding our arms stiffly to the front and making scything motions. At the same time we do this, our legs are to take us forward in groups of four running steps and one limp, or plié, as we are supposed to call it. The counts are *one*-two, *one*-two-three, with the limps on the *ones*. If we want, we can count *one*-two-*three*-four-five, or even, as the class wag suggests, *five*-four-*three*-two-one. Having learned the step, we're then divided into two groups and take turns limping in curved paths around the dining room to the guiding thump of Miss Humphrey's cane. After a while the scything, the limping, and the counting are fun and almost make sense.

Meanwhile, unmoved by prospects of seeing me in *Song of the Wasp*, or *Song of the Whisp, Wong of the Sist*, or whatever it is, the New London draft board has been preparing an ominous invitation. My presence is requested at a training camp in two weeks' time. I immediately picture myself being carted away with other poor saps inside a barred cage, wearing chains and tattooed numbers, being photographed for official records, then flung into the jaws of a pointless war. My beautiful career to be nipped in the bud! Old Tacet is telling me, "Dodge, my boy, dodge the indignities of soldier life, cling to your inalienable rights as a Creative Artist." The date of my induction is to fall on the day after what is to be my first stage performance.

The afternoon of the student concert Skelton excuses me from backstage duties. While on my way to warm up, I notice him introducing a new curtain puller to the mysteries of the two inscrutable ropes. Skelton pauses, looks toward me, and a sarcastic grin crosses his face. "I don't know how in the world I'm going to get along without you," he says.

"Yeah, but it'll be worth it. This is a historic day—my first debut ever," I tell him.

He scratches his giant Adam's apple with one bony finger and sighs. Skeleton looks skeptical. (Strange as it may seem, in a few short years he is to become my company's lighting designer, stage manager, and road manager all rolled into one—not to mention one of the best friends whom fortune's ever bestowed.)

I've gotten to the theater much earlier than the other students. We're to dance two reconstructions—*New Dance* as well as *Song of the West*. The fun of being a heat wave lessened when I found out I'd be spending most of the dance toting June Dunbar. Without taking off my dungarees (the

mail-order tights still haven't come), I begin to warm up, keeping at it for
about two hours, even though my two parts add up to but a small fraction
of that time. Having worn myself out, I go onstage and, just to make sure
not to forget my steps, run through them several times.

As curtain time approaches, a handful of teachers and students trickle
into Palmer Auditorium. After they've scattered themselves in bleak ones
and twos among the rows, the house looks even emptier than before. Lights
dim, the curtain jerks up unprofessionally, and some of the student performers stick their heads out from the wings to see if any of their friends
have come.

I want to look too, but can't. My body is being inhabited by an alien,
otherwise known as stage fright. Some clone, not me, is cowering offstage
and covered with icy sweat, his palms and soles slippery, temples booming,
tongue dry, seizured, sizzled. It's plain to see that the reason for greasepaint is to prevent your skin from betraying its cowardly color. Trying to put
my mind on the dance, I can't remember which step is to come first, or
even what any of them are. Once the curtain's up, however, my body
remembers them for me. Through repetition at rehearsals the muscles have
gained a memory—like when you get up in the morning, half asleep, and
your hand automatically reaches for the toothbrush. I relax, forget about
anyone watching, and let the dance take over my programmed limbs.

June Dunbar seldom unstraddles herself from my shoulders, and as I lug
her to and fro, her shiny long hair eclipses me. I'm anonymous from the
neck up. Some debut.

When *Song of the Waste* is over, the audience is still in for more. They
didn't get in for free and get off that easily. For *New Dance* a lot of old gray
boxes are placed side by side across the back of the stage. They could be
leftovers from the first Olympics. The boxes are to allow the dancers on top
of them to be seen behind the other dancers in front. This was a thoughtful
idea of Miss Humphrey's—democratic, too, because the back dancers eventually get to trade places with the ones in front.

It is a theme-and-variations piece. The theme is step-step-spin to the
right, step-step-spin to the left, and so forth. While the back dancers do this
theme over and over, solo variations—hoppity-hoppity twirls and such—
are taking place downstage. There are eleven solo variations, and I've been
given the honor of doing mine last. Until then it will be necessary to repeat
the spins approximately three hundred times. To make matters worse, my
spins have to be on top of one of the highest boxes. Those of us who are
lucky enough to do their variations early on can get as dizzy as they like
afterward, but those of us who are last are praying that we'll be able to get
through our solos vertically. This part doesn't seem so democratic.

Everything is going fairly well until the eighth variation, when I notice someone next to me get nauseated and run off. The stage lights, unused at rehearsals, have been disorienting. My step-step-spins start to change into step-step-oopses, and pretty soon, stumble–stumble–good griefs, and then trip-lurch-craps, and finally *oh, shit*. There is also a language problem. Mine wasn't strong enough. It isn't quite time, but I'm thinking that perhaps no one will mind if I get off my box a little early before I break something.

Arbitrarily, I pick a direction, hoping that it will lead downstage, where I can do my solo, and edge forward only to find myself at the upstage wings, where Skelton is beaming his evil grin at me. I choose another direction, this time the correct one, and angrily complete a cockeyed and overly expressionistic variation. Later, everybody accuses me of tampering with the choreography.

New Dance over, we take a bow for no particular reason. The empty seats out front have multiplied. If people are still there, they are hiding. Miss Humphrey has been watching. When she comes backstage, looks at me, and says not a word, I think her a very great lady indeed.

Then I go to the student lounge for coffee with my college girlfriend Anita Dencks. She's come up from New York to see the festival. As anyone can tell from her nubby dress and copper earrings, she is now living in Greenwich Village. She says that although she enjoyed the concert, I danced as if I didn't like my parts. I stew and fume and think it gross that anyone could tell anything about my attitude, my face being covered by someone else's hair and all, but in the end I have to admit that it's true. As Martha has told everybody, the body doesn't lie. Until I can develop a stronger technique, there will be nothing to hide behind.

By the summer's end many have helped and encouraged me toward a pursuit that seems more to have chosen me than to have been chosen. Besides Martha's and José's offers, Doris has said that my compositions for her course were pleasing. This is unusual, as she is known to be sparing with praise. Bill Bales, the dance director of Bennington, has offered me a scholarship there. Graham teachers have been generous. Betty Jones of the Humphrey-Limón company has been supportive. Even Irving Burton, whose solo I'd profoundly affected by giving it new music, has said nice things. I'm receiving largesse from artists who are welcoming a newcomer who they feel will be an asset—not to them personally but to their field. It's like being accepted into a house of unlimited accommodations, a house with as many rooms as there are dance clans.

Well, if modern dance were a house, its mama and papa would be Graham and Limón. Though on good terms, they are in no sense married.

When Martha visited the campus, a rare event occurred. The two appeared together on the same stage, not to dance, but to speak. The curtain opened and they charged out of opposite wings toward each other to meet center stage, where, to a roar of approval from the audience, they hugged. Though highly theatrical, the moment was more good manners than a meeting of creative forces. They had separate, and in some ways conflicting, outlooks. José prefers that dance be open, outward, and up. El Greco and Bach are his ideals. Martha, also no stranger to monumentality, is fond of inner landscapes and chooses to use modern composers exclusively, but not too modern (John Cage types are "bad boys"). José believes that Doris is the greatest choreographer; Martha never even mentions Doris's name. But when the two giants hug onstage, their differences fade into the background. The hug represents a common bond—their mutual commitment to the one art form other than jazz that can be called truly American.

Bowing her best Oriental bow, Martha girlishly backs up and gestures to José to speak first (she can then wipe him out with a brilliantly articulate splash of poetics). José, with the dignity of a grandiose Mexican peon, then proclaims that the body is the soul, elaborates on that for a while, adds that dancers are the only ones who know this, then goes on to say that artists feel passion and formalize it into dance, that artists give but businessmen take, that artists Live, Feel, and Seek Truth.

When it's Martha's turn, she totally hypnotizes the audience with foot imagery, several other natural wonders including spiraled sea shells, and states that all movement stems from the genitals. Nobody bats an eye. The effect is magnificent.

Martha and her company haven't danced in the festival this year, so I haven't yet seen any of her work. I've seen Doris's *Night Spell* and *Day on Earth,* also José's *The Moor's Pavane,* and have thought them wonderful. Even so, the Graham classes and the woman herself make me certain that I'd rather work for her.

The summer over, my plans are to find some sort of job in Manhattan, where I intend to rent a cheap railroad flat, whatever that is, and to study at the Juilliard dance department while taking night classes at Martha's school. By giving the New London draft board a change of address, I've been able to postpone my induction. With even more luck, I hope to go on dodging indefinitely by giving other changes of address.

Ever since a childhood of rapid relocations, I've been looking for a permanent spot. The bike trip through Mexico put an end to all wanderlust. Travel, even if you're a touring dancer, is for the birds. Even so, where dancing leads, that's where you have to go. And the future, zigzag or straight—whichever, wherever, whatever it is—it all looks bright.

Juilliard

Assorted sounds—twitters, scrawlings, tender thonks, bright squeaks—are all merging together and filling the halls of Juilliard. Young musicians, as seen through their windowed practice cubicles, look too intensely involved with their specialized noisemakers for me to interrupt. At least that's my impression when I rap on one of their windows to ask where dancers are supposed to go. This was in the spring of '52, just before New London, when entrance auditions were being held for budding dancers who hoped for admission the following fall. I'd not only expected to pass mine but was fairly confident that I'd do well enough to be awarded a scholarship.

Juilliard was then at West 122nd Street, a block up from Riverside Church and directly across from International House. Its new dance department had been added two years before, founded and headed by Martha Hill, an enthusiastic woman deeply committed to contemporary American dance. As a dancer she'd studied with Graham and Humphrey, performed with Graham's early women's group, and also been responsible for starting dance departments at Bennington and at Connecticut College. Her loud, clear voice easily transcended Juilliard's noisy halls, and being an authority on all types of dance matters, she knew exactly what she was shouting about. A minor influence left over from Graham days was still noticeable in the way she wore her hair—a topknot which in her version had migrated off to the left, where it clung precariously, giving her a sprightly, humorous look. Like Bessie Schönberg, she was to become a Rosetta Stone to me—as well as to the thousands of others whom both great educators enlightened, guided, and egged on.

Juilliard classes were given by many of the same teachers who taught at the American Dance Festival. In addition, the curriculum included Cecchetti-style ballet taught by Margaret Craske, Antony Tudor, and Alfred Corvino. Louis Horst taught composition; Ann Hutchinson, Laban dance notation; Norman Singer, social science (he later non-sequitured over to run City Center). Other subjects included something called rhythmic training, a course that came early in the morning. Nobody but the teacher ever knew exactly what it was.

The audition was to be judged by Hill, Tudor, and Craske and turned out to be on the concert-hall stage. Besides executing whatever steps were asked for, auditioners were expected to perform a short dance of their own devising. Mine was made out of moves from the dancelike duet that Anita and I had done in the park at Syracuse. Anita had also decided to transfer to Juilliard.

What to wear for the audition had been a puzzle. I'd decided to wear sweat pants and sneakers, which, at the time, no serious dancer wore. Anita said that they made me look gauche, so I returned to the dressing room and came back wearing my old basketball shorts. Then she said I still looked like a jock, and started criticizing my feet, saying that they were too big and too bare. Though critical, Anita had a good eye for appropriate apparel, so I went back and borrowed somebody's ballet slippers. Then I remembered that we were expected to dance modern as well as ballet, so I went back again and solved the problem by padding out in my socks.

After the judges had seen enough of my socks and asked me to remove them, they asked for jetés, turns à la seconde, and pas de chats. Not wanting to seem ignorant, I showed them some other stuff that I hoped would look French enough. Tudor either was being rude or was simply unable to hide his snickers. Later I was asked why I wanted to be a dancer. I'd overheard some of the other auditioners' answers—mostly about inspiration and other cosmic-sounding claptrap, during which I'd noticed Miss Craske yawn six and a half times. All the fancy words were making me feel lowbrow and tongue-tied. I stood there in front of the panel and couldn't say why I wanted to dance.

"Come now, dear, you must have a reason," says Miss Craske.

I tell her I don't know, and she nods in an understanding way, urging me on. "Dear," she calls me again. I like her, so I tell her that it's just because I like to move.

She says, "That is a very good reason, dear." (For many years she kept reminding me of this with a smile.)

I've never found out if it was my steps, my motivation, or what, but after a short huddle with the other judges Miss Hill turns toward me, happy as if she'd won the scholarship herself, and blares, "Paul, you've *got* it!"

Plans for a place to sleep shape up at nearby International House, a residence hotel for foreign students, where, in return for a room, I rise every morning at five to cook eggs down in the cafeteria. Being among foreign students makes me feel at home—after all, I'm a foreigner myself, a Southerner in Yankeeland, where everyone but me has strange-sounding accents.

After each day's classes I usually take an evening class at the Graham school. I used the phone number that Martha had given me and am being given free classes there. It's at Sixty-third Street east of Third and is, or is going to be, a gift to Martha from her patroness Bethsabee de Rothschild. There is an intimidating spiked gate out front and then a sturdy burglarproofed door. Inside, an impressive stone Buddha sits cross-legged in the vestibule, usually with seasonal flowers placed in its lap. It reminds me of Martha, but thicker around the waist, and it presides over a place that seems pretty ritzy.

There is a studio upstairs on the third floor, and two on the first—the larger one is where Martha births her creations. And there are a couple of offices on the second floor, where her good-natured sister Geordie pastes press clippings into giant scrapbooks. Noguchi sets are stored in the basement, and there are two large dressing rooms with showers for Martha's nine-or-ten-member company and for about fifty students. Martha frowns upon any girl perspiring, but it's okay for the guys to sweat if they have to.

Next to the main studio is a small suite—a dressing room with sofa, bathroom, and kitchen for Martha's private use. Some of the older members of her company are allowed to use her fridge. Martha lives a little ways down the street in a high rise. I suspect that she sometimes takes taxis from there to her school, but usually she hoofs it. Her crêpe-de-chine rehearsal gowns are made to order, and she wears the latest in streetwear, including a black seal coat and a lot of gold Noguchiish-looking jewelry. Sometimes she's seen rag-picking at Bloomingdale's or other department stores where she finds fabrics for costumes.

Though the school is ritzy, and though it is very exciting to be around its highly charged atmosphere, the minute I step inside the vestibule I always sense something I can't quite put my finger on, something that smells suspiciously like the odor of friction. Nobody smiles much except Geordie, and if you hear laughter it probably means that Martha isn't around. Everyone takes the place dead seriously, even Geordie's droopy cocker spaniel, Roderick. And the students are very intent, very fraught, like religious converts. Each hopes for a blessing dropped in passing from their heavenly host's lips, and each jumps for joy if sent to Third Avenue for her wonton soup.

Girls have to have long hair worn in a big bun on top, keep out of the sun if they are white, and stay that way, the whiter the better; guys are encouraged to have longish hair, and it is good to be as dark as possible—carryovers from Denishawn days, when the ancient Oriental idea of light women and dark men was the rage. This seems a bit much, and on being asked to let my hair grow, I start a beard, but it may be only a way to get Martha's attention. Like everyone else, I'm smitten with her.

If a certain red cloth has been knotted onto the outside handles of the main studio doors, it signals that she is in there and not to be disturbed. Nobody dares peep. The building's leaden silence—no, not silence; a sort of swept-up and refrigerated sound—is sometimes shattered by the slam of a door. The slams are well staged, and Martha always has her reasons. Her generation's theater etiquette probably demanded that great personages regularly display stylized fits.

During my first year in New York I don't do much else but take classes. Learning to dance keeps me too involved to make close friends or even a single enemy. Don't remember going to an art gallery, music concert, or anything cultural except a Merce Cunningham performance. My body is being stretched, firmed up, strengthened, and converted into practically a new model, and it screeches in open rebellion. Some dancers say that theirs doesn't hurt, but for as long as I danced, getting out of bed in the morning was an exquisitely slow process.

The year had four highlights. One was when the draft finally caught up with me, discovered that I had a heart murmur (perhaps caused by the swimming or the scarlet fever), and classified me 4-F.

The second was seeing a rehearsal of Martha's *Canticle for Innocent Comedians:* Except for her dancers, no one was allowed inside the Juilliard concert hall, but who was to know if anyone was watching through the slit of the lobby doors? Anita, some others, and I stacked our faces like a totem pole with eyes glued at the crack. *Canticle* was one of the few dances Martha wasn't in, and was about the sun, moon, stars, water, fire—a nature lover's dance. Martha loved nature but preferred artifice (I loved nature and hated Art). At the beginning her dancers were standing inside what looked to be a large circular nest, their arms draped along its upper edge. The set was designed by Frederick Kiesler to be sound bouncers for Juilliard music concerts. When the sections of the nest were slid apart by the dancers, it was as if the planet earth were unfolding to show all its wonders. (Later, a dopey French critic is to interpret this as a street scene with overcrowded pissoir.) The set pieces were then used singly in various ways for the suite of dances that followed. One became a sort of firmament for the sun, Bert Ross, to roll around on. Among other solos were one for Yuriko as a womanly moon and one for Helen McGehee as a mermaid who made her entrance from under a bridge. A duet had Stuart and Linda Hodes fooling around with a big symbolic rose. At the end a mysterious door opened to reveal beauteous Pearl Lang as Death. The whole dance was the loveliest, most impressive, most magical thing I'd ever seen.

The third high point that year might also be called rock bottom. It was a dinner party given by my teacher Antony Tudor, a man not only known for his great ballets but for his deflating remarks. At this time there were certain things that I felt absolutely sure of, not the least of which was myself. The puffed-up Tacet part of me was getting the upper hand, and I had made the mistake of telling Tudor that I'd had a flash in college and felt practically foreordained to dance. Hugh Laing and other stellars were at the party. I was eating half an alligator pear stuffed with shrimp and listening hard to the interesting things being said when Tudor rose from the table like a bird of prey, quieted everyone, and sarcastically proposed a toast to someone to whom he said the whole dance pantheon—Nijinsky, Pavlova, Graham, and the rest—was but a mere footnote in history, as compared with their new lord and master, the lately emerged cock of the rock, the great (here I had a feeling something bad was about to happen) Paul Taylor. My ears related to the rest of me in the way purple relates to pink. I'd never before run across such an effective method by which the older falcon generation puts young rabbits in their place, and for a brief time took classes with new humility and much less fluffy-tailed assurance.

The year's fourth highlight was seeing Merce Cunningham perform. Carolyn Brown also went to Juilliard that term and had been taking Merce's classes on the side. She urged Anita and me to see his *Sixteen Dances for Soloist and Company of Three*, a dance more dramatic than its title implied. It consisted of vignettes, some poignant, some satiric, and a few just plain goofy. At this time, although very much admired as a dancer, as a choreographer he was considered by most of the New York dance community to be an unimportant upstart. I'd seen pictures of him and knew that he'd danced in Martha's company and had been collaborating with composer John Cage. The steps in *Sixteen Dances* were related to Martha's vocabulary, but the choreographic approach was completely different—whimsical and airy, sometimes with little diddling motions of the hand and alert-eared snaps of the head. I liked the dances so much that I skipped a few of my Juilliard classes to take some classes from him. Anita was also impressed, and so a couple of times a week we joined Carolyn and subwayed down to the Village to his small studio over a laundromat at Sheridan Square. Others taking the classes were Viola Farber, Remy Charlip, Merriane Preger, and Jo Anne Melscher. Merce had few students and no regular company. The class material was difficult, included more footwork than other modern techniques, and the combinations often involved coordinations that were tricky in the way that simultaneous head patting and stomach rubbing is. Very few of the combinations gave me the feeling that I was dancing in a very physical way, but this may have been because I couldn't do them well enough.

Merce was polite and patient, his large hands clapping and snapping out the rhythms as he paced back and forth in front of us. Whenever he paused, his feet seemed to root into the ground, and when he demonstrated a jump, his landing was amazingly soft and quiet. He could twist his torso further around than any mortal should. Anita thought his face interesting rather than handsome, and she was nuts about his nose, which she likened to a snail. Taken all together, the six slender feet of him gave the impression of a large wood sprite or sea horse. Although genial and gentlemanly, it was easy to see that he was a private person.

Sometimes John Cage accompanied the classes on a piano that he had "prepared" by placing pieces of paper and oddments between the strings. He imposed gamelan-type rhythms and tempi that had little relationship to whatever rhythms Merce was teaching. Once in a while a few matchings of sound and dancing happened accidentally. The idea was for us to learn not to listen to the music, thereby avoiding the usual ideas about being musical. Although by nature instinctive rather than mental, Merce had begun trying out John's philosophy about chance.

Curious, I went home and made several dance studies for myself using chance methods. After putting a number of steps in six or seven different random orders and then rearranging the same steps in several other orders, both accidental and intentional, I concluded that sequential order of steps, arranged either way, made little difference to the end result. What seemed more important than sequence was the *type* of step used, so I devised some combinations of movements by chance, both simple and complex. These all turned out to be not as unusual looking as one might expect and tended to look and feel very sticklike when executed—that is, without "natural" flow, muscular density, or sensation. It felt stingy, like something I'd not particularly like to do or see. And instead of being "abstract," as I'd expected, most of the movements looked like a wooden marionette having difficulty in expressing emotion. So much for making up abstract dances by chance, I reasoned.

The Cage mystique, already then in evidence, seemed to me built along the lines of the Emperor's New Clothes, or the pastime of standing at a busy street corner and staring straight up to see how many others will do the same. The quip credited to the composer Lou Harrison—"I would rather chance a choice than choose a chance"—seemed honorable. Still, though they were incompatible to my own ways of thinking, these methods served Merce and his audiences in a valuable way. He once told me that before using chance he had been going through a reclusive period and had found it difficult to work or even leave his loft much, and that John had come to the rescue by encouraging him to use chance methods, thereby relieving him of the strain of decision making and enabling him to return to his creative work. My view is that any method is legit as long as the results are valid, which I believe Merce's to be.

But chance choreography wasn't often on my mind. To develop a strong dance technique was what I needed. It was much too early to be getting critical about Merce's methods or anyone else's when learning to dance required intense single-mindedness. I was eager to dance with both Martha's company and the one Merce was planning to form. Martha's was often inactive and gave only one short New York season a year. Although neither choreographer would be apt to enjoy sharing dancers, I felt optimistic about working for both.

Something happened at the end of my year at Juilliard that shows how quickly I'd forgotten Tudor's lesson in humility. Believing that the college credits from Syracuse combined with Juilliard ones would earn me a degree, I went one day to Miss Hill's office to make certain this was so. Disappointingly, I learned that the dance department wasn't yet set up to give degrees and that if I wanted one, I'd have to return for another year. Not wanting a degree all that much, I puffed myself up and told Miss Hill that I had no time for another year, that someday I was going to be a well-known dancer and would never willingly allow Juilliard to use my name for fund raising. After a year, finding the outside world a pretty tough place, I became a little less arrogant, and a year after that I was ready to eat my hat. Eventually, I was proud to be an alumnus.

Black Mountain, Hell's Kitchen, and Broadway

Soon after leaving Juilliard I stuffed practice clothes, Ace bandages, Infrarub, and a few other less important items into a laundry bag and headed south to Black Mountain. I had been invited by Merce to spend the summer with him and his other five company members at an artists' colony in North Carolina, where after two months of classes and rehearsals we were to perform a concert of his works which would include *Septet, Dime a Dance, Banjo,* and *Collage.*

At rehearsals Merce wasted no time on theories or verbal explanations of what his dances meant. He simply showed us their steps and, except for telling us their counts, said nothing about how we, as performers, should interpret them. Presumably, the dances were not about anything, and as performers, we were to execute rather than interpret. This puzzled me, because the dances seemed to have subjects, or at least emotional climates, and because Merce danced his own roles dramatically. Each of his movements, be they sharp or soft, shouted or whispered, startled or stealthy, clearly meant something to him. For instance, at the end of *Septet*, instead of merely tiptoeing in a line with the rest of us, he seemed to be deeply involved in some kind of religious procession, perhaps one that related to the Catholic altar boy he had once been; in *Untitled Solo*, an obviously psychological study, he was communicating personal but unspecific conflicts. Yet, to his dancers, he wasn't letting any cats out of the bag. We never knew if he chose not to tell us the meanings behind his dances because it might make us overemote in our own performances, or because such tipoffs would give glimpses into a personal life that he preferred to keep private. At any rate, undramatized steps and performances were what seemed to be expected from the rest of us.

We all adored Merce and rehearsed beaverishly to learn his dances. The two months were filled with uninterrupted work and more work, and the only one of us who did anything other than dance was Anita, who caught the mumps.

At the end of the summer, soon after we left, Black Mountain folded due to financial difficulties. Unfortunately, I may have contributed slightly to the collapse. Although I had been led to think that the summer would be expense free, the head administrator, poet Charles Olson, presented me with a bill for room and board, which I was unable to pay.

Back in New York, and sporting a beard which in '53 was far out, and needing a place to live, I went around knocking on tenement doors. Landlords were unimpressed with the beard, my occupation, and especially the fact that I had no source of income. With help from Graham classmate Murray Gitlin, I was finally able to convince one of the landlords to let me rent his fifteen-and-a-half-dollar-a-month railroad flat in Hell's Kitchen. Even in '53 the apartment wasn't much of a bargain. It was called a railroad flat because of its three lined-up closet-sized rooms, the caboose being the communal john out in the hall, I guess; and it had no heat, though for mild warmth in wintertime, a cast-iron gas stove could be illegally lit. There seemed to be a strong possibility of setting off an explosion from the neighborhood's abundant garbage and cat-urine fumes.

Later on, when subletting to Joe Layton, who was soon to become an affluent Broadway and Hollywood director, I would have earned myself three dollars a month profit had he not been so hard to collect from.

After furnishing the flat with "objets trouvés," most of which were local street gleanings, I sat down on a pseudo–art deco chair to survey the results of my decorating efforts. There on the newly enameled black floor and matching black walls, scuttling industriously, were communities of water bugs and various types of roaches. Most were dull brown, a color that went poorly with my color scheme, and none were nearly as attractive as the bugs that I'd been chums with at Edgewater Beach. Possibly I was losing my zest for insect life, or else these New York ones had lost their charisma. I then noticed a brave little mouse scaling the leg of my brand-new packing-crate table. On making it to the top, it brazenly sat there expecting a handout. Being no longer sheltered by institutions, and hungry myself, in fact getting hungrier all the time, I was unable to drum up much compassion.

Up to then I had received scholarship handouts from Syracuse, the American Dance Festival, and Juilliard. Classes at Martha's school and Merce's were also gratis, and the ones from Tudor and Miss Craske at the Metropolitan Opera Ballet School, cut rate. Rehearsals with Martha, Merce, and lately Pearl Lang I did for love, as did their other dancers; and so, the subject of food being foremost on my mind, I began to leaf through *Variety* and *Show Business* to find out who was holding auditions for what. Although show dancing was not what I had come to New York for, any kind of performing experience was bound to be worthwhile. I started making the rounds regardless of what the auditions were for, as long as the job would pay.

After other hopefuls and I had lined up like so many hunks of ham or slices of cheese, we were asked to tap dance, sing, act, and do acrobatics. Just because I could do none of these didn't keep me from wasting everyone's time. Instead of tapping, I flapped ineptly, then got a "Next"; instead of a circular series of Russian cartwheels, I used my hands and barely managed a single, which of course got me another "Next"; instead of singing a current show tune, I mumbled "Happy Birthday" and earned myself the rarely heard "Get out of here and don't you ever come back!" It was slightly discouraging that no one could recognize a star when they saw one.

Continuing the rounds, I eventually came upon the perfect audition, one where I was the only applicant. The producers of a TV commercial needed someone who could be a gorilla and fit into the costume, size medium, that they had already rented. After squeezing into it (I hardly popped the seams at all), and after assuring the director that I ate bananas well, I was hired.

It was to be my professional debut, one that would have been more auspicious if I had been allowed to dance, or at least waddle a bit. Too bad only vine swinging was required.

On rushing straight from Merce's rehearsal, I arrived for the taping late and was quickly sewn into the costume; and then, the eye holes being too high, someone had to lead me in front of the camera, where I was handed something that felt and smelled like a bunch of wax bananas. The director or someone else said, "Go, guy, swing your heart out!" No one seemed to care when I complained that I was being jabbed by a coat hanger that had been left inside the costume.

I began to get other commercial work, at the same time dancing with various modern dance companies and taking two classes daily. Just remembering my schedule and getting to the rehearsals and classes on time was an accomplishment in itself. Merce had been rehearsing us all fall for a mid-winter week-long season at the small and inadequate Theatre de Lys in the Village. He had his own scheduling demands, and so, though nothing was said, it was a safe assumption that he was not pleased by my being late to one or two of his rehearsals. On my part, I was beginning to indulge in a dangerous thing. I'd started to look at his dances with a critical eye and picture how I would make them if I were he. When a dancer does that too often, there's only one thing to do—make your own.

Things came to a point of no return over *Dime a Dance*, a suite of short solos, duets, and trios. Each company member had learned all the parts of all the sections, but we were not to know which part to perform until after the curtain went up. From a basket onstage different objects were to be drawn which would denote who would perform what. Unfortunately for me, the object that signified what I would dance was never drawn. Several weeks later, disappointed at not dancing in *Dime a Dance*, I asked Merce if future opportunities to dance were also to be decided by chance. He did not answer my question, or could not, but said that if I disapproved of chance methods, he thought it sensible for me to leave the company. I had gained a lot from Merce, was very fond of him, and admired the steadfastness of his beliefs. Had he indicated a preference for me to stay, and if I could have forced myself to agree with chance methods, I might've flipped a coin to decide about leaving. (A dime would've been appropriate.) As things stood, I chose to give Merce my notice. Since then we have remained friendly and I still admire his strength of belief and the clarity and lack of sentimentality of his dances.

When working with the American dance pioneer Charles Weidman, and although under his direction, I saw very little of him. He had already contributed much to the field but was now past his prime. His *Lysistrata* was to be presented in tandem with Robinson Jeffers's play *The Cretan Woman* at the President Theater on Broadway. I auditioned, was selected, and then rehearsed at an Eighth Avenue ex–funeral parlor where Mr. Weidman lived. Since he was rarely well enough to attend rehearsals, his two assistants and some of the cast set most of the dance. Just before we opened, the costumes were taken back by the costume makers, who believed that the producers were crooks and not likely to pay for them. Without sets, however, and wearing our own practice clothes, we went on anyway and performed the dance twice before closing.

One day in '54, while trudging from one rehearsal to another, I stopped off at the Stable Gallery near Columbus Circle to see what was up in the painting world. After giving the main floor a quick once-over, I went downstairs to see what was in the basement and found a copper-haired guy of about my own age sweeping dirt into a pile. He introduced himself as Bob Rauschenberg, said that he was a painter and that he supered the gallery for its director, Eleanor Ward, in return for being allowed a basement show of his own. The basement was featuring his latest work, something that he called dirt paintings. One of them had just fallen off the wall. Charmingly, he went on to say that he had made them by planting birdseed in earth-filled frames and that after grass had sprouted, and although he had sprayed fixative by the quart, it had been hard to get the frames to hang on the wall without everything falling out. Nevertheless, in spite of a minor gravitational problem, he believed his work to be an embodiment of the concept of art being nature, and vice versa. In addition to the dirt paintings, his show included some enigmatic stones and a few small boxes filled with curiosities that he had scavenged from beaches and streets. To me these all seemed very beautiful, mysterious, darkly comical, and somehow atavistic. Bob had at least two gifts—imagination and gab—and I immediately complimented him on his work, although it crossed my mind that he might be more of an idea man than a technician. While he talked I became convinced that, like me, he was bound to become important, but for the time being he was struggling and flat broke.

He lived in a ramshackle loft on Pearl Street down at the densely packed skyscraper tip of Manhattan, where he had been daubing an enormous white canvas with white oil paint—no painted shapes, just the real ones from the thick daubs. Since he kept running out of paint and having delays until he could afford more, the canvas was taking a long time for him to complete. By the time it was done it had yellowed with age because of the cheap paint, but that and other of life's picayune impediments didn't seem to bother him.

In '78, twenty-four years after he and I first met, both of us were awarded life achievement medals from Brandeis University. Others receiving similar awards were Saul Bellow, Grace Paley, Jessica Tandy, and Hume Cronyn. The ceremony was held at the auditorium of the Guggenheim Museum, and my old ballet teacher Antony Tudor was in the audience. Bob, by then a multimillionaire, was print-making at his portion of Captiva Island in Florida, and so a friend of his, Tanya Grossman, was accepting his award for him. My off-the-cuff acceptance speech was taped by her and later sent to me:

"There's a sort of coincidence going on here tonight, and it's about Bob and me. You see, we—uh—well, we both came to New York at the same time and we met, and he was one of the first people I ever met in New York, except he wasn't a New Yorker. He was from Texas, I think, and— ah—that we should be getting these same awards at the same time here seems like—umm—[*something garbled*], and I wish he was able to be here because, well, uh, I did very much want for him to see me get my award. Well, I guess maybe I'll have to tell him I got mine first.

"Anyway, when we met Bob said something to me that—I don't know why, but it's stuck in my mind all these years. He said . . . let's see . . . well, it was so stupid that it's no wonder I've forgotten [*awkward silence here*]. Oh yeah, now it comes back. Ahem. Bob said, 'All hot water is, is cold water heated.' You see? It was sort of dopey, right? But not really, because where I lived there wasn't any heat or hot water, and in the wintertime the whole place would freeze solid, and you had to wear hats and gloves inside to rehearse in and you had to write home with a pencil because of the ink freezing and cracking the bottle, and all, you know? So when I mentioned the cold to Bob he knew that I had a hot plate, so that's when he said, 'All hot water is, is [*rumble from passing bus here*] . . .'

"Anyway, what Bob said showed a kind of optimistic attitude—I mean, that anything, anything at all you wanted, was possible. And I think I must've caught a little of Bob's attitude and it's helped my company and me over some bumps. Sure, I remember what he said, and I sure hope he knows that I . . . Tanya, will you tell him that I remember what he said? And so these awards prove Bob right, that anything's possible, and this award is very [*more mumbles*] umm—and I appreciate it, and—uh, thank you."

After leaving Merce's company in '54, I began to work fairly regularly with five or six acquaintances and classmates. This loosely formed fly-by-night group was the original of the one in my name that exists today and was created mainly for the purpose of gaining performing experience rather than as an outlet for my choreography. Three or four times a year we shared programs with other fledgling dancers and dance makers at small stages such as at the Henry Street Settlement House, or Master's Institute, an Upper West Side residential hotel. Most of these shared programs were under the aegis of Dance Associates, a conglomeration of groups that were selected and encouraged by James Waring. Besides dancing and making dances, Jimmy generously arranged the dates, sent out fliers, and in general organized the concerts. He could have been called business manager except that we were not a business—that is, little or no money changed hands. The concerts were given without backing, usually went unannounced in the newspapers, and were performed practically in secret. There were few production costs. Costumes were made out of dime-store wares and refurbished hand-me-downs. We improvised with whatever could be begged or borrowed in the way of rehearsal space. Although the management of International House had not given permission, some of us used the gravelly, railingless, and risky roof there to rehearse on.

Some of the dance associates whose work later became better known were choreographers Richard Englund, Benjamin Harkarvy, Marvin Gordon, Paul Sanasardo, and Lee Theodore; composer John Herbert McDowell, who wrote dance scores for us and others by the hundreds; painters Bob Rauschenberg and Jasper Johns; dancer/costume designer Ruth Sabodka; and two dancers who danced mainly with Waring—David Gordon and Toby Armour. As far as I know, all of these people donated their time and talent. Two or three dance critics usually reviewed us, but probably only because there was much less dance then going on in New York.

Jack and the Beanstalk was the first dance that I made while connected with Dance Associates. It had original music by a young composer Jimmy had recommended. Bob did the costumes and props, which included a self-illuminating golden egg and a beanstalk that was merely a long string held up by gas-filled balloons. The dancers were Viola Farber, who was in Merce's company, Alec Rubin, Leslie Snow, Don Boiteau, Anita, and, of course, myself. The dance was supposed to be a nonnarrative fairy tale— that is, its six sections had no story or character delineation, but were separated one from another by still poses meant to resemble story-book illustrations and which were intended to get the narration over with in a hurry. Any hint of Jungian psychology as typified by Martha's interior landscapes was carefully avoided, as well as anything of a heroic or weighty nature. The dance was neo-old-hat-ism; I was taking a stand for brainlessness and physical fluff.

At the dress rehearsal the score's barely completed orchestration was heard for the first time. It did not sound right to me, so I asked the musicians to play it at low volume in a back room behind the stage, explaining to them that the dance would then be improved by an atmosphere of mystery and remoteness. Even keeping the door closed didn't help much.

After the dance was performed the audience just sat there. No boos, no clapping, nothing. This was not surprising to me, as I had assumed that the dance was neither good nor bad. It was never performed again, and its transitoriness was celebrated by a small ritual which Bob and I conducted.

Taking the beanstalk and its balloons out into the alley behind the theater, we released them and watched them disappear into the sky. "Isn't it just great, the way dances are so easy to erase?" said Bob, and I wholeheartedly agreed. We were not the least interested in leaving monuments to the future—in fact, we saw a kind of glamour in impermanence. Bob had lately gotten hold of a valuable de Kooning drawing, erased it, and hung it in his own show. As I understood it, the main idea was to flush a painting or a dance out of your system and then go on to the next one. (In the distant future I was to change my mind.)

After a summer spent dancing in Pearl Lang's company at Jacob's Pillow in Massachusetts, I return to the city and again make the rounds. There's an interesting rumor on the dancer's grapevine—Jerome Robbins, Broadway's top choreographer, is directing Mary Martin's *Peter Pan* and needs an acrobat who can dance a little. There has been no casting call in the trade sheets, but the show has already been performed on the West Coast and is to open in three days at the Winter Garden. Naturally, I rush right over as fast as I can. Unquestionably, working for Robbins would be a valuable experience.

At the Winter Garden a stage doorman tells me that there's no audition being held, but after telling him that I have an urgent message for Mr. Robbins, I'm allowed in. My eyes being slow to adjust to the dark, when stepping onto the stage I trip and almost fall. From out front someone yells, "Hey, what the hell are you doing in here?" The voice is deep and I assume it to be Robbins's.

"I'm the dancing acrobat, sir, the one everybody says you need," I reply, swelling my stomach and hunching a little, since I've heard that most acrobats are short and stocky.

"Bub, what's needed around here isn't a dancing acrobat but more cleaners. This goddamn place is filthy."

My eyes now adjusted, I can see that a cleaning woman has been speaking. She runs her vacuum up and down the aisles for a while, and then the real Robbins and his dance captain come in and I repeat what I said to the cleaning woman.

I'm then asked to do back flipflops, but not having any idea what they are, I say, "Don't you want to see me do some ballet first?"

"Later, maybe. Your flipflops, please."

"How about if I sing something?"

I'm told that my singing isn't especially needed and am again asked to flipflop. There seems no point in giving myself away, so I explain that mine are a little rusty and ask to show them later, intending to take a tumbling lesson somewhere as soon as possible.

Robbins says I can have ten minutes to brush up and gestures to the front lobby. There I find a group of little boys, the show's lost children, who are jostling each other around on thick carpeting. When I ask one of them if he can tell me what a flipflop is, he looks pleased, vaults into the air, arches backwards, comes down on both hands, and pops back onto his little feet as if shot from a toaster. The stunt seems to be on the risky side—a scary direction to take—but the show is apt to run, and a job is a job. After several attempts to copy the kid—each time landing on my head—the ten minutes are up, so I return to the stage, where I announce that my flipflops are perfection, then ask Robbins if there is anything else that he'd like to see. But he insists.

This is the moment of truth. Adrenaline courses through my veins. Eyes shut, I heave upwards and, after an endless moment of panicky disorientation, come crashing down on my feet. They sting like blazes, but I'm grateful not to have broken my neck.

"Umm . . ." he says doubtfully. "Now do them fast, one after the other, and make sure to travel in a straight line."

There's a limit to what adrenaline can do, and the straight line turns out to be a slow zigzag. However, perhaps because he has no time to find anyone better, Mr. Robbins hires me.

I'm quickly taught the part of one of Captain Hook's dancing, singing, brawling, slightly simian pirates. At rehearsals Robbins seems like an enthusiastic camp counselor explaining the rules of an enjoyable rainy-day indoor game. The dancers, several of whom have worked with him before, are terrific and do the show's charming and beautifully crafted song-and-dance numbers with pizazz.

The flipflops are needed during a fight aboard designer Peter Larkin's red velour pirate ship, part of which, at Robbins's insistence, has been junked in order to leave more space for the action. Dancer Don Lurio, soon to star in his own TV series in Rome, is dancing the role of a boxing-gloved kangaroo. He is to beat me up, and as a result of a final punch, I'm to exit backwards through an opening downstage right which is disturbingly close to the cement proscenium. Don says for me not to fret, that I'll be able to aim myself in the right direction by lining up on him. To gain more control and less panic, after rehearsals I take a couple of flipflop lessons at a gym.

On opening night I line up as planned, pull off a fairly decent line of flipflops, but veer a bit too far right and crash into the proscenium, breaking my nose and squashing it flat to the left. After crawling offstage, I see Mary Martin's maid passing by with a load of clean towels. "Hey, may I use one of those to wipe blood with?" I ask.

" 'Deed, no chorus boy ain't gonna soil up my Miss Martin's towel," she says stiffly.

"Well, that's all right," I say back, snatching the top one. "I'm sure she won't mind. You see, I'm going to be a big star myself soon."

After the opening kangaroo bit Don helps me to an emergency ward, where an intern tells me that though my septum has been deviated, he can do nothing for me, since noses aren't really his bag. But I persuade him to push while I pull, and between us we're able to shove it back into place.

Several days later I still can't breathe through it, so I go to a surgeon, who agrees to repair it, and since this is to be his first operation ever, he agrees to a reduced rate. Some weeks later, after removing the bandages and looking in a mirror, I'm sorry to see that the nose, never very long to begin with, has gotten even shorter; but when I mention it, the surgeon sets me at ease with assurances that all noses lengthen with age. "Just be patient," he says. "It will eventually grow back to its original length." (These days, over three decades later, I'm still patiently waiting.)

There being no understudy for me in *Peter Pan*, it never occurs to me to miss a performance. Heavy landings out of the flipflops keep jarring the tender nose and sometimes cause me to bite my tongue. And, though continuing my lessons, I never learn to land gently. I partially solve the tongue-biting problem, however, by having a dentist file down the two sharp points of my incisors. And then, after about two months of performances, my wrists begin to go and I sprain one of them. When I ask the dance captain if the flipflops might be replaced with back somersaults, I'm told that since I'm hardly seen because of everything else that's going on in the fight scene, I can leave them out until my wrist gets better.

Robbins has long since stopped coming to see the show, but that night he or someone else notices the flipflops missing, and I get a pink slip the next day. There's nothing much to complain about—understandably, performance standards have to be maintained.

It's possible to find another job, one more within my range. Cyril Ritchard, the show's elegant Captain Hook, generously recommends me for a nonspeaking part in a TV production of *Mysterious Island*, which stars Rita Gam. Big silent types are needed to leer and lurk around in a plastic jungle.

In a few years my company receives the first of several grants from the Robbins Foundation. Jerry has always been interested in what new dance makers are up to and, having seen or read about my concerts, is not only helping but showing me that he thinks my work worthwhile. Later on, in '84, he again aids my company, this time with a twenty-five-thousand-dollar grant, for which, should I ever work for him again, I'd gladly flipflop as often as possible.

* * *

Instead of lessening with familiarity, fear of flipflops and concern for the hardness of the proscenium increased with each performance. Show biz demanded a lot more fortitude than I thought, and, in a way, it's a relief not to have to go back to the Winter Garden anymore. In spite of what I told Mary Martin's maid, I'm not at all sure about ever starring in anything, for, since I left Juilliard, the preordained future has begun to seem less rosy. Taking a cue from old Dr. Tacet, I've begun to ask myself, "Have you the heart of a lion, the soul of a saint? Or even, dear boy, the fecundity of a hare?" Comparing myself with other dancers causes reassessments to be made. Living economically makes my stomach rumble. When funds run out, I resort to eating canned dog food, sometimes swiping it from super-markets. To restore dignity, however, I make up for such moral lapses by snitching caviar from Bloomingdale's.

As always, the cloistered world of Miss Craske's ballet classes has smoothed the difficulties of city life. While they last, her classes are shel-tering isles of order—something like my old barred and bubble-decaled haven of a crib back at the Brighton Hotel—and it's tempting to think of her classroom as protective insulation rather than as something that builds technique. The unequivocal Cecchetti system which she teaches is com-fortingly symmetrical, and she herself radiates perfect calm. Having studied with the Italian master, even teaching for him in her native London, she had then met a guru, Baba, and followed him across German U-boat-infested waters to India, where she'd proven her devotion to him and his teachings by living an impoverished life of servitude and, it's said, by hanging with other Babaites from the ledge of a cliff. After that, she re-turned to teaching ballet, Tudor being one of her students.

Though her classes sometimes seem tedious, and are not what I consider dancey dancing, for the hour and a half that they last, just being there gives me an illusion of well-being. She is admired by all, and her wisdom and peaceable manner are those of a woman who's passed an ordeal by fire with flying colors. Although I never mentioned it to her in so many words, the perilous bouts with the kangaroo probably wouldn't have been possible for me without the fortitude that she'd inspired.

Not employed often enough to collect unemployment insurance, I've been earning enough to scrape by and continue concert work. Paid to be a dragonfly in the Jones Beach Marine Theater's *Arabian Nights*, for which Rod Alexander choreographs an insect dance, I back up Nirska the Butterfly Lady (bugs always my leitmotif). Madam Nirska sports twenty-six-foot China silk wings and platform shoes—an impressive sight to behold, especially in a wind storm. Tenor Lauritz Melchior makes his entrance on a portly elephant—a well-matched pair—but the elephant isn't housebroken and leaves the stage unsanitary for those of us who have to follow in bare feet. Also included is a water ballet, the swimmers having their own problems, with sea nettles. My favorite sight of the two-month run is when a fellow chorus boy foolishly mistakes depilatory for hair bleach, then molts.

Rehired by Jerry Robbins for his TV version of *Peter Pan*, I managed one last flipflop, this time merely crashing into the key grip.

In modern concerts I've partnered Natanya Newman, an extraordinary dancer who's been in Martha's company, also in Merce's *Sixteen Dances*. Beautiful Pearl Lang begins to give me solo roles, including some of Glen Tetley's old ones. Some of these are performed at the ANTA in a Broadway season advertised as "three weeks of the greatest in contemporary dance." (Through a printer's error, my name in the *Playbill* comes out five times the size of Pearl's.) Bethsabee de Rothschild presents this season of twenty repertoire pieces and eighteen premieres performed by seven companies and six independent soloists. The notices are less than raves. Winthrop Sargeant, music critic for *The New Yorker* and Martha's sister Geordie's ex-husband, writes that "for those who attend the theater for uplift, a lot of the season has been lugubrious." John Martin of the *Times* thinks that the mixed programs, which seem to be trying to offer something for every taste, also automatically have something against every taste. The *Herald Tribune*'s Walter Terry, a nice guy who can be counted on to like almost everything, says he does, but probably nobody believes him. The thumbs-down on this panoramic view of modern dance is likely discouraging for Bethsabee—also annoying, in that she's had to put up with many of the choreographers' complaints over unequal allotments of performances, stage rehearsal time, billing, and other ticklish matters. After the season is over, for whatever reasons, she limits her backing solely to her friend Martha for a while, then moves to Israel, where she founds the Batsheva company.

When not dancing, I work for my painter pals, Bob Rauschenberg and Jasper Johns. Their careers haven't yet quite gotten off the ground, and so they're bolstering their meager incomes by designing and making department-store window displays, paying me by the hour to help at their loft on Pearl Street. Some of the displays are commissioned by Gene Moore of Tiffany's, a man known for his taste and discrimination as well as for aiding many rising artists by hiring them. At present he's still doing it, and I'm proud to be included as one of his artists, whom, in my case, he aids by donating the set and costume designs that he often creates for my dances.

Bob and Jap's loft is so small that in order to make room for the display work, Bob sometimes throws out a few of his old paintings. Once, when I find his last remaining dirt painting in the trash, I ask him for it and he signs the back "To Pete." This early work, like all the paintings of both artists, is soon to be coveted by major museums around the world. For reasons of sentiment I've never sold it—not that I couldn't have used the cash.

While working on the displays, Bob and Jap often talk about art. As far as I can make out, their main intent is to glorify, or at least present in a new way, ordinary objects. These things—Coke bottles, coat hangers, light bulbs, etc.—aren't supposed to be symbols. The idea is to appreciate them for their own beauty. If there's a message, it seems to be a recommendation for everybody to expand their vision, to get a kick out of stuff that's usually considered homely, corny, or even unsightly. Neither paints pictures of anything, exactly—they recycle the thing itself. Both disapprove of likening things to other things. Both have a fondness for the same objects, but Jap can get more wrapped up in American flags than Bob can, judging by his large numbers of them. And Jap likes numbers better, large numbers of numbers done in wax. Bob sometimes slips into exoticism, such as a stuffed angora goat with a tire around its middle. Jap is a fine draftsman. Bob can't draw at all, even if he wanted to. Bob's works, mirroring his own nature, have a high gloss of humor and are collages of enthusiastic charm and dark mayhem underlined by strong commitment. Jap's works, in my inexpert opinion, are less charming, almost frighteningly spartan, and so strong that I find them hard to relate to. Bob's I can laugh with; Jap's, for all their virtue, laugh at me. Both painters seem to look askance at most contemporary realists, as well as at the expressionists and impressionists, preferring Man Ray and some of the other dadaists. Monet's water lilies and Whistler's portrait of his mother are two of the exceptions. The window-display work bore a certain kinship to the two future greats' own painting. For instance, one set of Tiffany windows, a job that didn't take long, had plain ordinary dirt dumped in them, over which were strewn cut diamonds. Much of what I absorbed from the two artists strongly affected my early dances—one of the most useful things learned from Bob being that sometimes the quick, easy way is best.

Babe

So as to have space to practice and make dances in, I move from the Hell's Kitchen flat to a nearby building where I'm able to rent three floors, two of which are sublet at a profit, enabling me to afford the top floor, where I live for the next three years. There is no heat, shower, or bath—for that matter, no water at all. At some former time a fire has left large gaps in the building's roof. These I cover with clear plastic so that it's still possible to look up and enjoy seeing patches of sky. My second-floor tenant, Roland Vazquez, who dances with the New York City Ballet, lets me use his sink and john. The heating problem is partially solved by always wearing several layers of wool in the wintertime. Since everything freezes, there's no need to use the fridge and, since living in the building is illegal and firemen periodically come to inspect, a sleeping mat is rolled up and hidden in the daytime. Having space to dance in more than makes up for these inconveniences.

The first dance made here is *Circus Polka*, a solo which is soon enlarged into a group work and retitled *Little Circus*. David Vaughan, a fellow Dance Associate, performs the part of a dour and slightly menacing ringmaster wearing a string of large cow-bones around his neck, which Bob has suggested. When the part is later danced more menacingly by Jimmy Waring, it osmoses from what was intended as comedy into something more macabre. The cast change and its resulting effect kindle an interest in the differences between light and dark types of humor, an area that I hope to investigate in future dances.

Bob has also suggested an idea for the dance's two-man horse costume, but his concept seems too sophisticated for the rest of the piece, so I ask a recent acquaintance, George Wilson, to execute a cruder design that I'd thought of. He paints a backdrop in a childlike way on newspapers glued to old sheets. The costumes and drop are mostly my designs, but since I feel that being credited in the program as both dancer and choreographer is enough, I use the alias of my imaginary childhood companion, George Tacet.

It's unremarkable that old friend Tacet and new friend Wilson are both named George, but it seems too coincidental, almost predestined, that the correct spelling of my pseudonym turns out to mean "he is silent," and that George Wilson happens to be a deaf-mute.

I first saw him at Riis Park, there on the beach amusing other deaf-mutes with an energetic imitation of someone. Several months later I notice him again, this time at a Third Avenue beer joint. He's standing still and stony at the bar, alone and seemingly lost within an enveloping mantle of unadulterated endurance. When a drunken stranger comes over to ask him a question, George responds by pointing to his own ear and shaking his head, then turns away. The stranger mistakes deafness for snootiness, spins George around, and socks him in the mouth. Out of sympathy, or maybe curiosity, but probably because of his craggy looks, I go help him up and, by scratching a note on a matchbook cover, get him to show me some deaf-mute signs. He demonstrates the ones for "boy" and "girl," "father" and "mother," and how to spell his name by using letters made with the fingers of one hand.

Going on to give more than I can take in at once, he then flutters out the whole alphabet. His hands are calloused hams. His fingers, moving through clear, delicate shapes, look strong enough to break a piano. On further questioning he pulls out a pad and writes that his mother was an American Indian and his father Irish (no visible traces of Indian, but his big, stubborn chin is definitely Irish); that he's one of twelve children, three of them born deaf; and that he himself was born hearing (something he seems very proud of) and would still be able to hear except for falling off an ironing board as a baby when having his diapers changed.

As he writes, he's making little grunts and effortful mutterings, so I take the pad and ask him, if he can make sounds, how come he can't talk. He answers that it's because he's never been taught and that now, at thirty-four, it's too late to learn. He *prefers* not to talk. Things are better that way, otherwise he might be drafted and killed in the war. Whatever the reason, he seems quite adamant about it and, though handicapped, seems well adapted.

The pad soon fills with further background: a Catholic charity grade school for the deaf in Michigan, the crabby nuns there, a hearing girl he'd married, the marriage ending in divorce. Also criticisms of the hospital where he now works as an orderly, and even less enthusiasm for the two people he shares an East Side flat with—a hustler and a whore. The hustler has been building a cardboard-and-cellophane scale model of Manhattan which entirely fills the flat, and nobody can have sex there without knocking over the Chrysler Building.

More pages are scrawled with other unusual, yet somehow familiar, details of his solitary, pauperish life. The words rush onto the pages as if bottled up since birth. I try to picture the isolation endured by him but don't get far. Compared with his, any lonesomeness that I've ever experienced is chicken feed.

After the last page is filled, I treat him to a foreign film with subtitles, either *Children of Paradise* or the one about two war orphans who make a game out of burying dear departed house pets. In the dark he reacts compassionately to the movie, a lot less aware of the loudness of his sobs than I am.

Later we sometimes have a beer at the same bar, go to other subtitled movies, or just walk around town. Sometimes we play a sort of game where I try to guess the words that he bashfully tries to pronounce. His version of my nickname, Pete, comes out as "Beedah."

Pads and pencils aren't needed after a month or so, when I've learned to sign. Though now able to communicate more easily and quickly, we often fall into long stretches of comfortable silence. My mind is usually full of dance, a topic of little interest to him. At these times he becomes almost invisible, more of a presence than a fact, and being with him is to enjoy company and solitude at the same time. He gives my mind the luxury of space to move in.

Then one day at my loft, when looking in my cardboard closet for something to wear, I find that all the extra coat hangers are being used for clothes that aren't mine, and in a carton at the back are some alien odds and ends. One is a beat-up snapshot of a worn-looking woman surrounded by a dozen rag-tag children, all clustered in front of a rundown house that seems much too small to hold them. On the back in child's lettering is "Mother. Cadillac, Mich."

Finding these things shouldn't have been a surprise. Though I've noticed George's visits getting longer, somehow I haven't realized that he's been moving in. When he brought his pet hamsters over, I thought them temporary guests. However meager, my loft is a castle, which I feel territorial about. I'll have to tell him that I don't need a roommate right now and urge him to take everything back, starting with the hamsters, which tend to leave small brown marbles on my bed pillow.

But the more I think about it, the less I know how I'll be able to get him to go. Though he can be bull headed, the nobility of his heart is as congenital as his chin. I admire, feel sorry for—what's more, have become fond of— him. That is, I'm fond of who I imagine him to be. Admittedly, there are great gaps to him which have been filled in with whatever traits I've fancied. George was a cardboard cutout waiting to be colored. With a deaf-mute this has been easier than ever. Dr. Tacet was simple enough to imagine, although a little effort was needed to keep him consistent; but tangible George was a pushover, his basic framework already existing. Facts always fled from fantasy, and the realities of silent chums can be whatever one wants. I've made him faultless—it would be foolish to allow George to ruin George.

So it'll be tough to tell him to go. But I've made up my mind, and just as I'm folding his clothes, packing them with the other things, I hear him come puffing up the stairs. Unlike most, he never tries to hide or excuse his puffing. "Babe," I spell (calling him Babe usually buttered him up), "Babe, you've got to understand, I'm territorial, see?"

He doesn't see. He wouldn't know the word "territorial" even if I could spell it right. I'm weakening already, my fingers stuttering.

Starting over, I spell, "Babe, you see . . ." He spots the packed clothes and turns away. This always happens whenever we disagree. All either of us has to do to prevent an argument is turn away.

He starts returning his stuff to the closet. I back him into a corner of the loft and force him to look at my hand, telling him that if he won't go I'll have to call the cops. He twists free and leans his head in the corner. Sobs start shaking his back. He's locked there, won't budge. I steel myself to make good my threat.

When the cops come, I show them my lease. Babe glances at a note from one of them, picks up his belongings with exaggerated dignity, and leaves, stamping each step of each flight on the way down.

The next day those stamps are still reverberating. Otherwise the loft seems very quiet. Too quiet. As the day wears on, I become aware of other echoes—the booming of thunder that he uselessly wanted to know the sound of; the horrible explosion of his sneeze, which he adamantly called a cough; and, most deafening, most annoying, the clunking of his spoon whenever he stirred his sugar-thickened coffee. "Please stop it!" I'd sign impatiently, then warn him of the dangers of too much sugar and, while at it, criticize his inflexible notions of nutrition. To him an ideal meal consisted of macaroni, powdered instant potatoes, and Wonder Bread. That was what they ate in Michigan.

Intending to fix myself coffee, I find that, as usual, my hot plate's been left unplugged. Besides being sure that appliances work better if their cords are kept untwisted, Babe is deathly afraid of them starting a fire—reasonably, since the warning crackle of flames would go unheard. Unheard horns, too, present peril. When jaywalking, I often had to stifle an impulse to grab his hand; but you couldn't fool around with his proud independence, or buy him a beer without him treating you back, and . . .

The furniture. Can't get the furniture off my mind. It's somehow connected with the Babe, this junk that's stored downstairs on the second floor—beds, tables, chairs, you name it, all belonging to a charity organization, some sort of Jewish Salvation Army—all scratched, dented, used or misused, loved or endured by God knows how many past owners in how many homes, belongings rejected, then replaced with shinier, less imperfect pieces. The whole floor is stacked to the ceiling with a tangled mass of aging wooden bones. Of the unfilled space there remains only a narrow zigzag tunnel—dark, tubular, airless, and somehow obscene as it winds through so many once personal belongings.

So up here in my loft it's very quiet. No more clunking of spoons, stamping, or coughs that are sneezes. Yet it's a nagging quiet. A couple of days have passed, and Babe hasn't come back to visit. Something's beginning to nibble at the outer edges of my reclaimed territory. Compassion maybe. It's awful.

I go look for him. He's not at the bar, not at the hospital or under the Chrysler Building. He's not anywhere. Finally there's only one other place left to look. In the furniture—all the way back in there, right by the back wall—a cozy nook's been hollowed out and set up for habitation. There he is, a bull-headed Minotaur within a Cretan labyrinth.

If he couldn't live with me, nobody could stop him from setting up shop nearby.

There's nothing much to say. "Hi, Babe," I sign.

His chin juts, drops, and he exclaims, "Beedah!" It comes out too loud but is recognizable. I gesture; he follows me upstairs, where he flattens out the cord to the hot plate, fixes us some coffee, then starts that damn clunking again. A hunch tells me that I'll be hearing it for a long time. While I'm trying to ignore the noise and put my mind on dance, he's sitting there, solid but less stony than when we'd met. And he's talking to himself with the fingers of one hand, his dear, forceful letters spelling out "Until death do us apart."

Martha and the Orient

And then a sudden change from lowlife loft living to five months of luxurious hotels. The English cuisine at the Raffles in Singapore comes first to mind—and the bills—yet there's been more, much more, to Martha's '55 tour of the Orient.

Well, we might as well start with Martha. So far, of all the sights along the way, she's been by far the greatest. More exotic than the stilt houses of Bangkok, more mysterious than the sea of saffron-robed mendicants at the Temple of the Sacred Bone (did I ever tell you she likes bones? caves too), and more intense than the burning ghats of Calcutta, if not as aromatic. But comparing her this way is probably misleading. Clearly, she's like nothing else. Martha is Martha. And though many have tried to imitate her, she remains the definitive portrayal of herself.

As a statistical matter, however, she's hard to put your finger on. In particular, her exact age, her annual income, and the source of her sorcery. As to her powers of steerage, or whatever you call stubbornness after you've gained respect, without going into a lot of detail it has become clear that what Martha doesn't want to do, Martha doesn't do, and what Martha wants to do, Martha does.

It really isn't much of a problem. She wants mainly, like Ruth St. Denis before her, to perform for a discerning public, drop pith at press conferences, stay at the best hotels, take short rides in long limousines, and wear fur. And when she doesn't want to do any of those, she wants to roam bazaars and add to a rapidly rising pile of jade, silks, stone Buddhas, and such.

But don't get me wrong. Martha isn't merely grand; she can also be a regular guy. Lately, for instance, on the way to the Elephanta caves of Bombay, while bouncing along through the jungle in a sightseeing bus with the rest of us, she's said, "Pablo"—that's what she's started calling me on good days—"darling Pablo," she says, "please instruct our driver to pause over there by those fronds beneath that lovely palm tree. I shall now have a rest stop." And then, after being peeked at and scolded by a family of gibbons who've been playing around in the top of the tree, she resettles herself in the bus, saying, "Bethsabee, those monkeys up there are darling, but, really, their concepts of modesty are terribly old-fashioned."

Martha's companion, Baroness Bethsabee de Rothschild of the French banking family, besides making the tour financially feasible, has joined us as wardrobe mistress. For all I know, the tour being my first, wardrobe mistresses are always baronesses. Bethsabee supervises the laundering and packing of our costumes with quiet efficiency, almost as if born to it, and by looking at her own outfits, you can't tell she's an heiress—that is, if you don't know that expensive dresses are sometimes the dumpiest.

For Martha to be overcoming the rigors of this tour is no small accomplishment, considering the strain of performing, the discomforts of travel, and that she must be somewhere in her sixties, or at least too old to have birthdays. Besides giving numbers of lectures and press interviews, she performs in two out of three dances on every program. Though the rest of us wilt with the heat and sometimes drop out from dysentery, she never misses a performance.

Naturally, her technical abilities have gone a little beyond their peak, but she can still regain her feet without too much trouble after knee crawling ("trills or bourrées of the patella," as fancy Tacet calls it), and one of her best steps is still the backwards skitter on her heels done with locked knees. When that one gets going good, it sometimes travels her to a spot farther than intended—that is, clear into the wings. But it doesn't matter—she usually bounces off a wall and right back to stage center again.

As to her interpretive powers ("para-ambulatory luminosities," quoth

Tacet again), nothing can hold a candle to them. Her dark portrayals of monumental ladies of history are amazing and always being enlarged into a truer image of herself. Take Medea, for instance. Medea couldn't possibly have eaten the evil snake of vengeance as avidly as Martha does, or coughed it up as copiously, or scattered venom so lavishly while wearing Noguchi's four-legged wire contraption of glinting metal rods—which, once she takes it off, sometimes walks itself down raked stages to the apron, where it drops out of sight into the pit.

And Martha presents herself in a wonderfully stylized way. Her wide gapes of the mouth and pinwheeling eyes seem to have been distilled from experience and are larger than life. It's as if she's taken an already stylized personality and enlarged it for the stage, or vice versa. It's puzzling. I mean, maybe she hasn't been stylizing herself for the stage but simply heaping all her artifices one on top of another. You know—art for art's sake. And there's a lot more to get excited about, things such as her complete commitment, her spooky Circe-ness, and how her bun stays on. Even so, I guess I'm not yet able to appreciate the finer points of her dancing quite as much as her other dancers do, but I'm working on it.

The older ones are Helen McGehee, Bob Cohan, Ethel Winter, Stuart Hodes and his wife, Linda, Bert Ross, Matt Turney, and David Wood. Of the men, Stuart is most often featured. Ellen van der Hoeven, Ellen Siegel, Christine Lawson, Donald McKayle, Donya Feuer, and myself are the newcomers, making us a company of fourteen. The road staff numbers nine.

As individuals, one to one we get along well; and as a group, our belief in what we're doing is high—indeed, comes close to being a fetish. But our morale is always hitting rock bottom due to company intrigues and frictional undercurrents. A past master at spotting people's weak spots, Martha is usually the one who's sparked off the squabbles, and few of us ever realize that they aren't entirely due to our own natures, but more to our being used as pawns. Nevertheless, whenever the curtain goes up we perform as pros do. Martha always makes it possible for us to be better than ourselves onstage. Offstage, we sometimes find that we've been maneuvered into situations that make us worse.

Except for Donnie McKayle, who's already an established and much-admired dancer, we newcomers have been chosen from the school and have been cast in minor parts in five of the seven works in the rep. I've been put into *Diversion of Angels* and *Ardent Song* and am expected to understudy other parts, an assignment that I'm not taking too seriously, as nobody's ever had time to teach them to me.

Before leaving New York Martha had gathered the company at her feet to give us some dos and don'ts. "Sweeties," she said, "on this tour we are to be affiliated with the State Department. Your presences will be required at formal occasions at which, gentlemen, you are to wear ties and dinner jackets. All dress, grooming, and conduct in general is to be impeccable, and everyone's hair is to be kept at the prescribed length. By the way, Paul, we shall speak in private later about that naughty crew cut and recurrent beard of yours. Ye gods—wilderness above and scrub brush below!"

Yes ma'am, and the dinner jacket, too, I told myself. I can't afford it, and even if I could, I don't want one.

"And Paul," she continued, "you may as well know right now that when plans were being made for this tour, some of my more experienced dancers suggested that someone, anyone, other than you be selected to go."

"Oh, Martha, how can you say that?" Stuart adventurously interrupted. "We were all for him. You were the one who wasn't, but you were just pretending not to be so that we could all have a good scrap."

Then Martha said to me, as if Stuart hasn't spilt the beans, "However, darling, in spite of the others disapproving, you have been entirely my own choice, even though I have already begun to wonder if it was the right decision."

Then she said that on arrival at each airport there would be a press conference for all of us to attend and that if any of the reporters should ask us questions, we should make our answers brief and to the point, always keeping in mind that we are representing a long and honorable modern-dance heritage.

On the four-day flight to Tokyo, our first stop, where we'll be for two weeks, obi-attired stewardesses serve elegant bits of Japanese food, warm sake, and strange little damp napkins. While the other dancers are chatting with each other, I go around collecting their leftover sakes. Things are turning out better than all right, and the high life is also right up Tacet's alley.

The plane touches down at San Francisco, Honolulu, and Wake Island before arrival in Tokyo, where we are greeted by a cluster of shorties gracefully waving banners that say WELCOME MARTHA GRAHAM. After customs we're corralled into a VIP waiting area, photos are taken, and our first press conference begins. Martha speaks of Life, the Landscape of the Heart, and then dwells awhile on Small Deaths, whatever those are. When she finally finishes, some of the rest of us are asked questions, and I'm picked to define modern dance, something that none of the reporters seem to have heard of. The question is a toughie. My answer—one that gets me excused from future conferences—is the best I can come up with. "It's like this," I explain. "You know ballet? Well, modern's just the same, but uglier."

After settling in at the Frank Lloyd Wright earthquake-proof Imperial

Hotel, we go to a theater (don't quite get the name, but it sounds like Moo Goo Gai Pan) to rehearse a demonstration of Graham technique during which we're to show and Martha's to tell. Someone hands me a regulation practice outfit; I put it on and get set to do my first Graham stage rehearsal—except I've never been told what to do, so I stand at the back behind the others and try to follow. A lot of the steps are familiar, and for a while I'm able to keep up, but then we get to an unfamiliar back fall that's done in slow stages at first, then all at once—bam, right on the count of one. Before I know what's happening, everybody else is neatly curled up on the floor and I'm still standing there like a dope.

From out front Martha waves at me. "Go," she says. "Get off the stage!" She's in one of her uncompromising moods and means business, but I don't want to go, didn't come all this way to get off, so I only go behind a nearby piano and hunch down to wait till things blow over.

But in a little while she waves again. "Paul, what are you doing? I said *get off!* You have had plenty of opportunities to learn the back fall on one. Even beginners know the back fall on one. Do you expect me, *me,* to give you special coaching on the back fall on one? Oh no, sweetie pie, you are a big boy now. I am not your mother!"

Sweetie pie? Not my mother? Ouch! Though about the same age, Mother would be shocked to hear anybody getting her mixed up with Martha. Some nerve, bringing my dear mother into it. I don't like it. Go stuff your back fall on one, I'm thinking.

So I sort of stomp off to the dressing room, and when the rehearsal is over the other guys come, and Stuart nudges me in the ribs and says, "So Martha's not your mother. Ha ha, ho ho!" I'm wild to go at him with an upper cut but don't say anything back. Stuart's been fairly friendly and is almost the only one who stands up to Martha. In fact, sometimes they're a regular Punch and Judy act, so I let his dig pass and don't let on that Martha's stabbed me in a tender spot. He offers to teach me the back fall, and when the curtain goes up I go out and do it with the others.

So far, that's been the only time Martha's ever "lashed her tail" at me, as she'd put it. Since then her mood has been mostly cordial, or at least polite. It's hard to know if this is because she thinks me untasty game or what. Maybe she's gone on a diet. Anyway, as long as her tail isn't aimed at me, I'm looking forward to watching it lash.

In Tokyo there's time to absorb some ceremonial teas, colorful Kabuki, and achingly long Noh drama. To tell the truth, the superrefinements of the Japanese appeal to Tacet more than to me. They make me feel too tall and, well, slightly out of place. Sitting at miniature tables makes my legs cramp up, and low doorways are leaving a continual lump on my forehead.

It's a big relief when we take a chartered plane to Seoul. Or maybe Manila. Bangkok? Already the tour is a puzzling pile of sights—confused shards, mostly unclear as to location. Even if neatly stacked and identified in correct order, they'd effervesce, leaving less than you might expect. Travel, though a stimulus to the senses, jumbles geography and deadens thoughts on dance—even dance, up to now my only clear direction.

We're passing crazy quilts of rice paddies and reeking canals, and a seventh-century temple where I've taught a tot to tic-tac-toe (unsteadily the name Mahabalipuram creeps back); and at an outdoor stage built especially for funny American dancers, tropical moths flutter toward our mouths, sometimes missing, getting stuck in our greasepaint and flapping there piteously. And there's ancient gamelan music, as it used to be before being polluted by Western missionaries, and samurai swords and wicker soccer balls, and all the eternal Buddhas, reclining ones, emerald ones, ones with glittery pinnacles of crowns.

And the depressing views of India's filth. Partially ghat-burned bodies floating down the Ganges, disease everywhere, seas of mauled street people, some crippled at birth by parents who'd thought to make them better beggars, and others who come to wait in front of our hotels, offering themselves as guides or whatever, then following us everywhere, and Matt and I on New Year's Eve tossing our salaries off a hotel roof to the misery below. Crazy us—as if that pittance would matter.

And, in constant contrast, the king of Siam's bejeweled baby white elephant, perfumed, spoiled silly, resentfully shifting its weight in place and seesawing back and forth with a band of wildly whirling yak-buttered dancers from Tibet, very drugged, very smelly, very unlike the elephant; or the mincing classical Indian dancers who reek of Art; or the naturally sweet-smelling children who dance in the temples of Bali.

And lingams. Lots and lots of lingams. Before knowing what they represent, I'm having my picture taken while sitting on one. Everybody else knows what they are and, as the more lighthearted of our audiences have, are laughing like all get out.

And now, folks, we've come to as good a place as any to open Pandora's box—one of the trip's more distinct sights and one that until now has been pretty private.

Up in some mountains near Colombo, somewhere past the outskirts of coffee plantations, we're getting off a bus to stretch when out of the steamy forest a seerlike youth emerges, pauses as if having a vision, then floats straight to me. He's somehow known that of the twenty or so of us, I'm the only one who'll go for what he's carrying. It's the box. Hand carved, teak, satin smooth. He holds it out and I open the lid to see a lepidopterist's dream. Tropical butterflies of staggering charm, lemon-tipped wings and velvety abdomens tufted garishly, shaggy pitchforks at both ends, mauve, scarlet. Fritillaries, monarchs, swallowtails, skippers, satyrs, all splayed and pinned around the external skeleton of what must be Asia's largest scorpion.

Naturally, I'm netted.

The box is mine for almost nothing, and while I'm lost in its contents, the youth—he's that well-formed combination of Dutch and Ceylonese stock—floats back into his forest.

He was as beautiful as the scorpion and twice as unsettling, and in my hands is left an old familiar question, wide open, whirring up from the past, and then I'm realizing that besides a future filled with dance, a second kind of die's been cast. Martha's advice to me about shelving my urges is rushing back, and since I'm now twenty-five, it seems I've waited plenty long enough. Dance is life's main event, sure, but not all there is to it. Shouldn't be. Won't be.

Back in Rangoon, Bethsabee treated the whole company to a Christmas dinner. On the long candle-lit linen-covered table, beside the place cards, were set little suede pouches for the older dancers, each containing a cut gem—rubies, emeralds, sapphires. The five other new dancers and I each got an agate, uncut, and no pouch. According to company seniority, this was to be expected, and none of us minded. Much. But there was consolation. At least we, too, were generous. By us giving Bethsabee nothing, she ended up with the more valuable gift. Nevertheless, we never forget that she's financing the tour. How can we when our salaries barely cover our bills at the fancy hotels where we have to stay? On one side, Bethsabee's bountiful; on the other, thrifty. Not ambidextrous; her right hand doesn't seem to know what her left is doing.

On arrival in Dacca, I think it is, after Martha has given the press an extrauplifting address which has included the ever-popular "It is easy to be yesterday or tomorrow, but difficult to be today," her limousine passes under a large banner that says WELCOME TO MISS HUSH—the name given her by a popular radio quiz show way back in the forties. Poor Martha. Life is full of pestilence. A locust from the past has infested her landscape of the heart. Maybe she's even been nibbled by one of her small deaths. Naturally, the banner is quickly removed when Dacca's welcome committee learns that she prefers to be known for her present status.

At the next press conference she drops the business about the difficulty with being today and tells everyone that "a dancer is a symbol of the person who truly lives" (which is misquoted in a paper as "a danger is a symbol of the person who truly lives"), and then she expresses her desire to see an example of local dancing. Again there is a misunderstanding, and another paper mentions her wanting to see a strip-tease.

We are invited, however, not to the burlesque, or even to the temple of Dakeshwari, but to a private performance given by Mrs. Alfronza Bubul Choudbury and troupe (not Mrs. M. Moeharam Wiranatakoesoema, as tease Tacet tried to tell everyone). The dancing is awful, but afterwards Martha, tapping great resources of tact, bows to each dancer, saying that she was impressed by their passion and belief in what they were doing.

So far, most of what has been written about Martha's own dancing has been favorably inscrutable. One *Pakistan Observer* critic has written that in "*A Long Day's Journey into Night*" (he meant *Night Journey*), Martha is "full to the brim of sorrow and shame, but never once passes more than a bottle in the smoke," and also that "nowhere there is a sign of whipping herself into a lather for nothing."

Another reviewer approves of her "groping through the dark and the dense ways for a meaning in every motion," and goes on to say that "her ecstasy is other than the projection of an enlarged scale of the pladsome aspect of her personality" ("pladsome" being a pompous nonword that Dr. T immediately adds to his vocabulary).

And another enthusiastic critic calls her "a grand old lady with a load in her heart." That's one review that probably won't get glued into a scrapbook back home.

In Teheran, planned as the tour's last stop, we learn that some performances in Israel have been added. Martha summons me to her suite and says, "Pablo darling, I am so sorry, but Bethsabee cannot afford to take the whole company to Israel. Therefore, since you are in only two dances, we shall have to do without you. I hope this is not too disappointing, but you can look forward to dancing with us next year in New York."

It is disappointing. Very. I'd like to finish out the tour with everybody else, but it's best not to let it show.

So I go back to my room to try to look forward, but it's not easy, because I'm feeling pulled in two directions. Things need to be sorted out, and it's times like this that old Tacet comes in handy.

For openers he says, "How darst she dump you! She is merely using Bethsabee's parsimony as an excuse. The indignity of it! What inadequate appreciation of your adoration, what . . ."

I let him go on for a while, then say, "Maybe you're right, Pops, maybe not. Gee, and I thought Martha was getting to like me. It looks like I went and shaved off my beard for nothing."

"Mark my words, Sonny, that woman is a Delilah and wants to clip our career short, not to mention other unkind acts such as the abridging or enshrivelment of our most treasured anatomical gift. These games that she plays are quite quite perilous."

"Yeah, and I don't get the game rules. But don't let's come down too hard on her. You know how she needs stress. She's like some type of tree that thrives best in a windswept place."

"Yes, and fragile anemones around her get their stems snapped. Let us not forget that certain of her dancers have required Band-Aids, even psychiatric services. Do you recall that stormy performance of *Seraphic Dialogue* in Kuala Lumpur?"

"It was Jakarta."

"No, Dacca, dear boy. Madras? Let us not be finicky. We, for one, shall never forget the shamefulness of that interlude. It occurred during Joan the Martyr's transfiguration, did it not? Precisely at her moment of exaltation as she was suffering flames of destiny and death. The scene, I must say, was staged in front of an extraordinarily bogus cathedral—the geometric monotony of all that tasteless copper tubing!"

"Nah, you've got it wrong. It was afterwards, down in the dressing rooms."

"No, no, do not contradict. It started before, when the two supernumerary saints, Ellen and Christine—delectable young morsels, heh heh—were supposed to step off their pedestals in perfect unison. Martha, as you know, had previously envenomed the two dears with a rivalrous antipathy, and in so doing caused them to stop speaking one to the other. When Ellen refused to give Christine the accustomed cue to step down, their synchronization was spoiled. Both furious, they restrained themselves from trading blows until after the curtain's descent, good professionals that they are. But then, my oh my, have you ever heard such dreadful screeching, crashing, and yelping in pain? And how Martha hastened to and fro transporting teensy paper cupfuls from the water cooler—how gloatingly she grimaced while anointing her two saints!"

"Sure, she probably rigged the whole thing—but except for Bert, who slipped in a puddle and banged his back, nobody got hurt, and Martha hit the jackpot."

"Frictional games are uncouth, and being rejuvenated by one's winnings at them is worse."

"Who cares? She's great. And when you get that great you can do anything you want. Besides, she's picked me out from lots of other dancers who'd give their eye teeth to work for her."

"Nonsense. You have your own path to hew through the wilderness that is contemporary dance. Forget this old-style Graham folderol and form your own choreographic statements."

"Well, maybe someday, but not now."

"NOW! Tempus fugit, Sonny. Swiftly return to Manhattan, forthwith presenting the fruit of your imagination in a concert which will reshuffle and reshape the very fundaments of the universe."

"I getcha, Pop. That'd show her. But concerts cost money. You got any idea how I'm going to rent a hall?"

He had no answer for that one, but he goes on and on, and the more I listen, the more my resentment for being let go grows.

A couple of days pass, and then Martha summons me again. This time she's wearing one of her ornate Chinese robes and she's got herself all arranged in a thronelike chair. There's strong sunlight hitting my eyes from the windows behind her, and I can't help having the impression that things have been set up for me to be a victim of the Inquisition.

"Come closer, Pablo," she says.

I'm thinking, "Uh-oh."

"Come sit by my feet," she says. "No, come around behind and rub my neck."

This was high privilege. "Yes'm," I say.

"You were once a champion swimmer, were you not?"

"Yes'm, I was."

"And what a superb athlete you still are! And an excellent neck rubber, too," she purrs. "A little more to the right, if you please. You won many gold medals, didn't you, darling?"

"Aw, come on, Martha. This is embarrassing."

"Tut tut, no false modesty now. I hear you've bought a straw raincoat and a box of butterflies. How darling. Were they a good buy?"

"Yes'm. And some Siamese birds, too. Seven. But they're stuffed. Hey, Martha, how about coming to the point? How come you've sent for me?"

"Well, darling, there is good news, a change of plans. Bethsabee has said that you may come to Israel with us after all. Isn't that nice?"

Nice? What was this? She's running hot and cold, playing cat and mouse again. Who's she think she is, some kind of marionette master knotting up people's strings, yanking, snipping, then being lady bountiful and tying them back together again? It isn't nice. Not nice at all. I'm thinking that I'd better leave before she eats me up, and so, to be polite, I lie a little. "That's real nice of Bethsabee, but I can't come, because I've already made plans for a concert of my own. Everything's all set and rehearsed, the hall's even reserved and paid for."

"Well, then," she says, still purring and looking sleek, "I suppose that's that. Good luck, Pablo. I shall be with you in spirit."

This was a surprise. The tigress should've been lashing her tail. For a while I continue to rub her in silence, hoping she'll ask me to change my mind, but she's not one to beg and I'm not wanting to seem wishy-washy. I start to go.

"Wait," she says. "There's something else that you perhaps should know. When the other dancers learned that you would not be going to Israel, they got together and persuaded Bethsabee and me to have you come along."

I'm touched and almost waver, would've wavered if she hadn't needed persuasion. But in the end I take Tacet's advice and fly home.

7 New Dances

Back in New York, as I told Martha I would, I'm working out some new dances—*The Least Flycatcher, Tropes, Untitled Duet, The Tower,* and a couple more. The cold wind that's whistling in through my loft's see-through ceiling is forcing the dancers and me to rehearse in hats and gloves. Blue-lipped and unpaid, the dancers are finding it hard to sustain their interest. Even so, they are enthusiastic about one of the dances, *4 Epitaphs,* which is intended to be lyric and lovely. When it begins to look too pretty, however, I switch its Debussy music to some lugubrious Southern band pieces and change the lyrical movements to leaden ones. Bob says that it's either the saddest or the funniest thing he's ever seen, and costumes us with black hoods that cover our faces. Unhappy about looking leaden, and even more so about being anonymous, the dancers then lose interest, refuse to rehearse anymore, and I have to find another cast.

All these dances are eventually performed, not on a single concert of my own, but on five or six shared ones at small theaters around the city. Income from weekly unemployment checks, occasional TV bit parts, and part-time display work with Bob and Jap have provided enough income to live on, yet not enough to cover the cost of giving a whole concert of my own.

Bob, when speaking of these performances, is probably right when he describes my dancing as being of the don't-bother-me-now-I'm-busy type. I've been too occupied with steps to pay much attention to the audience's reactions. My one-time composition teacher Louis Horst, writing in *Dance Observer,* a monthly put out by him, has found no influence from his classes in my work, but is broad-minded about it anyway. There haven't been any mass exoduses during the performances, and afterwards people have clapped, or at least not booed. I've the impression that I'm an up-and-coming arrival.

The next eight months are spent working on an evening-long suite. The preceding dances, mostly made in haste and on intuition, seemed nice, but not nice enough, and when I try to analyze what I've done, several confusing questions arise. There must have been some kind of structure somewhere, but where? And what type of style? What was the point of view, if any? And what was a dance in the first place? Could it be anything? When you thought about it, "dance" turned out to be a very meaty word. Some defining was needed.

The solution doesn't take long, however, as old Tacet supplies all the answers. He says that dance is as limitless as the universe, so full of possibilities and golden dreams that it can be anything that one cares to call it. "Hence, dear boy," he says, "simply decide what is irksome to you in other artists' work, eliminate it, and what is left over you can pilfer and pass off as your own."

Considering Tacet's advice, I realize that when getting right down to it, there is little in others' work that doesn't irk me, even in Martha's, Merce's, Anna Sokolow's, and Sybil Shearer's (my favorites), so I decide to start over from scratch. Some kind of building blocks were needed, some clearly defined ABCs that could be ordered into a structure that would be antipersonality, unpsychological (no Greek goddesses), would achieve a specific effect (no Merce dice decisions), and would have a style free from the cobwebs of time (no ballet). So it is easy enough to know what not to do, and since it seems unlikely to find a solution in other people's work, I go out and look around in the streets.

Everywhere the city's inhabitants are on the move—objects just waiting to be found, make-dos of an untraditionalized piebald nation, milling and walking, sitting in vehicles or on benches, tearing off after a bus, some drunk and lying flat out. Lines of restless people at banks, theaters, and rest rooms. Wads crammed into elevators or spaced artistically on subway platforms or leaning against skyscrapers. They are standing, squatting, sitting everywhere like marvelous ants or bees, and their moves and stillnesses are ABCs that if given a proper format could define dance in a new way. All is there for the taking. There's no need to invent exotic climes or bucolic Edens. An array of riches surrounded me daily, and its timeless beauty needed to be pointed out and shared.

To begin, I amass a collection of natural postures, stick-figure drawings which fall naturally into five stacks—ones of legs standing, squatting, and kneeling and two other categories of arm and head positions. (Later on, I run across an article on posture in *Scientific American* in which the author has made similar groupings.) Because my fridge is empty, my collection is stored there. Each category is then pared down to representative examples and strung together. Like in butterfly collecting, the idea is to net the best beauts for scrutiny. *Epic*, a twenty-minute solo, is to be the first section of a full-evening work titled 7 *New Dances*.

There is also the matter of music to redefine. If dance could be broadened to include everyday moves, so could its accompaniment. I choose the sounds of heartbeats, wind, rain, a complicated collage of background noise, plus two compositions by John Cage, one of which he writes for me to be played on quasi–musical instruments (a pan, a radio, and a piano lid). Besides myself, the dancers are Donya Feuer, Toby Armour, and Cynthia Stone—well-trained professionals whose past accomplishments give them the right to toss their technique out the window. Bob suggests that the costumes be our own everyday clothes, and that the set for one of the dance's sections be a live dog sitting on a mat.

Much of the eight months of rehearsals—mostly at night, since we all work during the day—is spent unlearning dancerly habits, because the natural movements, when done in a dancy way, look unnatural, and so we have to find a new, yet equally stylized, way to do them. We memorize vast amounts of uneven counts in order to give rhythmic variety and to keep from falling into monotony. Learning these counts is like memorizing a page of numbers in a phone book. It also takes a lot of time to learn exactly how, and with which dynamic, each move is to be performed. For instance, the light turn of a head, the heavy drop of an akimbo arm, the slowing down of a run into a walk. When done right, there is much appeal to the tilting of Toby's shoulders as she stands with her weight on one leg, and the soft settling of Cynthia's arms as she folds them, and the way that the pointy heel of Donya's shoe digs into the floor as she lifts her toes—also, when the girls gaze downwards, the lovely arching of their necks.

We find that each posture tends to get blurred when executed consecutively, and so it's necessary to surround each with stillness. The sequences take little physical exertion, make it impossible to rely on our muscle memories, and are difficult to remember. By isolating the postures in stillness, we are left with no chains of uninterrupted movement. There are few chances to use our muscles, and our brains are forced to spin through a good deal of mental gymnastics. Discovering how to hold still and yet remain active in a way that looks vital is the most difficult of all. The stillnesses are important and are to be on a par with the moves—as important as the negative space in paintings, the yin of the yang—as important as, if not more so than, silences in music. For dancers whose training has been in movement, this is like a springtail losing its tail, or a snail losing its pace. Many of the rehearsals are devoted to nothing but holding still.

The walking, running, and isolated postures are built into what's intended to be a formal, objective, practically scientific format. Surprisingly, much of it turns out as if it were saying something dramatic. For example, in *Events I*, when Toby and Donya are spaced near to each other, their long series of shifting postures seems to indicate a restless sort of waiting, as if something dire is about to occur; and then when Donya finally walks away, she is not merely moving to a different spot—she is *leaving* Toby. The sound of wind adds to the tension, and an emotional relationship between the two girls seems to have built up, then dispersed on Donya's departure.

With no dance steps for us to hide behind, even more than is usual the sequences are revealing us as people. Undisguised, our individual traits are laid bare, and our shapes, spacings, and timings are establishing definite emotional climates in all that we do. In context, what was meant to be "scientific" has turned out to be dramatic. Posture has become gesture. It is surprising to find the two so closely related, in fact inseparable. I'd intended to present posture pictorially and uncolored by emotional connotations, but I'm now forced to accept that the piece contains not only a collection of "facts" but the inescapable body language inherent in all types of dance. Abstract and representational elements are battling with each other—an age-old situation that always makes arbiters out of choreographers.

By careful allotment of income, I've been able to rent the Kaufmann Concert Hall of the 92nd Street YM-YWHA, where my company of three and I are to show *7 New Dances* on October 20, 1957. A few days before the concert I'm making a twenty-minute tape of the phone lady who announces the time every ten seconds: "At the tone the time will be . . ." I've decided that her spiel is supposed to match the exact time during the concert when I'll be performing *Epic*. The phone automatically cuts off every minute or so, causing a lot of tedious retaping and splicing, also a skyrocketing phone bill. I'm beginning to wonder if all the eight months of rehearsals will be worth it, and it dawns on me that I've been so involved with investigating the exciting realm of natural movement that it hasn't occurred to me to imagine how the audience might react. It's a chilling thought. The dance is pretty stark, certainly less flashy than flipflops. Maybe folks won't go for this sort of thing. But I shove the notion aside—aren't the girls and I proven technicians who've earned the right to scrap dancy dancing if we want to?

The program begins and I'm standing there under Tharon Musser's lighting in a freshly ironed suit that I haven't worn since coming to New York. The phone lady is making her announcements and I'm remembering the tricky counts and executing interesting street gleanings, but, sooner than I would've guessed, a few of the audience rise from their front seats and head up the aisle. I conclude that the correct time must have reminded them that they had to be somewhere. Even so, I'm becoming more unsure about *Epic*'s ability to establish and sustain interest. Each slow ten-second interval is passing excruciatingly. Several more people leave at a polite but firm pace; then others accumulate into a solid mass and practically canter up the aisles. Inwardly, I'm sinking; outwardly, tics of my neck are betraying nervousness. By the time the solo is over, the hall has been emptied of all but a small handful of stalwart friends, friends who are able to enjoy my embarrassments best.

The solo over, I go offstage and tell the girls not to expect a large house.

After *Events I*, performed without further events out front, I do *Resemblance*, the item with the dog as its set. The dog's name is Duchess, and she's a mongrel rented from Animal Talent Scouts in the Village. When Bob saw a llama there, he asked for it instead, but it was too expensive. Although inexpensive, Duchess is the only one of us who is being paid and has a no-biting clause in her contract. At the dress rehearsal she reacted poorly to the moment when pianist David Tudor banged down the piano lid. She then raced to the basement, barking hysterically, and her trainer had to give her a tranquilizer. Now, as I'm performing my walking dance, she is poised on her mat, half-risen, staring at the piano worriedly, whites of eyes glistening and ears laid back. She is usurping all of the audience's attention. I'm sensing that I may as well not be there. Then, tail curled under, Duchess starts creeping off stage. Her trainer's finger appears from behind a drape, sending her back, but she attempts to exit again and again, each time being reprimanded. Her intelligent legs are fighting with her valiant heart. Instead of being a disciplined stage set, she's letting unprofessionalism get the better of her and ruining my dance. I'm thinking never to let a dog upstage me again, and that if Bob should ever suggest anything live, even his stuffed angora goat with a tire around it, it will be the end of our beautiful collaborations.

And now the girls do *Panorama*. My studio mirrors are the set. These are to remind the audience that what they are seeing is a reflection of the postures that they themselves hold in real life, but since there's almost nobody in the hall, the mirrors are reflecting empty seats and probably not reminding anybody of anything.

The concert continues with Toby and me in *Duet*. This dance is to feature nothingness taken to its ultimate. Before the curtain goes up, she sits on the stage and I stand close by. We start looking calm in an exciting way. The curtain lifts, exactly four minutes pass, and then it comes down. Not having batted an eyelid, or moved anything at all, we feel moderately satisfied and go prepare for our next item. This time everything has come off perfectly. It's been the limit.

Then we all perform the finale—rather minimal, but like fireworks in contrast to *Duet—Opportunity*, and immediately following it I go to my dressing room, where the manager of the concert hall has been waiting to inform me that if I should ever rent the theater again, it will be over his dead body.

A few weeks later Louis Horst's review comes out in *Dance Observer*. It consists of four square inches of blank space with the initials LH at the bottom. My first reaction is outrage. The review wasn't even very long. And then I realize that my own worst suspicions have been confirmed. Folks have indeed misinterpreted my beautiful ABCs of posture as being a nightmare alphabet. Other reviewers, all except friend David Vaughan, are very stern. Even the usually forbearing Walter Terry headlines his article with "Experiment? Joke? War of nerves?," then accuses me of trying to drive him insane. *New York Times* critic John Martin, one of the first to go up the aisle, predicts in a Sunday column that the Horst review is to become a collector's item. It's been an ignoble fall, and in the months that follow, teachers, fellow students, and dancer friends regard me suspiciously with sideways glances. Martha shakes her gnarled finger and accuses me of being a "naughty boy."

Yet there are certain benefits. I've more or less defined for myself some roots to work from. The relationship between posture and its pal gesture has become clear and might be something that can be applied to dance steps. By failing to find a completely objective approach, and by failing to disguise the dancer's individual body language, my awareness of the communicability of dance has increased. By assuming that dance could be anything one wanted it to be, I lost an audience, but this tells me to bear them in mind next time I try to communicate private dreams. And then there is what no amount of paid advertising could have brought—immediate notoriety. Almost everyone in the New York dance community has now heard my name. Having accomplished more than what I set out to do, I decide to get back to a more kinetic approach, and dive into new dances with a vengeance. I won't get mad, I'll get even.

Clytemnestra

Midwinter '58. Snow sifting gently through roof. As usual, no heat in loft. Am thinking about spending the weekend in bed when the phone rings. It's Martha saying that rehearsals are starting. Hang up feeling elated and eased—elated to be picked for a part in her new dance, eased to be forsaking my own choreographic plans. Only need to remove pajamas and put on sneakers to be fully clothed, last night having been too cold to undress. Hot plate on fritz. Investigation proves all electrical outlets inoperative. Make mental note to pay overdue Con Edison bills. After stuffing practice togs, BenGay, Ace bandage, iodine into a plastic bag, and saying toodeloo to Tabby, who's too involved with mouse patrol to answer, I slog through slush across town, going out of my way to pass the Adelphi Theater, where Martha's season is to be. Strong tingles of expectation.

It's been two years since her Oriental tour. During this time, except for a filming of *Night Journey* (blind seer was me), her company has been inactive. I've been giving concerts, having the pleasure of dancing in a couple of Anna Sokolow's fine pieces, and, to keep solvent, working intermittently in TV. Less pleasurable has been the musical *Li'l Abner*, from which I was fired. (After the tryout in Boston, the director's first choice became available.)

I cross Madison, Park, Lexington, secure in the knowledge that the order of consonants in the word "maple" always clears up my confusion over which street comes when, then stop off at a shell shop near Bloomingdale's to select belated Christmas gifts. After heavy deliberation, I decide on a nautilus for Martha.

The serious stone Buddha is still sitting cross-legged in the vestibule. I change clothes, place my sneakers on the radiator to dry, and greet the rest of the cast in studio number one. Since it's only two months after my unusual concert at the Y, some are regarding me suspiciously. After waiting a respectable amount of time for Martha to show, she doesn't, so we leave.

Eventually, by the following spring, the new dance is made and is about to be premiered.

"Pablo," Martha says, "I am just frantic, absolutely a boiled owl!"

It's very late—the opening is tomorrow night. On one side, the Tacet side, I'm proud to be keeping her company. On the other, I'm not anxious to be kept up so late when I should be home getting some sleep. She's refitting me in my costume and, her mouth full of pins, not saying much.

"Hold still," she mumbles, then jabs me in the rear.

"That's the fourth time," I tell Tacet. "She's doing it on purpose."

"My boy," he replies, "take the advice of a master phrenologist and say 'Ouch.' "

"Damned if I will. That's exactly what she wants."

"We must be generous. She is fond of you and these jabs are but mere bites of love."

"Love, my foot. She's using me as a pin cushion, trying to give me a bad case of nerves, getting mine just as jangled up as hers. She's got a lot on the line—*Clytemnestra* is her summation of everything she's ever done, her first evening-long work. It's a big deal. Might be her best yet."

"Great personages deserve to be placated. Henceforth you are to say 'Ouch.' "

"Oh yeah? I'll tell you something, Doc. She may be great, but she's just as human as anybody."

"Sonny, do not befool yourself. She is supersaturatedly special, and, like all legends marked for magnificence, for the sake of her cosmic mission, this extraordinary woman has laid what most people consider to be life's pleasures and pleasantries upon the sacrificial altar of Art. She willst be immortal."

"Nuts—I don't believe in immortality. She's ruthless and should leave my rear end out of her cosmic mission. Hey! Shame on her, now she's worming her fingers down inside the back of my shorts."

"Do not flatter yourself. That is only to prevent pins from penetrating."

"It's not. She's getting her kicks."

"Pablo, darling, turn around and face me."

"Oh my God, Doc, now what's she up to?"

"Really, my boy, can you not show more leniency? In her geniushood she has distended the distance between herself and mere mortals, thusly eliciting uponst herself a vast sense of isolation. Such as she find themselves fated to reach ever downward toward the cups of human kindness, yet must remain true to their pedestals."

"Pops, if you ask me, she's about to reach too far."

"Darling Pablo, you seem so far away. What are you thinking of? Are you

going over your role, remembering what I told you about the characterization?"

"Yes'm. Aegisthus, he's the bad guy."

"No, no. He is not bad, he is simply lusting for Agamemnon's throne, and
effete. You do know the meaning of 'effete,' don't you?"

"It means slimy. Don't worry, I've got my moves down cold. Aegisthus
will be pure slime."

"I know he will be, darling. And have you been reading the *Oresteia* as
I suggested?"

"Uh, it's a little long. I've been too busy. And what's to know but that I'm
old Clytemnestra's young lover, my part's not as big as Bert's, and I better
make the most of it? OUCH!"

"Sorry, darling."

"Doc, what did I tell you—she's a spider in the middle of a web, yanking
on people's nerve ends, and she's over the hump. Fat fat fat. Get the spare
tire on her."

"How darst you malign the mighty Martha! Fie! The tire, as you call it,
is but a beguilingly unanorexigenic condition of the abomastic area."

"Well, maybe. But that doesn't give her the right to go sticking pins in."

"She has every right. Have you forgotten the rehearsal?"

"You mean when she brainwashed Gene McDonald?"

"Gene, being new in the company, needed to be filled with inspiration.
She was duty bound to do so."

"She said we were going to rehearse, not sit around hearing all that poetic
stuff about the miraculous little bones of the foot and all. It drives me
crazy."

"Not Gene. He was totally transfixed."

"And how. So when she finally finished and headed for the door, for his
own good I had to tell him that the poetics were all a pile of shit."

"You never should have said that."

"Yeah. But how was I to know she was still within earshot?"

"Lowbrowed lump! You have been loutish to a legend and sullying the
bright bubble of her enchantment. She rightfully reapeth revenge by reaching down and jabbing back."

"YOUCH! Martha, please! I'm real tender there."

"Darling, we must suffer for our art. Put your mind on something else—
have I ever told you of the teensy weensy metatarsal bones of the dancer's
miraculous foot? . . ."

The overture is starting and the curtain's soon to levitate. Other dancers
and I are waiting in the wings, some chatting nervously, others trying to get

in the mood to, as it says in the program, rape Troy. Tiny Martha is standing alone upstage center on a blue-carpeted ramp, looking very calm. In fact, her stillness might be taken for complacency, even boredom. But it's not. She's a monumental mote, a doughty dot, an electron at the quiet center of a spinning atom. Her hairdo is towering higher than usual, and her giant eyelashes have been heavily beaded with wax. Protruding from under her brocaded skirt is a big toe which, either from so many years spent dancing or from being crammed into too many small shoes, or both, has grown in an unnatural direction, crowding neighboring toes, and now slanting sharply outward. Eyes cast down in Buddha-like contemplation; her face is as durable as a porcelain mask, one that is to express Clytemnestra's story of treachery, murder, disgrace, and final rebirth. Her concentration breaks for a moment, and she turns her head to the wings to hush us with a queenly hiss.

I've probably mentioned that my feelings for her aren't simple? Love, awe, fascination are spliced to a dimmer view, and, once in a while, stresses tug at my commitment to her. Yet, right now, seeing her stand so monumentally, so alone, I feel nothing but admiration for this small, feisty woman who, for at least thirty-two years, has been lifting dance to new heights. Besides, her knowing eyes have seen something wonderful in me, and I'm determined to be worthy.

Two curtains lift, one after the other (overpaid stagehands finally get the order right). An interesting but not quite Mycean throne sits downstage right. There are two singers, one at each side of the apron. A third curtain— a row of vertical golden bands—rises, and Martha stands revealed. The audience scrambles to their feet and welcomes her warmly.

Drowned out by this ovation, Halim El Dabh's music becomes inaudible. Considerable delay before Martha's first move. When the commotion quiets, she begins a series of repeated clenched-hand gestures and in-place treadings, almost matching herself to the corresponding thonks in the music. When the music goes on to something else, however, she soon goes right along with it, doing only one or two thonks too many before regaining her bearings.

Precision in a lesser dancer is not nearly as great as Martha's inaccuracies. Personally, I like her mismatching of steps to music, for then the steps don't seem so obviously phrased. I also enjoy seeing her choreograph her body into snarls and then find such wonderful ways to get out of them.

But right now I'm putting my mind on the rape of Troy. It's the only part of the dance when I'll need to be in unison with the other dancers, and it's quite a challenge. Something about the way I move—shades of timing, force of attack, not sure what—makes me stick out in a group, and even though I've worked hard at it, fitting myself in has been a problem. Maybe it's because my approach or mental outlook isn't the same. Being an ex-swimmer, I remember how nice it feels to press against water. I can't resist using air in the same way. Counterbalancing the imaginary weight of space makes my body feel that it's accomplishing something. Though I've tried many times to dance with less pressure and weight, that always feels weak, willowy, and extremely stingy. Martha's probably just about given up on me being in unison, and, to tell the truth, I don't really mind. But tonight I'm determined to do my best to rape Troy exactly like all the other guys.

They dance great—Bert Ross, David Wood, Gene McDonald —even the others who only get to clutch spears, tote dead bodies off, and such. Except for David, all of us are six feet or over; all move forcefully and archaically; all conform to the concept of a flat, two-dimensional figure that seems to be Martha's idea of a man. Naturally, her dances stem from her own point of view. We're usually stiff foils, or something large and naked for women to climb up on. A few of us would like to be more 3-D and think that less beefcake would be a good idea, but have been scared to say so.

The girls—Ethel Winter, Helen McGehee, Matt Turney, Yuriko, and the newer ones, such as resplendent Ellen Siegel—are all terrific, too. Helen, usually cast in ingenue roles, is wonderfully wiry and vengeful as Electra; Yuriko, movingly dramatic as Iphigenia; Ethel, glorious as Helen of Troy; Matt, always a favorite with audiences and company members alike, makes a gracefully broken and appealing Cassandra (unison dancing isn't her strongest point, either, so she's easy for me to identify with).

All of us have been thoroughly trained at Martha's school in a methodically developed vocabulary. We are seasoned performers with strong techniques and understand Martha's choreographic aims clearly. None of us are all that young; the majority have had college educations. Most of the men started their training later than the women, in our early twenties.

What happens for two hours after *Clytemnestra*'s opening curtain is to be described, photographed, analyzed in depth, and stored in libraries for future reference. There seems little left for me to add, except a few unrecorded, and probably unimportant, impressions. Most have to do with feelings and sensations difficult to describe, ones that, even if described, may seem unlikely; yet they're true, or as true as remembered feelings can be.

Inside, at a million m.p.h. or more, corpuscles are zipping around and filling me with a sensation of great speed. Otherwise, I'm experiencing a feeling of superslow ooziness. This, of course, has little to do with actual rates of speed but is because of something that, for lack of a better term, I'll call the dancer's clock. Focus or concentration makes time different for when you dance and for when you don't. No ordinary timepiece, like a drug, this clock stretches stage seconds, implanting eons in between—also compresses performing years into an outrageously short span. So I'm both speeding and oozing at once, scooting through space, slithering through time, eating it up and savoring each swallow. A flick of the foot and I'm airborne.

Bright stage light is coming from all angles. Clinically. Like under a microscope, or on a vast, borderless desert. Basking there. Adding to the hot light, internal rays are traveling out through each of my pores.

Besides the music, such sounds as street traffic, murmuring from the wings, and burbling from the plumbing are magnified to a high pitch. Lint on a drape, the flavor of sweat, the odor of a stagehand's ground-out cigar are noticeably present. Hearing, sight, taste, touch, scent have become paranormal. Present is also a sixth sense—let's call it will power. I can will myself into midair, hang there forever. By means of another, even more mysterious power, I'm able to control what the audience sees, can direct their eyes to any particular part of my body: my left shoulder . . . my right elbow . . . both bunions at the same time. Anywhere. When a dancer is hungry, determined or motivated enough, anything is possible.

Steps are Aegisthus's voice. Lunges bellow, spins scream, skitterings whisper insidiously. From someplace down low a carefully controlled spasm ripples up through torso, arm, and finally out through the tip of a recently acquired limb—Aegisthus's black leather whip. It's as if he's saying, "Look, everybody. Slime! Fury! Sadism! Dementia!" There is no doubt in my mind that I've been given a franchise on wickedness.

Great greedy gulps from an empty Noguchi wine cup. Rapturous reelings, slow darts. While in the midst of a cartwheel, I study the details of an upside-down proscenium. Hedonistic burning sensation of soles whisking across boards. Softness of a leap's superslow spongy landing. Softness of blue-carpeted ramp against rump. Softness of featherweight Martha in my arms.

For her safety, I shift into low gear, support her gently, treat her as spun glass. According to the whorls of my fingertips, her silky-smooth veil feels roughly corrugated.

Wantonly, we plot the murder of Agamemnon and the usurpation of his throne.

Aegisthus motions: "There is the dagger. Take it."

Queen motions: "Oh no, I could not possibly."

Aegisthus motions: "Sure you can. Just let me help you to place your hand on it. It's over here in a pocket of the throne somewhere. Somewhere

Left: My mother.
Below: Me, c. 1931.

Left: Edgewood, Pennsylvania backyard. Left to right: Sophie, me in Mammy's lap, Tom, my father, and Bettie. *Below left*: Me at age 2. *Below*: My Brighton Hotel days. *Opposite above*: With Anita Dencks in student musical at Syracuse called "The Rose and the Briar." *Opposite below*: Syracuse swimming team. Coach Webster is at far right. I'm second from left in front.

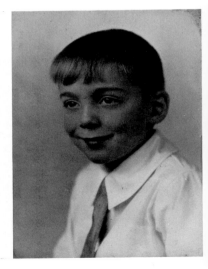

Left: Martha Graham's *Embattled Garden*. Next to me is Yuriko, then Bert Ross and Matt Turney. Set piece is by Isamu Noguchi. *Above*: Martha Graham and me in *Clytemnestra*. *Right*: More *Clytemnestra*. Behind is purple veil with famous safety pin.

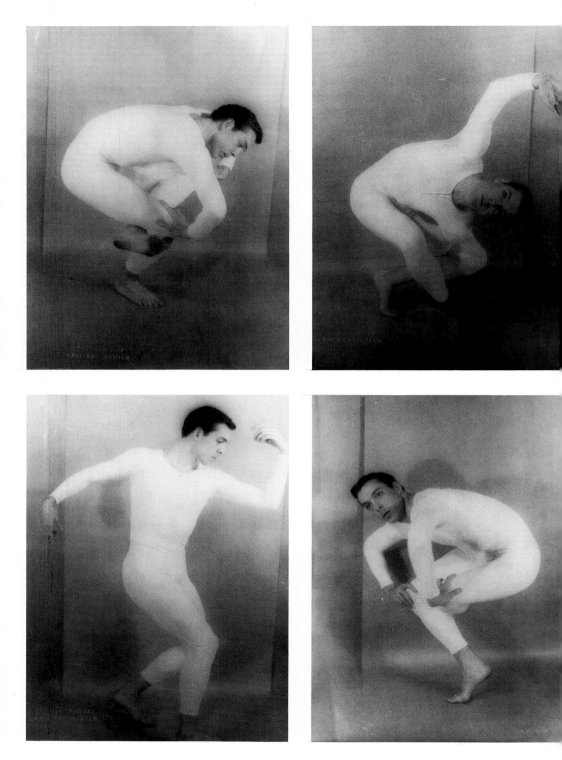

1960 Van Vechten photos of *Episodes*.

In George Balanchine's *Episodes*.

As Hercules in Martha's *Alcestis*.

here. . . . Rats! The stupid prop man's forgotten to preset it. No, here it is after all. Grab on, O Queen."

Queen motions: "Mercy, it does feel nice. I do like daggers."

Aegisthus motions: "Wait a minute. Your dress has gotten caught up on something. May I be of assistance? There. Now you can go do your dagger dance."

Leaving me sitting on the throne with the purple veil in my lap, she begins a long, demanding solo. Since I'm downstage in bright light, it might be easy to draw the audience's attention away from her, but this wouldn't be cricket.

I've figured out that I'm here because she needs a strong presence onstage, a kind of energy bounce to help keep her from lagging, to be a presence for her to battle. I should keep alive for her, stay in character, yet do nothing distracting. I've placed a safety pin to mark a place in the veil that I'll be needing to hold in order to manipulate it right. Keeping my face down so that it's in shadow, I slowly, unobtrusively inchworm the cloth through my fingers, maintaining the tension until, safety pin found, her solo completed, I fling the veil over both of us and spin her off.

When the curtain goes up on Act III, Clytemnestra and I are draped over her bed. She's having a bad dream. I'm going to be there for thirty minutes or so, so I've tried to get myself into as comfortable a position as possible, which isn't simple, the bed being not exactly a bed but one of Noguchi's stony and treacherously tilted abstractions.

I'm sleeping the best I can when suddenly, from out of the blue, Martha starts pummeling my stomach. I'm thinking that maybe she's come up with better things to do than the planned ones—something that the older dancers have warned me about. (Ad-libbing at premieres is not unknown. Later on, things get more precise.) I flick her fists away, then roll over and go back to sleep. She likes it when you play along with her. She soon comes back to pummel some more, and I keep flicking, rolling over, and trying to keep myself from falling off the bed. After a while she leaves me alone and goes off to dance with Bert, Helen, and Gene.

After the final curtain, on her way to her dressing room, she says, "Pablo, I noticed what you were doing on the bed. Naughty! Let's keep it in."

Clytemnestra is a resounding success. Both public and press immediately accept it as a masterpiece. Among many other tributes, Martha is praised for her merciless integrity (no mention of merciless pins) and for being a colossal figure in a theater of her own intellectually preconceived goals. John Martin of the *Times* writes that "the girl still holds promise." A more heartening and sincere tribute could scarcely be paid to her.

Her company is also extolled, and I'm singled out for praise. My part of the duet, with partial thanks to the safety pin, is deemed a deep characterization. This is very gratifying, since my role, though an important one, isn't as large as I would've liked and could have been lost in the shuffle.

The last performance over, I pack theater gear, return to wet sneakers, cold loft, Tabby's mouse patrol, occasional disagreements with Tacet. Within a batch of fan mail is an eviction notice from the Housing Authority, accusing me of illegal living. I relegate it to the trash basket and hide the hot plate.

Episodes

Dance these days—spring '59—is decidedly split into two main factions: modern dance, personified by Martha, and neoclassic ballet, by George Balanchine, so when it's announced that the two giants will collaborate on a new work, it comes as a startling surprise. No less so since the man engineering the collaboration is Lincoln Kirstein, founder and general director of his and Balanchine's New York City Ballet, whose militant and well-known diatribes against modern dance have, if anything, firmed up the firing line between the two camps. The new work is to premiere at City Center and is to be titled *Episodes*.

An invitation for me to dance in the Balanchine section of the new piece has come after a series of invitations from Kirstein more episodic than *Episodes* itself. Two years before, in '57, my work had been recommended to him by the dance writer and poet Edwin Denby. Lincoln, rummaging around for novelties, even ones that might contradict his view of what a dance should be, had then asked me to create something for his company, but the invitation was withdrawn for several reasons, the main one being that I wanted Bob Rauschenberg or Jasper Johns to design the decor and Lincoln didn't. (That a large painting of Jasper's was to be prominently and permanently hung in the lobby of City Ballet's future home, the New York State Theater, would be another of Lincoln's surprises.)

However, a second invitation, one sounding more like an order, came about a year later. "Geek," Lincoln had said—by then he was fairly familiar with my work—"Geek, you big piece of irrational pulp, you're getting another chance. A new company is being formed that will consist of thirty black dancers and is to perform in Spoleto. You're to be its only white."

The chance to be easier than ever for audiences to spot was attractive, so I accepted with pleasure. Yet this plan didn't work out either. I eventually danced in Spoleto, but not as a token white.

Then came a third invitation. This time Lincoln said, "Geek"—I was getting to like his term of endearment, if that's what it was—"Geek, you're being drafted. George says he wants you in a new ballet of his." Presumably, he'd put the bug in Balanchine's ear.

The dance was to make a meal of Anton Webern's entire orchestral output and was to feature a bevy of ballerinas who would spread out in a line close behind me and kick up their legs. Though this sounded risky, perhaps painful, and suspiciously like another of Lincoln's anti–modern dance enterprises, I accepted. The role would be a feather in my cap, as I'd be the first dancer ever to be kicked by so many ballerinas at once. That this project was also scrapped wasn't a relief but a disappointment.

In six months or so Lincoln, still determined to find a way to take advantage of what he referred to as my "maverick talent for oddball dancing," said, "March over to George's rehearsals. The Webern piece is back on again, but now half of it is to be choreographed by Martha."

George and Martha. Martha and George. Martha and George and Lincoln. American history was repeating itself.

"You bet," I answered, saluting snappily. "Am I to march over to Martha's rehearsals too?"

"Don't get greedy. For now, you're on loan from that old—"

Sallie Wilson and three other Balanchine dancers are to be in Martha's section. It's as if we're being traded around like hockey players. But I haven't forgotten the previous plan and am expecting to end up as the puck.

Despite what public and press are told, no further collaboration is to occur, Webern being the only unifying element in the two giants' widely differing approaches. Martha's elaborately costumed Part I is to be a dance about Mary, Queen of Scots, at the moment of her beheading; Balanchine's Part II, performed in practice clothes, is to be a less specific visualization of the music. Neither choreographer keeps tabs on what the other is doing, and the only known communication between them is when Martha runs out of music and asks Mr. B for some of his, a request that he graciously grants by ceding Six Pieces, Op. 6. Each half of *Episodes* turns out to be as self-subsistent as two towels—His and Hers.

Compared with Martha's rehearsals, those with Mr. B are a complete switch. At the first one (we'd not met), he arrives on the dot and shakes my hand while bowing half-humorously. I'm bowing back and, taking him in from his feet upwards, see that he's wearing smart shoes, freshly creased slacks, cowboy shirt, and one of his famous string ties. His handshake is run-of-the-mill, and his medium-sized body, though aged, is trim, but it seems never to have been particularly physical. When I get to the eyes, in color and depth of experience they twinkle back darkly. His manner is dry and businesslike yet easy and agreeable. It's plain that if given the chance, most any dancer would happily break his neck in hopes to please him. When he releases my hand, I notice something unusual about his fingers: the middle three seem to be of the same length, and I'm wondering if this is true of all geniuses.

After bowing to the rehearsal pianist in the same old-worldish way, and a brief huddle with him over the score, Mr. B indicates some opening steps to me, giving precise counts and speaking in abbreviated sentences with a heavy Russian accent. An intriguing twitch sometimes wrinkles his nose. It's as if he's been exposed to too many *Nutcracker* mice. The speed and craft with which he works are astounding, the rehearsal time being used economically, none of it taken up by explanations of concepts, poetic imagery, or motivation.

Before setting each phrase he refers to the score, occasionally picking out a few notes on the piano, then creating sequences that closely correspond. Since he's suffering a spell of arthritis and moving with difficulty, the steps that he demonstrates aren't always clear to me. I try to copy as best I can and he nods, seemingly satisfied, then continues to the next. There is no use for me to listen for a tune, for there is none, and no discernible beat, but the counts keep me from going too far off the track.

Each phrase is densely packed with complicated moves—knotted arrangements that, spatially, all stay in one small spot. Very few of them come from the traditional ballet vocabulary, and when they do, are usually reshaped into flex-footed versions or inverted. Much of the movement could've been derived from German expressionism—something that, to me, seems laughably old hat—and the way that the steps are being strung together feels arbitrary. It's hard to make them flow one into the other, and my limbs feel as if they were being sharply jerked around by a succession of invisible strings.

I'm being reined in, I'm thinking; pent up. It's disagreeable. Hurts. Besides, keeping to the music is too tricky, and this whole business is totally foreign to my usual way of moving.

The fact is, I'm drowning at sea and coming to the disheartening realization that as an apt instrument, as a manifestation of Mr. B's genius, I'm probably not going to be up to snuff. Creeping doubts. Hints of panic.

At the end of sixty minutes, precisely, the rehearsal over and my insecurity now blossomed full force, Mr. B executes another pleasant little bow, one suspiciously smaller than the first, and before forgetting everything that's been set, I tear home to practice. Clearly, a lot of homework will be required if I'm to justify this marvelous opportunity.

Having been evicted from the Hell's Kitchen dump, I'm now living in a different one, on Sixth Avenue not far from sleazy Forty-second Street. There, for three or four hours each day during the following weeks, I practice like a crazed worker ant. Though the body's always been pretty loose, several of the knotted positions are too pretzelish for it, so I make up and spend much time doing special stretching exercises. A classical triple turn in second position is also a problem. In ballet classes I've never been able to manage even a single turn in second without falling off the standing leg, so I practice them by the hundreds. By standing still on one leg with the other held out sideways at hip level for minutes at a time, I build up enough strength to keep it there during the turns, and eventually I'm able to pull off approximately two correct triples out of every five attempts. Since the Webern is hard to fathom, I go buy a record of it, and after wearing it out I go buy another one. Those moves that have been vague to me, I shape and clarify for myself, then check them out later with Mr. B.

Most professionals wouldn't need, or have time for, rehearsals at home, but the additional work is necessary if I'm to make a decent showing. It would be a disappointment, not only to Lincoln, Mr. B, and Martha but also for modern dance in general, if I should end up with egg on my face. Mostly I want to please Lincoln, as it was his idea to use me and I've come to admire him tremendously. In fact, I even associate him with "sponsor" Tacet, even daydream of what life might have been if he'd fostered my work as he had Balanchine's. Generalissimo and his Geek—what a duo we could have been. Too bad I'd come along too late.

There are three more rehearsals after the first, one each week for the next three weeks, allowing me more than enough time to practice at home. The line of ballerinas that I'd expected never shows up, Mr. B evidently having decided that my section of Part II is to be a long solo.

At the end of the last rehearsal, since the solo seems to be about something, yet its subject a mystery to me, I ask Mr. B if there is any particular way that it's to be performed. "Umm," he answers, nose fidgeting and sniffing out a proper image. "Is like fly in glass of milk, yes?" The picture was perfect. The convoluted dance, resembling the buzzing circles of something subhuman caught within a deadly vortex of its own making, seemed to be an epigram about self-ordained patterns and death. (Although there was no way to know it, Mr. B's metaphor was a prediction of a performance in '74 which, as with a drowning fly or a moth unable to resist a candle, is to snuff out my dancing days.)

*   *   *

On the morning of the premiere I keep bumping into my loft's furniture and dropping things. I've overrehearsed myself. The body's shaking, aching, and feverishly cold and hot. Coordination gone kaflooey. I'm not ill, just sick with fear—bone-rattling, ice-sweating fear. It takes all my willpower to force the hands to pack practice duds, and the feet to walk the nineteen blocks up to City Center's stage door. Once past the huge, ominous carriage lamps outside, I hesitate at the stairway to the dressing rooms. It's looming there like an unscalable mountain. Buffaloed, I collapse on the bottom step and seriously consider a quick retreat.

Just then a bunch of Balanchine dancers come over and introduce themselves, say they've heard good things about me and that they can't wait to see my solo. One of them, corps member Patty McBride, probably senses my nervousness and makes a special effort to be friendly. Jacques d'Amboise shows me up to a dressing room that I'm to share with Frank Moncion, Nicholas Magallanes, and Herbert Bliss—principal dancers whom I've seen only from the faraway reaches of City Center's top balcony. Not being able to afford tickets, I'd sometimes snuck in during intermissions.

The three stars move their makeup over to make space, and one of them even goes to find me a chair. As any alien to the world of ballet would be, I'm feeling pretty much like a dewinged insect, but everyone is doing his best to make me feel welcome.

When the dress rehearsal starts, since my solo is next to last I get to watch the rest of Part II for the first time. It's full of distortions, eccentricities, and is deliberately fantastic. It seems that Mr. B has been examining some of the unappetizing sides of human nature—inabilities to communicate, knacks for neuroticism, etc.—paring them down to raw bones, each episode an increasingly dark view until, after my solo, the dance is capped with a finale (one that I see later) which, perhaps because the previous sections have been so relentless, seems to me not quite the affirmation of wholesomeness that it was perhaps meant to be. I'm especially moved by several terse consecutive duets danced by Diana Adams and Jacques. Scathingly, their episode sums up the pitiful way people fail to make human contact. Grotesque it often is, but never fumblingly slapstick.

When my turn comes, Mr. B asks me to synchronize my entrance with that of David Hays's portallike set piece so that as it's being flown down, I pass through it to stop center stage as it comes to rest behind me. Though my timing is right on the first try, for some reason the effect isn't to Mr. B's liking and, after having me enter in other relationships to the set piece, he eliminates it. I'm trying to ignore a hunch that tells me that I'm next to be eliminated.

The stage now empty, in silence I walk directly to place and get into my opening position—one of the more tangled floor-bound ones. Conductor Robert Irving's stick tells me to begin. Immediately the orchestra has trouble and falls apart. This happens over and over. Then, when the players can get through the whole piece without stopping, they play it through three more times. Each time, since nobody says not to, I dance the solo full out. By the end of the third repeat, the dance being vigorous and long, I'm completely exhausted. I flop down on my back, lie there panting and hoping that Maestro Irving is now satisfied enough to go on to the last section.

Just then Lincoln, great brow beetling, emerges out of the dark and plows over. He's wearing his rumpled, ill-fitting black suit with the tarnished metal buttons. Eisenhower jacket and battle helmet would've suited him better. He's in his early fifties, quite large, big boned, with a strong, beaky nose and a less-than-marvelous dentist. Highly educated, he is camouflaging his sensitivity and shyness with bluster, as he often does. Take a tall Diaghilev, an undersized Frankenstein monster, a masculine Madame Curie, scramble them all together, and you'll get a fair approximation of Lincoln on the rampage. This wasn't just another pretty face.

He towers threateningly as I struggle to my feet. "Poor, poor," he growls, averting his eyes in distaste. "You look *poor!*"

"Gosh, I'm sorry, Boss. Maybe I'll dance better tonight."

"It's not your dancing," he says. "Your costume looks poor."

"Oh, that. Well, you see, no one's given me one, so I thought I'd wear these practice clothes. They're my best. I was planning to sew up the holes later."

"You look poor, POOR!"

Cut it out, I'm thinking. If you were as poor as me, rich man, you'd look poor, too. And the measly twenty-five bucks per performance that I'm getting paid won't be all that much help.

"Go up to the costume room, Geek," he says, flicking me a dingy smile. "They'll find you something else."

Up on the top floor someone hands me a new pair of tights and T-shirt. They're white—a color that I've often worn in my own dances and feel at home in. It's a good omen. After pulling them on I'm feeling a little less alien, more like myself, and I peer into a full-length mirror—which is, of course, reflecting Tacet in the form of a gigantic white fly that's nervously twining its forelegs together and shifting from foot to fluffy foot.

During the performance, while waiting an endless wait in the wings for my turn to buzz, my nervousness builds and locks into frozen terror. It's imperative for modern dancers to be well represented; we must match up with the best in ballet. Though ballet could learn a thing or two from us, rumor has it that if dancers aren't capable of ballet, then they have to settle for modern. What hogwash. No one's ever been given a better chance to hush the rumor and prove the point. That it's now up to me is a fearful load.

To relieve the pressure, I'm trying to watch the dancers onstage. They're coming through in multiple images, as though through a prismatic eye. Each seems secure and blithely free from care, the girls bourréeing around on boxed toes, trilling a premeditated and coolly artificial song. Seeing them dance with such ease, even though they belong to the dance world's twitty side, is humiliating.

By the time Diana and Jacques are dancing their scathing duets some of the audience has become uncomfortable. Nervous tee-heeing, then rude guffaws, rise through the music. At this point Jacques begins to change his performance style into something comical. It may be suitable to the situation—after all, he's a seasoned pro and should know when to adapt—but to me, playing for laughs is in conflict with what I think Mr. B has intended. I liked the duets the way they were and am astonished, disappointed, and depressed by the audience's reaction. My solo, being by far the most grotesque part of the piece, is apt to seem even funnier.

When it's my turn, stage fright forgotten, I stride out filled only with angry determination to dance in a way that will prevent anyone, even Cecchetti's ghost, from laughing.

No one does.

With minor reservations, *Episodes* is favorably received. As was to be expected, the accolades come according to whichever genius each critic cottons to. Reservations in the press such as "inhuman," "ludicrous," and "perverse" are lightly sprinkled by Balanchine's nonlovers; ones such as "melodramatic," "dull," and "the same old steps," by Martha's. But mostly there is high praise for both choreographers. The dance is considered revolutionary in that two major masters have joined forces, even though the so-called collaboration is in separate chunks. Both casts are also praised.

As to my own performance, it's certified A-1. Not a few people mention to me that the solo looks uncannily like something I've invented for myself—a puzzling observation. I didn't change any steps but only, after much effort and a certain extension of my range, found ways to join them one to the other in an attempt to make the choreography make sense to my particular body. I was just interpreting, serving Mr. B's intent in the best way I knew.

There are eight more performances of *Episodes* during the season. Mr. B often watches from the wings and bows politely when our paths cross.

Though I'm curious to know if he approves of my dancing, it seems inappropriate to ask. Then one evening he says, "You there"—calling me by name was maybe too informal—"your dancing is . . . umm [*twitch, twitch*] umm . . . umm . . . tasty. How you like to learn other ballets? *Apollo, Four Temperaments*, Cullberg's *Medea*? Tomorrow, come early. Jacques and others will teach you."

In hallways and briefly emptied rehearsal studios I'm taught the three dances, and after seeing me rehearse them, Mr. B invites me to join his company. It's a flabbergasting honor, but I can't accept. Guesting was one thing—but to be a regular member, a ballet dancer? I can't. I'd never be able to think of myself that way; I feel strongly that it just isn't how things are meant to be, that I have to keep heading in my own direction.

The Balanchine Part II is performed independently of Martha's Part I during the City Ballet's next City Center season. I continue to perform for two more seasons with them, and when I stop, the solo is deleted, at which time I offer to teach it to whomever Mr. B selects. That my offer isn't taken up is perhaps because Mr. B feels that he doesn't have another dancer he wants to see do it. Whatever the reason, *Episodes* continued to be given without the solo. Unrecorded at the time, except for undecipherable notes of mine, the glass-of-milk dance evaporated up into bug heaven.*

Spoleto

In May of '60, right after a Graham spring season, my last and final performances of Mr. B's *Episodes*, and a concert here and there on my own— all done more or less simultaneously—rehearsals for Spoleto are starting.

"Akiko, guess what? We're going to Italy."

"Leary?" she answers, switching around her Ls and Rs as usual.

"You betcha. Lincoln's recommended us to Gian Carlo Menotti, who's asked us to come dance for a whole month in a beautiful old opera house in Spoleto."

"Goodie. Akiko rike go Sporeto."

It's the first time my dances will go abroad. The Festival of Two Worlds,

* A reincarnation occurred in 1986 when the solo, or something fairly similar, was taught by me to New York City Ballet dancer Peter Frame and laudably performed by him in its original context.

of which this is the fourth, has an international reputation for presenting top talent and is a big deal. A group of thirteen dancers are to perform an all-American rep by Donald McKayle, Karel Shook, Herbert Ross, and myself. I'm to choreograph a new duet and expand an old trio, *Meridian*, into a full-company piece, for which a new score by Morton Feldman has been commissioned. I've gotten permission for Dan Wagoner and Akiko Kanda, both members of Martha's company as well as mine, to be included among the dancers, and Pina Bausch, once a classmate of mine at Juilliard, is to be dancing the new duet, *Tablet*, with Dan. (By '84 Pina is to be a well-known choreographer with a large company in West Germany. Some of the views in her darker dances I find admirably put forth and uncomfortably easy to relate to.) An Italian orchestra is to be under the baton of Jorge Mester, who taught at Juilliard and is now a highly respected and sought-after conductor. Young New York painter Ellsworth Kelly is to design the decor for *Tablet*; friend and playwright Louise Thompson, that for *Meridian*.

Akiko-san has gotten to the Sixth Avenue studio early. I'm not pretending to understand her clothes—a strange egg-shaped coat worn over a loosely knit, asymmetrical jumper, piebald pedal pushers, Mexican huaraches, and a sailor shirt. But this kind of thing has never kept her from being adorable. Men go nuts; girls turn green and back off. She's a miniature bundle of refined and disciplined Japanese fibers, possesses the spiritual stamina of a heretic; yet when sensing that she isn't being treated like a fragile flower, some sort of aboriginal critter inside her emerges to right the wrong. If her costume turns out to be unbecoming, or her part unsuitable, her temperature goes up and she swoons gracefully to the floor. Dan and I often find ourselves dashing around for cushions and aspirin.

While sitting on a chest that cages Bob Rauschenberg's wild stage stuff, she and I are waiting for Dan to arrive. He soon comes puffing up the four flights of stairs, blinks his little flea eyes, purses his Kewpie-doll mouth, and prattles cozily about the long climb. Dan enjoys being from Paw Paw, West Virginia, and runs being a bumpkin in the Big City for all it's worth. "Sho' am sorry to be late," he drawls. "I was cooking up Granny's recipe for buttermilk griddle cakes. You want some sometime?"

"Don't care for them," I reply.

"Well, how 'bout a corncob pipe?"

"I've given up smoking."

"Then I'll give you a root beer."

"I don't drink."

"So I'll buy you some perfume."

"I don't smell."

"That's what you think!"

This has been mostly for Akiko's benefit, but instead of laughing she says, "What are gliddle cakes?"

Though I usually end up playing straight man, Dan's corny barbs make him more likable, and we've been getting on great. He and Akiko go change into sweat clothes while I putter around at the tape machine. I've been too busy performing to form any specific ideas for the new duet and am counting on something to occur to me soon. Pina has been called to another rehearsal, so Akiko has agreed to stand in for her. The two girls are no more alike than a watercolor and a wood block. Akiko's dancing is daintily decorative, edged with something deep and heartfelt. Pina, at least a head taller and one of the thinnest human beings I've ever seen, seems to care little about looking pretty, is able to streak across the floor sharply, though a bit unevenly, like calipers across paper. She's also able to move slower than a clogged-up bicycle pump. At Juilliard she was one of Tudor's favorite students, and he seemed to enjoy seeing her go up on point. Besides causing her a sorrowful expression, this made her look even skinnier. Gian Carlo, knowing Italy's preference for fleshy women, has warned me that audiences there may not take to Pina. Personally, I love watching her and suddenly have an idea for the duet—am eager to turn her into a black widow spider or praying mantis.

When Dan and Akiko-san are ready, I ask them to try a few moves. One leads to another, then I throw everything out, start over, make up several entirely different sequences, and ask to see the first one again. Dan remembers perfectly, but Akiko remembers only the steps she likes. I urge her to put the stark, jagged ones back in among the pretty ones, and she halfheartedly tries, but everything comes out looking streamlined and lovely. I insist that she try harder to be angular—"Do like Pina would," I tell her. She begins to drag herself around in unconvincing agony, as if each separate part of her were being nailed picturesquely to the mast. Finally, I say, "Akiko-san, honey, maybe you'd better rest. Dan and I can work this out."

"But Akiko must stand in for Pina," she says in a barely audible voice while investigating her forehead with a fingertip.

"Uh-oh, Dan, let's get the aspirin," I say.

Oriental anemone wilts decoratively for a while, then, apologizing profusely, wafts home to take a scalding bath—the traditional torture ceremony which always purges the terrible sins of inadequacy from her sensitive soul.

A seventy-five-mile train ride from Rome, the Umbrian hill town of Spoleto had been snoozing for centuries until Gian Carlo came to rouse it with his arts festival. Many of the townspeople at first thought him mad—"Il Matto," they called him—but when convinced of his seriousness, they began to swoosh their brooms, slap their paint brushes, and bang their hammers. Flower boxes lined the curbs; new plumbing was installed in hotels and restaurants; and nightspots mushroomed up along dark narrow streets and chiaroscuro squares. The profuse weeds that long had been growing from ancient walls were left undisturbed for picturesque effect, and the town soon became a tourist mecca for titled dolce vitas, jet setters, and film stars as well as ambassadors, politicians, poets, and other international types.

Had they dared, the townspeople might have raised Maestro Menotti to a level above the Holy Trinity. As it was, their tributes only included bag after bag of fan mail thanking him for what he'd done for their once neglected town, and they gave annual torch-lit processions with triumphal petals strewn in their Second Savior's path in celebration of his birthday. Another composer might have made Spoleto a showcase for his own works, but so far, up to 1960, Menotti's been represented by only one opera, *Vanessa*, for which he composed the libretto and Samuel Barber the music.

A get-acquainted party for some of the festival performers is given at his small palazzo on the cathedral square, attended by his protégé, young conductor Thomas Schippers; the program director of chamber concerts, Charles Wadsworth; several patrons and others who've been important to the festival's success. Gian Carlo, a slim sophisticate with dark hair and an absorbed, mobile face with Roman nose, moves smoothly, humbly, almost oilily among his guests, introducing us to each other and making us feel welcome.

On the day of the opening the other dancers and I find that the opera house, like most old opera houses, is well designed; it seats twelve hundred, has good sight lines, a large, pleasantly proportioned stage, and, most importantly, comfortable dressing rooms.

My dance, *Meridian*, has been programmed to follow the first intermission, preceded by Donnie McKayle's *Games*, a very likable and well-made work which takes as its source street games remembered from Donnie's Harlem childhood.

During the *prova generale*, or dress rehearsal, some of the trumpeters in the pit show their distaste for *Meridian*'s delicate and far-out score by flutter-lipping too often, but, like good sports, they play the performance almost as if they can bear it. Mine is the most cryptic dance on the program. Even so, many persons in the large opening-night audience clap and stamp. I can't tell if they understand the dance, but wouldn't be surprised if they didn't. I don't; why should they? At any rate, understanding never seems to hinder their appreciation. They probably enjoy being confused. In short, the opening is so painless that it leaves me very little to remember.

During the weeks that follow, swarms of males hover around Akiko-san, making a lot over her. Bug-eyed tourists, paparazzi, fashion photographers stop her in the streets and click their cameras. She likes "Itary velly much."

Pina begins to get homesick for Germany or New York or anywhere else and cries a lot. When I suggest that she might try eating larger meals, it only seems to deepen her misery. "Never mind," I tell her, "things will be better after everyone sees your duet with Dan."

Through some oversight, a program that is to include *Tablet* and to be given at the Caio Melisso—a small jewel box of a theater on the main square—turns out to be too short, so Gian Carlo asks me to add three more dances. There are four days to prepare them. I condense the twenty-minute *4 Epitaphs* into a fourth of its former length and retitle it *3 Epitaphs* (even though there are now only two, the third epitaph being omitted except for starting it and then quickly giving it up as not being worth the bother—a joke that no Italian is ever to laugh at). I also revive *Rebus*. *Circus Polka* is the third addition to the program, for which I have a backdrop painted by the nine-year-old son of the festival's chief set builder. The drop needs to give a childlike impression, but the little boy turns out to be a much more advanced painter than expected and comes up with something more suitable to a *New Yorker* cover. In her *Tablet* tights Pina looks thinner than ever, so two flaps of cloth are added that will perhaps take the edge off her sharp bones.

The dress rehearsal at the Caio Melisso is late getting started. For one thing, the musicians have gone away somewhere. For another, I haven't finished choreographing. When I'm in the midst of yet another difficulty—the arm holes of Pina's costume have mysteriously gotten sewn up, and I'm having trouble getting her into them—the backstage phone rings and the stage manager says that Gian Carlo wants to speak to me. "Ask him to call back in an hour," I say; but he tells me that Maestro sounds upset, so I take the call.

"*Dio mio!*" Gian Carlo says, voice sliding up and down operatically, "we must not keep the critics waiting."

"Critics? What critics?"

"All of them, of course! Hasn't anyone told you that here in Italy, instead of the performances, it's our dress rehearsals that are always reviewed? Critics are out here in the lobby complaining that this late start is leaving them no time to get their reviews into tomorrow's papers."

"Oh. By the way, sir, have you seen our orchestra?"

"Aren't they in the pit?"

"Well, someone told them that they wouldn't be needed for a while"—me—"and I think they went to their favorite cappuccino joint on the other side of town—except for the drummer, who wanted something stronger. You know how drummers are."

So, after asking someone to round up the orchestra, we wait awhile, and then the stage manager tells me to take my place onstage. The curtain rises, but nothing comes out of the pit, so I step forward to have a better look—there's nothing but empty chairs in there. The curtain comes down resoundingly, and the critics, having read about my minimalistic dances at the Y, the ones that got the blank review, believe that they've seen the entire program and start leaving to go write their reviews. After a while the orchestra shows up, the critics are herded back, and Gian Carlo tells the ushers to stand by the exits and not let anyone leave for at least two hours.

In terms of a praying mantis, Pina's performance is superb. Afterwards the audience remains silent for a time, then chatters about happier things. I've heard some dancers say that their performances were "over the audience's head"—the most foolish of all notions. I believe that anything is good enough for audiences, and that if you horrify them enough you'll become a star with a following all over the world.

Just before the Spoleto performances are over, I get an invitation to choreograph for a ballet company in Holland. Choreographer Karel Shook, whose ballet opened the opera house program, has recommended me to Sonia Gaskell, the artistic director of the Netherlands Ballet. There's no particular rush to get back to New York, so, taking anemone Akiko as my assistant, even though she's most reluctant to leave "such a nice prace," and though it takes a lot of tugging on her petals, we board a train to Amsterdam, or maybe The Hague, where we find ourselves experiencing something so horrible that I'm able to recall its every detail in indelible clarity ever since.

Holland is an incongruous match to Spoleto. Weedy, crumbling walls and hot Italian dispositions are replaced by neat stair-stepped roofs, flat fields of orderly tulips, and northern no-nonsense. Akiko-san and I check into a hotel and go meet Madame Gaskell at her rehearsal hall. She's a fluttery lady, full of animation, who seems to believe herself to be the Sugar Plum Fairy. With her invisible wand she indicates her dancers to us, remarking that my ballet should feature her favorite ballerina, Sonja van Beers, who, Madame tells me, she has had to have injected with hormones and who otherwise would've remained too short. Sonja is now of almost normal height, looks to be a fine dancer, and, more importantly, speaks English, so I agree to feature her.

Madame also tells me that Joop Stockermans, who has no English, will be composing the music for my ballet, and that I should start explaining to him what the ballet is to be about. As usual, I've no idea, but point at my watch to indicate that it will be about a half-hour. Mr. Stockermans then seats himself at the piano expectantly, as if poised at the threshold of greatness, and Madame scurries away, leaving Akiko and me to deal with no fewer than forty dancers, most of them very young, who've now slumped to the floor where they seem to be sleeping.

"Up, up!" I say. Some look towards us in a noncommittal way, but don't budge. "They are tired," says ballerina van Beers. "And besides, they speak only French or Dutch."

"*Avanti!*" I shout, and having gotten them on their feet, wonder what I want them to do next. Running is as good a way as any to start, so I indicate that everyone should run around in his or her own little circle; then I settle back to see how many of them will bump. The ones that do, I plan to get rid of in order to narrow the cast down to some manageable number. But nobody bumps. Even so, Akiko and I sort of nudge about half of them out of the room.

During the following week the cast keeps growing. Akiko and I suspect that the rejects have been sneaking back in. There are definitely more dancers, but we can't tell which of them shouldn't be there. The whole company looks alike, and it's somewhat hard to tell the girls from the boys. One of them, Billy Wilson, I pick to partner Sonja van Beers because he's black and the easiest to tell is a guy. Every day there are more and more dancers, and many of them keep sitting or sleeping at the edge of the room and have to be urged to go away, but they misunderstand and keep trying to worm back into the dance.

There are many difficulties in choreographing for a large number. Let's say that you wish to get the job over with as soon as possible, but you've had little past experience. Then one or all of the following things may prevent you from accomplishing your task:

The dancers keep showing up to rehearse.

They want to know what to do.

The dancers are stupid.

You show them the dance, they can't do it, but you like your steps better that way.

The dancers keep marking, and you suspect that either they have changed the choreography or are practicing someone else's dance.

The boys are too girlish.

The girls are too girlish.

Everyone wants to do only attitudes and arabesques.

You can't stand attitudes and arabesques, don't want them.

And so you now turn your attention to other elements, over which you have even less control:

Dogs and children wander in and get mixed up in the dance.

The children don't get hurt.

The dogs are very noisy.

One of the dogs is always hugging the ballerina's leg.

She likes it.

Nobody wants to hug your leg.

It is a very lonesome business.

At the final rehearsal, our allotted time to finish having run out and the half-hour of music more or less filled up, I say so long to the dancers and hurry Akiko to the door before Madame should come and ask to see a runthrough. The dance doesn't look to be one of my better works. Then, as Akiko-san is pausing at the door to bow her dainty farewell salutation, Madame sails in, accompanied by her business manager and a gaggle of critics, this time the ones who splatter their droppings all over the Netherlands.

"My dear Mr. Taylor," she says, wand waving overhead, "we are all here to preview your new—your new . . . what *are* we to call it?"

Thinking quickly, I say, "How about *The White Salamander?*"

"Excellent! We know we shall enjoy it. But—ahem—who are all these young people you have here?"

Humoring her, I reply, "They're your ballet company, Madame."

The wand wilts. "But these are not my dancers. No, no, no! Oh, now I see—many of them are only students at my school, children who've been given permission to watch your rehearsals. Dear, dear, now we shall have to hire them."

As the critics seat themselves for the runthrough, Akiko and I slip back to our hotel, where we hurriedly pack. Once Madame Gaskell has seen the dance—a big mistake from beginning to end—I'm doubting that I'll get my full fee.

While checking out at the hotel desk, the clerk tells me that there's a phone call for me. I ask Akiko-san to take it. Hanging up, she says, "Nice Madam say clitics rike our dance and for us to come get pay enverope."

As a mildly satisfying revenge for a horrible experience, *The White Salamander* stays in Madame's repertoire for the next two or three years.

Italy

Winter '61. Sidestepping meaningful messages, I begin a new dance, *Junction*, which is intended to be about musicality—that is, some ideas have lately come to me about the interplay between movement and sound. I want the dance to be like two old troupers whose conversation overlaps and interrupts, like chums whose compatibility is so strong that they even have the right to ignore each other. The dance is not meant to be a visualization of its Bach score (selections from the suites for solo cello). I still don't agree with folks who say musicality means Mickey Mousing—simplistic aping. *Junction*'s steps are mostly to contrast to the music and, though sometimes matching its tempo, more often than not are to be faster or slower. The concluding section—an interwoven mass of bodies tumbling in slow motion—will occur during fast and agitated music. Sometimes the silences between musical sections are ignored; the dance continues through them. By alternating contradiction with agreement, I hope to establish structural tensions and unexpected contrasts.

Somehow in the process of working out the dance I've found that certain unintended emotional undercurrents have cropped up. Moving slowly to fast music sometimes seems to give the dancer a look of inner excitement, and its opposite—moving fast to slow music—perhaps gives a look of interior nonchalance.

But communicating different kinds of emotion with steps depends more on how the steps relate not just to the music but to all the dance's trappings—its title, gestures, images, decor. For instance, painter Alex Katz's bright, multicolored leotards and Bach's exuberant sound probably help to give *Junction*'s steps a lighthearted appearance, although the steps in themselves are not especially lighthearted.

From the minute the curtain opens, viewers tend to "get" *Junction*: they see it as being happy, then seem to maintain their first impression throughout. To me, the dance contains several different emotional colorings, but some folks out front are able to see only one and tenaciously cling to it, like cat lovers who deny the existence of dogs. Yet, to me, the world is multicolored, a rainbow mix; why shouldn't a dance be? I'm hoping to make other dances that will be more clearly pluralistic.

Anyway, though *Junction* may not have been the ultimate answer to the knotty question of musicality, it had been easy enough to work out and had fair success in New York. At least one critic, Edwin Denby, liked it enough

to praise it to a lady who, during intermission, asked him if it was interesting. He told her that it was, and she then returned to her seat confident
she would enjoy the rest of the concert.

Perhaps we should've had Edwin along when we took *Junction* on a tour
through Italy.

As a door to the future began to open, some sort of ominous crack should
have been letting in misgivings. But how were the dancers and I to know
much about trouping? Blind to the future, we don't know of the bumpy
decades of global crisscrossing that lie ahead. Instead, we're thinking we're
just out on a lark, just a short, pleasant ramble in the hinterlands until we
can zip back to Manhattan, where our big-time future is supposed to stay in
one spot. And instead of having second thoughts, we're giving our attention
to our stage manager, Tommy Skelton, the same Tommy who bossed me
around when I was a student at the American Dance Festival in New
London, and who is now standing in line at a ticket window of Milan's main
train station. He's hopping on one foot and pretending to be shocked at
some lady's silky-haired little lap dog which is trying to bite his ankle. Both
are squeaking. It's almost as if two teapots—one large, one small—have
gone mad. The lady, unaware of what is going on at the far end of her leash,
is quietly intent on lighting the wrong end of her cigarette.

Strange, the way life's coincidences and minor schisms steer your thoughts
away from the future and lock it to the present. Today: December 2—by
another coincidence, the Babe's birthday. Back in New York he's likely to
be puffing at a cupcake at Poly Print, the plastic-bag factory where he
works. Short on details, he's never been too clear about exactly what he
does there. Nurses machines and sweeps up, probably. Because of preparations for this trip, the party that he'd hoped for at my studio got lost in the
shuffle. But he understood, covered his disappointment with a jaunty shrug
and spelt "Oh well." It's inspirational that Babe speaks with his hands,
especially to us dancers, who can relate easily, speaking as we do with our
feet.

And here in Milan the station is Babel—we can't even hear ourselves
laugh. Besides the squeaking of Tom and dog, bustling travelers are shouting in a jumble of tongues, porters groaning, train steam hissing, babies
howling. Overhead there is a metal grid of crisscrossing struts which seem
redundant, unsure of where they are headed. Compared to the purposeful
hubbub below, they look indecisive. Yet there are no doubts as to where
we're headed—Trieste, our first stop of the troupe's first foreign tour. After
relentless rehearsing and some last-minute snags, we're on our way. Nothing indecisive about that.

Tommy is now gently, discreetly, trying to detach the pooch from his cuff, but he can't. And it's now, right this instant, that I've decided to like Tom Skelton. Us Americans always root for underdogs.

I'm fortunate in that besides being our stage manager, Tommy has come along to design our lighting and guide us from city to city. He is much more experienced at trouping than the rest of us, full of indispensable know-how, broad-minded, generous, and a big source of entertainment, not to mention being attractive to animals.

"Enough!" he's saying. "Good grief, can't one of you pull this mixed-up mutt off my leg? Nice doggie, go bite Paul for a while."

Getting the Italian tour was beginner's luck backed by providence, but more like pure willpower. Louise Thompson introduced me to Jim Spicer, a friend of hers who helps run the Becks' Living Theater. Since the troupe had had fair success at the Spoleto Festival, he offered to arrange a tour for us of seven cities in Italy through Annie Guerriere, the Living Theater's agent in Rome. I eagerly accepted, but on the day before we were to leave, Jim told me that our air tickets hadn't come through and that because there was no way for us to pay for seven one-way tickets, the tour would have to be called off. When I pointed out that only six of us were to go, he said that he had misunderstood and signed our contract for seven. Determined not to lose the tour, I got loans from friends and acquaintances, just enough for the seven one-way tickets. All that remained was to find an additional dancer, or anyone at all who could come on short notice.

Someone, I forget who, suggested Barbara Tucker, an ex–Erick Hawk-insite whom I'd never seen or met, but who was unemployed, trustworthy, and svelte. It was also said that she tended to have a problem with gravity, but it was no time for pickiness, so I phoned her anyway.

"Hello, Miss Tucker. Do you have an updated passport?"

"Yes, but who is this?"

"That's great. Do you like Italy?"

"I really don't know. Who *is* this?"

"Name's Taylor. How's about meeting me and my company out at Idlewild at the Alitalia counter tomorrow morning at nine? Somebody will teach you a dance or two while we're over the Atlantic."

"Well, I don't know. You see, I—"

"Don't worry about a thing, okay? See you there. Try not to bring too much luggage. Bye."

In Milan, after Tommy buys the tickets to Trieste (his pidgin Italian all but lost beneath his New England twang), we put into action his tried-and-true seat-saving operation, one that he's guaranteed is bound to work. While he flags a porter to take care of our costume case, I squeeze ahead of the crowd, locate an empty third-class compartment, place my hands and feet across the seats, and, as instructed, glare at the people who seem about to come in. When the troupers catch up, I help haul them and the luggage through the window.

The seven of us then sardine into six seats. But through our window we see our costume case sitting on a flatcar that is slowly klunking off in the wrong direction. Dan Wagoner and I fly out the window, catch up, and grab the case. By now our train has begun to pull out. As it picks up speed we race back, toss the case to Tommy, and then are barely able to grab onto the caboose. As we scramble aboard, everybody's long sighs of relief are in counterpoint to the train's accelerating clickety-clacks.

To make sure we're all here, I count heads. There's Maggie Newman, sitting straight spined and certain. A sports enthusiast with hard-edged hands and the kind of assurance that comes to those who've mastered karate, a superperfectionist and the one of us who when rehearsals bog down from exhaustion, wants to do everything all over again. Though her calves and thighs are a little not little, mostly she is streamlined and is a dancer of endurance and deceptive delicacy. Having been with Louis Johnson's company, she's clocked more stage mileage than the other girls.

And squashed between Maggie and the window, here's Liz Walton. We met at the Graham school, where she studied briefly—about four classes. A luscious mover, possessed of an outgoing disposition with matching smile. Given good reason, however, she can display a truly goosebumping temper.

And enthusiastic Elizabeth Keen. Her specialty is devil-may-care flights and fearless flinging around. Bones like rubberized steel with extra joints. Though attractive, she's not quite as pretty as the other girls, yet she's the only one with breasts worth mentioning. Underneath her bravura there's a deep pensiveness; also a strong feeling for fantasy simmers there. I suspect that one day she'll tap it to use for making dances of her own.

Barbara Tucker. She learned 3 *Epitaphs* on the plane. Maybe it isn't gravity but narrow aisles that she has problems with. She's a game gal, but it's a little early to know much else about her.

And Dan Wagoner. Good wag Dan the dancing man. We've known each other from the Graham company. After earning his college degree in West Virginia, then working as a pharmacist in Manhattan, he soon switched to dance. His background, I guess, accounts for the scientific or methodical way he dances and his on- and offstage down-home charm. Not some flitty mosquito, he's stalwart and moves with weight from a thick core, and he can be cooperative—when pressed, he agrees with me that I'm a great dancer.

And if I treat his scalp to a knuckle rub, he even agrees that I'm the world's greatest dancer.

The relationship of all of us to each other is mainly one of fondness, but sometimes, such as now in this crowded compartment, is a matter of mutual forbearance. Like some families, we've begun to feel stuck with each other.

Making the best of things, Dan now lays one of his jokes.

"Hey, y'all, what do you call an unwashed sailor who's crossed the ocean for a second time?" Giving us no time to guess, he pops the answer. "A dirty double crosser! Haw haw, hee hee!!!"

"Wow, what a good one," I reply, humoring him. "Think I'll write it down in my tour journal."

"Y'all get it? Anybody need it explained?" he asks in mock innocence.

During other quips and bright banalities Tommy produces a quart of Chianti, and, taking communal swigs, we wobble on toward Trieste. Rounding sharp curves, the dancing train causes us to jar our teeth against the bottle and dribble on our clothes.

We had no hint of things to come; the dribbles were not seen as omens. But Tommy then produced a rancid pizza, and that was when we should've had second thoughts about the whole trip. Nobody remembers the impression that we made on Trieste. Perhaps it was stronger than the one Trieste made on us. It's best to say that we didn't stop there.

Arriving in Venice, we unscrunch, detrain, and arbitrarily pick a direction that might lead to a cheap hotel. Along the way we glimpse St. Mark's and other stagy structures through a blurry scrim of sleet. As we've heard, winter-time Venice is a closed-down carnival, laughless and spook ridden.

Already we've had just about enough scenic hinterlands. We're soaked, sore, and starving, and there don't seem to be any affordable hotels. We investigate Harry's Bar, but it turns out to be too expensive, so we slosh across the street, or maybe it's a canal, to a nice Venetian greasy spoon.

While we wait for menus, nobody is saying much about the tour. Taking a stab at optimism, Maggie is glowingly describing at length a certain kind of padded bra that she thinks Liz Walton should try. Liz is listening patiently, but some squishing noises from under the table sound very like her wet shoe tapping in fury. The foot is a long one and would be looking like the fuse of a damp firecracker.

After an eon of growls from our stomachs, a waitress takes our orders and brings linguini with clam sauce. Tommy twirls fork against spoon professionally, opens his mammoth mouth as doth the baby bird, lowers a wormlike complexity into it, his Adam's apple bobs, and, zip, a little leftover tail vanishes from sight. We all copy and in no time order seconds, except for

Maggie, who orders thirds. Her calves and thighs put mine to shame, I'm thinking, but it's best to be kind about them. Every once in a while I've dropped hints for her not to eat so much. Now I'm saying, "Maggie, honey, please keep your mitts out of my plate."

Tommy has a great knack for improvisation and is spinning one of his yarns for us, says we're not in Italy, that our trains haven't gone anywhere. The views from our windows have been panoramas painted by a crew of gnomes hired by the Pope to build up the tourist trade. To make it seem that our train was moving, the views have been constantly jiggled by the little guys as they raced over the railroad ties. And this here spiffy restaurant is a set that he, Thomas Skelton of stupendous theatrical renown, has designed and lit at high cost and great care just for us. (Laughter and applause here.)

Even better than his performances is his Adam's apple. Nature added it as a preposterous afterthought, and Tommy, countering with forethought, is always trying to mask it with a fine collection of turtle-neck sweaters.

By the time we get to Siena, pretty panoramas have gone up in smoke. What was expected to be a pleasant ramble has become a rat race, our trouping a treadmill thing. Travel days are a drag, performance nights worse. Nobody's getting enough sleep, and it's easy to forget why we've come.

Always sapping our energy are the stages to mop and the costumes to wash, mend, and pack. Our bare feet need constant desplintering and bandaging. Our theaters and hotels are crummy. Secretly I'm worried that our fees won't cover salaries, and that there won't be money for the air tickets home. Sponsors are being reluctant to fork out. Slow trains cause doubts about making it to the next city in time. Lazy stage crews do little but ogle the girls.

But I guess it's the press interviews that bother me most. Sponsors insist that I do them to help ticket sales. At one of them a long-haired aesthete asks, "Signore . . . er, um, Taylor, is it? . . . with *Junction* have we not strayed a bit too far from the music?"

"Yeah, yeah," I answer, winningly. "But too far ain't far enough."

"I see," he answers, unimpressed. "*Signore*, our readers are fascinated by the mysterious wellsprings of creativity. How would you define the esemplastic power of the poetic imagination?"

"Come again?"

"Your creative juice, from whence does it come?"

"Oh, I getcha. You mean sperm. Gosh, you know, the usual place."

In Siena my clenched jaws ached.

*   *   *

Florence turns out to be a town after my own heart. It's full of contradic-
tions. On our way to Teatro Piccolo (not that it contradicted its name), when
rounding a corner (no contradiction there either), I run across Michelangelo's
statue of David (at last, a contradiction—by someone who later said that it
was a fake). It is unavoidably white, so blinding in the winter light that it
takes a moment for my eyes to adjust. Although I've been seeing pictures
of it all my life, it's bigger than I expected. There's that nudity again, but
more of it. I'm kind of mortified, and squirming inharmoniously inside. I
mean, the nakedness isn't embarrassing—it's the passersby who may be
noticing me stare. The adolescent hands and feet are disproportionate,
contrary, too large even for the rest of him. When he grows up to match
them he'll be bigger than Goliath. And the abdomen is off—femininely
pubescent and white, too white, and billowy soft.

You don't have to go all the way to Florence to see David when they have
plenty of smaller, more practical, plaster ones for sale on Forty-second
Street. Porn stars all and, like this one, blatantly liberated. But it's astounding to think of the countless people—basic, bent, or both—who've craned
their necks and fallen for this guy.

So I've had enough and look away. I notice that an ant has been crawling
up from the cobblestones and has just arrived at my pants cuff. Appears to
be the superdiligent type. Aiming for the heights, he obtains my knee, then
loses ground. My pants are too shiny for him. Nevertheless, feelers waving,
feet scrabbling, the little trouper achieves traction and continues his upward trek. After a couple of serious backslides he climbs all the way up to
my belt, where, forelegs suspiciously investigating a strange new terrain,
he attacks the perilous slickness of the buckle. Come on, sport, you can
make it. Never give up the ship.

He seems to be the type that goes around humming while he works,
single-minded, unswayable as to his goals in life. I scoot him back down.
What will he make of that?

Undeterred, programmed for fortitude, he's coping with wrinkles, lint,
treacherous surfaces, all obstacles in his upward endeavor. I shove him
down again. Getting a little weary, are you, Mac?

Before restarting the long climb, he's tossing his head as if to shake out
all wavering thoughts, then sallies forth, but now limpingly. A leg has
become dislodged and a feeler snapped. Poor little guy. On reaching my
buckle for the third time, he's stymied by my finger, which is blocking the
way. Momentarily confused, friend ant drags back and forth along the new
barrier, probing at it gingerly, questing a less steep place to cross. Come
on, crawl on up—you can make it, you single-minded little scamp.

The inside of my closed hand is being tickled by a frantic attempt to escape. Ineffectual nips from microscopic jaws. Opening my fist, I study the ant as he thrashes valiantly, roll him between my fingertips, then flip the corpse at the statue.

That little jerk, he was too inflexibly single-minded, and too hung up on travel. And that big David, he's just the opposite—damn inharmonious, embarrassingly ambivalent, too soft. . . .

Insects and heroes—nothing if not contradictory.

At the Teatro Piccolo, while the crew is taking one of its many hour-long breaks, I'm resting in my dressing room. There is no cot, so I'm lying on the floor when I look up to see Tommy's apple bobbing. He has dropped in to ask if I'd like to visit the Uffizi Gallery. "Come on, lowbrow," he says, "this may be your only chance to soak up some cultcha."

"I hate culture, and Florence is wearing me out," I groan. "Can't you see I'm dead?"

"Sure, you're floored in Florence."

"Very poetical."

"And you've been menaced in Venice."

"Agh! You got any more? Let's get them all over with."

"The gallery's just down the block," he persists. "If we hurry, you can rest for at least ten whole minutes when we get back. The others are coming, too."

Pulling street clothes over wet practice ones, I follow him and the gang out into the cold. As we hurry past the statue of David, pigeons rise and scatter under low gray clouds that are gaining in intensity. The light has gone flat, and the buildings we pass are photographs from a big, slick, overfamiliar coffee-table book.

The long, poorly lit halls of the Uffizi are filled with a thunderstorm of footfalls that echo from wall to wall as we race past masterpieces and slow down slightly for corners and guards.

"Hey, Big Cheese, that Caravaggio was neat!"

"Oops, troops, there went the Botticellis!"

And oops, there went Florence.

And somewhere, lost in the crisscrossing agenda, is Turin, where Liz finally explodes from unreasonable demands imposed by the touring life (I had asked her to lay off the sightseeing), and Maggie gets fed up with being anonymous. She has noticed that the papers carry only photos of the other girls and writes a long note, delivered to me at curtain time, with instructions to see that things don't go on this way. Since I have no pull with the press, there isn't much I can do. Maggie and I stop speaking to each other for the remainder of the tour.

Bone tired, mirthless, dragging our imposed-upon feet from stage to splintery stage, by the time we get to Rome I have the distinct impression that the dancers are about to quit. Pacing my room at night, wearing down already threadbare carpets, I'm picturing the troupe's sad demise. And having scrutinized the parts of my dances that I'm not in, I'm questioning their worth, even doubting the dancers' commitment to the steps. Am being devoured by a dragon named doubt.

And, for some overly fastidious reason, I've begun to think of the girls as errant young wards who need chaperoning. In the Teatro Parioli's communal dressing room, the looked-for trouble gets found: one blue spot each on three of the four girls' derrières. Assuming the worst, I lash out like a compromised father; responding in kind, the girls make clear their low opinion of snoopers. In the crowded area between the Spanish Steps and the Trevi fountain, they say, some awful Lothario-type signores had administered terrible tweaks. It was dreadful. Rome was dreadful. The tour, the world, and the whole darn universe were dreadful, and they wished they had never come. During this, Dan has been whistling "There's No Place Like Home," and he now tells the girls not to fret, that he'd beat up Italy's whole he-man populace for them—had he but the time.

But even if it is sometimes bumpy, road life is offset by our growing awareness of each other's strengths and weaknesses. We're gaining something that is perhaps one of the reasons for our onstage togetherness—a tribal unity that all audiences notice right off. We've developed the mutual trust that is so necessary when coordinating onstage physical risks. Have also caught on to each other's timings and projections, and have developed other knacks which enable a mishmash of egos to become a unified band of individualized troupers.

The Roman audience does not seem to notice any signs of offstage friction and applauds warmly. After our second and final performance, the Theater Club of Rome gives an elegant supper, which includes *gambrelli alla Lucianna*, and something hot *con funghi*, and other unfamiliar but delicious dishes. Afterwards, during our *vini tipici*, a distinguished gent with *tipico* Italian fervor makes a long speech and offers me a large eighteen-carat award beautifully sculpted in the shape of a Promethean flame. It quickly passes from his warm hands into my hot ones, and while I stumble through a few words of gratitude (about two), my mind is racing ahead to a pawn shop, an airlines ticket counter, and the return trip that is now possible.

As it works out, the award does not need to be pawned, since the American ambassador, John Brown, hearing about our shaky finances, makes a kindly donation.

Before we can go home there is one last stop. Messina, Sicily.

Messina, to bagged and bloodshot eyes, looks pitiful. Parts damaged eighteen years ago during World War II are still evident. On the way to the Teatro Savoia we carefully step around unrepaired bomb craters. Our theater, once an opera house, is in disarray and is now used for movies, its antique boards full of wide gaps and thickly layered with grime. Out front, in what were once plush seats, rats are nesting. The chief and only stagehand, Luigi, is an elderly hulking bald-headed man with fleshy little excrescences on his forehead, each flourishing several long hairs. And, among other things, he looks like he won't be able to get his grand drape up. But he does. Except that it sticks halfway and hangs there looking as groggy as our eyelids.

Luigi then disappears, and, used to this sort of thing by now, Tommy locates a bucket and mop and swabs the boards. Padding here and there as he looks for a nonexistent clean bit of floor to warm up on, Dan jokes annoyingly about getting his feet wet.

During our dress rehearsal Luigi returns and heaves himself up a shaky ladder to an even shakier overhead grid where he prepares to take a nap. "We're in luck," I tell Tommy. "As long as he's up there, maybe you can get him to do our snow for *Insects and Heroes*." Tommy communicates to Luigi the way tissue paper snowstorms should work, and, after Tommy surmounts a language barrier handicapped by Luigi's halfheartedness, the snowstorm is arranged. Eventually, a good fifteen minutes after Tommy has given the cue—in fact, after the rehearsal is over—four or five stingy flakes come drifting down.

"Mr. Luigi, sir," Tommy calls, "for the performance tonight, can't we have a little more snow, and sooner? Not too much, not too little, please— let's say exactly one handful, okay?"

"*Mamma mia*," says woebegone Luigi, and then, "*zzzzzzz.*"

At curtain time, he furrows his brow, climbs back up to the grid with a fistful of snow, and perches there like a great bald bird of doom. Surprisingly on cue, just as Dan takes an upside-down position, a soppy snowball plummets down from Luigi's sweaty fist, hitting Dan squarely on the butt. We, the audience, even every rat in its nest, then hear a basso boom from above: "*Basta?*"—Enough?

Other surprises. Snagged toes and trip-ups, late or entirely missed entrances due to a dark crossover, prolonged intermissions due to a sparking light board, a rat's shrill squeaks and squeals during the quieter sections of Bach, and so forth.

After we take our bows and return to our dressing rooms, the audience lingers awhile before realizing that the grand drape, still stuck, is never coming down.

And it's just now that some of us are beginning to suspect that our future, like that half-open curtain, may be a gaping, possibly voracious, abyss.

Phaedra

Later on that same winter, the first rehearsal of *Phaedra* was to have started at seven p.m. It's now almost nine. Martha's other dancers and I have long since finished our warm-ups and are sprawling around on her studio floor and waiting for her to arrive when her sister Geordie comes in to tell us that Martha has just phoned. Looking sweetly apologetic, Geordie says, "She wants you to know that she may be late . . . if she comes at all."

Another hour passes, yet she still doesn't arrive, so we all get up off the floor and go home.

Martha's entrances seem to be getting later and later. When starting a new piece, she seems more reluctant to come, and once started, seems to find it hard to sustain interest. But she's wearing her years amazingly well and, all things considered, is still very much Martha. Admirers and detractors alike have long agreed that her gifts are greater than mere talent. I guess she's gotten too successful for ambition; certainly her sense of identity is too strong to need flattery. Maybe she's slowing down from sheer apotheosis. Anyway, it is only fitting that now, after creating roles for herself that include St. Joan, Jocasta, Clytemnestra, and Mary, Queen of Scots, she is planning to add Phaedra, Queen of Crete, to her gallery.

The second rehearsal goes better. We're back down on the floor, this time sitting with our spines in stiff attention. Martha has arrived. Martha is speaking. Martha is sitting on one of the kidney-shaped platforms that her friend and collaborator Isamu Noguchi has designed especially for her studio, her legs in the lotus position, the outside of her knees impossibly flat against the platform and covered by the crêpe de chine skirt of her long black rehearsal gown. Though her legs are perfectly good ones, hardly any of us ever get to see them.

While intoning the legend of Phaedra to us, her voice takes on the deep purr of an idling ice-cream truck, occasionally leaping several octaves up the scale to a sound that resembles the giggly piping of a little girl. The contrasting tone colors are effective. She may have learned this technique in Denishawn days, when theater folk spoke more vibrantly and manicured themselves toward total stylization. In her voice there is a Kabuki element, or a banzai.

Too entranced to notice the hardness of the floor, we learn that Phaedra's mother, according to top sources, was known to be unusually lustful. Martha likes this part of the legend very much. Martha is tipping her head a little to one side, holding her chin down demurely, and fluttering her eyelids. After a pause timed to perfection, she adds that the mother was highly attracted to bulls—"spotted ones with great big horns, great big enormous . . . HORNS . . . Well!"

Pictures of these white-and-brown bulls as painted in Cretan frescoes are offered, and, while we pass them around, Martha unfolds her legs and lurches toward the studio kitchen. Her lurch is like Bette Davis's in *Elizabeth and Essex*, or more likely, since Davis at one time studied under Martha at the Neighborhood Playhouse, Davis's lurch is like Martha's. A tinkle of broken glass escapes from the kitchen, then a yelp from Geordie's elderly cocker spaniel, Roderick. Martha is fond of animals, all types, and, though Roderick is always getting underfoot, she certainly never would mean to step on him, if that was it.

I've heard that there was a time when Martha's patience wore shorter quicker, and her temperament was longer. It is said that she used to slam doors right off their hinges, but that was before I was taken into the company. It's too bad, I'm thinking—a shame that I've come along too late and missed the really good shows. Probably, in order to rev up creative juice, she has to let her temperament fester inside until ready to burst out all transformed into inspiration. What were a few busted hinges compared to that? But there hasn't been much temperament lately, and I can't help wondering if maybe her best dances weren't made in the old days—*Primitive Mysteries* was a miracle, and *El Penitente*—when she was more temperamental. Those dances were deep and rough-hewn. Ethel Butler in Washington taught me some of the style, and I ate it up. The movements weren't like now, not decorative—not done with such slick, long limbs and pointy feet.

Looking refreshed, Martha returns, resumes her lotus position, and starts the legend over again from the beginning. Going at a leisurely pace, she finally gets back to the place where she left off, and then, as if about to let us in on a dark secret and arranging her face into the mask of a sharp-toothed demon, she tells us that although Phaedra's mother was highly attracted to bulls, the bulls had been not at all attracted to her, so she then ordered the court inventor, Daedalus, to build a hollow cow-shaped contraption into which she could crawl. Being inside there worked very well, and having enjoyed successful consummation, the mother gave birth, not to Phaedra, but to Phaedra's half-brother, the Minotaur, a creature part man, part bull.

At least the logic of the Minotaur's genetic inheritance was believable.

Martha has been glancing out at us slyly and giving satirical nods. She really knows how to tell a story. Her slow, majestic gestures and abrupt pauses are supreme, and if she says one more word about the mother, we're all going to crack up.

But then she sobers and says that she wouldn't dream of asking us to dance that part of the legend. "No, no, this we shall never do." For the sake of good taste, the matter would be merely hinted at, or, as she says, abstracted.

To Martha the word "abstract" means "essence." She had often said, "Darlings, the word 'abstract' means 'essence,' and so the abstract of an orange is orange juice."

Now she is saying it again, sort of owlishly, and then, as if she'd reminded herself of something, she rises from the platform and returns to the kitchen. The fridge door slams, a glass tinkles again, and Roderick repeats his yelp. While she's gone, some of us get up off the floor to rub out our cramps. Martha returns, motions us to be reseated, then tells us that the abstract of an orange is orange juzzzz. She is slurring the "juice" a little, and some of the newer company members are looking puzzled over what kind of juice may be in the kitchen.

After a while Martha veers away from the legend and into a different story, which is so neatly spliced to the first one that at first we don't catch the change. Then we realize that she is telling us about a ghost, one that she says is haunting the top-floor studio.

By now it's about midnight, and we still haven't gotten to dance. Martha is obsessed by the ghost. It's haunting her mind, echoing, ricocheting back and forth in there like a terrible tennis ball that won't stop bouncing. Suddenly she rises, forgets that her legs have been crossed, and careens across the room to a corner where Roderick has gone to sleep. She drags him back, his stiffened forelegs resisting every inch of the way, and, pulling herself up to full height, points imperially at the ceiling and proclaims,

"Roddykins knows about the ghost! Don't you, darling?" Poor Roderick then creeps back to his corner, where he cowers and blushes with skepticism.

"There *is* a ghost, my darlings—a wicked, wicked ghost upstairs. Roderick has seen it, Geordie has seen it. And they have heard it woo-hooing and clomping. I tell you no lies. Every night it tosses its horns, lashes its long tail, and . . . "

Though we want to believe it, we can't. The details are getting too much in the way. Sibyl-like, Martha drones on, but none of us have the nerve to mention the time. At about one o'clock she releases us, and that's the end of the rehearsal.

After two and a half months have gone by, the interlude which is to hint of the mother's offbeat appetites has been set. Since Martha has spent a lot of time away from the studio, it has been necessary for some of us to help set this bull session, based on her idea of having Linda Hodes poked at by four men with phallic horns (actually, ten-inch pieces of broomstick from the kitchen). The interlude turns out abstract enough for Martha's taste but, after the premiere, too juicy for several of the critics. One of them writes that the dance is "more risqué than anything presented on Broadway within recent memory."

Helen McGehee, according to another, is "appropriately aloof" as Artemis. It could also have said "aloft." Assigned to a high pedestal, she's aloof, aloft, and, what's more, mad, since she hardly ever gets to dance.

The first time I saw Helen perform was in *Canticles for Innocent Comedians*. When she repeatedly rose on one leg, going from low squat to relevé, the rest of her Juilliard students and I nearly croaked. She's basically a lyric dancer, but she can turn into a spark-ejecting demonette when cast in dramatic roles. At these times her intensity takes me by surprise, as her offstage nature is one of perky friendliness. Her talents are wasted on the pedestal, and it's no wonder she isn't happy about being stuck up there.

As for myself, I'm more than content to be Theseus in *Phaedra*. It's a leading part, like all the other parts given to me in the five years since *Clytemnestra*. My roles now include the Seer in *Night Journey*, the Stranger in *Embattled Garden*, Antony in *One More Gaudy Night*, Hercules in *Alcestis* (one of the very few good guys Martha had cast me as), and Samson the Destroyer in *Samson Agonistes*. I was paired with Akiko Kanda in an *Acrobats of God* duet. As is usual for some of the leading dancers to do, I choreograph some of each of my roles, sometimes putting in my two cents' worth for group sections as well. If our help is needed, those of us who sometimes set segments work within Martha's vocabulary, adding variations of certain movements or inventing related ones. Martha lays out general guidelines and then oversees, making changes or not, as she sees fit.

In the years since I was taken into the company, my billing has gone from cow's tail to third place. Martha, of course, is first by far; Bertram Ross, second. Bert partners her more often than I do, and is an unusually fine and dramatic dancer—especially, I think, in *Seraphic Dialogue* and *Canticles*. His duets with Martha and his devotion to her and her work are both considerate and considerable. He is practically indispensable.

Phaedra, like other of Martha's pieces during the sixties, has a polished theatricality, superb lighting by Jean Rosenthal, and Noguchi's beautifully sculpted three-dimensional set pieces, and is popular with New York dance audiences. The unequivocal vocabulary used in Martha's dances, honed and polished over the years, is now more balletic looking than it was in the forties, and is one that her dancers have absorbed thoroughly. Her steps are second nature to us; in fact, if required, on very little notice we can practically improvise in unison—and sometimes need to at premieres when some of the choreography has been left open-ended. Our strong techniques and the security that this common vocabulary gives us frees us as performers to go from proficiency to a higher level of communication. That, and our desire to embody Martha's visions, may be what produce the unusually cohesive company, one of the strongest she has ever had, yet one valued for each soloist being very much an individualist.

Mary Hinkson's lyricism is more linear than Helen's. Within the company, hers are the most pointed feet, and the most envied. It seems unkind that they have to go through the punishments that the profession demands. Her great natural beauty and talent are immediately apparent to audiences everywhere, and she's always one of their favorites.

Mary graduated from the University of Wisconsin with Matt Turney, and both girls joined the company in '51, representatives of a curiously high number of modern dancers with college degrees. Matt, probably the member dearest to the rest of us, dances like a long blade of grass. She has an ability to bend to onstage and offstage winds of Graham weather. Other attributes are her warm dignity and vulnerable look. Though she seems at times as if she might fall down, she in fact dances with complete control. This deceptive frailty belies an inner strength in both her dancing and her nature.

Yuriko dances like a serene female Buddha. She can squat the deepest, sit cross-legged on the floor the easiest, and has the longest hair. Once, when dancing *Embattled Garden* in Israel, Bert accidentally stepped on it. He then stepped on a detached hairpiece belonging to Glen Tetley, which, because of wet spirit gum, stuck to Bert's foot. Kick as he would, he couldn't shake it off. The serene mask of Yuriko's Buddha face then cracked for a moment to give me one of the biggest laughs of the tour.

Yuriko is a moon dancer—cool, remote, mysterious, and capable of producing the main ingredient of dance's magic, unnameable and never understood, the wondrous invisible that we all seek.

David Wood, alias Pepper, whom I first met in New London when he danced with the Dudley-Maslow-Bales group, has an uncanny Graham technique as well as more ballet technique than most of us. He has great elevation and speed, consummate grace, crystalline purity, but because he isn't as tall as the rest of the men, isn't cast in major roles as often as he deserves, Martha preferring to use taller men. (Sometimes I think she views us men onstage as giant dildos.) One of David's best roles, and one where he dances opposite Martha, is the whip-wielding taskmaster in *Acrobats of God*. He's also terrific as a bald-headed, pole-thumping seer in *Clytemnestra*.

Pepper often runs rehearsals in Martha's absence, and with his talent for discipline and organization he's a logical choice. His help was particularly appreciated during the creation of *Acrobats*. The choreography had turned into a group project, and David kept things from falling into chaos as we pitched in to finish up one of the sections.

At the theater during the dress rehearsal, we keep bumping into each other. Martha was late to the rehearsal, and so David straightened out the mess. When Martha arrived, we showed her David's neatened-up version, and afterwards, when David asked her what she thought of it, she replied, "Don't bother me now," and then, on her way to her dressing room, was heard muttering, "Dear Lord, I am being nibbled to death by a duck!" But she didn't mean it. As I've said, Martha was fond of animals—dogs, monkeys, all kinds of creatures, even David. Noticing how crestfallen he looked, our lighter, Jean Rosenthal, went over to say, "Sweetie, you should know Martha by now."

Martha, too, wasn't always absolutely sure of her own steps, so during the performance Cameron McKosh, our rehearsal pianist, called out her steps to her from the wings—things such as "Three knee crawls to stage left!" or "Now go upstage and stroke the set." At one point the audience started laughing, and so Martha began to give a satirical imitation of herself. Since she usually portrayed tragic heroines, this was an unexpected change, and the audience loved it. David did not burlesque his role of whip master and made a very good straight man for Martha to bounce off of, sometimes literally.

Ethel Winter is a many-pointed star—spiritual as St. Joan, lascivious as

Aphrodite, flirtatious as Cleopatra—variable according to how she is cast. And she has nerve, too—dares to look younger than Martha when she dances Martha's role in *Appalachian Spring*. Though Ethel's portrayals demonstrate a talent for varied roles, her individuality always comes through clearly. None of us have that homogenized look that's found in some companies. Our style is unified, but, encouraged by Martha, not our stage personalities.

Three other dancers, who at this time are billed somewhere toward the bottom of the Graham roster of big-print people, are Dan Wagoner, Richard Kutch, and Richard Gaines. Terrific, all three. And somewhere toward the bottom of the lineup, her name in the smallest print, is a statuesque slip of a girl who, to me, is to be the most impressive and important of all: Bettie de Jong.

Linda Hodes is also very special. As a child, she studied with Martha, and in her teens she entered the company. She later married Stuart Hodes, who was to be Martha's leading man. Later a daughter was born—easily, Linda being no stranger to contractions—and Martha had a namesake. If anyone did, other than Geordie, Linda loved and understood Martha best. Like David Wood, she became a rehearsal director, a position that she presently and beautifully holds. One of the Graham trademarks, an often-used fluid S of the arms, was based on a certain way that Linda moved hers and later codified into the official technique. A liquid and lushly moving dancer, she was in the original cast of my *Insects and Heroes*, along with Graham crackers Dan, Akiko, and Matt. In Martha's company, Linda's uncompetitive nature, and her awareness of whatever Martha's casting needs may be, probably leave her with roles that demand less than she is capable of, although in the dancing that she does get to do she is spectacular.

Samson Agonistes is acclaimed by the press even more glowingly than it was the year before, when it was titled *Visionary Recital*. After the premiere I suspected the critics of writing their reviews beforehand, because to me it had been pretty much of a farce. At rehearsals a ball of yarn representing Samson's fate had been unwound by the cast and, as we danced with the strands, had been cat's-cradled into a snarl that none of us ever learned to get out of gracefully. One day in frustration I intentionally snapped a strand, and Martha said, "That's *it!*" and incorporated the action into the dance's opening scene.

At the premiere a large stage spike that was needed to hold a previous set securely in place was broken off by the stagehands and left with its sharp tip sticking two inches out of the boards. The first of us to puncture his foot was Dan, who, deep into his character of Samson the Tempter, felt hardly a thing. When Martha spotted a shimmering red pool leaking from him, she hissed at me to tell him to get offstage. Besides being concerned for him, she probably didn't want to get her treasured white silk sari soiled. Dan then exited, soon followed by Martha. Leaving gooey footprints, Bert was the next casualty to exit, then two others. Martha's dressing room was turning into a beehive of spiked people. From onstage I could hear the turmoil, Martha's voice rising above everyone else's and threatening to get whichever stagehand had been the culprit. Geordie was there too, and Roderick was yapping ecstatically.

It wasn't long before the rest of the cast exited, leaving Akiko and me alone onstage. She was determined to stay, at least for the duet which, no matter what, she intended to dance with Dan. It didn't look as if he would be back, so she sidled up to me and whispered, "You do duet with me, yes?"

I'd seen the duet only during a single runthrough and wished I'd paid more attention, as I had no idea what Dan had done, only that the duet started with him on his back with his foot raised and with Akiko picturesquely resting her hand on it. I assumed that position and we began. Akiko fluttered sweetly around me, and I faked whatever it was that she seemed to expect me to do. Then the duet music was over and she was gone.

Left with the whole stage to myself and Robert Irving's baton still swooping in space, I somehow threw enough steps together to take me through the rest of the music. After the curtain had come down, I couldn't tell if it was my blood on my feet or someone else's.

The reviews were amazing. They spoke of another Graham masterwork, another seamless, flawless, quintessence of a masterwork. But to me the new works didn't seem so, not because of the injuries that night, or other open-ended openings, but because the new dances seemed to be becoming self-consciously glamorous, and the style was getting to be more balletic, less satisfying to perform than when I first entered the company. Yet Martha had given me dance experiences of inestimable value and more than a glimpse of the workings of genius. And she had given many things that I could not appreciate at the time. Although I still could have learned an enormous amount from her, and though I still would have liked to try, she herself was now seldom available. I think her dark, wise orangutan eyes had always known that I would eventually need to leave.

The time had come. I gave a year's notice. Martha did not storm or object the way she often did when dancers left, but stated her belief in me. She had been attending my New York concerts and had made it clear that she was proud. I suspected that wherever I went, she would always think of me as Pablo.

During the year after I gave notice I taught all my parts, some to more than one dancer, and at later times returned to her studio to teach the roles to new members. The teaching sometimes did not produce the results I would have preferred, but Martha had very much made use of my personal movement traits, and many of them seemed to be untransferable, or at least I wasn't able to teach them very well.

It had been six wonderful, hideous, bewitching, boring, tickling, vivid years. Hardly a week has gone by since then that I haven't thought of her.

Paris

Bettie de Jong is Dutch. The "Jong" is pronounced "young," or is sometimes mispronounced "Long," as in how she looks. A slender five feet nine inches tall, she has small hands, small feet, and a small head that perches gracefully on a long Dutch neck. Her eyes are gray blue, except for the left one, which is half brown. Straight ash-blond hair is skinned back in a tight knot. Cheekbones and other facial features are spaced exactly the right distance apart to project well from a stage. Picture a lovely reed dancing.

It is impossible for my company and me to picture her not being with us. She is not only with us, but necessary. Besides brightening our dances, she has become our company "auntie." Resourceful and so self-reliant that she almost never accepts even a free cup of coffee, she is our Dutch treat.

Me, mostly I love her, but sometimes I don't. Once in a while both these feelings are like a furry noose which slowly tightens around my neck, but always I'm very grateful that she is with us. Whether lifting me up or dragging me down, dear Bet makes me certain that I'm an appreciative person. And she's the trouper who is to stay the longest.

She was born in Java, where her father was an agricultural botanist specializing in the development of an improved variety of potato. After World War II she moved with her family to Holland, where she performed with the Netherlands Pantomime Company and saw the touring Graham company perform. Feeling that modern dance would suit her better than pantomime or ballet, she then came to New York, where she did secretarial work at Martha's school in exchange for classes and also worked as an au pair girl for Ethel Winter and family.

While studying at Martha's, and occasionally teaching beginners' classes there, she was selected to be one of *Clytemnestra*'s Furies. During a rehearsal break, while fixing Martha some egg drop soup, she mentioned that she had heard I needed dancers and said she'd like to join my company. Although we had both danced in John Butler's *Carmina Burana*, it was the first time we had spoken. Since she was a fine dancer, and appealing— especially the alien accent and two-toned eye—I invited her to join. There, over Martha's soup, a happy dialogue started that is still in gear. It rolls along, coasts, and grinds uphill, swerves and fish-tails, takes breakneck chances and slows down for corners. It is sometimes stalled out by mutually stubborn silences and put into reverse by overheating, yet it always returns to caring purrs, if not to the words themselves. The usual subject is the weather, and, whatever it's doing outside, her sinuses merge with the landscape. If the humidity is high, it worsens them; also if it's dry. If it's cold, hot, sunny, cloudy, it still worsens them. There have been times during our long dialogue when I've been able to free my mind from her sinuses and, inserting automatic "aw"s and "um"s, dream up some of my best dances. Probably, no one has ever had a muse like dear Bet.

An invitation for my company to participate in the sixth annual Théâtre des Nations, a theater arts festival in Paris, has come from its director, Claude Plasson. Representatives from twenty-three nations are to compete for the festival's awards. The representatives are mostly large, state-supported classical ballet companies, the largest being the Frankfurt Opera Ballet, which boasts some three hundred dancers. My self-supporting troup of six is known in Europe only by whatever word may have leaked out from Italy the year before. Our inclusion in the festival seems somehow suspicious to me. With all the larger and more prestigious American companies that could be representing our country, it's unusual, to say the least, that we've been chosen.

Exertions to prepare for the Paris trip have been exhausting. Rehearsals at my studio have been wedged in around my final season with Martha. Because my dancers also have other commitments, it's seldom been possible to schedule more than three or four of us to rehearse at the same time. Foot by sleepy foot, we've been working far into the night, often long past twelve. Like Martha's, my dancers are committed to their work and are rehearsing for free; in modern dance at this time, paid rehearsals are pretty much unheard of.

Since Maggie, Barbara, and Liz Keen decided to leave the troupe right after we returned from Italy, we were short on women, so Dan and Liz Walton helped me give an audition. Choosing the three replacements was easy—only three showed up. The new girls are Bonnie Mathis, fresh from Wisconsin and one day to star with American Ballet Theater; Shareen Blair, who was switching from Merce's company to mine; and Bet. Actually Bet didn't need to audition, since her dancing was a well-known commodity.

A new piece is needed and time is short, so I curb flights of fancy in favor of practicality. It seems a good idea to make up a slow dance, as that kind can be set quicker, needs fewer steps than fast ones, and takes less energy to perform. Dan's schedule has been almost as heavy as mine, so he's agreed to sit the new dance out. It is to be called *Tracer*. Bet and the two other new girls are to dance it with me. A specially commissioned score has been written by James Tenny. Bob Rauschenberg's set piece is a stationary bicycle wheel which is spun at various rates of speed by an onstage motor. He has also designed the costumes, which are marked with tire treads and look as if they've been run over by a car.

For the time being, Tacet has consented not to design decor. Although he pretends to envy Bob's designs, in private he considers them a bit too dada for his own taste, and is critical of the choreography on the grounds of its simple patterns and leisurely tempi not being Byzantine enough. However, the old geezer has consented to come to Paris with us as official Aesthetical Executor.

There were the usual problems in raising travel costs. Again I had to borrow in order to buy cut-rate air fares.

At Idlewild Airport, when the dancers ask Tacet to watch their luggage while they go to check out the gift shops, he agrees grudgingly, but, after picturesquely draping himself over it, takes a snooze instead. Cushioned by the bags and snoring like a banshee, he looks quite the aesthete in his new cream-colored cravat. Though he tends to be beset by obscure illnesses, we see him as, on the whole, salubrious and likable, but sort of complicated.

Aboard the plane, sitting first with one of our girls and then another, he reminds me of an aged but still ravenous bee. Though his continual buzzing about Art and Life sometimes grates, it's only done for theatrical effect and usually nonmalignant. But we've suspected that there are impure motives behind his insistence on coming with us to Paris; and, just as we should have anticipated, the first thing he does on arrival is to investigate Pigalle. Accompanied by a new "wife," he then returns to his hotel room, and on emerging several days later, he has an awful time explaining his broken bed to the concierge. Fearful that he might spoil our troupe's reputation, we have to send him back to his real wife in Perth Amboy.

We are to give five performances, not at one of the main theaters of the festival but at the Lutèce, a second-rate theater on a street on the Left Bank that many dance goers have trouble finding. The stage is so small that when the six of us line up across it, two disappear into the wings. The same thing happens to our hands if we raise them. Leaps, even low ones, have to be scaled down or eliminated. There are a number of immovable stagehands taking up all the wing space, and since there's no room for them and us both, it's necessary to remove all exits and entrances from our dances. Besides these disadvantages, the company's small number of dancers and our shoestring productions make us darker than a dark horse in the festival's competitions.

That we win first prize for choreography proves, I guess, that the French aren't all bad.

April in Paris starts with a myth-eroding drizzle which is to last for almost the entire month. On the way to the Lutèce, the dancers and I pause beneath dripping chestnut trees where a poster-plastered kiosk reconfirms that we are really there. The others read their names with ritual fascination, but, feeling uncomfortable with most types of publicity and somehow believing that being anonymous is more dignified, I pretend not to see mine.

At the theater, after a long search for Tommy, we spot his hands waving at us from out of the prompter's box. He says that he will be running the show from there. Since the theater's cigar-smoking stagehands are forbidden by their union to operate our tape machine, and since Tommy has no room for it in the prompter's box, we are going to have to run it ourselves. After learning how, and snapping several tapes in the process, we barely have time to make up and put on our costumes before the performance.

The house lights blink out, the curtain rises, and ten or more nervous heartbeats later Bonnie throws up—or as someone else says, "burbles with *mal de mer.*" The *3 Epitaphs* head bag that she's been sewn into hasn't filtered out fumes from the stagehands' cigars, and, to make matters worse, horrible little eddies have been trapped inside there. It is Bonnie's debut performance with us, and I'm thinking that it won't be long before she'll be opting for other employment.

While dancing, we experience another distraction—the sight of Tommy's bony wrists inexplicably flicking at us from below the stage with his Adam's apple bobbing behind them. (The prickly red splotch on it is where shaving always causes him the most trouble.)

At the end of our performance, in order to all be seen at once, the six of us have to stagger our line. The audience's tumultuous booing and stamping tempts me to turn around and bow backwards, but the closing curtain is too quick for me. After squeezing past one of the fat cigars—he'll be lucky if he doesn't run into my fist someday—I stomp off to my dressing room. Before I can record the words "Stupid Frogs" in my journal, Tommy rushes in to say, "You ninny, they're not booing, they're shouting 'bis.' "

"So?" I reply blackly.

"So that means they like us! Go back onstage and take some more bows."

The following performances are jammed. If the Parisians, by nature cerebral and analytic, had been as warmly emotional as the Spoletini, they might have carried us through the streets; but instead we're invited to socialize formally. At the residence of U.S. Ambassador and Mrs. Gavin I ask what our chances might be for receiving financial help from our state department. In kind and tactful words, the ambassador tells me that performers who represent our country abroad are aided only when the state department sends them to cities where America's image needs bolstering. That was that.

On our night off, the dancers and I go to the Paris Opéra to see a typical French ballet, a full-length extravaganza called *Gala*. Except for the obvious difference in production costs, there is very little of it to compare to our own dances. To begin with, the theater itself, very unlike the Lutèce, is wall-to-wall magnificence. It rises solidly in front of a beepy boulevard which is forced to detour around it in the way that Park Avenue is forced around Grand Central, or the way that State-supported French dancers seem to be forced around costly tons of decor.

At the opera house Maurice Béjart is the choreographer whose dances are strangled beyond salvation, and deservedly so. He or someone else has thought up a clever plan that isn't cheap, simple, or tolerable. Moreover, it backfires and doesn't work. The dancers are cranking themselves around in dozens of costly wheelchairs, an ineffective theatrical effect that is its own reason. Amateurish collisions are happening in front of one of Salvador Dali's backdrops—a gargantuan reproduction of his autograph. Señor Dali, evidently, isn't one to mind publicity. Another backdrop of his depicts a cyclopean eye that's exuding the usual weird limpnesses and framing the ballerina Ludmila Tcherina who, in turn, is exuding French pizazz. Constricted by having to remain in front of the eye, she is able to flourish her rigidly correct pointes only while sticking in one spot. As an occasional attempt to seem modern, however, a flexed foot is daringly displayed, as well as other feeble distortions of classicism's put-upon vocabulary.

As American modern dancers, free from European harnesses or overly binding debts to tradition (who makes the rules, anyway?), we can see the futility of distorting the same old ballet steps to make them appear new— that is, nobody can tell us that we have to make a silk purse out of a sow's ear. Only the French or their near relatives the Hottentots would want to distort classicism by adding decorative flexings and feathers.

Next, an oversize bivalve, evidently a papier-mâché hat box but meant to be a closed scallop, is bumped across the stage by scraggly male dancers of a lower financial bracket who are dressed in Grecian tunics. It is fairly easy to predict that an aping of Venus's rise from the sea is on the agenda—though it has nothing to do with the rest of the ballet, it's a way to let us know which dancer is the ballerina.

Doubled up in the seclusion of her scallop, Mlle Tcherina can hardly wait to rise from the sea. There are some eager exploratory probings of her fingers at the crack of the scallop's lid, then frantic pushings. The lid is malfunctioning, something is stuck; and the scallop toters are showing their concern by jerking their heads back and forth from wing to wing. One of them now exits, perhaps to locate a crowbar. Another one, recognizing a fine opportunity, improvises a small jig to fill up the lengthening interim. After a while Mlle Tcherina, in a sudden surge of energy, heaves suddenly into view, but a glimpse of her perspiringly dramatic face is all that we get. The lid rebounds, gives her a good whack on the head, and knocks her back down into her scallop.

We are very much enjoying this part of the ballet. Having experienced pains and discomforts onstage ourselves, it is something that we can relate to. At last we have discovered exactly what it is that we modern dancers have in common with French ballet. In fact, Venus's rise and descent has been so impressive to us that it is to be re-enacted by generations of my dancers, each initiating the next with the ever popular ritual, eternally popping out of costume trunks as they play Ludmila-in-the-Box.

A few days after our opening at the Lutèce a cable comes from Anne Guerriere, the booker who arranged our Italian tour. She is offering us TV work in Turin—a much-needed source of income—but the work isn't to start for another four weeks. We have nothing to tide us over until then. But since we have to be out of the Lutèce in two days, and since we're having sold-out houses, it seems logical to try to continue our performances at some other theater. All of the festival's theaters are occupied, so I ask Mark Rudkin, a past classmate of mine at the Graham school who now lives in Paris, to help me find an available theater. He gives me one of his suits (which, by the way, soon died from a molting disorder) and tells me that if I'm to rent a theater, I should put it on and go find a benefactor.

A certain Mme Bousquet, renowned as a social lion around the turn of the century, was still passing out tea on Tuesdays. Although not actually invited—a postal blunder, no doubt—I'm intending to drop by her salon, my visit to be the buildup for a shakedown.

It's still raining and the Paris edition of the *Herald Tribune* is not working so well as an umbrella. At 3, Place du Bourbon, apartment 10, after climbing a creaky stairway and waiting in front of a flaking door, I'm greeted by a slow old lady who is still assembling herself. One hand is groping for a fallen shoulder strap, the other straightening a blowsy red wig. Not moving at all is the glassier of her eyes. She then voices cheery French chirps and makes turn-of-the-century welcoming gestures. I'm looking around for the other guests, but, although it is Tuesday, there are none.

Mme Bousquet waves me to a dusty settee, then rattles around with her tea service. I'm not understanding a word she says but am studying her mouth which is making funny French shapes. As we sip I tell her my name, and that I'm a ballerina—the masculine equivalent in French has escaped me. At the same time, I'm feeling disappointed and planning my retreat. Before I can excuse myself, however, she's popped a piece of hard candy into my mouth and dismissed me. In one of her eyes there's a kind of knowing twinkle.

The next day a message is left at my hotel that says there is something waiting for me at Mme Bousquet's. What? A pair of pointe shoes and a tutu? When I return to her salon, her shaky hand offers me an envelope stuffed with francs. Not being sure that I should accept them, I ask who they're from. From her energetic gestures and a few French words which I'm able to grasp, I get the impression that the francs are from an anonymous donor. She wishes me well, I boo-coo a lot, then fly back to hug the dancers and tell them that we'll be able to rent a theater and dance longer in Paris. Maybe it's my imagination, but a few of the girls don't seem too pleased with the idea.

In a day or two an extension of our season is announced. The newspapers mistakenly congratulate festival director Plasson for his opportune decision in keeping us on. No comment.

We move to the Théâtre des Arts, where we're to give nineteen performances. It has five hundred and thirty seats and a comfortably large stage and is in the red-light district.

On the way there, we're all intrigued by milling mamsells of the night who are flashing their bare white thighs under dark umbrellas. Tee-heeing with delight, Bonnie exclaims, "Golly, this is different from back home in Wisconsin." Bet, her company role now risen to a level somewhere between auntie and virgin queen, shoos her girls through the spellbinding streets of Pigalle in a Dutch no-nonsense fashion.

The des Arts is owned, operated, and lived in by a Madame Roubejansky, or some similar Russian name, who has, it is said, received, or maybe inherited, the theater from a former lover. We knock on her apartment door. The odors that are coming from behind it are permeating the theater. (Later on we see her fumigating it daily with generous squirts of eau de cologne from a lace-encased atomizer.)

Inquisitively, Madame's head emerges from a swirl of steam which is escaping from a shuddering pot on her stove. A flurry of flutters from her Japanese fan and the rest of her materializes—short, pale, plump body swaddled in a diaphanous peignoir and topped off by pale pink curlers. The total impression is one of ectoplasmic domesticity.

She says that, although she will soon be involved with a dinner guest, she will loan us the theater's only keys, and that if we will come quickly with her, she will now show us how to lock up every night after our performances.

We follow her light-footed steps—those of Jackie Gleason spring to mind—through the foyer and out onto the street, where, plumbing the depths of her floating veils, she locates something, winks, and holds a well-warmed key above her head triumphantly. She then demonstrates the exact procedure for locking up. "Watch carefully, I wish not to show it twice—this drizzle, I must be *très vite*."

Her increasingly transparent garment is already beginning to cling.

"These inner doors must be closed up tight. So! But not locked, no. Oh, no, no, no! And then we close, close, close my outer gates." (Old geezer would've preferred them to stay open, the wider the better.) "Like so! *Alors*, now then, we lock the gates—*mon Dieu*, but I am becoming—how you say?—soaked? And now we reach through the bars and push open the inner doors. Just so. And then we throw the key into the foyer like this." (Vibrato-laden high C on the "throw.")

The shining key soars in a graceful arc, landing with a ping on the foyer floor.

"And that, *mes cheris*," she says proudly, "is how you must do."

And then, wild eyed and wringing desperately at what has just been a scintillating frock, she reverts to her native Russian—"WHAAAAAGH!"

She's locked herself out. It is now raining torrents. We have no idea how to help Madame and are just as anxious as she is to find shelter. After assuring her that we'll always do just as she's demonstrated, we race to the nearest Métro.

Performing in the des Arts at night leaves our days completely free. Since we have the time, and the stage is available to us, this is too good an opportunity to pass up. We begin a new dance, a plotless one which is to be called *Aureole*.

It's the first time, and perhaps the last, that I get to choreograph on a stage. Besides the luxury of having enough space, I'm able to see what the dances will actually look like from a seat in the house. Working in my small studio in New York, where I watch dancers while practically on top of them, much guesswork is involved. Here at the des Arts I'm discovering that movement looks different from a distance. Strain is less noticeable. On the other hand, energy is watered down. It's reminding me of when I first saw Martha in the distance on New London grass and as she came closer, what appeared to be a smooth glide turned into a lurching swagger. Distance made large movements seem smaller, and small movements seem even smaller. The grander the movement, the farther it would project from a stage. As is said, distance lends enchantment, but Martha was the exception that proved the rule. The closer she got, the grander she was.

I'm also becoming aware that distance tends to make dancers look less personalized and more abstract. Small human flaws that I've become fond of in the studio—their momentary perplexities, soft grunts of determination, microscopic recoveries from dares that don't quite come off—become all but invisible onstage. The onstage god or goddess whom the audience sees often suffers clay feet when off. Surprisingly, certain dancers who aren't all that terrific looking offstage become knockouts the minute they hit the boards, and the reverse can be true too.

Stage light has much to do with the transformation of mortals into immortals. Thick and thin bodies both, when lit from the side, appear thinner and taller. Faces like Bet's, which have features that are well-spaced from each other, and faces that have no deep eye sockets or other dark depressions, are easier for an audience to read than close-featured faces, and take light better.

While working on *Aureole* in the des Arts I've begun to be able to tell which formations and patterns will be effective from a distance and which not; which steps project; which gestures will read; which dancers have inherited physical traits, or crafted ones that will benefit by being framed by a proscenium.

My old friend Mark Rudkin, who has not only given me his suit but has had his tailor alter it for me, is culturally oriented. He is a seasoned theater goer, well educated, literate, paints, and sings. He is also the son of Maggie Rudkin, the Pepperidge Farm tycoon who baked her first bread so as to nourish him when he was small and sickly. But to get to the point, Mark possesses a large record collection. On hearing that the dancers and I have begun a new piece, he dipped into it and came up with several Handel string concertos which he says I will like because they sound like a bunch of mice. After splicing various excerpts together, he has urged me to do something with them.

To reciprocate Mark's generosity, I've composed for him a middle-aged pun about an old suit and a young dance.

Rudkin's tailless tailor tailored Taylor,
Then Taylor tailored a taleless dance.

Working on *Aureole* is a good way to keep my mind off company concerns. Tommy is planning to leave soon and will be designing the lights for other troupes in New York. It will be difficult to do without him. Before leaving, Tommy finds a replacement: Raphael, a gracious Peruvian, is our new stage/road manager and, evidently, has no qualms about the job. It's puzzling, because even a cretin would have thought twice.

The new dancers are dancing well enough, though they gripe some and aren't as consistent in their performances as others. In a way I miss old pro Maggie, and am at times almost certain that, as she did, everyone will leave after this trip. Dark wings are swooshing around in my head, and I'm picturing the company needlessly wasting away in Scranton. Perhaps we'd do better if I could offer them bigger wages and less splintery stages. Yet performing each night and working on *Aureole* usually pushes these concerns into perspective.

Just before we leave Paris for Turin Liz hits the ceiling. Eyes flashing, neck stiffened, chin lifted, she says that she is not doing any traveling just now. "I can't," she proclaims. "My sole black dress is at the cleaners."

Admittedly, in my efforts to provide work, I've forgotten to tell her about Turin, but it's an understandable oversight. Usually I can tell something to one dancer, and the telepathic others instantly know. Bet, however, will be able to soften up our rebel.

Our costume case in one hand, my suitcase in the other, and with the impediment of a bicycle wheel pressed insecurely under one arm, I attempt to hail a cab with my head. Bet and Liz have better luck, and, after the whole troupe wedges itself in, the cab takes us to Orly, where, still mumbling about her darn black dress, Liz lags at the end of our line as we weave through the crowd. Bet urges her on with soothing words about all the black dresses she'll find in Italy.

"Yeah, I know," Liz moans. "The old-woman kind. I won't be bossed around like this! He should've told me. Who does he think he is, anyway! I have my own life, my own plans!"

As a tactic to distract him from what might be a misleading first impression of Liz, I draw Raphael away to a quieter spot. He's listening carefully as I go over his new responsibilities. To begin, I explain that my company is one that's proud of the harmony that exists between members and is unusual in that we all get along so well. Just then Liz's voice interrupts. "Paul thinks he's God!" she yells.

I pretend not to hear.

"I'm sick of this gypsy life! What about my boyfriends back home? We've been away too long and they're getting impatient!"

"Liz, would you mind? Raphael and I are talking business," I say. "Now, Raphael, the salaries must be paid on Fridays, and you should notify each hotel management to—"

"Hey, dancers, we should all get together and tell Paul to go—"

"—management to take care of the . . . Bet, I see a boutique over there. Would you please take Liz over and buy her a—"

"I won't be bought!"

"Gosh, Bet, can't you get her the heck out of here?"

After Bet tugs her off by the hand, Liz rumbles on like a distant volcano.

In Turin *Insects and Heroes, Tracer*, and *3 Epitaphs* are taped for Italian TV with only minor mixups, the main one being that I'm expected to direct the cameramen and can't tell a boom from a zoom. When we've finished the taping, Raphael and I take the company earnings to my hotel room, where we deal out seven neatly balanced stacks of lire—it's better than solitaire. Then I call down the hall, "Come get it, everybody!" A sudden gust beats them to it, scattering the money like confetti. All the dancers gather around my bed and I redeal. "One for dear Bet, and one for good Dan, and one for . . . okay, for sweet Liz," and so on back and forth across the bedspread.

The next day the dancers depart for short European vacations, except for Bet, Dan, and me, who are waiting at our hotel until our different departure times. Auntie Bet is to visit her mother in Holland and is to be the last one of us to leave the hotel. It seems strange to be saying "So long." On our way to the airport, Dan and I squeeze into a midget taxi, and, as we pull away, it crunches around a gravelly curve. Through the back window we catch a last glimpse of dear Bet standing tall and reedlike at the hotel's front door, long Dutch neck resolute (two-toned eye misting?), and the movement of her small waving hand is receding into a distance that, somehow, holds not much enchantment for me.

Snoozing across the Atlantic, I have half-dreams of French drizzle blending with Pigalle's fragrances. Mists and ectoplasms merge with hard-edged people, and there's a confusing interlude featuring George Wilson and George Tacet.

I spot Babe George on the observation deck at Idlewild among a crowd that's come to meet arrivals. As the plane taxis one way and then another, Babe scurries back and forth along the railing of the deck, waving and trying to match his steps to the plane's unexpected changes of direction. When we meet by the customs exit, he's eager to tell me of all the new "improvements" that he's made at the studio, and I'm having to brace myself. His decorative skills, when applied to the cherished plainness of my territory, instead of at his own place, are pretty scary.

When we get to the studio, he proudly points out his new additions. This time there are only two—a king-sized plaster Michelangelo David hot from Forty-second Street and a nightmare table lamp with bulbous base that's been spat at with silver paint. These objects are so tasteless that they've become high art. Instead of offending Babe by heaving them into the night, I decide to live with them for a while.

Among a stack of envelopes containing bills that have been waiting for replies is one with a foreign stamp. Brushing the others aside, and hoping that the mystery of our mysterious French benefactor will be solved, I tear it open. Written in delicate loops on elegant stationery, the letter says that it had been a pleasure to assist us, that our extended season had been a delight, and that now, at any time of my convenience, I can repay the loan. The *loan*! After dropping the letter, I pick it up to see that it's been signed by the fashion designer Hubert de Givenchy.

By return mail I apologize for misunderstanding Mme Bousquet's French, promise that the debt will be paid, although it may take a while, and send my thanks.

In a second letter from M. de Givenchy, he stylishly says that if I had thought it was a gift, then it was a gift. This message was as thrilling as if I'd been given a blank check.

Aureole

After returning to New York we immediately resume work on *Aureole*. What's been set in Paris looks terrible at home and has to be started over from scratch. Good Dan, sweet, peppery Liz, two newcomers, and I are its cast. Dear Bet was to have been in it, but by the time she's returned from visiting her mother in Holland the dance has more or less jelled. Though I've promised her a part and feel funny about breaking my word, I can't see a way to squeeze her in. It's certain that *Aureole* would be an entirely different dance were she in it.

Paris has been a little too much, or too little, for Bonnie and Shareen, I guess, and Sharon Kinney and Renee Kimball have been taken into the troupe as replacements. Whenever allowed, Sharon assumes the airy movements of a winged creature returned to its element, and her delicate frame is matched by a gentle manner, although, like Liz, she isn't above getting her dander up. Sometimes she makes the high-pitched chittering noises of a wren having its nest raided. Paradoxically, she has an aversion—a phobia, really—to birds, and objects to being compared to one. Whenever I call her Tweety, for instance. Humid, dark eyes with giant pupils make her an atropine or bella donna type.

The other arrival, Renee, could be mistaken for a *Mademoiselle* cover or Palmolive ad. Her kind of alabaster beauty seems hardly real, in fact is almost intimidating. Her energy is extraordinary, and she has such strong ankles that if there was any logic to them, they'd match the circumference of her waist.

Last summer the two were students at the American Dance Festival, where I'd handed them costumes and asked them to stand inside two of the scrim-doored cubicles that were part of Rouben Ter-Arutunian's set for *Insects and Heroes*. Extra dancers had been needed, not to dance but to slide the doors open and shut, turn lights on and off, and look ornamental. Not a challenging assignment, though pleasant enough to the girls, who perhaps thought they'd someday be given less confinement and more dance steps. And so they have. Remembering their good-sported stasis, not to mention their noticeable knack for dancing which was apt to soon bloom full force, I auditioned them in the fall and invited them into the ranks.

While working on *Aureole* Renee seems to have less assurance than Sharon. Her self-doubts are betrayed by excessive energy. She transforms the safest of simple steps into feats of peril, and in her risky revolutions seems half-squiffed, something I think just wonderful—that is, if she doesn't injure herself or anyone nearby. Therefore I set in motion a plan to bolster her ego by becoming tact itself. Instead of correcting her at rehearsals, I dole out dollops of encouragement. This causes me no end of heartburn.

The ulcers, by the way, were to accumulate one right on top of the other and prompt my doctor Harvey Klein, the best duodenalist in town, to remark that mine are the worst he's ever run across, an honor I'm almost but not quite proud of. But Renee mustn't get any credit for them. I'm mentioning this only because it's while working on *Aureole*, the dance that was to be loved by my mother for giving her such a happy feeling, that my stomach began its burny feeling.

Anyway, part of the plan to enlarge Renee's assurance is to take Sharon aside for a private talk. "Look, Tweetums," I say, ingratiating myself (choreographers have to be sort of psychological).

"I asked you not to call me that," she interrupts. "Dancers shouldn't have to stand for this kind of thing."

"Okay. Look, my fine feathered friend—"

"Cut it out!"

"Oh, all right. The thing is that Renee's a victim of her own clogged concepts, see? Being new in our close-knit dance family is making her feel insecure. I need your help. How's about taking her under your wing and—"

"Watch it!"

"Sorry. I mean take her under your whatever. You know—give her some helpful hints, butter her up."

"All right, but that'll be difficult. We're not speaking."

"What? I thought you two were college chums at Ohio State."

"We were, but we fell apart. Now she won't even look at me."

"You're jealous of each other?"

"Well . . ."

"Sharon, there's no time for this sort of stuff here. We're all going to be together a lot on the road, and there mustn't be friction within the company. Try to patch it up, will you?"

"Okay, I'll try. But it isn't gonna be easy."

And so by the time of the next rehearsal the rivals have declared peace, the ice has melted, their friendship revitalized by its temporary dip.

In a way, Dan and I are also rivals. Though not jealous of each other, there's always been some healthily competitive sandpaper between us. Like me, he's anything but petite, and his body is bigger than you'd think— that is, like most performers', his body looks different onstage. Most dancers look larger than themselves, but somehow he manages to look smaller. Maybe he does this so as to make me look too big. Am not sure.

Wanting to give him a nice fat solo, yet not a real long one, I scatter several shorties here and there among *Aureole*'s five sections. This is for a reason: it's so that he won't become too winded to be able to pull off a vigorous finale. In other words, so that his part won't overshadow mine. After all, it's my dance, and I'm supposed to be the main event.

Nevertheless, Dan is holding his own. Most of the steps given him are fast and footsy—lots of small hops and jumps in parallel position rather than turned out. He doesn't get much running to do, as his stride isn't a long one, and on him running looks slightly finicky. He's excellent at tongue-twister coordinations, so I toss some of those his way, along with other moves that he neatly executes in the down-home Wagoner way.

At this time—'62—modern dance is still keeping its distance from lyricism, "pure" or unexpressionistic kinds of dance, and reassuringly melodic music. There are a few exceptions—José Limón and Pearl Lang have done pieces that are primarily movement structures meant to match their Bach scores. But most modern choreographers are still oriented to asymmetrical angularities and use music such as Bartók or Wallingford Riegger—modern, but not too modern. *Aureole* has been commissioned by the American Dance Festival, where anything old is out. Unable to resist quirkiness, and always eager to ignore trends, I've accepted Handel, hoping to rankle anyone at the festival who thinks modern dance has to limit itself to modern music and weighty meanings. Am also hoping that a change of diet will be good for both audience and myself.

In another way, the dance is an attempt to get what I've learned in Louis Horst's classes out of my system. As Louis would've wanted, the dance's steps have been limited to a few basic seed steps—themes to vary in speed, direction, sequential order, and any other way that might make them seem less redundant. My favorite step in *Aureole*—a certain run with flyaway arms—is a direct and intentional steal from Martha's *Canticles for Innocent Comedians*. It may be a little off, but it's the closest I could come.

Something about simplicity has been on my mind. No puzzlements for folks to ponder, no stiff-necked pretensions from classic ballet, or even any of its steps. Just old-fashioned lyricism and white costumes. By the way, Dr. Tacet, who's designed and sewn the costumes, isn't happy about having to use the elastic from Jockey shorts for the girl's waistbands, or about me substituting a white bathing suit for tights. And he pouted some when I ripped his ruffles and suppository-shaped decorations from the girls' skirts and tossed them into a trash can.

The dance's many entrances and exits are an attempt to give an illusion of a larger cast than five and to open up the stage space so that the dance will seem to be happening in a larger one than is bounded by the proscenium. The best parts of *Aureole*, to be seen only backstage, are the dancers' hurtling races through the dark crossover in order to make their next entrances on the opposite side of the stage. There are likely to be graceless collisions with unwary stagehands, the dancers' onstage expressions changing into ones of something less than angelic serenity.

As far as choreographic invention goes, and virtuosity, there isn't much of that in my duet with Liz, but at this time there isn't a high premium put on these things. Even in this "pure" piece, feelings are foremost. "Dance" is a meaty word, and, naturally, there's more to it than firework displays. The duet is built on my own feelings for Liz—part fantasy and part real. As she changes from a cute kid with scrawny shoulder blades into a radiant woman, my admiration is on the upswing. I intend the duet to be easy and warm, also formal and distant. It's hard to say if the formal part is fantasy and the easy part real, or vice versa. Liz and I never discuss it, but the duet is a reflection of a real relationship, one that, as usual, is loaded with inexplicable duplicities.

The solo for me isn't set until the rest of *Aureole* is finished. This is due to procrastination pure and simple. I've told myself that the other dancers must first be well rehearsed and secure in their parts. But now rehearsal time is running out, and the long solo, which I'm beginning to wish in the worst way wasn't so long, is set on the commuter train to Adelphi, where I sometimes teach. In order not to attract attention, I stay in my seat drawing little stick figures in a pad and later copy the anatomically possible ones with my body. It's like learning a dance by mail—deciphering one of those Arthur Murray Teaches Dancing in a Hurry footprint diagrams. The main difficulty lies in keeping the flow going by passing through, rather than hesitating in, each position. It's been irksome to see other dancers lock themselves into positions as if to say, "Get this, everybody, I'm perfect— think I'll hold this pretty arabesque a while longer in case your slow eyes don't notice." Though I'm able to get the hang of it, the matter of flow, as well as other things particular to the way I move, may become a problem if the role is ever taught to someone else.

The solo, done almost entirely on the left foot, is also unusual in that it's an adagio. Usually, in classic ballet anyway, adagios are danced by women. Though I haven't intended to get too involved with meaning, the Handel has a hymnlike sound, and, to amuse myself more than for any other reason, I've made the part as if it's to be performed by some kind of earth father who goes around blessing things. Doesn't travel much, but indicates expanding space with développés of arms and legs toward the four cardinal points. If done in a gestural way, these slow-motion semaphores may give the effect of being in an open plain which extends beyond the theater and out into the stratosphere. I have myself a pretty big image—Father Nature, religion, and the cosmos. The balances are deceptively simple—the solo's hardest part is the entrance in silence. It's a simple walk from the wings to stage center which has to be unselfconscious, friendly, and seem inevitably right. No matter how often I've practiced it, this easy walk scares me to death. It's going to strip me of dance steps to hide behind and leave me stark naked.

When *Aureole*'s premiere is only a few days off, four of its sections have been set, but not the fifth and final one. By my bending Horstian rules, the seed steps have become unreasonably transmuted beyond recognition. They're twisted backwards, sideways, and inside out. I've hit the bottom of the barrel and can't think of one more blessed way to vary them for the finale. How to fill up the remaining music? I tell myself what I once learned from Bob Rauschenberg—that the easy way is best—and go over to the rehearsal tape machine to snip off the pesty last movement.

Just then Edwin Denby comes into the studio to see a runthrough. He often treks to nickle-and-dime performances and ratty studios, where, if asked, he offers hesitant and gentle criticism. It's late morning, and he's probably been up all night writing poems in a microscopic hand, then left them to walk his thin frame and long feet from West Twenty-first to Thirty-eighth, perhaps savoring some noteworthy examples of ironwork façades along the way. Another guess is that he's arrived with no change in his pockets, he being the city's softest touch. Also generous with his time to many unestablished dance makers like myself.

Bet offers Edwin some coffee and shoos the studio cat from the middle of the floor. Tabby's always underfoot and loves to bask in beauty in the golden rectangle of light that falls from the skylight. Tail twitching, the cat saunters off in dignified retreat, then veers around to take a picturesque pose on Edwin's lap.

After we show the dance, Tabby seems unimpressed, but Edwin blinks cheerfully.

"Well, what do you think?" I ask, deep down preferring a couple of choice compliments, not criticism.

He answers mildly. "I think that perhaps it could be even better if a little something is added to finish it off."

"But, Edwin, there's no time! And ending this way gives more importance to the duet. It makes an unexpected ending."

This is wishful thinking. I know he is right.

Wishing us luck on the premiere, he apologetically nudges Tabby off his lap, rises, then shyly backs out the door.

With little time to lose, the dancers and I tackle a concluding apotheosis, or coda. Unable to bear the dull prospect of more tinkering with the same old used-up steps, I throw together the first that come to mind. A bunch of dizzy tilts, turns, breakneck cavorting. Even if the dance is no good, at least we'll have a workout.

And then on a bright day in August, Bet packs our costumes and magnetic orchestra into one small case and we all train up to New London. During the trip she completes a pair of tights she's been knitting for me, needles clicking away like Madame Defarge's. Dark-eyed Sharon is looking nicely complementary sitting next to Renee's fair splendor. Liz is radiating enthusiasm, and Dan prattling. I'm a million miles away and scanning fields for butterflies—whites and sulphurs to match the fluttering ones in my stomach.

Arriving at Connecticut College, seat of modern ferment, ivied asylum of creative sweat, we go backstage to hug our lighter, Tommy. He smiles and bobs his Adam's apple up and down for us, looking a lot less skeptical of me than he had in this same place ten years ago. It's a homecoming. Merce and his troupe are the resident company this summer, along with José and his. I trust that Tommy's student stage crew will be more adept than I was. They're beginning to look awful young. Larry Richardson, who's pulling curtain, will one day, like me, be taking to the road with a group of his own. Here we are, all one big family. Am supposing that I can put up with a little generational repetitiousness.

The gang and I are to share a program with Katherine Litz, a dancer of delight whose solos are delicate flights of whimsy, a phantasmagoria dreamed up by an eternal ingenue. She does dilapidated aristocrats, fragile souls at their toilets in the twilight, romantic matrons with girlish tremors. My favorite is a dithering enigma in a sack. She never ceases to cheer her audiences, never seems to mind that her work isn't widely recognized, and never mentions her solitary struggles to continue work that deserves higher acclaim. We, her friends and fans, are nuts about her, but sometimes there are a few in the audience who seem confused by Katy's ladies. Let's face it, these are insensitive jerks. No art and no genius can ever be without touches of haziness and mystery. It's a big honor to be sharing the same program with her.

At the dress rehearsal in the darkened Palmer Auditorium a large piece of plywood has been placed across the back of some center seats. On it is Tommy's usual clutter of cue sheets, shaded desk lamp, metal ashtray brimming with Gauloise butts, and something new—a flashlight. Also as usual, Tommy's headset has gone stone deaf, and so technology is being replaced by primal shouting. "Put another amber gel on the special that's over stage center," Tommy calls to the crew.

Preoccupied with a sense of impending doom, I've finished a long warm-up and, curious to see what Tommy has up his sleeve in the way of lights for *Aureole*, jump down off the apron and grope up the aisle. Noticing the flashlight, I ask nervously, "Does that mean you're expecting the light board to blow?"

"Nar," he twangs. "Your solo's going to be lit dark. It's for you so's you can see your way around the stage while you're dancing. I'll have a giant spotlight follow Dan."

"Skeleton, I'd have thought by now you'd have gotten rid of your New England twang. Hey, what's that ugly rope dangling down over there stage left? And what's that wrinkle in the cyc? And why does this proscenium look so slanted?"

"Don't worry. Everything will be fixed by tonight. We'll have the audience all lean to one side so the proscenium will look straight."

Tommy's wit knew no bounds. Right now, though, I'm thinking he's not so funny. "Dancers, come out onstage so we can see what your costumes look like under light," I call, wondering how everyone can be so cheerful when we're about to dance the worst mess since spaghetti.

Tommy says, "Paul, how do you like this sunshine effect? Pretty gorgeous, huh?"

"Everybody looks yellow. If I'd wanted Orientals, I'd have gotten some in the first place."

"But that's the color of sunlight. We mix green light with lavender and out comes sunlight, see?"

"Yeah. I see green and lavender edges on their faces. Can't we just have plain white people in plain white light? Let's dump the sunshine this time. Also that soft focus you use for ripe old stars. Who needs it anyway?"

In professional lighting circles uncolored light is considered poor taste. Tommy, like his teacher Jean Rosenthal, favors shaded depth over flat visibility and has learned to mix his palette not like a painter's but according to unfathomable laws of light. However, more out of friendship than out of artistic beliefs—"compromise" being another word for "friendship"—he humors me by yanking all the gels.

After the dress rehearsal, I go downstairs to a dressing room where I make up to fateful ticks of my watch, indulging in as much fear and insecurity as I want. Involuntarily, my left big toe is twitching a little dance of its own. Can't help wondering if that might be a sign of approaching insanity. I get up to put on a dry dance belt, put it on upside down, take it off, put it on wrong again, sit down, get up, sit down. (Recollections need to be somewhat choreographed.) Noisy watch tells me to get into costume. I skid into Bet's room next door and say in a totally expressionless voice, "My costume. I can't find my costume."

With a double gesture, one hand denoting pity, the other disdain, Bet replies, "Oh, *Paul*—you have it on!"

How stupid of her to be so clever. Dutch Treat was always saying annoying things. Miss Treat is her other name. And she peppers her food, too. Heavily.

What happened, and how *Aureole* felt to perform, are things that are nearly impossible for me to describe. To pare it down to basics: the curtain lifts, we depart from this world, find a far more vivid place, and then the curtain closes.

Toweling off quickly, reveling in relief for being not too tired to still walk, the dancers and I grope for each other's hands and force our leaden feet to scamper back onstage for a speedy bow before the audience gets a chance to escape. I'm making an effort not to look overly humble when a tidal wave crashes into us. They liked it; we like them—in that order. Catching a sideways glimpse of Sharon, I notice her brown eye brimming.

Friends and faculty come backstage to say complimentary things. Pal Babe's hand appears from between two people, offering me his program. On it are written the numbers of bows for each dance. By *Aureole* is a circled "12." Across the cover is lettered "I like Katy best." The Babe, bless him—tact was never his strong suit.

Wonderful Merce drops by to say he's thought my dancers wonderful, and grand José is gracious and supportive. Other than the experience of dancing itself, these rewards are best.

None of the troupe has any idea that this has been the first performance of a piece that we'll be dancing hundreds and hundreds of times. On five continents, in world capitals and Podunk towns, in North African desert heat, at the edge of Alaskan glaciers, in the moonlit Parthenon's shadow, under banyan trees. With happy hearts and grapefruit ankles we're to dance it in Rotterdam, Rosario, Riga, Rio, and Istanbul—in more corners of the globe than you can shake a leotard at. *Aureole* is to be performed in big, fancy opera houses and on shaky postage-stamp platforms, on slick parquet and splintery planks, on wax and linoleum and broken glass. It's to be danced with amoebic dysentery, Montezuma's revenge, bleeding hearts, and yellow jaundice, with sprained backs, split soles, torn ligaments, popped patellas, and a hernia or two. The usual. Orchestras of all ilks will play astounding tempi, often the correct ones. Magnetic tapes waver and sputter out, but the dance persists. We're to get quite tired, yet Handel never falters. He's our novocaine.

There are to be garlands of jasmine, too, often looped around our necks by almond-eyed strangers. At times paupers or great fortresslike socialites come to say that they've been touched in some meaningful way. Kings, queens, and bag ladies are to see it.

Today it's strange to imagine the many *Aureole*s that are danced by other companies, casts in many places, mostly dancers I've never met whose limbs move through the same shapes as ours, and who've probably grown similar calluses. God bless their poor little bare toes.

After the premiere, critics express surprise at the American Dance Festival for including a "white ballet" on its programs and write that *Aureole* typifies just about everything that modern dance has been trying to do away with. Allen Hughes of the *New York Times* says that it's "different, daring, and delightful."

"Delightful." I was to argue with the *Times*? Yet there's something . . . If I could only duplicate myself and send one of me out front to see what it looks like.

Later on, when out with an injury, I was able to see it, and my nagging doubts were confirmed. The dance had been good to me. I appreciated it, valued and trusted it, but was out of sympathy. Though I understood its audience appeal, for me it had little. I too enjoyed seeing dances that required little effort to understand, ones that gave uplift and caused a smile. Yet I was not smiling. I couldn't forget how relatively easy the dance had been to make and how previous dances, both larger and smaller scaled, had stretched my goals much further. *Aureole* had been child's play compared with others that I had to dig for, grapple with, and slave over, ones that had a more developed craft to them but weren't as popular. It was impossible to know if it would continue to be appreciated; yet for all its success, perhaps because of it, *Aureole* filled me with resentment. I was wary of it. It caused me to see a time coming when a choice would have to be made—to remain on the comfortably safe side of the doorway to success, or to pass through it and into a tougher and lot less familiar place.

Charlie

The roof at the Sixth Avenue studio seems at the bottom of a crater. Skyscrapers crowd close, leaving only a patch of gray November cloud straight overhead. All around, a giant amphitheater of windows stairsteps upward, including those of the Dime Savings Bank. The Soot Bowl. Office workers could be equipped with opera glasses and concerts given, the least expensive tickets going to tourists at the telescopes on top of the Empire State. A quick estimate of the total income is staggering.

I haven't come up on my roof to dance, however, but to have a good think and solve a recurring problem. Usually my body tells me what to do. When the legs head south, then west, I know that I'm to take Miss Craske's class at the Met; or like when Tacet's early morning eyes fasten on the sink and his hand misses the tap. But every so often I get an urge to mull, to sort out what has been from what might be. This time it's money.

Income: Fifty-five dollars per week from classes taught at Adelphi and in

New Haven (minus train fare); two dollars per hour from renting out my studio to Katy Litz, Maggie Black, and Glen Tetley; recent grants from the Guggenheim and Robbins foundations—kindly of them, but too soon spent (Am still unable to purchase an across-the-room TV-control gadget, which I want even though in my small room my arm reaches anywhere perfectly well).

Expenses: mostly for concerts that never break even. Arithmetic unnecessary. As usual, am deep in the red.

Bet and Dan and other dancers have been donating their time and talent and shouldn't be expected to do so indefinitely. Something's got to change.

While mulling at the roof's edge I'm tucking in the grimy tail of my Ace bandage. It's a tattered Purple Heart for my lately purpled ankle. Am also nursing a grudge—those damn critics. Last week one from the *Village Voice*, essentially a lump in cruddy jeans and swingy beatnik beads, clomped across the room at an elegant East Side party, badgering me with, "We all know about you. You're just out to make a quick buck!"

"Pah," I said, or some other Tacet-like retort.

Now I'm concocting even better ones. "Sure, I'm just wild about money. You should be, too, so you can dress better." Or maybe, "Miss, I assure you that I am impervious to monetary corruption—and, by the way, your charming outfit tells me that you are of similar bent." Although buttering her up might have been foxier, it would've played havoc with my killer instincts. "Pah" was best, after all.

But maybe she was right. Am I becoming money mad? I'm thinking that since I took up dance, my early sense of mission seems to have gotten clouded with doubts and rude realities. What folks think of me may be what I am. I guess Tacet and I are sort of living in the reflections of ourselves in others— even been scouting out our names in print to make sure one of us exists. And cash, once a trifling nuisance—now it's supposed to be important?

It's turning cold here in the lengthening shadows. Overhead, a patch of gray is preparing itself for a color change. Dusky pink. Gel #342, if I'm not mistaken. Go down, heat water on hot plate for desiccated mushroom soup, return, sip, and set cup at edge of roof. BMT rumbles below, vibrating soup ominously. Beat-up orange-and-black monarch glides in and settles on cup, like as not mistaking it for milkweed. Poor little guy, he's missed migrating with his pals to Central America.

Dollars. Situation not good. Yet better than before. The company lately has been under the aegis of Theater 1962. Rouben Ter-Arutunian, who did designs for *Fibers* and *Insects and Heroes*, had gotten Richard Barr to a studio runthrough, Richard then persuading his partners, Edward Albee and Clinton Wilder, to present my work. Although the concert at Hunter College Playhouse was sold out (violinist Isaac Stern took standing room), it lost about two thousand dollars. Besides picking up the tab, Richard and partners had donated the use of their offices and staff, freeing me of my usual chores—placing ads, having programs printed, mailing press releases, fliers, presales, etc., not to mention liberating my taste buds from long nights spent licking stamps. Like Rouben (for his fee he wanted and was given a shoeshine kit), Richard is a past master at cost cutting and good at shoestring presentations. Grateful for his and his partners' help, I hadn't wanted to muff chances for future help by requesting a live orchestra.

But Theater 1962 can't go on sponsoring my gang year round, or get us the touring engagements that might guarantee our survival. Their aegis is wonderful, a rare kind of aid for a modern troupe, but, as Dick says, the arrangement is only a stopgap operation.

Like a giant firefly in the dusk, yellow light starts blinking on top of the Dime Savings Bank. It's as if old Tacet were up there with ideas flashing out from the bumps on his dome.

We probably need an agent, a full-time, professional one—not our current volunteer, Ruth Schneidman who, with generosity and good intentions, has been making me feel that my independence is being harnessed. Better ask her to please stop. Must then be careful about picking the right agent. Involvement with wrong one would be suicide—as bad as marriage. Suddenly, a flash of dancer Fred Herko, who hadn't married but had taken drugs and jumped from a window to his death.

A passing cloud covers the moon, and the roof becomes a dark, indistinct, and sort of scary place.

As usual, Tacet is waiting someplace in the gloom, wanting to express opinions. I'm needing career advice, so maybe it won't hurt to let him play devil's advocate. "Hey, Doc, what are you thinking?"

"Sonny," he starts, "definitely you do not desire an agent. They withdraw twenty percent. Your unpaid Mrs. Schneidman should continue with the booking."

"But it's like I'm a dangling marionette with her fumbling around at the other end of the strings. And yet, having tried to book the company myself, I know it's not my forte. The right manager could do a lot better. Don't you think we should get a professional, so then I can concentrate on dancing?"

"Absolutely not. An Artist doth not taint himself by collaborating with the world of business and hucksterism. Have you forgotten what José Limón said—that artists give, businessmen take? Real artists have no agents, thereby maintaining the purity of their presentations."

"Yeah, and like us they ain't got no big audience, either. Do we want my work to be seen or not?"

"Let us be content with a small select public. After all, sublimely subtile masterworks are digestible to but a select few."

"No. Good dance is for everyone. I know it. Lots would come if they had the chance. An agent will—"

"An agent is about as necessary as the plots in my collection of pornographic films. A de Rothschild will appear on the horizon one day to support and—"

"Doc, forget it. Private support has seen its day, and Diaghilevs are as dead as dodos. Time's a-wasting. Quick, let's go pro and aim for a wider audience. . . . Can I see your porno films?"

"Mark my words, wide acclaim and success means loneliness and awesome responsibility. Are you able to take on the dreadful difficulties and heavy load of a full-time company? Your life will be harnessed and hampered in a way worse than heretofore."

"You want me to settle for the gripes of failure? Sure, there's consolation in those. I see your point. It's tempting to let the company remain a part-time, far-out operation. Life would be much easier. But this is a big decision, and it's making me kind of confused. May I *please* see your porno films?"

"You have always been confused, yet you have done a great deal, and mostly without help. Keep your strings free and untangled. Your choreographic creations are too refined for general consumption. Large audiences accept mere surface values and will always reject meatier implications. Avoid the mainstream and allow yourself to become one of the all-time great dance martyrs, one sitting aloft in his appointed throne, not indulging in the gripes of failure but partaking in the hallowed joys of injustice collecting. . . . There are no films. Heh heh, I was just joshing."

That did it. As usual, the old geezer is proving to be nothing but vapor. I refuse to be taken in by the overly artistic side of myself.

A passing cloud uncovers the moon on the count of three. The ledge is no longer dark and dangerous. The question is settled. First thing in the morning I'll BMT up to Fifty-seventh Street, where all the concert bookers hang out, and ask one of them to take us on.

The first stop is Isadora Bennett's office in the Wellington Hotel. She's Martha's press agent, knows bookers, and maybe can steer me to one.

"Issie, you in here?"

Hidden behind a huge pile of paperwork, she replies from her desk, "Who's that? Come around here where I can see. Oh, hello there, darlin'. Sit right down and tell me how you are. Just move those papers off that chair and put them . . . oh, put them right on the floor. By those other stacks is fine . . . no, there better be walking space. Just pile them on that shortest stack."

"Sure, Issie. I think I can reach up there."

"Watch out not to knock the other stacks over, son. We don't want to be buried alive. Now then, have you met my new secretary? Myrna, come meet Paul. . . . Oh, I guess she's gone out."

A voice comes from behind some other stacks. "No, I'm here, Miss Bennett. Be right there!"

"Stop!" Issie says. "There's one about to topple!"

"Issie," I say, "maybe I'd better come back later. I can see you must be busy."

"Yes, yes. Oh my, yes! This place is in one hell of a mess." Her fingers are raking through her graying red hair, leaving it no less rampant. One of the buttons of her blouse is in the wrong hole. "Things never seem to get caught up, but there's always time for my darlin'. Now tell me, what can I do for you?"

"I'm looking for a manager, and thought maybe you could recommend somebody."

" 'Deed I can. There's a young man working part time for me who's planning to go off on his own soon. He's probably over inside there." She points to a closet door. "Charlie, are you still in?"

An optimistic voice with a New Jersey accent calls out, "Did you say something, Issie?"

"Paul Taylor is here. He wants to ask you something."

I edge carefully to the closet. The door opens a crack, then jams against Issie's archives. Half a mouth says, "Hi, glad to meetcha. The name's Charlie Reinhart." An index finger emerges. I give it a shake.

Chemistry, or the voice, or maybe the firm finger, tells me that this guy will do just fine. I'm not needing to know his job qualifications—Issie wouldn't steer me wrong. However, I'm thinking that bookers should be cool types, and I can't tell if he flaps easily, so I say, "What are you—some kind of closet queen? Do you like girls or boys?"

"Girls," he says. Then, after a thoughtful pause, "But they come second to guppies in black leather, of course."

Terrific. He's someone who's got his priorities figured out. There's just one other thing to settle. If he's willing to book us, it's important to establish our relationship right off. That is, it's best to beat him to the driver's seat and let him know that he'll be working for me, not the other way around. "Let's cut the crap," I tell him. "Be at my studio this afternoon at one and we'll show you some dances. Don't be late."

He shows up on time, breathing heavily because of the studio's four flights. After tripping on the doorsill and tossing around in stiff-armed gyrations, he regains his balance and settles into a wide, pigeon-toed stance.

I ask if he's ever seen my work.

"No," he answers, "but I asked Don Duncan"—a business cohort of Issie's. "He says yours is quality stuff."

"I guess you'd better see for yourself. Bet, Dan, Liz, Sharon, Renee, meet Charlie . . . uh . . . what's your last name?"

"Reinhart."

"Reinhart. Charlie Reinhart. Right, of course you are. Well, troops, I guess we'll have to show him a dance. Over on that bench, Charlie—sit!"

During *Aureole* he's beaming, his smile a dead ringer for Alfalfa's in the old "Our Gang" movies, and by the end of the runthrough he's fallen off the bench. We're all laughing, and Bet goes over to help him up. I'm noticing what look to me like dollar signs spinning around in his eyes.

"Okay, you're on," he tells me. "My fee will be ten percent of total income."

"Righto—but besides booking, you'll be coming on our tours as road manager."

"And after the troupe's gotten to be a household word, my cut will go up to twenty percent," he counters.

"Agreed. I trust you, Reinhart, and you can trust me. The hell with a contract. Let's shake." I offer my middle finger. He gives the tip a sharp pinch.

So that's how a long contract and palship begins. For the next eight years that he's with us, although we never quite settle the question of who works for whom, our unwritten trust is to remain unbroken.

Mexico

A January '63 edition of *Últimas Noticias* says that we are to perform in Mexico City at Bellas Artes, the National Palace of Fine Arts, through the "personal intervention" of Amalia Hernandez, director of Mexico's Ballet Folklorico. The announcement is accurate, overlooking a few spelling errors which Spaniardize Bettie de Jong into "Betti de Jova," Dan Wagoner into "Dan Wasonzer," and Richard Barr into "Ricardo Ricardo Bore." Lighter/stage manager Tommy has known Amalia Hernandez through designing Folklorico's lights and has been responsible for maneuvering her to see a runthrough at our studio. Since the engagement is to bring us a healthy number of pesos (two thousand dollars, plus travel costs and per diem for two weeks of performances), for the first time it has been possible to pay each of the five dancers a hint of rehearsal salary—a rarity in modern dance at this time, and good cause to be proud. Richard Barr has volunteered to come along on the trip as our business manager for the heck of it, Charlie staying home to book us other dates.

Lately it has seemed to me that the troupe is getting a little wayward— too much chitchat during rehearsals, snacks right before curtain time, rank leotards, things like that—and so, on the way to Idlewild Airport, I determine to be a more effective leader. Dutifully, I gather the troops in close formation at the Aeros Naves departure gate, explain the seriousness of our mission, then command them to sit in a quiet, dignified way while waiting for our flight. "And ladies," I add for good measure, "please try to keep your knees together for a change."

"You must be kidding," Liz snaps back. "Nobody can sit in any position at all. We're still aching from those darn tetanus, polio, and smallpox shots we had to have." The width of Liz's flared nostrils usually indicates the degree of her annoyance—in this case about seven point five on the Richter scale.

Ignoring her, I turn to Tommy and hand him the bicycle wheel that is our set piece for *Tracer*. "From now on you'll be carrying this," I tell him. (I've always felt self-conscious toting it through airports.) As we line up to board, a stranger asks Tommy what in the world he has there. "A wheel," he answers, holding it up patronizingly. "Doesn't everybody travel with one?" At this Liz laughs too loudly, I'm thinking—and her dress is too loud, too. The plain black one she usually travels in has been replaced with something a smidge too short and gaudy gold. Dan's getup could also have been toned down. What was with that rosebud-embroidered shirt and skinny little string tie? And why won't those undisciplined hands stay still?

After boarding the plane and buckling into the seat next to his, I soon tire of his bright banter and turn away to gaze through slanting dots of rain on the porthole pane. Outside on the glistening tarmac a squad of army jets is cueing up for takeoff. The precision of their well-spaced line is inspirational, and after our plane lifts, banks, and levels off, the militaristic sound of seat belts being clicked open is music to my ears.

With nothing much to look at except the boring billows of clouds below, I sink into my own fluffy half thoughts.

March to Mex off on the wrong foot. Will take time, but I'll be a Class A Leader yet. And maybe Charlie's future bookings will make us rich so that we can afford some kind of regulation uniform on the order of those worn by U.S. athletes on the way to the Olympics. Ours can be emblazoned with an insignia shaped like a bare foot, my five dancers represented by the five toes. To symbolize myself there'll be a big heel. . . . No good. No heel—better just have a mammoth sixth toe.

With sleeper's logic my thoughts then lead from big toes to dildos to Martha. Whenever she enters her studio her dancers always stand at attention. I should get mine to do that. And should visitors come, perhaps Bet can get Sharon and Renee to put on maids' caps and serve tea.

And then on the insides of my lids, a disturbing event—echelons of guppies in leather-belted battle array swimming at me, unsheathing sabers, rattling them. After a scaly Armageddon, a hasty retreat, a frightening fall, and our plane's landing jolt, I wake up in Mexico, D.F.

At customs we're delayed by a snoopy inspector. Overly curious about our costume trunk, he is muttering something in Spanish about impounding it. Irked, I order him to pass it through pronto. He replies with sharp words, but when I look them up in my Spanish dictionary they aren't there. Nevertheless, Richard is able to rescue the trunk by presenting our declaration form with some *dinero* folded inside it.

On the way to our quarters, the pseudosnazzy Hotel Regis (to be totally demolished by the earthquake of '85), I'm chewing out the dancers. "Jerks, if you all would only dress right, customs inspectors wouldn't be so suspicious and hold us up like that."

Later on, Bet gets me alone and says, "Paul, be careful. If you don't talk nicer to the dancers, we're going to have a revolt on our hands." It's another of her bothersome remarks.

"They're just babies and have to be told what's right," I reply with a shrug.

The Bellas Artes turns out to be in the center of a city that exudes the memorable smell of pineapples combined with open sewers, a city where galloping dysentery beckons from behind each sidewalk refreshment stand. Afflicted with a lighthearted yellow dome, the ponderous architecture of the white marble theater seems more suitable to a birthday cake. It's been built on a swamp, as was the whole city, and year by year has been slowly sinking into its site. Perhaps some fine day only the tip of the iceberg will show—a rusty replica of a snake-eating eagle perching atop the doomed dome. The sinkage problem has been temporarily solved by lowering the theater's immediate surroundings, and so we need to descend six or seven steps to reach the stage door. Armed with our bags of makeup and practice O.D.'s, we march single file down into our marble fortress.

Campaigning from behind, I then urge my mountain corps up several steep flights to the stage. On reaching the first landing, Bet and Liz plop down on the top step. "Come on, let's move it," I tell them. "Oh, Paul!" says Bet. "Can't you see we're tired? All of a sudden we can't breathe."

Always the same old excuses. So stubborn and Dutch. This is depressing—she should get in shape or see a doctor. (Not until later do we learn that Mexico City is at an altitude of seven thousand feet—future Olympic contenders would need to arrive several months early to acclimate to the thin air.) Leaving Tante Bet to sit there with our budding insurgent, I continue up toward the others, who have paused at the second landing. They're panting at an awesome clip, and their small bags seem to be weighing them down. "Keep going, get the lead out," I call to them. Dander up, Sharon looks back over her shoulder, knits her brow, and shows me the tip of her tongue.

Catching up at the top of the stairs, I find them leaning on each other like a teetery house of cards—a lightweight edifice within the marble one, both slowly sinking into a swamp. Eyes glazed, spirits gone flat, they're looking toward the stage as if experiencing some unnameable dread. Finally, after a spell of ineffective gulping, Renee manages to gasp, "Gosh, I don't think we'll be able to dance here."

"Nonsense," I reply, trying not to show total agreement. "Get dressed, then let's warm up on the double. Our dry run will start in twenty minutes."

But then we discover a three-foot cylinder of oxygen just by the stage. It's under the reign of a nameless hombre of Indian descent with a sunny something about him. Probably one of those hopeless softies who loves everybody. Gathering around the tank, we intently watch the twist of his hairless wrist; a valve hisses and he places a well-worn rubber cone over Liz's nose. She nods blissfully, and then, entirely without utilitarian purpose, a hairless tendril arm twines around her waist. She should know not to fraternize with the crew—will have to speak to her later, but right now I'm eager for my own turn with the nose cone.

Aided by whiffs from the metal lung, the rehearsal goes not badly—that is, until getting to *Post Meridian*. The dance starts with Liz and Sharon walking slowly out from the wings in unison—not the flashiest of openers, and I've often been tempted to frill it up, but this isn't the time or place to grope around for improvements. If the girls would walk with panache, maybe they'd pull it off. The music begins its jetlike drone and the two enter. "Stop the tape," I call to Tommy. "Go back, girls. You weren't

anywhere near being in unison. And please, let's be less casual. I know it'll
be hard, but try to look like you're somebody, okay?" They re-enter. "Wait
a minute, that's awful. Can't you two even walk?" Again they enter. "Stop!
Now you're too stiff. Where's your pizazz? Walk like you mean it, and for
cripe's sake get together!" The two lean brow to brow, whisper something,
then turn toward me to yawn in precise unison.

Some nerve. Obviously, they don't agree with me that pizazz could make
the entrance work. To them it's an uninteresting assignment, they aren't
even trying, and they're challenging my authority to boot. If a showdown is
what they want, they'll get one. "Liz, are you chewing gum? We don't chew
gum onstage. Get rid of it. And while you're off in the wings, stay away from
that boyfriend of yours on the oxygen tank!"

Backed up by the tape's loud rumbles, Liz and I trade trigger-happy
shots as armed neutrality explodes into full-out warfare. Overripe gripes are
clearly, if exaggeratedly, expressed. As a parting blast she shrieks, "We're
all fed up with being bossed around, you . . . you fascist toad!" Then, after
performing several frustratingly soft stamps in her bare feet, she streaks in
a straight line to her dressing room, soon returning to march center stage
with satisfyingly deafening clicks from her new high-heeled shoes. She's
changed into the gold dress and is accompanying herself with jangles from
a snarl of gold bracelets. Although a nonsmoker, she's bummed a cigarette
which is jutting belligerently from granite lips. Clenching, curling fingers of
smoke climb upwards as she pauses in splendor directly beneath the bare-
bulbed work light. "I'm leaving. Should anyone care to contact me," she
sniffs regally, "perhaps the night clerk at the Regis will take a message."

Crap. Now who'll do the *Aureole* duet with me? She's an ingrate, a sassy
brat, an upstart, a quitter, an awful flirt, and, last but not least, her nostrils
sure look pretty whenever she goes on the warpath. War, old Tacet calls it.
"*La guerre*—banquet of vultures, hieroglyph of misery"; he says it deter-
mines not who is divinely right but who shall remain. Oh well, who needs
her anyway? But it won't be easy doing her parts as well as my own. And
her *Piece Period* Empire dress would be too tight, not look nearly as lovely
on me. Perhaps . . .

"Bet, dear Bet, would you go catch Liz and tell her I'm sorry?"

"Oh, Paul, you'd better . . . "

"Yeah, you're right. I'd better tell her myself."

That night in the wings Liz and I wait to go on. For now we have stimulated
each other enough. Antagonism is laid aside for future flings, and we are
back to our customary starting place. Tommy has magically transformed the
harsh work light into a gentle wash, and the stage is freshly mopped. In a

moment dimming house lights will cause the expectant twin hushes that sometimes occur on either side of the front curtain. As usual, Liz reaches over to snap the waist elastic of my tights, and, also as usual, I fend off her hand with a slap. There was something more than déjà vu about the whole repetitious bit.

Though we fondly love and admire each other, her deep aversion to any form of dictatorship and my touchiness about traces of rebellion are what spark our periodic collisions. If we were able to recognize our differences, we might be more forbearing and less bewildered. But even if there's no permanent truce, we'll always be forced to cool off quickly. People out front have paid good money. Even more importantly, our profession imposes a rule that limits temperamental outbursts—an unbreakable law enforced by the great mediator Curtain Time. The troupe is a society in miniature, and we are both victim and product of our stage habitat. We dwell in a house that demands that clamor be transformed into music, heated gestures into steps, dreams into choreographic fact, and offstage chaos into onstage order. And so I'm beginning to realize that the dancers aren't babies and don't need military leadership. Curtain Time, commitment to our profession, and each of the dancers' own personal whips of discipline are plenty militaristic enough.

Leaving Liz standing in the wings, I make a quick trip to the oxygen tank, where I store up enough to last a week. As I step out onto the stage, the world suddenly becomes a giddy place. Am happy, very very happy, so happy that I've forgotten my dance. On looking through a haze of bright cobwebs to find out what costume I'm wearing, the name of the dance comes back, but none of the steps, and so I puzzle the public with some off-the-cuff doodling, and don't even care.

Afterwards, instead of leading the dancers out for a bow, they lead me. To a cot in my dressing room. With leadership tables now turned and the dancers heady with a newfound responsibility, they command the hairless hombre to strictly ration my intake for the rest of the run.

After a week at the Bellas Artes we pile into a bus and head coastward for a single performance at the Playa Hornos, a movie house in Acapulco. The bus driver warns that there may be stray cows on the road, recommends that we hang on tight, then treats us to a roller-coaster descent to the Pacific. At the outskirts of town he deposits us at an inexpensive hotel which, because we seem to be the only guests and because of a faulty neon sign, Dan dubs "Hotel Vacancy."

Left behind like a snake's shed skin is any determination to conquer Mexico with terpsichorean ammunition. Acapulco sunshine and a humid holiday atmosphere cause a kind of unshriveling to occur. Sugary sea breezes untense our minds and muscles; a covenant is made with gravity—a temporary alliance, certainly not surrender; ambitions are locked away, lassitude reigns, and Bet's sinuses are again on the loose.

After checking in and dumping our luggage, we rush right out to buy bikinis, wiggle into them, then ooze to the nearby beach.

Eager to examine some tropical flora and fauna, I leave the others and walk along a well-trod path that runs close to the most unpopulated part of the shore. Landward rises an early Aztec mango tree, perhaps, with the remains of a silk stocking snagged on one of its lower branches. Disturbed by my passing, wads of offal-eating gnats disperse in dark puffs. Sea urchins, sharp spined and easily able to penetrate the feet of careless waders, are guarding their tide pool homes, sucking and rasping on the rocks there at the bottom, nestling against rusty cans and broken *cerveza* bottles. Invisible presences, the voracious Acapulcan viruses and joyous self-splitting amoebas are crowding crevices, ledges, any old nook, loving and multiplying at an admirable clip. Tide lines, explosive nature's flotsam garlands, deserve particular attention, seeing as they're displaying a profusion of prophylactics. Draped there, lying limply, as if having failed to make some statement concerning mankind's reproductive tendencies, the little castaways are but sad representatives when compared to the prolific Pacific. But, though outwardly forlorn, they're still impressive, assuming that potent juices are still alive, brewing and stewing inside there. How great that in their afterlife the bladders now serve as breed shelters. How thrifty, how practical and paradoxical, how to be envied.

For some time now I've been toying with the idea of brewing progeny myself; but not caring to marry, I am drawn to the possibilities here. The isolated semen in its manufactured womb, unaided by ovaries, is perhaps making the best of a lonely situation by reproducing all by itself!

For the time being, however, I've had enough ecology. Preferring to leave my discoveries untouched, I return along the path to see what the others are up to.

All have been for a swim and are now clustered inside a not quite primitive beach hut featuring white plastic walls and a roof of plastic thatch. Richard has treated everyone to rum punch, and they are rollicking and turning red from the sun or the rum, or both. Dear Bet is rendering something that she has promised would be "America the Beautiful" but which has turned out to be completely unrecognizable. Feeling extremely embarrassed for her, yet more concerned for the others, I grab a towel and perform the necessary act of kindness by muffling her mouth.

After more rum the party becomes very meaningful to each of us. To Bet it means Keep Croaking. To others it means Take a Nap. To me it means the merging of sights just seen along the path and the present one, and I can't help viewing my gang as a wad of thirsty gnats or joyous amoebas crowded moist and warm within a plastic womb. Swaying there inside the hut, as I look from face to shining face, from sea to shining sea, each seems light years away. And they are of a different species. Happier. More content. I'm much more alone than on the recent walk.

I should've guessed that boozing would bring bleakness. At some point—impossible to know exactly when—I'm deeply saddened at not being able to recognize Bet's song; or maybe it is the unlikelihood of male self-propagation that comes crashing down; or perhaps it is the realization that not only me but each of us will never be free from isolation. Each is a solitary alien, each is ever to be a stranger. Anyway, whatever the cause, maudlin tears roll forth, if not now, then later, back at Hotel Vacancy.

There, lying on an indecently swaybacked bed, one crippled by the romps of former guests, I grimly watch the ceiling darken. Crickets in cracks are stridulating, and tropical moths are bumping into things. Now is to come one of the minidramas that I sometimes invent and always star in.

It's Christmas Day. Martha and Mr. B have recently added to the holiday spirit by creating a new jewel for their combined companies. Deservedly, the two giants are being given a Christmas dinner by the President and his wife in the White House. Because of a blunder made by some uninformed social secretary, my company and I have been uninvited, but thanks to six black raincoats with bogus security badges under the lapels, we are able to gain admittance. Having been delayed by Liz, who has made a scene over wearing black, we arrive too late for the dinner but in time for the President's after-dinner speech. We are surprised to see that white sheets have been placed over Martha's and Mr. B's vacated chairs. After quieting everyone by hurling his plastic wine glass into the fireplace, the President hops nimbly onto the damask tablecloth, lifts an oversized silver chalice etched with a Mexican eagle, and shouts, "Here's to America's two greatest crackpots! May they rest in peace." Then, hopping down and coming over to throw an arm around me, he whispers benevolently, "Take it from one as wishes you well, *mi muchacho*, and never eat none of our plum pudding."

At eleven the same evening, movie goers are leaving the last showing at the Playa Hornos cinema and Tommy is removing the big beaded screen. While he goes on to tighten about eighty bulbs in an overhead strip, all but three of them turning out to be duds, the rest of us do a quick warm-up, put on our costumes, and sit down to wait for an audience. We're blistering from the afternoon's sun, the more exposed portions of our skins lifting and sliding around and doing a little dance of their own.

"Oooooh!" moans Liz. "Let's hope and pray the audience never shows up."

"Eeeeek!" trills Sharon, while daintily testing a reddened teaspoon shape rising on the top of her foot.

"These tights are too darn tight," Dan says, while attempting to rip both seams at the ankle.

As tormented souls unified by misery, our only hope lies in quickly removing the raspy costumes and remaining totally inert. But we're professionals; to dance is to live. But we don't want to live. However, two or three people begin to enter the house, and then a few more. Enough to be called an audience, and that's that.

Everything isn't all bad. Here's the perfect time to try out a new approach to leadership, the very chance I've been waiting for. Instead of bossy orders given from the rear, I now intend to get in front and lead by setting an example.

"Well, old pals," I say optimistically, "there's at least ten people here. I'm going out and lay them in the aisles."

"Well," Sharon chirps, "good luck!"

"Yes, have fun," Renee chimes in. "If you've decided to dance tonight, that's your own business."

"So long for now," says merry Dan. "We'll be seeing you tomorrow morning back at the Vacancy."

Nuts to the new approach, I'm thinking and, menacing them from behind, growl, "Get out there and take your places, you jokers!"

Sighing resolutely, Renee goes to stand downstage right with her nose pressed against the front curtain. Grouchy wren Sharon migrates to midstage left. Liz does a slow, resentful flounce over to a spot that is a yard to the right of upstage center, where, at the last possible moment, Dan hauls her into their opening lift.

Whenever *Aureole* is performed, these paths lead to these precise locations and in this precise sequence. Only this time, instead of walking lightly, they're edging in agony, and their costumes seen in contrast to their skin is making a study in magenta and unlaundered white—which, by the way, is a color scheme that would make tasteful Tacet cover his eyes and reel backwards. As for myself, I'm too absorbed by my own blisters to bother about much else.

But Renee doesn't always press her nose against the front curtain. She only does that at very shallow stages where every last inch of space is needed. Built to accommodate celluloid shadows, the Playa Hornos stage is fairly wide, but not much deeper than the thickness of its movie screen. We have not rehearsed or respaced the program. Exactly what will happen is anybody's guess. Passing each other is likely to be a problem. To pass by climbing over one another, or by jumping down off the front of the stage, are the likeliest possibilities.

Off in the dark wings Tommy is poised with his hands on the rope that opens the curtain, standing there like a self-illuminated stalk of rhubarb. His unearthly glow is emanating from a spectral source that even such lighting experts as himself cannot understand.

The flimsy curtain, hemorrhaging with modernistic lozenges, is an open-from-the-center kind, not a guillotine, its lower edge permanently hung a foot off the floor in order for a janitor to mop without getting it dirty. That everyone out front is now presented with a preview of three pairs of feet (not counting Liz's, she being cradled in Dan's arms) is no surprise to us, nor a terrible imposition, trouping having hardened us to the heartbreaking compromises required by quirky janitors.

"Here we go, gang," Tommy whispers. It never seemed to make much difference to most people that an occasional malfunctioning sound system allowed only the audience to hear his whispered cues.

"Here we go," he whispers again, just to make sure we hear.

"For God's sake, hurry up," Dan whispers back, his grip on Liz in their cradle lift beginning to weaken. Tommy tugs at the rope, but the curtain has gotten stuck, so Dan lets Liz's rear sag down until it's resting on the floor, thereby giving the audience another and better preview.

But Tommy has most of his attention on the fouled-up curtain, tugging and jerking on its abundant folds as if fixated, rippling its rope with loose little flicks of his bony wrists, then turning away in a pretense of giving up, only to spin around and attack with renewed vigor. He seems to believe that if he's foxy enough, the curtain can be taken unawares. Calling upon resources of strength that no one has ever seen in him before or since, he takes a deep breath, drops into a low squat, and hurls himself halfway up the rope, where he clings, knees pumping through the air like pistons. The curtain suddenly unsticks, dumping him into a heap on the floor with the rope still clamped in his hands.

Never has there been such a quick, abrupt, lightninglike curtain. Its flimsy folds billow and fly as if hit by a tornado, and the swirling eddy of lozenges wraps itself several times around Renee, swaddling, swallowing, and whisking her off to the farthest reaches of the wings. *Aureole* then begins with three dancers instead of four. Fortunately, Tommy and I are on hand to unwind her from her cocoon, otherwise she might be up for pupation. Although the experience has been disorienting, Renee emerges bravely.

"You okay?" I ask.

"Sure."

"Well, can you go back on?"

"Of course," she says, zigzagging vaguely and ending up against a backstage wall. "Uh, if you'll just point me in the right direction . . . " Helped by a hefty shove, she joins the others.

Soon we're all streaking back and forth along the ribbon of a stage trying hard to avoid each other's whooshing arms and dangerous elbows, sometimes successfully. Sand from the beach has somehow gotten into my dance belt, causing me to reinterpret my role: benevolent earth father converted to St. Vitus. The night is a scorcher and the theater is not air conditioned. We leave salty puddles all over the stage. In an effort to avoid one, Sharon careers into Renee, who bashes into Liz, who, in attempting to avoid Dan, has to hop down off the front of the stage. Dan, dodging everyone, steps into a puddle, throws up an arm in abrupt spasm, regains his balance, and then is immediately mowed down by me.

Soaked and heavy, Tacet's costumes stretch to unfashionable lengths, the girls' skirts plastered between their legs, my sleeves flapping out beyond my fingertips and flinging bright arcs of sweat into ten clearly visible faces in the front row. But we do not let our public discourage us. We do not let the costumes tangle and trip us. We do not seriously injure ourselves, or others. No.

When *Aureole* and the rest of our spectacles are over, the curtain all but down, the audience gives no indication of being amazed or delighted or repulsed, or anything. No one can interpret hands that pat politely, then dissolve quietly into the tropic night. In a way we are grateful to them. Never have so few been so lenient to so much.

The troupe is left tired, sore, and slaphappy. Me, I'm all that and also feeling the way some people do when they've let an opportunity for martyred death pass them by. It's very disappointing. I'm also sensing that my fame isn't firmly intact. Where were all my fans? It's been fifteen years—surely I should be at least semifamous by now.

Old Tacet, he would have things in proper perspective. He's telling me not to be discouraged, and saying something or other about the vicissitudes of celebrity. Yet the more I dance, the more I believe it to be the right thing to do. The basic truth is that I'd gladly trade my life for the chance to dance, would perform at a moment's notice with pride and fervor on any old stage in any old circumstances.

*   *   *

Small shreds and flakes of scorched skin were left at the Playa Hornos.
Nearly two decades later I still wonder where those specks are now. It's
scientifically certain that they do exist somewhere, if only in a gnat's stomach, or in the genes of that gnat's gnats. Less certain is the existence of any
other traces of us in Acapulco. I sometimes think it was a shame that our
trip didn't end more tragically. We would have preferred hearty boos to
being condoned with kindly politeness. Personally, I would have liked
being entirely devoured by gnats—a truly tragic touch that would have lent
nobility to our journey's end. When written right, sad endings nearly always leave the strongest impression; readers of obits tend to feel they've
gotten their money's worth. All earthly doings eventually descend, Mother
Nature downs ups, dancers fall, even the lightest of leapers must land. That
our steep climb to the stage of Bellas Artes was followed by a roller-coaster
drop to the Playa Hornos was, if not exactly tragic, at least both geograph-
ically and aesthetically correct.

And so the Mexican jaunt ended, not with big-bang nobility but only with
a piddling whimper of baggage. On the way out of the country, rather than
being delayed again at customs while searching for a list that had been
misplaced and which was needed to legalize the departure of company
belongings, I declared our costume trunk as my personal luggage. The
customs inspector was a decent, incorruptible-looking type, not at all like
the one encountered on arrival. When asked, I told him that the trunk
contained all my best clothes, and he then asked me to unlock and open it
for him. After gazing for a moment at Sharon's plumed *Piece Period* bonnet,
which was lying among a sweaty tangle of bras, he slipped me a knowing
wink, closed the lid quietly, and, glancing heavenward, waved us on.

The Midwest

By now, March '63, Charlie has booked his first tour for us: Studebaker
Theater in Chicago on the eleventh, University of Illinois Auditorium in
Urbana on the thirteenth, Hanley High School in St. Louis on the fifteenth.
As the tour isn't all that extensive, it seems best that he again stay in New
York to book another. Jennifer Tipton, whom Tommy has been training, has

agreed to come along as stage manager, Tommy having left to light an impressive string of Broadway shows, St. Mark's Square in Venice, and other big things. Jenny—recently his secretary—is an ex–dance student of the American Dance Festival and in years to come, like Tommy, is to be one of the finest and most sought-after lighting designers anywhere. She has also agreed to help drive, which turns out to be most of the time, since she's the only one of us able to back up our rented station wagon and U-Haul without denting anything. If we're to get from one date to the other in time, we don't need delays.

The long, flat drive to Chicago is uneventful, and except for a word game called Break the Code introduced to us by the multitalented Jenny, it would seem endless. The game needs no pencils, spinning arrows, or boards to spill, and is to assume a major place in company annals. Jenny starts us off by saying, "It took three days to drive to Toledo." From that we are expected to deduce the name of a famous person. Unable to come up with any conceivable clues, we promptly admit defeat, and she tells us that the answer is "Clara Bow"!

" 'Clara Bow'? That's nice," remarks Dan, immediately losing interest and going back to his needlepoint. My passion for solving puzzles having been whetted, I say, "Just as I thought. Hot diggity, this is fun. Let's do another."

"All right," Jenny agrees. "Since you've broken the code, this time it's your turn to give the clues."

"Oh well, you go right ahead. It'll take me a little while to think up some really good ones."

As is so often the case with fads, diversions, and springtime infatuations, the game seems to offer an endless future of joy, but I'm wondering how long it will be before we're at each other's throats, and how much of a threat the game will be to company camaraderie in general.

Jenny keeps giving the code to break. Our brains thrash to nowhere. Getting into the spirit of the thing, Tante Bet mentions the name of a Dutch celebrity for us to decode. Since all of us now know who it is, he's dropped—nobody's ever heard of him anyway. Sharon, under the impression that she's come a little closer to unravelment, chirps, "I think I've got it!," then darkens her brow with doubts and plummets into the depths of despair. It's pitiful to see hopes soar, snag, and topple. Renee offers Sharon a tidbit of sisterly compassion, then pleads, "Paul, why are you allowing Jenny to do this to us?" Although we keep trying, none of us are able to break the code. A few years later, in Natchitoches, under duress and in a moment of weakness, Jenny reveals the code to me, and from then on she and I are to inflict new generations of car-bound dancers with the game as a kind of initiation rite or test of their capacities for self-control.

A blizzard holds off till the afternoon of our rehearsal at downtown Chicago's Studebaker Theater. It continues through our single performance and is, we quickly assume, the reason why we do so poorly at the box office. Or perhaps that's because Chicago isn't ready to have its traditional concepts of modern dance dispelled, if it has any. Or maybe because, as far as we can tell, Chicago has no downtown. At any rate, we don't draw, and like the car game, the thing is a mystery.

Carroll Russell, who has personally financed our engagement through Contemporary Concerts, steadfastly believes that Chicago should see what is going on in New York. Although unable to recoup a cent of her investment in us, she is to continue bringing us as well as other modern-dance groups here. Her unsolicited donations, warm hospitality, and generous spirit make her a game dame with style if ever there was one, and that is a final pronouncement.

After Chicago we half-fill Urbana's auditorium, nearly, then empty Hanley's, but stop the show in Richfield—by teaching three master classes.

We're anxious to get back to New York as soon as possible. A TV job is waiting for us there. The return trip is as uneventful as the drive out was and except for three unfortunate distractions along the way, would probably soon be forgotten. The first of these concerns a stray dog; the second, another dog, which for all we know might be the same one; the third, an equally distracting dancer. When I think about them afterwards, all three seem in some strange way to be connected.

The dog, a short-haired, medium-sized mongrel with big bat ears and narrow nose, looks to be what all jackal-type dogs, if left alone from selective breeding, revert to. It has somehow gotten trapped on the median of an expressway, where it's rearing, spinning, and pawing the air. As it darts from edge to edge of the trash-littered island, we glimpse the frantic motions of its mouth, but the closed windows of our station wagon keep us from hearing the awful sounds of its distress.

"Oh no, did you see that?" moans Liz.

"Poor thing," says Bet, her cramped knees momentarily forgotten.

The sight was touching, cut close to the bone in fact. I guess some of us were seeing a little of ourselves in the dancing dog, and seeing the expressway as . . . well, that was our life.

After a few miles, Sharon exclaims, "Oh, golly gee, I've left my purse back at the diner where we had our last rest stop!"

Turning at the next crossroad, Jenny sighs soulfully. "Swell," she says. "This means a half-hour delay at least."

On the way back, we look for the stranded mutt, but it's no longer there.

The diner, like many others where trucks congregate, was once a trolley, or some other sort of vehicle; its outside is now stuccoed, or at least partially stuccoed, the rest being clapboarded. Having had little to eat for at least two hours, we decide to have a second brunch. As we enter, the drum of a coffee maker is reflecting a wavy tableau of familiar fat people. There are those ridiculous offbeat outfits again, the ones that by now I'm almost able to ignore—Dan's ersatz doublet (a deeply felt gesture to his early West Virginia heritage), Bet's made-over overcoat (updated to match the style of several years ago), and the other girls' inventive ideas of the far-out. Except for me in my classic blue-collar clothes, none of us go very well with the present surroundings.

The interior is gleaming with art deco black and chrome, and on the tables are artificial flowers. Someone sneaky has filled their vases with water. On the way to adjoining booths we step carefully over the corpse of a cylindrical dog which looks suspiciously like the one we saw on the highway. As Sharon goes to retrieve her purse, the rest of us contract ourselves into question marks, skitter sideways, and conclude the performance with a canon of resounding plops. Doggie-wog wakes up and comes to sit nearby, swishing its tail back and forth against the tile floor and enlarging a bald spot there on the underside of it.

While waiting for a waitress, it seems as good a time as any to bring up something that I've been putting off. "Listen, I don't like to sound like Emily Post, but when we get invited to after-performance parties—you know, like the one Miss Mertz gave for us in St. Louis—I think maybe we might be a little more—"

Quick to get the drift, and sensing criticism, Dan interrupts. "You mean the one where by the time we got there, the faculty-member guests had already eaten up all the food?"

"Yes, it was *so* awful," Renee adds. "And we weren't ever even introduced to them. We went over in one corner and they just stayed in the other."

"Well, that's what I was getting at," I continue. "Don't you think it might be a good idea for us to try to be better at these things? I mean, let's be more sociable. I mean . . . well, Sharon honey, maybe you shouldn't have gone and gotten that ham out of Miss Mertz's fridge and put it in your dance bag."

"Nerts to Mertz," says Sharon, her Irish on the upswing. "All the restaurants would've been closed, and we had to eat!"

Just then a waitress with a yellow pencil stashed in matching hair doles out little glass barrels. Preparing to take our orders, she funnels her tongue around her twirly pencil, and then, removing the pencil and rotating her lower jaw in a cow-cud way, she stands back to give us an intense once-over. Undecided whether to be amused or affronted, she asks, "You the Beatles?"

Bet, her mind on the sad decisions of balanced meals, replies absently, "Beetles? No, thank you, I'll have a hamburger. Without the roll, please."

"Oh, no, my dear—if you want the burger you have to take the bun." Omnipotently, the waitress takes our other orders: "Yes, you can have the cottage cheese instead of the fries, but it'll cost you extra, and anyway you'll have to take the slaw," and so forth. Somewhere along the line, Liz asks, "What's the soup du jour?" The waitress expands her breasts proudly, as if filling them with worldly wisdom, and replies, "Sweetie pie, that's the soup of the day!"

Then Dan's dancing hands indicate something outside the window. For a while we watch the resurrected mutt. It's now sniffing around an idling truck. Following a scent to the rear wheels, it leans forward, front legs braced, and crams its nose into the tailpipe. Eyes rolling, hind paws pawing in the gravel with delight, it's inhaling blissfully.

"Good grief," Dan says; "Gracious" and "Ahem," say a couple of the others. "Don't worry about a thing," says the waitress, patting the air softly, "Diana's hooked on exhaust fumes and just getting her daily jollies."

That's the second of the homeward trip's distractions. The third is about to come.

She's a little person with enormous magnetism and push—a brash but lovable Munchkin. "You're cute," I sometimes say. "You're friggin' nuts, I'm *big*," she'll reply defensively. She has a smart-aleck way of expressing herself. If you judge by the way her pale face seems about to ignite itself, it has the look of an underfed and slightly sour marshmallow before roasting. And, although it's galling to admit, I suppose that in matters of yet-to-be-popular dance directions, we share a certain kind of unreasoned ambition.

She appeared one day out of her Quaker background to take some classes that I was teaching at the Sixth Avenue studio. She expertly executed all the steps but, I suspected, without a whole lot of belief. Luigi's jazz classes were what Tacet told me she preferred. And then, before I knew it, she'd invited herself into my company.

"It's a deal, but you'll have to wait till summer," I said, leaving her and Geulah Abrahams, another student, to teach classes for me at Adelphi and in New Haven and Boston while I went off to Hoosierland. "While I'm gone, try not to injure the students," I advised. "And, Twyla, how about changing that odd last name of yours to something less percussive? Let's make it Young"—her married name—"instead of Tharp, okay?"

*   *   *

All merry mouth and gamy breath, Diana weaves back to our table at the diner looking more fulfilled, but practically the same dog.

I mention to the dancers that Geulah and Twyla are going to be in our next new piece. A span of stone falls.

Bet is the first to reply. "Geulah's all right, but Twyla? Paul, are you sure?"

"Uh-oh! Uh-oh! Uh-oh!" sings the canonistic chorus.

"Come on, troops. No kidding, Twyla's got lots to offer. Tons of talent, don't you agree?"

Liz whisks her fingertip across the table, slouches, then lets her hand fall heavily to her lap. Straightening up, she exclaims, "Think I'll have a double vanilla cone!"

"I thought you were allergic to ice cream," says Dan.

"I don't care. Right now I need some kind of lift."

Bet's small, humane hand disappears into her large purse. "Liz, try one of these desiccated liver pills. I also have a jar of powdered yeast here somewhere if you'd rather."

"Never mind," says Liz.

Sharon, pressing her temples and imitating the last twitches of a fatally wounded bird, cries, "Dear Tante, some of your aspirin, if you please!"

"Girls, you don't know her yet," I coax. "She's terrific. Trust me. You'll see."

In the gathering gloom we offer some morsels of french fries to the dog. Turning its head away, Diana momentarily studies the leg of the table, then makes a final exit without a backward glance.

Picky dog; picky dancers.

The Studio

In New York, after the ritual lugging of company luggage up the four flights of stairs to the Sixth Avenue studio, comes the ritual inspection of Babe's latest decorative "improvement"—this time a humongous tire that he says is to be painted white, filled with dirt from Central Park, and planted with artificial flowers. The word "flowers" he indicates by daubing imaginary

ones at his nose. "Artificial," or "lie" (its synonym), is communicated by
swiping a derogatory finger across persimmon lips. So as not to disappoint,
I pretend to be enchanted by the tire, though it's spoiling the stark simplicity of my beloved work space. Offensive. Lowbrow. And there have
been other additions. Catching the drift of Babe's taste, Tabby has artfully
shredded the lower edge of several burlap curtains. And in the bathroom,
created with lifelike accuracy, a masterpiece of little padded footprints is
depreciating the toilet seat. However, Tabby's kitty litter box, which usually sits under the sink, is missing; also the rectangularly routed flies that
patrol above it. When asked about the missing box, Babe proudly informs
me that Tabby has become more hygienic, now straddles the bowl, will
perhaps soon learn to pull the chain.

And as if our conflicting tastes weren't enough, a third party—old Tacet,
my obsolescent figure of fun—has lately become critical of both Babe's
notions of decor and my preference for none at all; and ever since Mexico
he's been questioning the studio's ambience. Feels the color scheme looks
accidental. Also that, as a seat of creative ferment, it's just too too banal.
Instead of being so plain, so unimaginative, so blah, one's studio should
match the levels of artistry toward which one is billowing and distending.
(True, we are headed somewhere, but not toward any existing taste.) He's
advising me to renovate every little tittle, right down to the dime-store bell
on Tabby's collar; and how his index finger arabesques as he dismisses our
costume trunk, recommending that it be replaced with a Mies van der Rohe
coffee table! Tesselated ferns in gamboge jardinieres, whatever they are,
are to mask the rusted radiators. "Tut tut, dear boy," he pouts, indicating
the cobwebbed tin ceiling and its bare bulbs, then demands that our brick
walls be plastered over and painted a color that he says should echo the tone
of the warmth that our public is soon to shower upon us.

"You mean the color raspberry?" I ask, then run right down to Nuts and
Bolts, a gay hardware store on the corner of Broadway and Canal Street,
where I pick out a vibrant lime for the trim and a mutated taupe for the tape
machine. Surely these colors were, as Lucrezia Borgia would have said, a
scheme.

But on the way back I grow fonder and fonder of my simple studio where
the bricks are only white, and the tape machine only tape-machine colored,
and when I think of the natural green of my avocado plants I want to prop-
osition them. The studio needs no changes, is already more than a place to
dance in, is brighter than its own whiteness, bigger than its dimensions, more
real than truth or reason. No studio can keep its mental health in conditions
of complete reality. Let other dance studios be demented—ours will stay one
of the sane ones that dream. On entering it, especially when it's empty and

quiet, you can see it for what it is—an illusionary place, a crenellated castle keep of smiles and sunbeams, a dream chamber, and this despite its aroma of perspiration and the sadness of baggy leotards.

Someday, if what Charlie tells me about financial stability comes true, moving to a more luxurious studio would be a mixed blessing. If we vacated the present one, perhaps it would shrink to an even smaller size, or become insane, less joyful. Perhaps subsequent tenants would ruin it with improvements. And I feared that if revisited, it might remind me of time's tricks and dear troupers come and gone. Our antiquated stomping ground, its blotchy skin of bricks and tin, its skeletal, subway-shaken beams, its lamebrain of a boiler in the basement, in fact its whole transitory soul—if it's to crumble and fall into Sixth Avenue, I never want to hear about it. That place is us.

TV

As part of a new series of half-hour-long programs called "Repertoire Workshop," CBS-TV is to tape segments of *Piece Period*, *Aureole*, and *Fibers* and air them from coast to coast. "Better a variety of segments than one long half-hour of the same old piece," says program director Dan Gallagher, and insists that there be at least three commercial breaks in order for viewers to escape to their kitchens.

Although TV seems an effective way to reach a lot of people all at once, my enthusiasm for the venture is not as strong as Charlie's. He appreciates the selling techniques of Madison Avenue and is optimistic about us becoming a household word overnight. After picturing myself among other greats—Babbo, Brillo, Drano, and even Geritol—in the end, I'm not sure I want us to rise quite that far.

Everything has to be adapted for the camera—allowances made for close-ups, spacial limits defined, traveling steps shrunken, camera angles found that might give some illusion of space. To me, trying to give three dimensions to what is basically a flat medium seems pretty hopeless; redoing dances made for the stage would be like trying to force them inside one of the viewers' fridges. We'd do better to start over from scratch.

At a CBS studio on West Fifty-seventh Street everything is looking distant and lifeless on the monitor, and no matter how we adapt, there's always something missing. Not just arms and legs due to misaimed cameras—the dancing has no goo, no kinesthetic response. And as seen on the screen, fast moves are looking too fast; slow ones, too slow. It seems to me that a machine for recording movement accurately has yet to be invented. "Incidentally," says our producer/director, Merrill Brockway, "can you get your girls to smile a little more? And do their jetés in one spot? And please, we should replace a few more of those other crosswise traveling steps—very difficult for the cameramen to catch. We wouldn't want any blank spaces on the screen, would we?" He is a nice man, is helping me to learn about TV, and is doing it in a friendly, gentlemanly way, and the hardest part of the whole job is not being able to tell him off.

Then comes the matter of Rouben's *Fibers* costumes, which program director Gallagher is concerned about. At one of our rehearsals, after presenting the troupe with a box of chocolates, he says he's sorry but the costumes will have to be redesigned. According to him, though not totally offensive, they're somehow giving him the impression of jock straps, or as he says, trusses. People did not like that sort of thing in their living rooms. Our white *Aureole* tights would also be frowned upon, because, he says, they're too revealingly male. In fact, all the costumes would have to be redesigned. I object, but he's firm about it, makes to leave, and then is stopped by Dan, who wants to know if we can still keep the chocolates.

In case the dancers should look too distant, something more is needed to fill up blank spaces. I'm told that each dance is to have its own special set for TV, designed by an in-house designer, but that I shouldn't worry because he is fairly familiar with all kinds of dance, since he's a weight lifter. Due to other commitments, he will probably not be able to actually see our numbers before designing the sets, but I'm not to worry; everything will be very modernistic and adventurous. We're to get the latest in plastic shower curtains for *Piece Period* and a network of grungy ropes for *Fibers*. For *Aureole*, the cement floor ("Sorry about it giving you and your dancers shin splints") is to be painted with stripes that gather into a vanishing point, thereby creating an illusion of unlimited space, supposedly.

Although feeling that our names are about to be associated with plebeian atrocities, Tacet and I stop grumbling, steel ourselves, and respond to fate with a small shrug of our shoulder blades.

The night before the taping—to take place in front of a live studio audience, with no possibility for reshooting—I'm attacked by second thoughts, tossing and turning and longing for a third side on which to sleep. Our exposure—in prime-time—would be misleading, backfire, and Charlie would be unable to get us any future bookings. With luck, maybe the program could be postponed indefinitely, or at least shown at five a.m.

The next day, not having slept, I swim onto a chair in the TV makeup room, get bibbed, and immediately fall asleep. After a groggy, underpar performance, Brockway and Gallagher accompany me to a viewing room, where the three of us watch the unchangeable results. A gentlemanly three-part silence ensues.

Babe's Finger

A couple of days before the taping, Babe, as usual, has been working on the night shift at the Poly Print plastic bag factory in Sunnyside in Queens, sweeping up and tending the machines there. Unable to hear their noise, he always has to be careful not to let the rollers of the machines catch his hands and pull him in. At about three a.m. I get a call from a policeman who is reading from a note which he says is bloodstained and signed by Babe. I am to hurry to Cumberland Hospital. Because of a poor connection, I'm unable to tell if the cop is saying that Babe is crying or dying, and before I can learn exactly where the hospital is, the cop hangs up.

After ripping through a phone book to find the address, I take the wrong subway train, to Brooklyn, then return to Manhattan to start over. Another train takes me to who knows where and I have to start over again. Each moment of delay is an eternity. I'm seeing the Babe on a slab and eulogizing—his importance, his devotion, the uncomplaining way he accepts his deafness and isolation, his simple needs, his monumental chin. He's a pal I've been taking for granted.

By the time I finally reach the hospital, the sky is getting light. A cold spring wind is blowing. Silhouetted tenements are changing into a row of black tombstones in the orange dawn. Halloween is early, and the world is in reverse, with light roofs darkened into shadow and dark trash rolling like beacon skulls along the street.

I rush into a men's ward to find Babe sitting up in bed, laughing and circling his finger at his temple ("nuts"), then pointing to the head nurse, who is a tight-lipped type. The other patients are chortling and nodding their agreement. Babe has already made fast friends with a little boy who has wandered in from the children's ward and is eating from Babe's breakfast tray. Babe's right hand is wound in bloodstained gauze. With the left he tells me that a machine has sliced off his index finger at the second joint from the knuckle, and, although he brought the severed piece to the hospital, the head nurse threw it into a trash can, but an Oriental doctor (here the pinkie slants an eye) rummaged around until finding it and then sewed it back on. Babe seems pretty chipper about everything except a ring that I'd once given him that now is missing.

The nurse gets rid of the kid with some indelicately signed thumb jerks and prepares to give Babe some kind of shot in the rear, then also jerks her thumb for me to go. She has her own rules, regulations, and lofty standards. It's as if four square inches of Babe's unsheeted rear was going to be shockingly indecent. I tell Babe not to worry, that I'll try to track down the ring.

In a few days he is released from the hospital. About a month later he returns for an unveiling and finds that the severed joint has turned jet black and is reeking. It hasn't taken, likely due to contamination from the trash can, and has to be cut off again and a patch of skin from his wrist grafted over the wound.

The shortened index finger is now permanently messing up his once strong and clear signing. Most of the letters come out misshapen, particularly the Fs and Ds, which are nearly unrecognizable, and when he attempts to cross his fingers to make an R, they don't hold and snap apart. As his voice had been muffled, so now is his right hand. Smiling apologetically, he relies on his left.

Hoping for Babe to receive workmen's compensation, I apply for a hearing for him and go along to translate. From a dais under an American flag a black-robed black judge asks what Babe's problem is. When I start to answer, the judge holds up a warning hand and says, "Hold it! What do you think you're doing? Let Wilson speak for himself." I explain about Babe's muteness and am reluctantly allowed to continue. The judge asks one or two questions about the accident, rules that Babe is to receive no compensation, and summarily dismisses the case. Stepping closer to the dais, I try to explain that for a deaf mute, losing a finger is as bad as a hearing person losing the tip of his tongue, but the judge, as if he were the Southern Cross shining down on the just and the unjust, points down at me and exclaims, "Don't tawk! Didn't you ever hear of court procedure? In here you ain't just out on the streets, you know." Then, like the head nurse, he jerks his thumb for us to leave. The gesture was as graceless as it was slurred—expressive enough, but not nearly as fine as Babe's lost handwriting.

About a month later I'm able to get Babe another hearing. This time we bring a lawyer with us, and a different judge awards an amount that just about covers the lawyer's fee. Babe returns to Poly Print. Soon afterwards, he receives a cake in the mail, sent by the mother of his little chum from the children's ward.

Somehow, on reviewing recent events, there seems to be a proliferation of dilemmas building up—Babe's sad loss, the disappointing TV program and midwestern dates, the car game Break the Code, the median-stranded mutt whose frantic barks we couldn't hear, the phone call from the cop who was unclear about whether Babe was crying or dying. Things were beginning to seem similar and connected—parallels that, strangely enough, all had to do with communication gaps.

Scudorama

Gaps and more gaps. And disappointment. When just at the brink of a solution to the question of communication, I'm told by Charlie that some hoped-for dates in Spain and a ten-week tour of South America have both fallen through. And then, while pondering what kind of dance to do next— what to express and how best to express it—I burn the toast. Things seem very serious. The dates, the communication, the toast: they are having to be shelved. Future looking dim. And as if all this isn't enough, when just on the verge of a simple solution to the universe, I get on a wrong bus.

But what would it all mean ten thousand years from now? By then our planet will have been obliterated, so what's the point?

To the dancers my despair is comical; some say it is like a beagle's. Yet when I'm happy it's even more of an enigma. I imagine that I'm being very clever, that everyone loves me, but probably that is not the case at all.

A capacity summer audience in the recently built Philharmonic Hall at Lincoln Center, however, has been amused, and the dancers have now worked long enough to collect unemployment checks—an impressive achievement, us being the first modern dancers that I know of to do so. And there has been an offer to choreograph a Broadway musical, also to do the dances for a new *Aida* at the opening of the Met Opera, and a pilot film to demonstrate a new type of wide screen that Hollywood has been developing, plus a lucrative offer from Margaret Erlanger to teach at the University of Illinois—all of which I've turned down. None of them were proscenium concert work. Modern is what I set out to do and, come whatever, is what I'm sticking with. Don't much care to branch out or gain a multifaceted career. The key to success is the art of saying no. No to incidental dances, no to high-tech gimmicks, no to classroom situations. Best to concentrate and keep priorities straight. Career should not overshadow dancing. It's better to be career free, be anonymous, just do the work. There's something noble in namelessness. Artisans and real gents don't give press conferences or sign their work. In fact, I'm thinking maybe to let Doc, that venerable old fraud, change the company's name to Tacet and His Terpsichorean Troupers. (When people say "in fact," that's the time to doubt them.)

The two new girls, Geulah and Twyla, now make us a company of eight. Wow, we're getting to be a lot. European impresarios have lately said that six dancers aren't enough to fill large opera-house stages. "The two new girls ought to fix things," I've told Charlie.

"But expanding to eight's not exactly the thirty or more they mean," he remarked.

"Don't worry about it," I replied, "it's not numbers that fill a stage, it's how large the dancers perform."

Even so, though we expected to be at the Berlin Opera House in the fall, we have been assigned to one of the Berlin Festival's smaller stages.

In the meantime—August '63—we are working on a new piece commissioned by the American Dance Festival and to be premiered in New London. Given my recent mood, a terrible plurality is calling, another zig of the old zag. The new dance is to be as dark as *Aureole* is sunny; fragmented rather than integrated. I had sought symmetry, now feel equal to finding anarchy. After all, life is pure chaos. The desperate dog on the expressway still haunts me and sends a creative shudder up my spine. Perhaps thinking of Twyla's fevered face also has something to do with it. I say "perhaps" because who knows what dark directives lurk within the nooks and crannies of my convoluted brain. And other images are gathering—distress signals, shrouds and thrashings, a ghastly pile of Grünewald remains, a duet between a corpse and its carrier. Why such morbidity? If I could explain the images to myself, or where they come from, it would be like a sorcerer revealing one trick by inventing another. "What does it all mean?" people may ask. "What were your objectives?" Well, I'm the sort who has only one aim—to get a dance out of my system as quickly as possible. But enough of Taylor trying to read his own mind.

Scudorama is slow to emerge. It took quite some time to invent *Aureole's* vocabulary, and I am now faced with the task of manufacturing a different and more complex one. I have found that self-imposed restrictions—what moves not to use—are a huge help. A restriction this time will be that any dance step ever seen before is taboo.

In Chicago I asked composer Clarence Jackson to write the music. Had heard a score of his for Donald McKayle last summer at Connecticut College, where we had met—at Dean Bloomer's luncheon for visiting artists, I think, or more likely at a backstage beer bash for the alcoholic student stage crew. Anyway, he agreed to write the music but said that it couldn't be ready for at least four months. I needed to start rehearsals before then, so in the interim I'm setting the dance to Stravinsky's *The Rite of Spring*, a record of which has been lying around the studio for years. Will transfer the dance to Jack's score when it arrives. To some folks this may seem a puzzling modus operandi, but it's logical enough to me. Not following music is a major element in my search for musicality. Have yet to be accused of orthodoxy.

After three weeks of rehearsals, totally unfamiliar steps are yet to be found, and the dancers and I have absolutely nothing to show for our efforts. At the end of each rehearsal I discard everything and the next day I start over. The dancers remark about me not seeming to know what I'm doing, so I make an effort to comfort them in hopes of winning their sympathy by presenting myself as a lonely figure trapped on an isle of desolation. Dan and a few of the others reciprocate by giving me a generous, if slightly naive, vote of confidence. And dear Bet, sympathetic gushings not her style, gives me a silent vote—a whole half-bottle of out-of-date vitamin pills.

Twyla, cackling unsympathetically, continues zipping through zany combinations like an energized fleck of flotsam. She arrives at rehearsals wearing granny glasses and floor-length scarves, these being her emblems of bravura. She's playing a style-conscious toughie, but not quite convincingly. Despite the disguise, the kooky cookie's vulnerability and fine sensibilities still show. Why a displaced Quaker would ever want to be different again is beyond me.

Renee, menaced by the recent presence of Twyla, increases the riskiness of her dancing in an effort to consolidate feelings of security that she has gradually gained over the last year. Her hard-won self-assurance now seems to be slipping away. To help build it back, another director might choose an appropriate moment to say something like, "Renee, your beauty drowns me." That might ease her; but me, I ain't got time for games of flattery. Am far too plagued by my latest itch.

Steamed up from radiating bodies and a hellish New York summer, the studio mirrors are framing a group of fuzz-edged Rorschach ink blots. The clarity of a contorted dance is being warped. Even at their best the lying mirrors annoy. Tall, thin Bet is unperturbed, as hers is the only reflection that retains some semblance of a reedy line.

I say, "Bet, let's work out the duet. Just let me tote you around as if you're a corpse." From a kneeling position I tell her to sit toward the back of my head and then wrap one of her legs around under my chin. "Climb on . . . there, that's it." With difficulty I manage to stand, but top-heavily and tipping. "Okay, now try to lean way out to the side. . . . Further. . . . Can't you lean any further? Woops!" She falls. "Oh, gee, I'm sorry! Did that hurt?"

"Yes!"

"Well, I said I was sorry. Try it again. This time I'll support you under your arms. Umph! Everything okay up there? Now if I can stand up again. . . . Okay, now lean way out. . . . Stop! My neck's cramping! Catch her, Dan!"

"What's the matter?" jibes Dan, "that head-sitting trick ought to be easy as falling off a log."

"Hush, you hick," I reply. Wagoner had no rival for the title of Great West Virginia Wag.

"You know, Bet," I say, "the lift will work if you put on a little weight. I mean, your sit bones really hurt the top of my head, so please try to grow some rear, okay?"

Babe pauses on his way to empty the trash, watches as I rub my head and neck, then catches Bet's eye and makes the familiar circlings of finger at temple. Continuing toward the door, he is careful not to step on a roach that is traversing the studio floor, followed by a smaller one—perhaps its child or, more likely, a midget species. Both are headed in the same direction—maybe because their feelers are telling them that other accidents of a more gory and appetizing nature lie ahead.

Midget Twyla gleefully bounds and slashes through space. Her piping voice can be easily heard over *The Rite of Spring*'s din. "One-ee-and-ee! Two-ee-and-ee! . . . " She has become dissatisfied with the counts that I've given her and is counting quadruplets in her own way.

"Paul," says Geulah, "this old towel that we're using for a shroud—I think Tabby's peepeed on it." So that she will never be confused with Twyla, Geulah has come with larger teeth, an unassuming nature, and a happy marriage. "So?" I answer, and getting a puzzled look, say, "You expected dancing to be sanitary? Just keep on thrashing your shroud, honey."

Two more weeks pass while the dance gains a bonanza of atrocious imagery. While portraying lost souls in limbo we're beset by imaginary hurricanes and pseudofloods. Leaning into the wind, our limbs nearly wrenched from their sockets, we partake of true angst and wallow knee deep in real discomfort.

During the long nights between rehearsals I feel porous and pregnable; in the quiet empty spaces before the dancers arrive, an oppressive listlessness comes over me, cold sweats, and spells of dizziness.

Then one day Twyla, leaving rehearsal, stops to inspect the narrow shelves that hold my collection of bibelots gleaned from Martha's tours—dust-collecting keepsakes such as seven stuffed Siamese birds, a Japanese tea stirrer, and a mummified Egyptian asp within a ceramic coffin. "This one— I want it!" Twyla states, patting a human skull that I had accidentally unearthed when cliff-climbing in Israel. To keep myself from falling into the sea, I had grabbed into the earth and a chunk of cliff had come loose to reveal the skull. After taking it back to my hotel and painstakingly removing several layers of dirt with my toothbrush, I was surprised to find that the ancient relic, by absorbing the tone of its surroundings, had turned a beautiful earth-colored pink.

There by the shelves I'm thinking that I definitely shouldn't part with the treasure. It's what Emily Dickinson would have called a "gay ghastly" thing, its gaudiness in contrast to its ghoulishness. It is reminding me of the shrouds that Alex Katz has designed for *Scudorama*. Instead of the usual white linen, he's come up with big Technicolor beach towels which reinforce what might be called the dance's ironic element. *Scud* is supposed to be a dance of death leavened by light touches, a serious-minded relative of *3 Epitaphs*. I mentioned to Alex the idea of having a few tombstones scattered about the stage and even went as far as selecting epitaphs to be inscribed on three of them:

The dust of
George Tacet
Swept up at last by the
Great Housekeeper

Here lies a father of twenty-nine
There would have been more
But he ran out of time

At threescore winter's
End I died,

A cheerless being
Sole and sad.
The nuptial knot
I never tried
And wish my father
Never had.

However, after deciding that those might reveal a little too much of my personal life, I scrapped them.

Station THARP continues to transmit static. An avaricious little voice is saying, "I want it! I said I want it! Gimmie gimmie gimmie!!!"

The skull was a favorite, but I'm fonder of her. "Are you sure you want it, Twerp? Really sure you do?" Then, although a strong hunch tells me that I'll someday regret it, I gently remove the treasure from its shelf. "Okay, it's yours," I say. She crams it into her dance bag unceremoniously, and down the stairs she trots. The round, clean place that is left on the dusty shelf is looking alienated and forlorn.

Later on, I'm dozing on the costume trunk and paddling through several well-formed misgivings, all dance related, when the phone jolts me to full consciousness. Its bubbly spasms are ominous and frightening. I answer, and composer Jack says that he is going to bring over a batch of sheet music for me to see.

"Thanks, but don't bother," I say. "I don't read music."

"Oh yeah, I forgot," he says. "Well then, I'll play it on the piano for you."

"We don't have any piano."

"Oh? . . . well then, I'll whistle it for you."

"Jack, I don't need to hear or see it. The dance is done—that is, rehearsal time's run out—and now all I have to do is synchronize the darn thing to the music. That won't take long, and we can do it at the dress rehearsal. The main thing isn't that *I* read the score but that the musicians be able to read it. To tell the truth, I was thinking that maybe we shouldn't use any music after all, but I don't care for silence. It's too loud. I mean, the last time we had live music the orchestra fell apart in the middle and we had to dance around to the sound of shuffling sheet music."

"Haw haw! That's really funny. I'll be right over."

Who hasn't writhed and rubbed right shin against left calf as the future mockingly leers down on him? As a dazzling Connecticut fog creeps up from the Thames, it is boding more than a touch of evil. The premiere is only an hour away. Distant thunder is rumbling cornily. The dancers and I are clustered outside the stage door to Palmer Auditorium. We haven't remembered the campus ever being so hot and pale and watery. Its buildings—great, looming masses of self-conscious red brick—now look strangely gothic and are barely visible through the churning banks of mist. The grassy green quadrant where I first glimpsed vivid Martha under her vivid parasol has become vague and colorless, and we are trying to ignore a sickly sweet odor that is being discharged from a lot of late-blooming privet hedges.

"Why are we waiting out here?" Sharon asks peevishly.

"And why are we shivering in this heat?" adds Renee.

Other than for finding security in numbers, we are waiting there for Jack's music. It has been sent from New York on a Greyhound bus which has yet to arrive. Alex's set of lavender plywood clouds is supposed to be on the way, too. Charlie, we fervently hope, will come sprinting out of the fog with them in his arms at any moment.

"Hey, that dorm over there—it's floating. I could've sworn it was further away a second ago," Liz says uncomfortably.

"Your eyes are playing tricks," I tell her. "You should get more rest."

"Paul!" moans Bet, "you forget we were up rehearsing till one last night." Her filmy bathrobe is clinging to her bones like old orchid petals. Next she's likely to start on her sinuses.

"Oh, my sinuses, this humidity . . . "

"Bet," I snap, "we're all really tired of your sinuses. Cut it out, will you?"

The heat and the waiting are beginning to get to me. If our stuff would only come in time, I'd go down on my knees to Shiva, god of dance—but not if it got my costume wet. A chilling thought crosses my mind—Shiva is also the god of destruction.

"Okay, you all, let's go in. It's almost curtain time. It looks like we'll have to do the premiere without music and set."

Gaps and more gaps. And premonitions. Down in the basement of Palmer Auditorium the bulbs that border our dressing-room mirrors are flickering in delayed reaction to the electrical storm that rages outside.

Alone in my room, jittery and hunched at the mirror, I'm trying to concentrate on the reflection of my chin. Through an outrageous slight of nature it is cleftless and always requires a line from my grease pencil. This time, instead of leaving a bold slash down the middle, the shaky pencil is leaving a row of timid dots. Something yowls somewhere and, startled, I straighten up. Suddenly there in the mirror hovers no other than the singular George Tacet, but looking even older than usual, wide eyes milky, nose and ear hairs sprouting rankly. It's as if I was seeing him for the first time. From under all his grandiloquent posturing peeps an eminently nervous soul.

After gawking at each other for a moment I ask why he isn't home in Perth Amboy, where he has promised to stay with whoever his latest wife is. He wasn't needed when I was getting into a performance mood. Ignoring my question, he opens his cavernous mouth, flourishes his tawny smile, and mouths the words, "Gird yourself, Sonny—yet another sharp-toothed unkindness is to occur quite, quite soon. One of you shan't dance tonight."

Now he's acting the soothsayer? Unsure of his meaning, I spin around to confront him directly, but he has left. Although he's only imaginary, sometimes his advice has been worth listening to. Even so, but feeling a bit foolish, I pull on a robe and go next door to Dan's dressing room to make sure everything is all right. He's not there, so I hurry upstairs, where I find everyone crowded around a couch in the green room. The place reeks of smelling salts and disaster, and the girls are cooing as a doctor applies a cold compress to Dan's propped-up leg. "I'm sorry, Paul," Dan says sheepishly. "When we were running through *Scud* I tore a muscle in my calf. The doctor says I'll have to stay off it for a while. What'll we do about tonight?"

"Gee, Dan, don't worry about it. I'm sorry, too."

Remorse is flying all over the place—his for causing us a problem, mine for maybe giving him dangerously harebrained steps.

After permission from the doctor, and assurances from me that certain of the dance's crawls and limpings would be improved by his disability, Dan spunkily agrees to try a limited number of them.

At curtain time it is announced that Dan will not be performing in two of the program's three offerings (audience murmurs its regret), but that he will be partially performing in *Scudorama* (a noticeable brightening). It is also announced that due to a last-minute decision, *Scudorama* will be presented in silence. (No mention made of fugitive bus or missing set. What audiences don't know wouldn't hurt them.)

I will dance Dan's part in *Aureole* as well as my own and, in *Scud*, attempt whatever steps he is unable to manage. Since I no longer have the slightest idea of what his *Piece Period* solo is, and there being no time to find out, it seems best to omit it.

The load is a mouthful. By adding his roles to mine I've bitten off much more than anyone should try to chew. Why was I burdening myself with such exhausting duple duty? Well, like they always say, the show must go on. But who was always saying that, and why? Just *why* did the show have to go on? We could have apologized to the audience, refunded their tickets, and delayed the premiere. It isn't so much that the show has to go on, I'm thinking; it's more that I have an obligation. A private matter, Tacetly oriented, so to speak, but not deriving from anything he ever invented. The obligation is the same as mountain climber George H.L. ("Because it is there") Mallory's. Yes, dances are like snow-capped mountains to climb. Yet we never conquer mountains. We may stand triumphantly at their summits for a few moments, or on the center of stages, but then the audience goes home and the wind blows our footprints away. The dances are to be climbed because they are there, and because if they were not climbed, we wouldn't be there, either.

Besides, dancing is necessary, has become a habit, a dangerous addiction; no more so than while under *Scud*'s mountain of Grünewald bodies.

Onstage, since I am the largest and least easily squashed, I have placed myself at the bottom of the heap. The others are flinging their full weight onto me and stacking themselves into a wormlike pile of pain which then rotates, slowly grinding me into near extinction.

A little later, having recovered enough to stand, I trip and hit the boards with a dust-raising thud. Fortunately, I can hear someone out front asking a neighbor, "Do you think he will be able to get up?" and so I must. And so it goes.

Twyla the Slitherer, completely covered with a shroud and elbowing herself across the splintery boards, though being occasionally delayed by a series of snags, is unstoppable. She does not like being so far upstage, but I have choreographed her there for her own good: it would give the cute little thing an awareness of the humble, selfless position required from new troupers. She is looking forward to the part of the dance when she will be allowed to donut herself around Dan's face. It will get her off the floor and for a short time make her more noticeably present.

Scud's images of death, futility, and panic take on new meanings to us, everything all too real. Agony, exhaustion, blazing lights, the hellish heat. Getting no lift from nonexistent music, we have to make do with our own sounds—thuds, groans, pants, booming pulses. The audience is increasing our misery by adding sounds of its own. As I unwind Bet from the viselike grip that she has on my head, we hear the hesitant beginning of a laugh, which is then picked up by others out front, echoed nervously, and followed by a scattering of preposterous little explosions. Tragedy has been weighed against comedy, comedy winning out.

Evidently, the dance is not as mordantly ironic as I intended, is only enigmatic; and, instead of treating viewers to scenes of jolly mayhem, I have placed them in the awkward position of being unsure of their own responses. Am thinking that, although off on a wrong track, the viewers are not complete idiots. No one can be expected to stand ambiguity for long; for some it is better to make a wrong choice than have no viewpoint at all. But in future performances, when the music's around to lend its steadying hand, maybe the dance's intended emotional tone will become clearer.

Further along in *Scud*, in place of Alex's plywood clouds, I'm seeing stars, and am by now too tired to be able to remember the final steps of a solo. I make for the wings, but Twyla prevents me from exiting. She is crawling in place and blocking the way. "Get back, get back, you haven't finished!" she hisses. She is upset, and tears of disappointment are streaming down her cheeks. My Twerp has fervently wanted the premiere to go well. I get back.

After the dance is over, the audience—mostly the festival's dance students and teachers—for the most part are very nice about it. Some of them tell me that they themselves have taken part in similar kinds of performances, or at least they have in their worst nightmares. They can relate; they can sympathize; they wish us better luck next time. So it seems that some sort of communication exists after all. Although the irony of *Scud* is yet to see the light of day, at least the disappointing realities of its handicapped presentation have communicated well.

Exactly and precisely ten years after the premiere, by an eerie coincidence that reminds us of spooky premonitions and shifting dormitories in the fog, a dusty package is delivered to Charlie in New London. He is now directing the American Dance Festival. The town's bus terminal is being rebuilt, and some member of a demolition crew has found the package in a cobwebbed corner, then conscientiously posted it. Charlie comes backstage and hands me the package. "Here you go, sport. It's the *Scud* score. Better late than never."

Pony

The '63 season of the American Dance Festival having ended with our performance of *Scud*, Tommy directs the student crew to dismantle the stage, store away lights and other equipment, then lug several cases of beer onstage for the students' annual closing-night party. Someone's collection of rock records begins vibrating the loudspeakers, and the stage is soon filled with young people celebrating their latest natural elements: the twist, the frug, the monkey, the pony.

Alone at the back of the stage, mostly masked by the other students and

oblivious to them, weaving through the music's pulse and inserting super-
sonic squats and unexpected levitations into the stratosphere, an energetic,
bandy-legged person of about twenty is deep into his highly individualized
version of the pony. His torso is too long, the limbs not long enough; his
shape in general, wiry and whimsical. His pants are those of a clown—low
in the crotch and high at the ankles. Abundant dark curls are whirling, an
intensely furrowed brow is flinging out a pinwheel of bright beads, and a
moisturized shirt is sticking to what an older generation would have called
a washboard stomach. Seemingly, he is on the verge of spinning off into the
future, or maybe transforming himself into antimatter. Liberties are being
taken, a defection to another country being made. The pony, having been
mutated into something that bears little resemblance to its origins, now
features odd, futuristic steps that have no particular tie-in to anything ever
before seen anywhere.

Where was he when I needed him during my search for *Scud*'s vocabulary? As an addition to my growing collection of troupers he would do just
fine, and so on the spot I decide to ask him to join up. While searching for
a piece of paper, a matchbook cover, a fortune cookie–sized slip, whatever
might be used to write the studio's phone number on, a familiar feeling of
something already seen takes me back to archives where other documents
are filed—the note on a matchbook cover that I'd given to Babe at the West
Side beer joint, the fortune-cookie phone number from Martha on this very
campus.

"Hey, Pony, or whatever your name is, stop whatever that is you're doing
and come here for a minute."

Becalmed, he has the look of a startled buck with wary head upright and
alerted ears funneled forward. His eyebrows, though raised, remain horizontal, are not at all the desperate diagonals of frightened game. The quiz-
zical face is tilting to one side, as if glimpsing evil and finding it laughable.

"You like to move, don't you?" I ask.

"Yeah, sure."

"Where you from?"

"California. But I've just moved to New York."

"That's nice. I may be able to use you. What would you say to joining my
company? I'm not asking, mind you, just want to know what you'd say if I
did."

"I'd say great!"

"Right. You'd be nuts not to. Well, I'll think about it," I say, handing him
the studio number. "By the way, what's your name?"

"Grossman. Daniel Grossman."

The "Daniel" part sounded suitable—like in the lion's den—but the

"Grossman," it's sort of ungraceful. "Haven't you got some other? What's your mother's maiden name?"

"Williams."

"That would be better. You'll be Daniel Williams, *if* I take you, and you might have to answer to Danny so as not to get mixed up with Dan, okay? But me, I'll call you Pony."

As if vaguely sensing an oncoming identity crisis, he looks puzzled, but then nods compliantly, as if having been told some antiquated joke.

"So long, Pony," I tell him. "Call when you're in the city."

Katy and the Gorilla

In August, after *Scud's* premiere and after dancing somewhere on Long Island, I think, but just before going to Berlin for sure, the company is to be at the outdoor Delacorte Theater in Central Park at a dance festival sponsored by Rebekah Harkness. (Her fortune and philanthropic inclinations were inherited from her father, who was a partner of John D. Rockefeller, Sr.)

The troupe and I are looking forward to sharing the stage with Katherine Litz—we shared a program when *Aureole* was first performed. Katy's great. In an effort to unify our Central Park program, but mainly because of wanting to dance together, she and I decide to co-choreograph a duet. At the first rehearsal she brings to my studio a phonograph record of a lengthy concertino by Leopold Mozart that is big on bird calls, asks if I think it will go with some old pink wings that she has been saving in her closet for just ages, and suggests that the title of the dance be *Poetry in Motion*. All this is okay by me. Catching the spirit of the thing, I say that I would like to wear a gorilla getup, then take my bows as a bear, and that is okay by her.

Katy works on an opening section while I make several visits to the Bronx Zoo to research gorilla and bear movements. When I return she shows me what she has made for herself. It's composed mainly of masterful oops-and-whoops-type catch steps which give the impression of wonderfully vague searchings and daffy aimlessness. Her hands and wrists are adding filigrees of girlishness, and there is a delicious dose of wanton spinster here and there. Though the solo might be a little bewildering to insensitive types, to most people it should seem inevitably right, even the most natural of activities. She is always totally universal in her communication of doubt, trepidation, and wonderment.

Due to my absence and her ability to compose quickly, her solo opening section has taken up more than half of the music. "Now, Paul," she says with kindly concern, "don't you think you should make some kind of entrance soon?"

I explain that the apes have been dormant, the bears hibernating unseasonably, and that the Bronx visits have been for nothing. "Oh well, when gorillas move it is probably this way," she says, then composes herself into a frowning lump on the floor, the back of her neck weighed down by the world. "Evidently, Bronx gorillas are not terribly active, but we may assume that they are very intelligent, and before moving they give it a lot of thought." Seeing her point, I sit down beside her and imitate. Thinking about moving is not easy. The remaining music is eventually filled with more of her butterfly flits and flutters. Me, I mostly remain rooted in place, my gorilla brain heavy with action.

Although the duet occasionally hints of a certain sensual relationship, it is far from being psychological or Freudian. Naturally, sex is not something that we disapprove of, but, unlike most others in the New York vanguard at this time, we think Freud to be old hat and that dance need not be serious to be serious; that is, we believe antic behavior and foolishness can be meaningful and worth championing.

The Delacorte's 2,267 free seats are all filled. New York's finest are patrolling a barricade at the front entrance and holding back a rowdy crowd larger than the one that's gotten in. (Have I ever mentioned that I can't *bear* being looked at?) Twilight is falling. Dogs are crying, hundreds of babies howling; with any luck at all our program will chase the noisy things away.

The rented gorilla costume is unhygienic, old enough to be Mycenaean, and reeking with ancient history and sweaty routines. After making sure that no coat hanger has been left inside—one learns the tricks of the trade from past experience—I put it on and go to hide below the back of the open stage to wait for my entrance. Since I will be coming from the direction of the Central Park Zoo, and since the rented costume has cost a fortune, it is expected that folks will assume that a real gorilla is on the loose. To get into the correct mood I've been thinking ponderous thoughts and contemplating my stomach of black foam rubber. One of the dogs from out front has sneaked back and is also contemplating and sniffing at it suspiciously.

Katy, onstage, eyes basking in blue lunacy, is wobbling around on high heels and adroitly fumbling with a purse, both of which have been added to her ensemble at the last minute. On cue I toddle out, then pick at the hem of her chiffon dress, either missing it completely or revealing too much, become infatuated with her wings, and so forth. Shrill whistles from the audience—sounds that usually make my back crawl—in this case are more or less appropriate to the theme of our bucolic love song. The bow in the bear suit goes over well, even though some lucky stiff, I forget who, gets to wear it, there being not enough time for me to change. Even so, I feel that the performance has been the most pleasurable one of my whole life, the most rewarding, the most fulfilling and sensually meaningful.

Letter to a Young Dancer

Strangely enough, considering *Scudorama*'s unfortunate premiere, during the months that follow a few students send me their resumés and ask about auditioning. One even includes some theories on dance as an art form and requests career advice. I never get around to answering her, but if I were to do so today, the answer might go something like this:

Dear Miss Girth [or Worth—the handwriting is a bit unclear],
    Thank you for your letter. As to my advice, perhaps the best I can give is to say *Beware*.
    You probably already know that a dancer's life means more than curtains and luggage lids going up and down; means more than stretched sinews, technical tricks, and musical feet; even means more than a riveting stage personality. So let's move on to the cautionary matters— have you thoroughly thought about what a career might mean in prac-' tical terms? But maybe rumination is something that shouldn't be recommended. It can lead young dancers to heartbreak. For instance, take my dog, Deedee (stands for damn dog), a fine example of good sense. She doesn't dwell on Mental Matters, she simply and humbly goes about her daily routine and, seemingly happy to live each moment to its fullest, is unworried by her dim past or uncertain future. When I'm getting ready to leave her, the five or six long hairs that are her eyebrows tilt worriedly. I depart, she endures a moment of misery, then pulls herself together. When I return there is no growly recrim-

ination or bitey revenge, just a circling flurry of delight accidentally whacking her tail against the walls. She has seen the futility of mental misery; she grasps an important aspect of time.

Most dancers I know, especially the talented and successful ones, seem to possess Deedee's knack for living moment to moment. You see, their idea of time is related to those infinitely short moments when they are onstage being their superselves. What dance audience wants to watch an ordinary person? Audiences expect, maybe deserve, a blow-up of reality—a god or goddess, a veritable miracle in the shape of a human being, which is what a good dancer is. [Not quite true, but let it go. Dancers are basically undefinable.] Anyway, these godpersons have the ability to play tricks with time, to stretch or compress it, to stop time altogether as they pause in mid-flight and imprint themselves on a viewer's memory. But both a dancer's stage minutes and his career days are numbered, and dancers have to accept this chilling fact. They can expect maybe ten years of peak performances. Sadly, just as their talent and experience begin to mature, their technique and their poor temporal bodies have already slid over the hump. "Oh well," they may tell themselves, "a one-legged backbend into a five-meter split leap without preparation isn't everything." They then persevere into the next day and into other areas of excellence. The whole thing is noble, or at least touching.

Dancers, good ones, know how to make the most of their short shining times. When they are onstage there is no waste, no moment of halfheartedness. Each millisecond is danced with commitment and largesse. Even in these dancers' stillnesses or controlled throwaway steps there is a giant generosity and inner energy. And these qualities are maintained at every performance, whether on a mammoth stage during a scary critic-packed premiere or on a disenchanting Des Moines postage stamp.

And a dancer's ego, his misnamed "temperament," is ever at the service of a more impersonal vision. Has there ever been a truly temperamental dancer of merit? It is usually the unproved ones we have to watch out for. Dance artists are, first and last, workers. Their ambitions, their needs for recognition or luxurious living (more often, just plain living), play second fiddle to the greater need to be an artist, a servant of Pan. Whole lives go by spent polishing that jerk's pipes, and all for the few seconds that the public glimpses.

How do they do it? Partly, I think, by learning to live by the moment. The discouragements are too great, the rewards too slim, to survive in any other way. Today they're the hottest ticket in town, tomorrow, completely ignored, then hot again a couple of years later. An injury may knock them into a hurtful and expensive therapy, yet they persist. Only Pan's whip of discipline and the dancer's race against the clock count. This kind of thing is conducive to humility—there is no time for temperament.

To sum up, dear dancer to be, let's leave theoretical matters to the philosophy majors, sharpen our senses of time, and dance in the present. In other words, let's listen to Merce, who puts things into proper perspective when he recommends to his dancers that they "just do it," and take our cue from Deedee, who adds her wise two cents' worth by scratching an ear with a back paw and shaking her head, thereby ridding herself of Rumination. If dance you must—above all, beware! Stop theorizing, look before you leap, listen to reason, and take your cue from Deedee.

Wishing you all the best,
Paul T.

Berlin

Dancers, beware. Beware of impracticalities, and beware of places that start with B. Back in October '63, I should have taken my own advice.

Charlie with us in Bloomington, Indiana—"Okay, okay already! Stop worrying about our future. The tours will get better. Just stay here and don't go 'way. Be right back with your milk and chicken soup."

And then Charlie in Berlin—"We'd better get you to a doctor, right? Right? Paul, please listen to me. Come on, no stuff, you've got to go to one. *Got* to . . . okay? . . . Okay?"

And then more bouncy travel days, bumpy butterfly nights. Berkeley, Los Angeles, Seattle, Bloomington—station wagons, poorly equipped university stages, so-called master classes, eight-dollar-a-night colonial motor courts—all these immediately following the engagement in Berlin, and booked by Charlie as a sort of domestic afterthought, an epitaph to Berlin. Our just deserts.

Berlin, Berkeley, Bloomingdale, bumps. Ordinarily, I'm not a superstitious person, yet I can't help noticing an accumulation of Bs, whole hives of places that start with B. Bethesda had meant scarlet fever—the reason for leaving my adopted family of beloved Buttses; Bar Harbor and Boston: a strawberry blonde and a blighted romance. Bellas Artes, Bangkok . . . I make connections, I think twice, my mind becomes mnemonic. Although as yet I've experienced no particular misfortune in the badlands of Brooklyn, I've always felt uneasy whenever anyone mentions the place. To dance there could mean being blasted to bits.

But if you dance, you tour, and take the bitter with the sweet, or, as is sometimes the case, the bitter with the bitter. If this sounds negative, it may be because of the ulcers. It's in Berlin that they start bleeding.

Our invitation to dance at the Berlin Festival came from its director, Wolfgang Stresemann. It seems doubtful that our three-thousand-dollar fee will cover expenses, but Charlie, always the optimist, assures me that at least the air tickets are guaranteed. Besides us, Charlie is now booking other groups, the Alba-Reyes Spanish dancers for one, and I suspect that the additional work is diffusing his energy and concentration on us, although there is little evidence of this, only the distribution of an eight-year-old press release which states that I'm presently dancing with the Graham company—annoying, but not a serious oversight. It's the other things that really rankle. Sharon has become engaged and is likely to be leaving the troupe. Also Renee. It isn't hard to visualize both girls soon trudging along side by side, preceded by swollen bellies. Marriage and pregnancy; to me they are the sublimation of a death wish.

On the way to Berlin a Lufthansa pilot is commanding us to listen while he informs us of our altitude, and telling us to observe the stewardess while she demonstrates the "opferation" of the life jackets. "Und do *exactly* as you are told," jokes Gestapo Liz. A stewardess would be coming around soon to deliver the other hoary line, "Coffee, tea, or me?" Bet and Jenny would then ask for double martinis. Dutch Treat's purse is bulging into the aisle and weighing heavily on her feet. Besides a massive assortment of dietary life preservers, it contains an electric transformer that she's volunteered to carry aboard so as to lower company costs on overweight.

Jenny is pretending to smile as Bet relives for the umpteenth time a misadventure at the Bellas Artes when just as the curtain was going up, after carefully rehearsing a group of dressers to help with extraspeedy quick changes, it was learned that a different and unrehearsed group was to help during the performance. Warming to her subject, cackling, shooting out her hand in a sharp karate chop, Bet gets to the part where one of the unrehearsed dressers then chased after her from wing to wing, arms outstretched and holding the wrong costume. The dresser finally gave up but, not to be put off, had forced irritated Sharon into the "allergitimate" costume. (Bet's portmanteaus are often better than her stories, sometimes even bulkier than her purse.)

Predictably, Dan leans over the aisle to add the part about how at the next night's performance, a rumor having spread that a striptease would be occurring in the wings, the stagehands had gathered round to watch.

Bet, not to be topped by Dan, now quickly adds the clincher—how Tommy had denied having anything to do with the rumor, but anyway had seized the opportunity to collect five-peso ogle fees.

An unexplained mixup lands us outside Cologne instead of Berlin, but Charlie rents a car and takes us for a sunny scenic drive, eliminating the landscape as quickly as possible. We get to someplace that only he knows the name of, and there we catch a bus.

In Berlin, on the way to the Kempinski Hotel, the bus takes us past the Kaiser-Wilhelm Memorial Church, a dark, sooty mass of stonework with decapitated steeple. Streets are teeming with dome-hatted hausfrau shoppers, their headware like hardware from the same mold, like felt helmets, like the deactivated pineapple that my brother Tom brought back from World War II. A rush of concern: Would *Scud* be misinterpreted by our German audience as a blameful reminder of former guilts and unforgotten days? How would Germans react to the dance's wormy pile of Grünewald remains? After all, as Americans, were we ourselves entirely blameless? Hadn't we been much too slow to accept what was being done to European Jews?

Passing other throngs brings more troubled thoughts, ones to draw back from. I don't feel up to absorbing and digesting any at present. Stomach is burning.

In the hotel we pass through a long, dark hall of antique mirrors to find the tubs in our rooms equally antique. While the dancers soak away travel cramps, Charlie drags me to a press interview, then to our theater, the Kunstakademie, where we sit in on the festival orchestra's rehearsal and meet festival director Stresemann, whose father had been chancellor and foreign minister in Germany before Hitler. We thank him for the opportunity to dance in Berlin, to which he replies graciously, then tells us that he is a baseball fan and that Koufax has just led the Dodgers to a two-to-one victory in the World Series. I don't know what the heck he's talking about, but Charlie does and so is able to make the appropriate responses of joy.

By evening I'm more than grateful to get back to the hotel. Things inside both me and my room aren't as they should be. Bleary furniture is shifting from wall to wall and my stomach is eating itself up.

Lately there's been a rosy tint to my saliva—only trench mouth, I've decided. This I can live with; it's the other things that bother more—the sandpaper-skinned maniac who churns around inside me with the wild, uncontrolled anticipation of a five-year-old on Christmas Eve; the back-aches and bloating stomachs; the temptations at rehearsals to give in to the discomfort by marking or lying down; worst of all, the heavy black blanket of negativeness that's been enveloping my mind. There are even times when I long for a final curtain's thump to close the scene. That's when I boost the angst up to a climax so that it can do nothing but recede.

Think pink, old Doc, think pink.

I'll design a grand finale costume to be buried in, an expensive one. Should start a layaway plan. But my novocaine fantasy isn't working very well this time, pain still not receding. Am switching to plan B (yet another B), the pinker one where I picture what it would be like to trade trouping for the career of a movie star. While checking out the day's shooting in my private viewing room, I'm pleased to see that director Tacet has achieved a lovely cinematic effect by having the camera zoom down from my private plane, then follow me in my limo across hill and dale, pan as I tunnel through dark hotel halls, dolly in for a wide-angle view of my expensively capped teeth, continuing on through them in a downwards direction for a sharply focused closeup of—*Gott in Himmel*, we're back to the ulcer again! Double speed, I run the film backwards and start over.

This time I'm on location at the Central Park Zoo. Many different types of creatures are leaping and whirling authentically around me, tossing off tufts of fur and bits of feathers. Three monkeys are being funky, two turtles being fertile; a deer, queer. (Someone has written lyrics and set the whole thing to music.) While I watch, the face of a bear is gently dissolving into my own. It's the most handsome and virile of bears. My shoulders are becoming magnificently compact, gaining a pleasing pugilistic slope, and my dismally androgynous thumbs are no longer thin necked and artistic. This time the fantasy is working. The bars on my cage have faded away, and with them the pain.

On the day of our Berlin opening I give in and let Charlie take me for a medical examination. Herr Doktor seems acutely bent, not so much be-cause of his spine, although it might have been less of a tilted-back Z, but because of the creepy motion of his hand as it skulks forward to be shaken, and the detached, compassionless, almost drugged blandness of his eyes there behind his thick glasses—glasses that, judging by their bandaged frames, have been treated to a lot of haphazard surgery. And there's a chilling aspect to the two black tubes of the stethoscope that snakes from his ears. The overall impression is of iced quack.

After poking at my stomach and listening to it through his dark device, he unplugs himself, then lets his neck be hugged by the two snakes while stroking them affectionately. What skill and scientific know-how have gone into their invention, he seems to be thinking, what wonderful technology! "Das is strange. I did not hear nudding," he says.

"How about if I take off my jacket and sweater?" I helpfully reply.

"Vat jacket undt sweater? You vearing jacket undt sweater? To remove dem, blease. Vee start ober."

The examination moves forward in a backwards sort of way. After misplacing his stethoscope but then finding it around his neck right where he left it, Herr Doktor moves on to administer a test involving barium, which, according to him, tastes just as good as edelweiss and makes you feel twice as high. He then pronounces me seriously ulcerated. Evil satisfaction and joy light up his face. He is not inhuman after all. He recommends an operation followed by at least three months of bed rest and a diet restricted to soft foods such as oatmeal and lager beer. Handing me an infuriatingly high bill, he warns me to watch out for lettuce because of its sharp edges. Just then my credibility for the whole medical profession snaps. It would have been easier to believe in the sharp edges of Kate Smith.

"But I must dance," I explain. "Tonight at the Kunstakademie, and then in California and—"

"Nein, mein poy, first vee must opverate undt denn der dietink undt der bed goink."

The thought of this guy going at me with a scalpel causes me to grab at my stomach and twist across the room to a sink, where I lose the barium.

In the waiting room, where I've left him, Charlie wants to know Herr Doktor's verdict. I tell him that there's nothing worth worrying about. We take a taxi to the theater and on my insistence stop off at a liquor store to pick up a half-pint of gin. It's probably not the best thing for ulcers, but perhaps it will get me through that night's performance. After downing some of it, I go onstage to see how Tommy is doing.

When with the Limón company in the Orient recently, Tommy has picked up amoebic dysentery. I find him on his back in the middle of the stage, waving directions to the crew with one hand, holding his hot forehead with the other, and clamping a thermometer between his teeth. The dancers and Charlie, who have been buzzing to themselves in a corner, rush over to tell me that they've been trying to work out some kind of program that can be done without me, and Charlie says that, although he's never stage-managed before, he will be running the show for Tom.

There is no way for the dancers to perform without me, and cancellation would mean a big financial loss, so I tell them to rehearse the scheduled program without me, that I'll be resting in my room, and for them to come get me at curtain time. Charlie takes Tommy back to our hotel and arranges for him to be hospitalized in Stockholm until well enough to rejoin the Limón company in Russia.

Onstage, while I'm doing a weak rendition of *Aureole, Piece Period*, and *Scudorama*, the lights are blinking off and the boards are angling in unusual directions, forming themselves into crisscrossed nonpatterns. The proscenium is lopsided, and the direction of the audience keeps shifting around. There are no right angles to be found anywhere. Worse, there seems to be no stage center, a loss that always addles me. It's as if I'm a magnet caught halfway between the North and South Poles.

As it turns out, all these architectural curiosities are in fact true: there are no right angles, no stage center, and so forth. The theater was designed to be ultramodernistic. Even the unexpected blackouts were real. Charlie, while shuffling through the sheets of Tommy's light plot, kept dropping, then retrieving them in the wrong order. To muddle things further, he had to work through a translator, so that by the time the cues were relayed to the crew, his directions were either completely misunderstood or executed too late.

Performance over, I'm slumping on something or someone in the wings, waiting there until enough energy returns for me to be able to change into street clothes, when up steps a small elderly woman. It's difficult to make out her features in the dim light. From her comes an aura of such authority and warm seriousness that it leaves me no choice but to immediately straighten up. She excuses herself for coming unexpectedly, says that she has enjoyed the performance, mentions several favorable things about my dances, and turns to go. "Please, ma'am," I say, "won't you tell me your name?"

"Oh," she says—"Oh," as if the name was unimportant—"I am Wigman, Mary Wigman." And then, before I can round up the gang to introduce them to the founder of German modern dance, she's gone.

No one else came backstage, and it was just as well. After Mary Wigman's compliments, no more were needed, nor would they be for a long time.

In less than twenty minutes, however, after changing into street clothes— the usual drop from dizzy peaks to drabness—I'm longing for someone else to show up. Anyone.

And then the tapping of champagne glasses telegraphs the arrival of dance enthusiast Nathan Clark of the shoe family. He sometimes surprises us and other of his favorite companies by showing up in New London, but also in Paris and even less likely places. His presence always satisfies our appetites for being appreciated, and his champagne also fills certain voids. "Gee, Paul," he says, "you looked great tonight."

Kennedy's Death

After sensational Berlin comes a sensational series of traffic violations when we return to our station-wagon game and a tour of western and midwestern motor courts, and after that some illegal subway rides in New York. (To save time when finding myself on a train that is going in the wrong direction, I sometimes hop off the platform, cross the tracks, and hoist up onto the right side.)

The sixties being rich in all kinds of antiestablishment attitudes and practices, the counterculture is rejecting such anachronisms as the legit theater. Broadway drama and musicals find their audiences dwindling and are attended mainly by the older generation. Not counting Martha's company, it has been about twelve years since any modern dance has been seen on Broadway. Most modern dancers prefer to dance at downtown places or ratty off-off-Broadway lofts, where they can remain untainted by establishment connections.

Being conservatively radical, or radically conservative, or maybe concertedly radial, my attitudes do not fit in with those of either the older generation or my avant-garde contemporaries, and so, ready and willing to cross the tracks from off Broadway to on, when producers Dick Barr and Clinton Wilder offer to present my gang at the Little Theater on Broadway and Forty-fourth I gladly accept. (Naturally, avant-garde friends are quick to disapprove, and when I run into a few of them later at a Judson Church concert they are to hurl accusations of flagrant funny business and scowlingly turn their backs. Was that nice?)

Perhaps because he's proved that it is possible to present such groups as us on Broadway without spending a fortune, Dick is soon to be elected president of the League of New York Theaters and Producers. He has kept our budget low by obtaining permission from the musicians' union to allow us taped music. At his suggestion, Tommy has been able to come up with an economical yet more than adequate light plot. In order to avoid stage-crew overtime, we do our dress and tech rehearsals simultaneously, taking a minimum two hours for them on the afternoon of the opening—an arrangement that the company is to continue in the future. No special floor covering is built or rented, Tommy being careful to warn the dancers not to get their feet caught in the metal track of the Little Theater's stage, which has been left there by a former TV production.

Thinking of all the economic limitations, I check my feelings, and the feelings are awful. Small stage, no live music, no sets, very little advertising. Yet we will be making the dances available to a general public. And the costs to produce us are infinitesimal compared with recent multimillion Ford Foundation grants, given only to classical ballet companies, an amount that is producing results in ways similar to what ours will be.

Party Mix—score by Alexei Haieff—is the new piece. It's an antic dance with no message to speak of, its intended humor meant to stem from unexpected juxtapositions of angular shapes and movement; an imaginary party, the social swim and sink of an unlikely hostess (Bet) and her unlikely guests; sort of an abstraction of a satire—an orgy of my imagination which no consideration of real people in the real world can stop.

At one of the rehearsals, as Sharon is perching precariously on Danny's rear, Charlie drags into the studio. He's just come from Dick's office, where they have been working out business details and signing our Little Theater contract. From his walk the dancers and I can tell that he is feeling low. We stop rehearsing and gather around. He's looking as if the world has just had the rug yanked from under it, is as close to tears as we've ever seen. His lips move once or twice, but nothing comes out. Finally he manages to say, "President Kennedy . . . dead. He's been shot."

We're stunned. Desperate glances are bouncing back and forth. Twyla inches over to a wall where she leans her head heavily. Liz starts to leave, turns back, and holds her hands out as if offering us a ten-ton watermelon. As Bet touches my arm I feel a swaying sensation, like being on a subway train without straps to hang on to, or one from which the motor has fallen.

Babe, sensing bad news, comes over from my shelves of tour mementos where he's been relocating dust to ask what's happened. I trace the shape of horns growing out from my temple—the sign for "president"—and not knowing the sign for "assassinated," have to spell it. After several false starts my fumbling fingers are unable to form even a rough spelling. The Babe's eyes are smiling at my ineptness, but when he guesses what I'm trying to communicate they immediately well up. Not wanting anyone to hear him blubber, he's able to hold off until retreating to the bathroom, where he inadvertently attracts attention by slamming the door.

Feeling that someone should do something, I suggest that we have a few moments of silence in the President's honor.

Then the music is rewound to start over, the dancers take their positions, and the rehearsal resumes. The outlines of our imaginary world begin to shift back into place, but the real world's would never be quite the same.

Babe's Pets

Babe is still refusing to be the quiet victim of my imagination, and what I've tried to envision as a stone colossus to lean on is turning out to be just another noisy person. Furthermore, he sometimes leans on me. Though not what I had in mind, our symbiosis is more durable than my house-of-cards company. Dancers keep coming and going, but Babe's bulldog face and craggy chin remain. Unlike the dancers, we've learned a fairly consistent balancing act.

And like the dancers, Babe's pets also enter and exit. Death hovers close, then drops down unexpectedly. Guppies overeat, bloat, and float to the surface stomach-first; gerbils get sat on. Tabby's being folded up in a Castro Convertible was indeed a tragic way to go. After proper mourning periods Babe has developed a new affinity for pugs, a breed that in a way resembles him. Pugs are squat, velvety-haired dogs with curly tails which they curl tighter instead of wagging. They squeal and snort and might be compared to porkers with bronchitis, except for having no snouts. One of the differences between Babe and a pug is that a pug is much quieter.

It will make him happy, so I decide to buy him one. When I bring it home from a disease-ridden pet shop on Fourteenth Street, just as we open its carrier, the darn mutt flops out and dies. It was defective, a lemon. Babe cries and cries while I search for a towel to wrap the corpse in, intending to return it to the shop for a refund. But then Babe reminds me that it's past five, that it will be Labor Day weekend, and that the shop won't be open for three days. My fridge is all full of dance notes, so I bundle up the corpse and take it to Babe's place nearby to store in his. What I don't know is that he's loaned his place out for the weekend. But, though his guests use the fridge, they don't bother to look inside the towel, so everything works out okay and I get my money back.

So then I get him another pug from somewhere else, and he names it Kim. He calls it that because he thinks it's a word he can say. "Glimb!" he says, or "Glimb, Ai lub oob!" (which means "Kim, I love you!") He says this over and over, very loudly, and Kim squeals and curls her tail tighter and tighter. I don't try to get him to say it right because Kim would only become confused. I once tried saying "Kim" to her, and she let her tail droop down like a sad sausage.

Anyway, just as we might have known, Kim soon falls down a flight of steps—the breed is known for faulty hips—and breaks her back, and when Babe rushes to her aid, she gives the scar where his finger once was a nasty bite. The whole thing is macabre, and for a long time I try not to think about it.

Nevertheless, Kim survives, although her rear legs have been paralyzed, and when Babe equips her with a pair of wheels, she's almost as good as new. Being the proud owner of a wheeled dog is a mark of distinction, and he loves Kim even more than before, and shows her off by rolling her around the neighborhood and by allowing her to zip among the dancers at rehearsals, sometimes tripping them. They don't care for her or her sappy smiles of delight, and since she never learns to go around the corners of the studio without getting hung up, everybody suspects that her brain doesn't work too well.

And then one day the Babe decides that what Kim needs is a pup to play mama to. We have to go all the way to Brooklyn to find the kind he craves—a Boston bull terrier. This one is also flawed, is the runt of the litter, with one eye bigger than the other and slightly in the wrong place; but it's the only Boston bull available, so we bring it back. He names it Elmer or "Albagh" and is ecstatic. But Elmer turns out to be uncongenial to Kim. After discovering that she has no feeling in her hindquarters, he assumes that it will be permissible to eat them. Babe walks in on the two pets and finds Kim, her tongue lolling as usual, panting merrily and being consumed from the rear.

A quick separation is necessary, and so Elmer has to grow up alone in a small, dark storeroom, where he develops an unpredictable tendency to either cower in the corner or viciously attack everybody. Around the time he reaches puberty he's become totally insane, but Babe doesn't mind and of course continues to adore him as always.

Kim eventually grows bored with her wheels and prefers to drag herself around like a seal—an activity that rubs her stomach bald. Surprisingly, unlike Babe's other pets, she reaches a matronly age before passing away uneventfully, after which there is the usual period of deep mourning. Though Babe's grief is magnificent, it seems a bit much. I'm unable to talk him out of sending off for a mail-order marble mausoleum, but after a while he gives in and settles for a Pampers-lined fruit crate. We bury her in the country along with her discolored coverlet and little rubber shoe. The cement tombstone that Babe painstakingly inlays with pebbles takes him more than a month to complete. Its inscription reads:

KIM

IN GOD'S CARE

I LOVE YOU VERY MUCH

GEORGE WILSON.

In a year or so another similar bereavement and burial occur after Elmer's passing. It's wintertime, so he has to be placed in a Poly Print plastic bag and squeezed into the freezing compartment of the studio fridge so as to last till spring when the ground is thawed enough to dig.

Much of the glamour of life has gone, and Babe regularly pays bittersweet visits to the graves. In the fall he takes a rake to tidy up leaves. In the summer he keeps the weeds at bay and cultivates his pretty plantings, which he believes to be forget-me-nots or bladderwort or some other pretty kind of wildflower. I haven't the heart to tell him that what he's planted is poison ivy.

If there is a conclusion to be drawn from Babe's beloved pets, you might easily surmise that they often carry with them a dark element of doom. Sure, we're all doomed, only some of us are more doomed than others. Since Babe loves me most, this gives me something to think about.

Gray Rooms

Trains, planes, and station wagons. Hotels, guest houses, and motor courts.

If one is as much of a home-lover as I am, itinerancy definitely poses a problem. Being the kind of person who is prone to territorial imperatives, I've always had to find a place where, unobserved, I can drop the role assigned to me by background or profession; a private place where, temporarily, I'm unobliged to live up to others' expectations; a retreat from the outside world, even from the dancers; a place where I can keep my own good company, although, frankly, once inside a retreat, I sometimes very much enjoy retreating from *it*.

In New York, and before, whenever moving to a new address, I always performed a certain ritual which confirms the rights of occupancy. Every square inch of each new habitat's walls, doors, and window frames had to be painted, whether they need it or not, and the smaller the brush, the better. I then mopped, scoured, and sterilized the floors. Instinctually, I became a three-legged canine setting territorial boundaries with liquid markers.

But, naturally, when I'm trouping none of this is possible. Complete privacy is as fleeting as our lives of labeled air luggage and roadside landscapes.

Early on I realized the pregnability of motel rooms. Most had no bolts on the doors and were more often than not broken into by maids with master keys, or sometimes by other people whose keys, with a little forceful jiggling, could open any of the doors. These uninvited pop-up guests were a common nuisance. The privacy problem came to a head in Hackensack, I think it was, on the morning that yet another cleaning woman woke me by letting the cord of her vacuum cleaner trail across my face. Naturally, I sprang out of bed, shoved her from the room, and chased her down the hall, barking loudly. She then disappeared behind a door marked Staff Only. Respectful of her turf, even though she hadn't been of mine, I returned to my room. On the way I passed a nice New Jersey-looking couple who did not return my nod but kept their eyes locked to somewhere down around my belt level. It was puzzling—you never know how folks from New Jersey will be. When I got to my door, right off I noticed two things: I had slept in the buff, and my door had swung shut and locked me out.

Good reader, much was gained from this experience. It is not for naught that I have visited Hackensack, or even worse places, or that together we have journeyed this far through these pages, for I can now tell of a benefit that, in a way, grew from being locked out: After shivering in the hall I came down with the flu and was prevented from working out a new dance— no, not *Private Domain*, even though its subject is bare skin and voyeurism, or *Public Domain* (two dances, by the way, that have absolutely nothing to do with each other). It was to have been about certain kinds of birth control devices, and its abandonment has benefited the Right to Life movement immensely.

It is difficult to recall any particular roadside room. There were hundreds of them and, in the U.S., very alike, yet imprecisely alike. Each had at least one disturbing element of change. Sometimes a tricky bathroom door which was to the left of the bed in the morning would slip way over to the right, causing sore noses in the dark. The phones, if there were any, also relocated themselves, and they never rang, or if they did it was nerve-wrackingly and only Bet telling me of the latest company disaster.

The beds, usually twins, one of them always seriously empty, were with or without vibrating machines built into their mattresses, usually of the Magic Fingers brand. They contributed little to my dance life; at best, their sensations were only what one could expect for a quarter, even though something, anything, was better than nothing. At first. When the novelty wore off, my moral fiber improved and I refused to stoop to such reprehensible sublimations.

Announcements from the management, sometimes glassed and framed, were screwed or nailed onto the inside of the doors, or stapled there, or perforated by ineffectual thumbtacks and then glued. They mentioned what would happen in cases of nonpayment, listed absurdly early check-out times, and strongly stated what was and what was not proper treatment of the plumbing. An ominous line toward the bottom hinted at the possibility of losing all your valuables, and under that, a sanctimonious "Have a nice day." The announcements were wasted on me. I always paid up, was free of valuable belongings, never left cash in my room, and was not once tempted to throw tampons into the toilet.

What I liked to do was stuff up the grids of air conditioning units with tissue paper (a particular lavender roll is jumping from somewhere in the Far East). There were no off switches, and the dancers and I had to be leery of cool drafts which tightened our muscles.

The pictures, only one per room if we were lucky, listed toward the kind of thing that's intended to charm the Moral Majority (a segment of our global population which no one in his right mind would ever admit belonging to). Very popular was the urchin with the soulful eyes, drippy teared, bathos-oozing, and making a strong case for sending all children everywhere off to concentration camps. Streetscapes, done in the smear-a-glob manner, lied of romantic France. Van Gogh's sunflowers lived in fear lest someone notice that their simulated brushwork of cardboard ridges didn't match the painted forms, and if it did it was strictly by accident. Expansion nails joined the pictures permanently to the walls—there was no way on earth to pry them loose. To obliterate the pictures a towel had to be draped. Coat hangers were usually wedded to their poles in the closet or hidden away somewhere where they couldn't be found and stolen.

These rooms seemed to be expecting trouble; their occupants were not to be trusted—a worldly attitude, no doubt, but off base in my case. My collection of hotel towels and ashtrays was gathered for purely unselfish and farsighted reasons, would perhaps be willed to a museum someday. But usually I left with less than I came with. My airline baggage tags, laundry slips, and shirt cardboards could have brought the maids a tidy sum if only they had sense enough to sell them to lovers of collectibles.

Gideon Bibles were on prominent display. From the looks of them they were virginal, had never been opened and, like most of us who were isolated far beyond the outskirts of town, seldom had the opportunity to penetrate or be penetrated. Since the mating of opposites is one of my dictums, I was always careful to shut the Bibles away in a drawer with one of my dog-eared hot novels to keep them company.

Since the dancers and I were of one mind about motels, each of us developed his own way to manufacture an impression of domesticity. Dear Bet, when deeming her room unsatisfactory, would repack and drag her bag to another, and then sometimes to another, and when at last she realized that all the rooms were going to be equally unsuitable, would settle in and rearrange the furniture. She and the other girls traveled with their favorite silk scarves, stuffed animals, frilly pink doilies—anything portable of which they were particularly fond and which could be used to personalize, perk up, and take the edge off of the gray anonymity of their nightly retreats. One of the guys used to travel with a cute little stuffed panda, which would have been okay if he'd just kept it out of sight around customs officers, who could be brutally surgical when searching for dope. Secretly I coveted the panda, and one day when we were in Calcutta I was very sorry to see that it had been replaced by some sissy crocheting.

Me, I spent my spare time in these motel rooms trying to sleep or nursing a bad ankle or reading. Mostly I avoided the dancers, as we saw so much of each other when traveling or at the theater. I was fond of them all but didn't want to overdo a good thing by wearing my welcome out, also felt it necessary to keep some distance for leadership reasons. I had once, maybe twice, made the mistake of becoming romantically involved with one or two of them and had always found that sticky complications resulted. What I usually did was close my door and get ready for the next scheduled event on the company agenda.

There were times, though, when the rooms seemed very gray indeed, drab in color yet glaring with social needs, loud and quiet at the same time. The benefits of isolation were ambiguous. Sometimes it was all I could do to keep from dashing to Bet or one of the others for company. Frustrating sounds of life and laughter came from the direction of elevators or lobbies. Through the walls, inches away from the heads of my beds came the real or imagined moans of the heated romps of strangers.

And as the tours rolled by, the rooms remained the same, were all an increasingly inadequate background for restlessness and solitaire. To me they were more than just an embodiment of exclusion.

By '71, not long after my mother became seriously ill, a time when both my stamina and my belief in myself were at low ebb, I had given in to emotional needs by allowing myself to fall for one of the dancers. Just before performing in Hawaii the affair ended disastrously. I won't go into the details, since they involve two other people, one now dead by suicide and the other still living. Although the road conditions described above contributed to this unhappy time, in all conscience I must say that they were not to blame. However, I feel obliged to include here the following occurrence, not for sensationalism or self-therapy but for the sake of presenting as honest a picture of my dancing days as possible.

In Honolulu our road manager had just phoned to tell me that a dancer had injured herself, our program would have to be changed, and a sponsor in Texas was about to cancel an upcoming date there—the usual variants of what had been going on for a long time, except that our luggage hadn't been lost. Given my emotional state over the busted romance, the news was enough to push me towards the edge. I took some Dexamyl, and would have taken sleeping pills, except that I was out of them. Bet might have supplied me, but I'd been crying and didn't want her to see my eyes. I did have a full bottle of scotch, though, and chug-a-lugged it. Instead of euphoria, my depression worsened, getting blacker and more insane, until, with great relief, I came to a simple solution. But my last single-edged blade wouldn't come out of the razor. The damn gadget would be of no further use, and so, intending to clog up the plumbing, I hurled it into the toilet bowl, along with a pack of Kleenex. I then spotted a clear plastic glass in its niche by the sink and threw it at the floor. It didn't break, only bounced a couple of times, and so I ground it underfoot, scratching my bare heel in the process. One of the fragments wouldn't cut at first, but after some clumsy efforts I was able to start a flow going, at which point I passed out. When I came to I felt like a flop.

At the theater that same night I explained my taped left wrist by saying that I had fallen and sprained it. Then I did the performance.

The more I think about this "slice of life" (though now I see it as a weak and foolish thing to have done), the more its inclusion here seems to fit. It's like putting the two books—the dog-eared novel and the unread Bible— back to back in the same drawer; it illustrates a tendency to join hot and cold opposites. I feel that it wouldn't be right to present the soars without the stumbles. It's reassuring to know that most dancers sail over bumpy terrain with more grace.

The Red Room

The three walls, the ceiling, and the sloping floor are the color of terra cotta. In place of a front wall there is a wide row of vertical strips, also two similar rows running across the middle of the walled space and at the back. Five discs—three yellow and two orange, each five feet in diameter—can be slid along on their edges or laid flat on the floor. Movable, the walls, strips, and discs can be raised out of sight or lowered. Dreamed up by painter Alex Katz and built in the Spoleto scene shop, the Red Room is where we are to serve a four-week term, its effect being that of a large cage or prison cell.

By coincidence, on a hill overlooking Spoleto's terra cotta roofs is a real prison built of stones scavenged from a nearby Roman amphitheater. It was once a castle inhabited by Lucrezia Borgia, a fortress for repelling trouble but nowadays used for caging trouble in. We can easily imagine being locked up in it—its clammy walls, the isolation, the loneliness. Better to imagine being in some other jail, one where American meals would be served, a nice, homey place where one could escape from daily responsibilities and, in our case, the strict and sometimes nearly suffocating demands of dance.

Though picturesque, the small town of boxed-in squares and tight, narrow streets could also be seen as a place of internment. But of course it isn't entirely Spoleto, the prison, or the Red Room that intensifies our view. More likely it is the confinements and restrictions required by dance and the trouping life. Audiences cannot be expected to come to us, and so we travel, stagebound and migratory, itinerant shut-ins catching glimpses of many lands through the windows of snug conveyances, dressing rooms, and small hotels. As the old Chinese proverb goes, it's like looking at flowers from a galloping horse. Being away so much keeps home life spotty, and we've found ourselves participating in all-but-impossible juggling acts when trying to balance a demanding profession with a personal home life. As for myself, I have seen dance as being a home, in dreams a family castle; but lately it seems to be more and more of a shrinking cell.

Gian Carlo Menotti has invited us to his festival again. For newcomers Danny and Twyla it is to be the first trip abroad with the company. They have been looking forward to it excitedly. It is to be Sharon's and Renee's third, Bet's and Liz's fourth. They are a little less excited. Not counting the tours with Martha, it's to be my sixth.

Momentarily mixed up about our destination, while preparing to leave I've written Mother that we will be returning to Mexico and have zipped a few tattered pesos into my money belt. Were they left over from '62? From '48? Who knows? Dates and chronology seem unimportant; dancing focuses, fuses us, to the present instant. Time seems to be without subdivisions; different stages merge, countries blend. But then, as Tacet says, "Such temporal unification and blendings of swirling colors should never be disdained by the retroflexive Artist."

Lighter Tommy and assistant Jenny are also coming, as well as conductor Simon Sadoff. We are to give ten performances, alternating in the opera house with Gian Carlo's production of *Der Rosenkavalier* and the Royal Ballet featuring Margot Fonteyn and her new partner, the recent Russian defector, young Rudolf Nureyev, in his staging of *Raymonda*.

Good old Charlie has worked out our travel arrangements, and his enthusiasm is infectious. At the Sixth Avenue studio he describes his vision of the coming trip. However, he's being a little vague as to the flight, one we assume will be on Icelandic, which past experience tells us is a cramped and roundabout way to go, but cheap. "Then from Luxembourg we'll drive through the beautiful French countryside," Charlie says, "stopping along the way for picnics of long bread, soft cheese, and big bottles of burgundy. And then we'll get to see the beautiful Alps, coast merrily down them and spend a couple of leisurely days soaking up the beautiful Riviera. Next will be the valley of Umbria, where we'll have more picnics, this time in the shade of beautiful olive groves and those other beautiful trees—holyanders or something—or are those bushes? Anyway, then in Spoleto, rested and refreshed and with plenty of extra time to rehearse, we'll open in the beautiful old opera house. Tommy will have gotten our lights all hung and Simon will have already rehearsed the Trieste Orchestra. And instead of another crummy motel we'll be living it up in—get this—a beautiful Italian villa of our very own with two housekeepers to take care of the cooking and stuff. And we'll be able to sleep—the villa's on the outskirts of town, away from all the noisy traffic. Nice, huh? Everything's going to be beautiful, *beautiful*. What a lark we'll have!"

Sharon, eyes glistening, utters high-decibel chirps. "Golly! No smelly motel! Our own house!"

Renee's often somber face melts, and she and her off-and-on chum Sharon hug as they haven't done for weeks and weeks. Joined by the others, Dan, Liz, and Danny bounce several times off the studio's low ceiling.

Standing alone and watching from the edge of the room, Babe also smiles. Unable to read Charlie's lips, he's glowing in the reflection of our excitement. After flapping his hand to get my attention, then learning of Charlie's plan, he spells with quick, forceful fingers, "Bring back presents! Bring Tabby ball with bell in it!" (ever his fascination for all types of noise makers). "And write, not forget to write!" Again, as his major source of communication, the mail will have to do.

"Okay, okay, I will," I promise, forming the O by curling my index finger to touch the tip of my thumb, then making the K in another curliqued way. At the I, I hesitate. The I is my least favorite letter. They're made by bunching everything loosely with pinkie uplifted like a matron at tea. They and a few of the other letters look too frivolous, but I'm finding ways to invest them with a more virile shape.

Babe is to stay at his apartment as usual, look after the studio and Tabby, and at night tend machines in Queens.

"Tomorrow morning we'll all meet downstairs on the sidewalk before busing to Kennedy," continues Charlie. "All bags there at nine."

As usual, dapper Dan adds the old company quip, "And bring your luggage too," then turns to chat at length with Danny, touching on aesthetical subjects—early American hooked rugs, Lhasa apsos, sassafras tea—and repeating quaint bits that he's heard someone else say (Tacet's niece Melissa Clarissa de Lavallade if I'm not mistaken).

When everyone has gone, Bet helps me pack our costumes and write up the carnet. After she leaves I stuff a few necessities of my own into a Valpak, including tweezers and enough elastic adhesive tape for all, because I remember the beautiful old opera-house stage as being a terrible mass of splinters.

In the morning, tightly clustered on the crowded sidewalk, we say so long to those who've come to see us off: newlywed Sharon's hubby, John Binder; a sizable number of Liz's boyfriends; Nathan Clark, our fan club of one, who as always is pouring champagne and offering it to us in plastic goblets; and of course old Doc T with his farewell hugs, pressing his frame against people he's barely met, finding other excuses to touch his delectable dancers or trying to blow in their ears, wheezing, waving, and displaying his tawny teeth.

After a wistful-looking Babe helps me rope my overstuffed Valpak, which has just burst its round-trip zipper, the troupe boards the bus. As it pulls out into Sixth Avenue traffic, Babe tears up, then runs along beside us for almost two blocks, giving parting toots from his toy horn.

After an endless wait at Kennedy, others at Reykjavik and over the Atlantic, we land in Luxembourg, where an old friend of Charlie's, Gusta (Gus) van der Wyck, meets us with a Volkswagen Minibus which she's lending us for the next six weeks. Its interior has been tampered with in an effort to convert it into a vehicle able to hold more people than are good for it. While the girls are looking dubious and snickering, the guys and I manage to pile all the luggage on top, cover it with a tarp, then lash down the whole teetery pile. Under its heavy load the minibus is listing to one side. "Quick, everybody in before it falls over!" says the ever optimistic Charlie.

The three smallest dancers—Sharon, Renee, and Twyla—crowd into the cozy backseat. The rest of us accordion ourselves and sit with knees ground together and shoulders overlapping. Charlie squeezes in behind the wheel, and with effort we're able to get the doors closed.

Gus stands outside reiterating to Charlie the best way for us to go. On a map she has drawn a red line along the quickest and most direct route. Handing the map through the window, she says, "Bye bye—have a nice drive. See you in Spoleto," then waves.

"So long," we say, our arms too squeezed to wave back.

"See ya, Gus!" calls Charlie as the bus groans ominously. "Uh, bye bye," he repeats.

But we don't go.

But the mystery of the unturned ignition key is soon solved, and, near to bursting, tilting and top-heavy, our tiny bus begins to rock rhythmically down the road toward France.

A mood of discontent is permeating the bus. Manicured French trees in a stiff geometric landscape are passing too slowly. We are becoming increasingly aware of certain compacted tensenesses. We are eyeing each other suspiciously and not at all happy that someone, we are not sure who, needs a bath. For a while nobody says anything, and then Charlie volunteers, "What sights we'll see! So what if we're a little snug?"

"When is our first stop?" Liz asks eagerly.

"Right here, I guess," replies Charlie, then gets out to retie our tarp, which has come loose and begun to flap.

We continue along a major highway that is smooth and familiar, a glossy black dance floor with a yellow Oz stripe tapering straight into the distance. Kilometers, or "clicks," as Charlie keeps calling them, rotate slowly on the dashboard. Instead of glimpsing scenic wonders, we're having to make do with the other vehicles that are coming and going alongside of us, every cliché under the sun: the vacationer's canoe-topped Volvo with shaggy, wind-flattened head of dog protruding; the speeding sports car, fender smashed, driven by the mustachioed hotshot with girlfriend pressed close; the family rattletrap with the towheaded tot making faces at us through its rear window; the rusty truck that grinds slowly up a rise, oblivious to the caravan of impatience that rages in its wake (and which when recalled is to be colored terra cotta and laden with a load of chickens imprisoned in their coops).

"Yuck! This road reminds me of the New Jersey Turnpike," someone says.

"Yes, Gus's route is boring," Charlie agrees. "Shall I treat us to a more scenic one?" We soon turn onto a narrow, potholed road, and after wasting time exploring uninteresting dead ends, turn back onto the highway. And then, at another stop to retie the tarp, we trade seats, find ourselves worse off than before, and trade back at the next tarp-tying routine. Farther along Twyla moans, "This van is humiliating! Look how everybody's laughing and pointing as they pass. Go faster, Charles!"

"No, we'd better stop. Maybe they've been trying to tell us something." We then not only make another stop but have to backtrack to retrieve a trail of dented luggage. "I was wondering why the bus was picking up speed," says Charlie.

Perhaps because of the difference between a mile and a click, or perhaps because of a mathematical error in the conversion of one into the other, or perhaps because the VW's top downhill speed is approximately 35 mph, or maybe simply because it's been foreordained, the fact is that we're making very little headway. An awful awareness of being trapped in tin prevails. Bet, never one to complain except indirectly through her Epic of the Sinuses, keeps shifting her positions, thereby causing me to shift mine. The door side of her knee is turning purple, and her sharp elbow is piercing my ribs. It's hard to bear the sight of her automatic smile as, bravely ignoring discomfort, she turns to the trivialities that she feels are required of her. "Lovely weather, isn't it?" she states. "Awful humidity, though." As usual, the sinuses are being quick to acclimate. If the weather were dry, then they'd acclimate to that, always switching to whichever weather we happen to be having. Always, always. Good God, they're consistent!

And then we round a sudden curve, surprising a bicyclist and hooking his sleeve onto our side mirror. "Stop the bus!" we all yell to Charlie.

"Oh, *now* what," he groans, then slows down enough for the cyclist to disengage.

And then we're delayed by a side trip to a station house, where a baboon in policeman's getup insists that we've been driving on the wrong side of the road. While Charlie forks over the fine, I watch two frail guards escort a hefty fellow into a back room, and I try not to let his arrest remind me too much of my own commitment to dance. Switching thoughts back to Charlie, I can't help wondering if he's paying our fine out of company petty cash or his own pocket; but in the end, never having had any reason to question his handling of funds, I decide not to ask.

*   *   *

Castellane is a small Alpine village in Switzerland or Italy or maybe France. Like I said, to troupers countries tend to be without borders, the patchwork world becoming just one big smear. We're having an impression of postcard Alps, ones seen better in airports; at least we aren't back in Luxembourg, the fuzzy place where our lark started. Castellane is perching high at a pass where a road that isn't marked in red, or even on our map at all, threads between two major Alps. A little north, just where the road zigs into a drastic zag, a plaster Christ stands enshrined, eyes rolled heavenwards, his feet and hands trickling with plaster blood. He isn't as gaudy as Mexican Christs, but is pretty gaudy just the same. According to a little roofed sign, the treacherous road has caused numerous fatalities.

Far below spreads a dark sea of greenery—larch, cedar, and pine— through which several unpaved roads crisscross bewilderingly. And at the close of a long summer's day, as rain trickles from the roof of the sign and thunder bounces from Alp to Alp, a vehicle is leaving one dark road to try another, nosing and prodding here and there within the panorama, moving tentatively and distrustfully, and whenever it changes course it stops, then spins its back wheels and spews up mud. And high above it the Savior's eyes seem to be saying, "Dear Father, that vehicle down there . . . see those tiny little tail lights way down there in amongst Your big dark panorama? Well, at the risk of sounding uncharitable, I would say that that vehicle looks to be cloistering a small congregation of halfwits."

And then the van snorts, coughs, and dies. Undoubtedly lost, we're unaware that only yards away is a road that can lead us out of the woods and up to Castellane.

His face shedding raindrops and taut with determination, good old Charlie sets out on foot to seek benzine, stubbing his toe on a stone and causing for himself and the rest of us a brief scene of general laughter. And then, after an hour or so everything happens at once. The rain stops, Charlie returns with the benzine, and Danny spots a glistening sign that directs footloose travelers to Castellane.

The walls of the restaurant there are sprouting a forest of cobwebbed antlers and a few trout on plaques. A doleful waitress leads us to a table pressed against a back wall. We are feeling dismal, but not from the murky room or the dusty taxidermy, not from anything tangible.

Scanning the menu, Charlie recommends that we try trout, the house special.

"Fish, ugh. I hate fish. What ever happened to our picnics?" frets Sharon.

"We're running just a bit behind schedule," Charlie explains unnecessarily. "We'll have them soon's we catch up. Aren't these Alps the greatest!"

"Who's looking," Liz says dryly. "All those chasms, they make my back crawl. I've never been on such scary roads. And the van is tossing us around in back. There's nothing to hang on to. Danny, from now on I'm in the middle seat."

"First you fought for the window," Danny replies, "and now—"

Cutting him off, Liz says, "That was when I could stand to look."

Dear Bet excuses herself and goes to find the ladies' room.

"Again?" I ask no one in particular. "That reminds me, gang, from now on let's all try to go at the same time. All these continual rest stops are holding us up."

"Good grief, next he'll tell us to go faster!" responds Jenny.

"Oh, come on, Jen, we have an opening to make. By the way, did we really have to make that extra stop back there in Nancy or somewhere just so that you could buy perfume?"

Defensively she says, "Have you already forgotten that in New York you asked me to bring back a bottle of Chanel for some friend of yours named Dr. Tacet? Who is he anyway?"

Bet returns gingerly. Her small feet always swell from long rides in all types of conveyances. As if she were an extra rib, she squeezes back in beside me.

"Bet, are you taking Tacet some perfume, too?" I ask.

She shakes her head in denial, knowing of my alias but not wanting to go along with the joke that I've been playing on Jenny.

"What about you, Twyla?" I ask, trying to prolong the game.

"You didn't ask me to buy anything, but you did ask me to be patient with Charlie if this lark got loused up!" And then she treats us to a particularly wicked and mirthless Tharp cackle.

"What!" Charlie exclaims, laboring under the impression that we are all stone deaf.

That troublemaker Tacet, I'm thinking—why was he always opening his big yap? He never should've questioned Charlie's knowhow. Out loud, anyway. Now the fat was in the fire. Trying to change the subject, I say, "By the way, Charlie old boy, wasn't that traffic fine a little steep?" and on saying it immediately realize that I've switched to an equally touchy subject.

By raising his menu a little and basking behind it in unconcern, Charlie refuses to recognize these unjust blows to his managership. There's always something sort of endearing and noble in the way that he won't stoop to defend himself. A dandy sort of Gandhiism.

In the end only three of us decide to order trout—Charlie, because he's recommended it; myself, because it might be a tacit (or atypically Tacet) way of letting him know that I'm sorry for doubting his abilities and would like to make amends; and dear direct Bet, simply because she likes it.

While waiting for us to give our orders, the waitress has been shifting her weight impatiently, looking as if she doesn't understand English, as if determined to be finicky should we try to speak French. So, to prepare myself, I whisper to Liz, asking her for the word "trout" in French. (Liz even knows "*Schliess meinen Reissverschluss*"—German for "Zip my zipper.") "*Du truite*," she answers. "Trois" I already know from pas de trois. All prepared, I order trout for the three of us.

"Tweet tweet."

No reaction from waitress.

"Tweet tweet," I try on the others.

Maybe at some other time, in a less dismal place, someone would have laughed.

Was the trout good? Although it's tasty enough, everyone is being prissy about the heads and the Christ-like eyes. Liz says that her blood sausage is okay, but a sad substitute for the Nedick's hot dog that she really wanted. Desserts are forsaken in favor of a downhill coast to the Riviera.

That, too, doesn't quite live up to Charlie's prediction. The narrow road is hemmed in by perpendicular heights on one side and sheer drops on the other. Frayed nerves and a frayed tarp dance to the music of fenders screeching against wet wheels with treads long gone. At some of the road's sharper turns Charlie goes into reverse and tries again. Undaunted by upgrades, he urges the van on with little forward jerks of his head, like a child whose tricycle is stuck. "Shall we get out and push? Will we make it in time? Can Jenny spell you again?" we plead.

"Leave the driving to us. Relax, just put your mind on dancing in the beautiful old opera house," he answers, tightening his grip on the wheel with grim determination. "Beautiful. Spoleto's gonna be beautiful."

The Alps behind us, and more uplifted by getting rid of them than we were by their grandeur, we creep through the next day and night without sleep in an effort to make up lost time. Since Charlie prefers for us not to tire ourselves by helping him drive, he stays at the wheel, and we take turns sitting next to him so as to poke him whenever he begins to nod off. We get to Nice about two or three the next morning, stopping somewhere along the seashore, where Charlie's chin nestles down on the wheel. Before drifting off he says, "Gang, you must be tired and should get some rest. Guess we'll have to spend the night here in a hotel."

A street sign tells us that we are on the Promenade des Anglais. Other than a strange porcupineish-looking tree like the one in *The Red Shoes,* all we can see is a big black void where the sparkling Mediterranean should be. Jenny misses seeing even this much, since she's snoozing inside the van. She's had a siege of cramps and is now giving us a good lesson in the healing power of sleep—sitting on her own hands, hyperextended elbows locked into position, head sunk craneishly into shoulder, lips loudly flubbered by small jets of relief.

While the others hearken to the hissing of wavelets against an unseen pebble beach—a romantic setting, except for the snores—I cross the street to a hotel, intending to ask about accommodations. Entering the lobby is like walking into an exhaustion-provoked nightmare. An injured man lurches out of the gridwork cage of an old-fashioned elevator, his neck slashed and blood squirting. He collapses onto the floor and several people—the night clerk and six or seven others who are probably guests—stand frozen for what seems an eternity, then rush to stoop around him while someone goes to phone for an ambulance. It isn't a time to ask about rates. I'm shaking and can't think of any way to help, so I return to the van, where, not wanting to worsen the troupe's already low spirits, I mention nothing of what I've just seen. I tell them that the hotel was too expensive. Further down the road we're able to find another place and some very much needed sleep.

The next day, the van's accelerator pressed flat to the floor, we pass through Monaco without paying much attention to it or its casinos; to Menton, San Remo, and Imperia we pay even less. Eyes clamped in the direction of Spoleto, we forget to look for the "beautiful olive groves and holyanders." Somewhere along the way we take a wrong turn, which leads us onto a rutted road impossible to turn around on, and we arrive at a place called Cortina to find ourselves staring stupidly at a dishwatery lake and a marker testifying to the demise of Hannibal's elephants.

The trip then continues like a treadmill, or worse. Other vehicles seem stationary as our jail on wheels slips backwards away from them. Two days late, we finally zero in on Spoleto, bump along its cobblestoned streets, and find Gus waiting for us. She wants to know what has held us up. "Heavens! I've been worried to pieces!" she exclaims. "What in the *world*? Was the red line wrong on my map?"

The walls are made of large rectangular stones, and there are nine front windows, a deep doorway, and a stoop: a boxlike structure that looks as if a five-year-old had drawn it. Strangely proportioned, weightless, off-kilter. Everything—walls, windows, doorway, stoop—is the color of spit; some-how we expected more terra cotta. Only the tiled roof is that color (as a matter of fact, it is terra cotta). Uncommunicative about its age, the place seems suspended in some pre-Christian time, a prototype of numberless progeny to follow. There is no shrubbery to soften the harshness of its shape, no trees in which to nestle.

Inside on the first floor is a living room sparsely furnished with nondescript pieces. Several of the rooms are locked and are to remain so. A staircase of listing steps leads up to five bedrooms for our use, as well as several more locked ones, each on a common hall. The interior walls are whitewashed yet seem curiously dark, even at places hit directly by the sun. Their surfaces are clammy to the touch and leave our fingertips chalky. Even to those of us who have little faith in things that go bump in the night, the place hints of swirling maelstroms of fiends incarnate.

There was no regulation cypress outside, no garden mosaic of dolphins playing, no antique statuary of urinating urchins—not the slightest trace of any accessory that can be associated with the word "villa."

We drag our luggage upstairs, relieved to be able to undo ourselves from the bus and each other and grateful for what we trust will be the end of a Siamese situation.

The next morning I wake to a rooster's frenzied communion with dawn— a nerve-wracking aubade embellished by songbirds, barnyard critters, and a chorus of neighborhood dogs. I remove my head from beneath my pillow, dress, and go down to inspect the grounds.

The nettles and overgrown grass at the front of the house hold little interest, so I continue around to the back, outsmarting a tricky barbed-wire fence on the way. From a kitchen window a face peeps shyly and then quickly disappears. A man with rolled-up trousers and purple bare feet comes out of the kitchen door, frowns slightly, and also disappears. Assuming that they are Caterina and Teodoro, the caretaker domestics whom Charlie has told us about, and sensing that I'm intruding on their domain, I continue on around the house to the front.

On my circuit the Borgia prison on its high hill has been nowhere in sight—it should've been easy to see from at least one direction. Nor has there been any sign of a town, only the unbroken expanse of a wide valley. We're miles from Spoleto, too far to walk. When they get up, the dancers won't be pleased to find themselves so far from town. I'm thinking that I'd better break the news gently. Until then, I fill up the time with a little nature study.

A few insects are droning and creeping in the grass, species closely related to my childhood chums back at Edgewater Beach. Florentine clouds, a Japanese rising sun, and a Texas sky are looking about the same as they do everywhere and are bringing on heavy ruminations. While weighing the

World against fly-specked Man and our piddling relationship to the universe, I'm filled with both joy and remorse over everything being part of a
Celestial Order. I begin to celebrate the sun for its belonging to such an
impressive spiral nebula, then lament for it being that nebula's prisoner;
pine over the earth being a slave to the sun, then hum a little hymn of
gratitude for its chains; chide and chuckle over each planet's being ruled by
both tyrannical and benevolent dictatorships; could bay at the transparent
morning moon for its being earth's chattel; and so forth and so on down a
line of duplistic servitudes and right back to the insects.

And always everything seems to be on loan to us—our lives, our fast slow
vans, our rock-hard tissue-paper bodies, our new old villa conceived by
ancient children, the villa so locked to the earth by its multitude of natural
dimensions, only one of which has been named gravity.

And the sleeping troupe? We're each locked to dance by a commitment
made freely, but one that sometimes causes hesitation when we're faced
with doubts and distrust. Are our efforts to create something for others to
enjoy, something of value that we can share, worth the losses of personal
freedom that are required? Are the talents that we've been given big enough?
Are we missing the mark? How long will the disciplined techniques imprisoned in our bones enable us to dance? Will our need to continually
travel as a group, and the resulting pressures and frictions against bodies
and spirits, eventually split us apart? We've formed strong attachments to
each other, but we also need solitude and independence. But, in our common commitment to dance, we aren't so different from other teams that are
deeply involved in their work and that make sacrifices and restrict their
lives for the sake of it. All people are bonded to their own particular gravitational force; all are in similar orbit around related spheres; each has eyes
that are commanded to focus inward or out. Corkscrew patterns all; all
heavenly devil dances being performed in mirror image.

At just about this point I notice something crawling in the grass. It's too
large to be an insect but smaller than a bread box. I try to grab at it and
miss. Instead of running off, it forms its body into a perfect sphere, buries
its bright eyes in its fur, and lies there under the impression that it's safe.
I've never seen anything so darling and stupid and decide on the spot that
it must be a hedgehog. Unable to wait to show it to the others, even though
they may still be sleeping, I pick it up and hurry to the foot of the stairs,
where I call for everybody to come look. Sharon is the first to appear. "A
bird—now he's got a *bird!*" she screams, making fleet Javanese gestures
with her hands and wrists. When she's caught by surprise, her bird phobia
tells her that all creatures are the dreaded avian type. Glancing hysterically
over her shoulder, she flings shut her bedroom door and bolts it. It's as if

she's trying to escape her phobia by locking herself in—trading in one sort of imprisonment for another.

The stark simplicity of Alex Katz's set for *The Red Room* magnifies any flaws of execution, and during the week before the rest of us arrive, he's been struggling to have it built properly. The men at the scene shop could turn out ornate opera interiors and complicated landscapes, but seemed out of their element when it came to simple sets. In order for the discs to be raised and lowered, their cables had been connected with large, ugly, clawlike gismos of which the builders seemed fond and loath to part; but after a lot of confused bickering through someone who translated Alex's Queensese into English into Italian, the gismos had been exchanged for smaller and less obvious ones. When in place, the rows of strips had hung far from perpendicularly, and asked by a stagehand to prove it, Alex had to use a plumb line before getting the strips trued up.

The language barrier has also caused trouble with the costumes. The cloth petals on the skirts tend to hang wrong or fall off; and the pants, in order not to rip when we plié, need to be fitted snugly at the crotch, but the Spoleto seamstresses are reluctant to fit them, either because they're shy or because they think snug crotches risqué. Pointing to the girls in their petal skirts, Alex, admirably nasal and repetitious, whines for more glass: "More glaaas, more glaaas!" But even those of us who well understand Queensese don't understand that he wants earrings. He then bounces the heel of his hand off his brow and says, "Forget it, forget it!" Nevertheless, when finished his designs are to me some of the best sights of the trip.

When the set is in place and the dancers and I are in our costumes, we start warming up for the dress rehearsal. The old opera house is ice cold, and we're still in knots from the long drive. It's great to see Tommy and Maestro Simon again. They've wisely decided to stay at a hotel in town. Karen Levy, an Adelphi student of mine, has come to take our company classes, and since she's talented and here anyway, I've added a small part for her to *Piece Period.* American duo-pianists Paul Sheftel and Joseph Rollino have come from their home in Rome to play Alexei Haieff's score for *Party Mix* and have sportingly agreed to let their pianos be placed on opposite sides of the stage, even though, as duo-pianists are wont to do, they've gotten used to playing close together. Unfortunately, due to the wide stage, the music's loud opening chord is to become two, each half as loud as the one is supposed to be.

When the Royal Ballet has finished its dress rehearsal, I go onto the stage to find a small, boyish man talking to designer Beni Montresor, whose *Raymonda* set seems to be both dignified and daring—even better, it looks transportable and would be perfect for a traveling company like ours, which Alex's set is not.

Montresor is saying, "I am sorry that you are not pleased with this set, Rudy," and then leaves. The young guy turns to me and introduces himself as Rudolf Nureyev. I suggest that since he doesn't seem to care for the set, maybe he will let me take it off his hands. "Yes, I was being a bit angry about how it looks. My 'yellow light' was on," he says, eyes twinkling. As we chat I'm struck with sympathy for this brilliant young Russian, who has lately defected, given up family, country, even his native tongue for the sake of broadening the scope of his dancing. Right off I like him. Even though we are of different backgrounds, it is easy for me to be sympathetic to his goals and his displacement.

As it turns out, his fast-growing reputation for temperament (his "red light") is based more on his bark than his bite. He knows that Spoletini adore temperament, always expect it from artists, and would feel gypped not to witness any. Invited to a jet set–type dinner party for the Royal Ballet given at Gian Carlo's after the opening, Rudy takes a while to towel off and dress and arrives at the party a little late. He's famished, but the food has already been eaten, so he generously gives everybody an extra performance by smashing several wine glasses against the wall—stylishly Russian and the only courteous thing to do.

He seems interested in my work, and in the weeks to come we see him in the wings trying to learn *Aureole* while we're performing it.

The Royal Ballet is representing tradition at the festival; my troupe, a new direction. Both are bringing nonnarrative dances, Rudy having removed as much of the story from *Raymonda* as possible, and my summer program having no stories to begin with. To the annoyance of Italian dance writers, abstract dance (or relatively abstract, there being no such thing as abstract dance) is on the rampage.

So we are about to start our dress rehearsal: *Raymonda*'s set flies smoothly out and ours kind of klunks down in fits and starts, getting snarled on something, and by the time Tommy is able to get the three walls, ceiling, and ground cloth into the right places, there's no time left to rehearse any of our dances except *The Red Room*. Simon does well with the Trieste Orchestra, Gunther Schuller's music sounding fairly recognizable, and we do a not-bad runthrough except for the girls losing some petals and me almost breaking my neck. A series of seven double air turns, each taking off and landing on the same foot without preparations in between, carries me to the apron of the raked stage, where I'm barely able to avoid falling into the pit. Afterwards I remember to warn the musicians that I might fall on them during the performance and that if I do, would they please push me back up onto the stage?

Immediately following the runthrough Gian Carlo gallops over, looking upset. "*Dio mio,* you need to soften up this dance!" he says. "That decor! It is much too harsh for our Spoleto public, too stark, too unrelenting. Can't we pretty it up a bit, or better yet, eliminate it altogether? Forgive me for saying so, but it reminds me of a jail."

At the opening that night the house is packed. As it was when we were here before, the audience seems more interested in who is sitting in the boxes than in watching the stage, and it's in a giddy mood, happy to be so well dressed and looking forward to intermission when their getups can be compared. But there is no way for them to know the agony we are in. The terra cotta floor cloth has been made of sandpaper or something rougher and, like the red coats of the British, is camouflaging the blood from our feet which we're tracking all over. Alex could be accused of plagiarizing a red-on-red Pollock painting. And we're having to dodge descending discs and rows of wooden strips, never certain whether or not they'll be coming down on our heads. By the time the girls make their final exit the stage is petal strewn. As Mammy used to say about fall foliage, "It's a perfectly beautiful riot of color." After we bow, Alex is relieved to be able to breathe again. He's been sitting in the house counting our pliés and waiting for our pants to rip.

Dank, chilly days, boring after-performance nights. Continual rains keep streams brimming, puddles everywhere, and no breeze stirs the tall, buggy grass at the villa. In our rooms the costumes that we hang up to dry stay perpetually wet. Mosquito larvae are maturing at an alarming rate and after breaking the surface of stagnant waters don't have to be told to know where to go for a good time. All of our welcoming windows are unscreened, but it seems that the most attractive is the one to the room shared by Renee and Twyla.

Passing their open door, I see Renee with her hair hanging in drippy points after its fifth or sixth shampoo of the week. She's sitting and contemplating the electric hair dryer in her lap. "Just look at this thing," she says. "Just look! Now what'll we do?"

"What do you mean, 'what'll we do?'?" I reply encouragingly.

"What I mean is *now* what'll we do?"

"Well, how about using a towel?"

"No, no! I mean now what'll we do *here* at this darn villa! What'll we do every day when Jenny is always making off with the darn van and we're stuck here miles from nowhere with nothing to do and noplace to do it in, because it's awful having only three performances a week, and there's too much time here. We've taken a hundred naps. We've practiced our makeup a thousand times. We've painted each other's toenails forever. I mean, how many times can you paint toenails? I tell you, there's nothing to do and absolutely no privacy to do it in. If I have to stay here another minute I'm going to scream. And just look at this dryer."

"So?"

"Well, can't you see it's all wrinkled and bent?"

"Oh yeah, it is. What happened?"

"Well, I loaned it to Twyla and she melted it."

"No!"

"Yes. She plugged it into this weird Italian current and melted it."

Looking to Twyla's bed, I see that it's unmade, with the bedclothes bunched up in the middle. Overhead hangs a makeshift cagelike construction. "What's that supposed to be?" I ask.

Before Renee can explain, the messed-up sheets metamorphose into a head and Twyla says, "Mind your own business!"

She's blinking in the light. There's something of the mole about her, or the recently hatched termite. "Come on, Twerp, tell me what you've made."

"Beg me."

"Please?"

"Okay. If you must know, it's my mosquito net. Like in a tropical rain forest. Heh heh heh!"

"But there's no netting."

"I *know*. And no place to buy any. No place to buy anything. This villa is disgusting, and the friggin' bugs keep eating me alive!"

"Now, Twyla, honey, let's not slander an occasional dipteron or two. You should get to be an insect lover like me."

Just then she experiences an excruciating itch, then smacks her little hands in the air all around her while launching a barrage of bad words. A mosquito being bitten by a mosquito.

"Let's stop this cruel squashing," I tell her. "Don't you care about ecology? Don't you care about nature taking its course? We must live and let live. Come on, Twerp, join up with me and we can prevent mad biologists from their chemical cruelties to the reproductive glands of our little friends."

"Oh, shut up!" she says, without a trace of biological insight or compassion, then retro-pupates by disappearing beneath a flurry of bedclothes.

Mosquitos, a hedgehog, and barnyard creatures. These and others at the villa were piling up into a regular menagerie. Have I mentioned somewhere that I'm just wild about nature, that nature is more impressive to me than religion, or even dance? Well, it is. I'm drawn to nature's magnificently programmed order, also its lovely recycling process—an eating contest where the worm always wins, a process that metamorphoses all life, even rocks, asteroids, and suns.

There hangs in the Sixth Avenue studio a needlework sampler that once said In God We Trust but now has the word "God" replaced with the word "Order." I trust Order a lot more than I trust Him. Dance is a form of Order, a minor form and unimportant to many, but even so it's one that should be played at reverently. And, though sacred, dance is an artifice, never natural. Ordered and mutated, yes; natural, no. Like other dance makers, I take my cues from such natural phenomena as the mechanics of water motion, moving formations of scaled, winged, and warmer creatures, the cyclings of spheres, odd spectacles such as weddings, funerals, and lines of depositors at banks. Choreography is monkey see, monkey do, and at best is second best. Some folks, especially those who find organized religion unappealing, may, like me, find in dance an ordered discipline that signals the existence of Order. Yet dance is only a symbol, not the real thing.

But it can relieve instinctive cravings for ritual, ordered magic. Something tells me that when churches started making their rituals more understandable, that was when churchgoers began to look elsewhere. Dance, like magic and ritual, contains ingredients—aural, temporal, and visual things, not to mention the dancer—that must be combined just so and in precise proportions or it doesn't work, there is no magic. The most important ingredient of dance, a truly mysterious ingredient, one that must never be missing but often is, one lucid and cloudy at the same time—that one is nameless. Poets know this, as do great religious leaders. It's the transforming alchemy that everyone seeks; it's inscrutable, cannot be taught, but when found it turns lead into gold.

But to mention nature, dance, and religion without referring to the other side of the coin wouldn't be giving the whole picture. Turn Order and God over and what've you got there in back? Chaos and Satan, naturally. But the back side is not the opposite; it's of the same cloth—some say it's exactly the same thing. And so it's only fair to mention such other evils as Sunday painters and objets d'art, dial-a-porn, blow combs, lobster bibs, and music—music in airports, elevators, and dentists' offices, the opera—handshakes of the left-handed type, convention name tags, people grouped for cultural uplift, therapy, and sightseeing. Last but not least, I should mention long dinner parties, and one evil meal in particular.

This meal, and the part of the Spoleto lark that follows, due to good taste (another evil) and the laws of libel, must be related without naming the culprits who were partly responsible for causing us several long weeks of doubt, disappointment, and distrust. They shall simply be referred to as GT, Ph.D., he being far away, and too occupied with writing his own autobiography to mind, and as good a scapegoat as any. That understood, we can now continue.

The road gang and I are crowded at a small round table in the dining room—the lesser dining room, not the nice one that has been unlocked only on the evening when Gian Carlo came to dinner at this so-called villa which isn't in Spoleto at all and is too far to walk to. And the meal is to be flawed by elements of joylessness and near hysteria. Nobody is at his best this evening, not even shy Caterina (a pity that her sleeve has to dip into the soup), not even our even-natured newcomer, Karen, who should be immune to echoes of past discords among some of the older dancers. Sharon and Renee (or Shanee, or Chaîné, as I have lately been calling the two of them), instead of occupying adjacent chairs, have again split up and are sitting as far apart from each other as possible.

We've endured a hungry wait for the slowest one of us to pick his way down the treacherous stairs, speaking grayly about Spoleto audiences or whatever. I'm not really listening, my mind having strayed to the Big City. It's a shame that dancing had to take us away from there, too bad that there are now so many cities, dances, dancers, all blurring together. It's unexpected and tiring and awful and swell. And my mind is doing this sort of disjointed dance when, out of the mist, there's this long meal beginning.

The dear reedy girl who's seated herself next to me is being wonderfully forbearing and brave. And there's good old debonair Charlie on the other side of her, and Danny directly across the table in his black-and-white striped shirt—too California for my taste and like a jockey's or something, but never mind—and in the spider-webbed corners of the room, batting there at the cold dank bright dark walls, moths are caught and confused. And maybe even terra cotta mice are standing by.

Our linguist Liz has planned a menu with Caterina for all to enjoy, but something has gotten lost in linguistics, and, as usual, Liz is in for a surprise. This time it turns out to be an encore of brook trout. Teodoro comes around with his homemade red wine, purple bare feet explained at last. My stomach feels burny, so I upend my empty glass. Charlie, after a gum rinse, a slow swallow, and a wince, asks for white. The others smile to themselves, but after a canon of similar winces has traveled clockwise around the table, pausing at sly Dan who declares that he doesn't drink anything but pink ladies, they all ask for white.

Bob Rauschenberg photo of me in my *Epic* suit for the first of the *7 New Dances*—the concert earned a blank review from Louis Horst.

Left: *3 Epitaphs*—Bettie de Jong is at left. *Below left*: *Tablet*, with Akiko Kanda at right. Backdrop and costumes by Ellsworth Kelly. *Right*: A shot of *Piece Period*. *Below right*: Bet de Jong in *Piece Period* corset with Sharon Kinney and Renee Kimball in back.

Aureole with Eileen Cropley.

Above: *Aureole*'s original cast members. From left: Sharon Kinney, Renee Kimball, Dan Wagoner and Liz Walton. *Below*: *Junction*. Left to right: Liz Walton, Bet, Shareen Blair, me, Dan Wagoner, and Bonnie Mathis.

Left: With Linda Hodes in *Insects and Heroes. Below*: Left to right: Liz, me, Bonnie, Dan, Maggie Newman.

Fibers. The costume is by Rouben Ter-Arutunian.

Right: *From Sea to Shining Sea*, with Liz, Bet, and me. *Below*: Me in *Scud-orama*. *Opposite above*: *Orbs'* full cast. Left to right: Janet Aaron, Jane Kosminsky, Bet, Dan, and me with mask. *Opposite below*: More *Orbs*.

Opposite above: All the dancers. Giza, Egypt. *Opposite below*: Round the World Tour. *Above left*: Charlie Reinhart with Taylor, my namesake. *Above right*: George Wilson, the Babe. *Right*: My favorite shot of Bet and me taken in front of Sadler's Wells Theatre, London.

Opposite above: Bet in *Big Bertha* title role. Eileen on my right arm, Carolyn Adams on my left in poodle skirt. Alec Southerland designed. *Opposite below*: *Esplanade*. *Above*: *Esplanade*'s premiere with Lila York in front followed by Christopher Gillis, Elie Chaib and rest of cast.

Noah's Minstrels section of *American Genesis* led by Carolyn Adams as Lilith.

Right: *Public Domain. Below*: *Private Domain.* New to the company: Senta Driver at center with Monica Morris at her left, Nicholas Gunn at her right.

Taking a stab at conviviality, Charlie says, "Well, things here are going very well . . . uh. Well, really going very well . . . aren't they?" Getting no response, he tries, "I hear that Rudolf wants to join our company."

"Where'd you hear that?" I ask. "He only said that he'd like to have my parts." I think I hear someone whispering "Good idea," but it's probably only insecurity speaking.

Liz, sniffily nudging her bug-eyed trout to the far side of her plate, says, "Paul, that's not what I heard. I heard that Charlie says *he's* taking over your parts—Sharon, pass the potatoes—that's why you've been taking our company classes, isn't it, Charlie?"

"Bull," says Twyla. "Charles just wants to show off his knobby knees in those birthday tights that Bet gave him. Easy on the potatoes, Liz. You are what you eat."

"True," Sharon chimes in. "Travel is *so* broadening. You won't be able to get into your lovely petal skirt."

"That ugly old rag," Liz replies. "I hate it. Tacet should've done the costumes."

"He's a dirty old mother!" cries Twyla with glee.

"Twyla!" says Bet, even though Twyla hasn't used the complete epithet. All of this was banter, not of high quality, but banter just the same.

"Old Doc's okay," says Liz. "Know what? The next costumes he designs, I'm to get the prettiest, brightest of anybody's . . . you know, yellow. He's promised."

"You don't say," snaps Twyla. "That stinks. You'll look like a five-hundred-pound canary. Yellow's always been *my* color. Just when did he promise you that?"

"Back in New York. He also said that he suspects you and a somebody else of quitting as soon as we get home."

With a pseudosmile of confidence, Charlie tries to steer the conversation back onto thicker ice, then brings up the beautiful old opera house, our beautiful successes there.

"Cut the beautiful crap," I tell him. "All right, company, let's have it. Nobody quits without proper notice. Who's quitting? Who? Ingrates! I want to know right now—Bet, keep your knee to yourself! Which of you?"

But no one will confess. Bet babbles about everybody just being out of sorts, that all we need is to get away from each other once in a while, that we each need to have a single room, and that we should persuade Caterina and Teodoro to unlock some for us. Although these are the only sensible things said all evening, none of us pay much attention because, though her glass is only half-empty, she's swaying in her chair and somewhat slurry.

During dessert many sharp remarks are made about the van and what a pain it is to always have to go everywhere stuffed in it together; intense futility expressed over the lack of an interesting social life; and much carping about the scarcity of hot water, to which Charlie suggests that we all take dips in a nearby brook. Lastly, long lastly, there is a shocking accusation that I've cheated at cards. Only then do we leave the table. The evil meal is all over, but disenchantment eats on.

The next day, as I'm looking for a corner of the villa in which to put one of Twyla's twin brothers, who has shown up with a sleeping bag on his back, I suddenly hear a loud commotion coming from Bet's and Liz's room. It sounds serious. I race upstairs to find Charlie and the girls screaming at each other. Bet has collapsed onto her bed, flat on her back and seemingly in shock. Charlie, standing at one side of the bed, is blasting across her at the girls, who are banded together in a tight knot, and using words that no one has ever heard him use. The girls are shrieking back their hatred for the villa and blaming him for building up their hopes for an enjoyable summer. Before he has a chance to resist, I yank him out of the room and a little ways down the hall where no one can hear. "Charlie," I tell him, pounding my finger on his chest, "don't you ever talk to my girls like that again. You could've been clawed to death!"

After cooling off, we plan the company's escape from the villa, and then I remember Bet, rush back, and find her alone and still lying flat on her back. She's moaning to herself, completely undone by the references to prisons and prisoners that have been accumulating ever since we left New York and wrenching up buried memories of a painful past—her childhood in Java during World War II, when she and her family had been separated from each other and interned in Japanese prison camps.

Once we've left the villa and found single rooms at different hotels in town, the rest of our stay is tolerable, if not pleasant. As it turns out, none of the dancers planned to leave the company, and, for now, it's to remain intact. Though we have escaped after serving an abrasive term in van, villa, and *The Red Room*, we're not quite free of that old fettered feeling—a continual one brought on by our commitment to a strict and restricting profession.

The following year, Alex's reputation growing, a group of his paintings are selected by the Museum of Modern Art in New York to be shown at the '65 Spoleto Festival. His set being too heavy for us to tour with, its discs, rows of strips, terra cotta walls and floor are dismantled and left behind. Washed in the blood of the lamb, minus set and redone to different music, *The Red Room* is to pupate, dry its wings, and eventually become *Post Meridian*.

Thanks to Charlie

Right after Spoleto, four months of American dates keep us dashing from stage to stage. Afterwards, when thinking back, I found it hard to know exactly what was accomplished. Of the tour there remained hardly a trace, either faint or focused, and so I scrabbled through a dull, fat folder marked " '64," hoping to find a clue—a car rental receipt, a laundry slip, a chiropractor's bill, any little excavation that might cause a tingle of recognition and bring meaning to all our perpetual motion.

Sure enough, at last a floor plan of the Guthrie Theater in Minneapolis surfaces, and with it, a tingle of annoyance. The musty diagram brings back a thrust stage with no front curtain and no wings to enter from or escape to, one which made us feel as though we were dancing on a low, flat peninsula endangered by heavy seas, or, whenever we faced front, as though we were dancing on an asymmetrical tongue sticking out at the audience. During the two hours preceding "curtain" time we struggled to solve its limitations by drastically altering the dances. Even so, no matter which way we faced, we couldn't rid ourselves of the feeling that we were being seen sideways.

As I hoped, the memory spreads and deepens as the Guthrie brings back other stages. We were booked onto quite a few defective ones that year— a shaky platform under a leaky tent on Long Island, a frosty barn in Massachusetts, a glassy basketball court in New Jersey which, as usual, had been laid directly on bone-shattering cement, plus other stages, each with at least one major fault. None of them had been good enough. We preferred the sumptuous boards of Europe, their dryness, warmth, and bounce. We had gotten used to them. We deserved and cherished them. We pined for pine—those boards had been easy to love.

For the American tour, having no one except Tacet to gripe to, I took along a spiral pad in which I logged the difficulties of life in general and inadequate road conditions in particular. It and several others were soon filled. Back in New York, I compiled from them a list which I took uptown to Charlie's office, hoping that he would be able to improve future tours. Possibly the road conditions were built-in and unavoidable, but I intended to get them out of my gripe pads and off my mind by dumping them onto Charlie's lap. I was a lot more interested in improvement than in complimenting him on his work for us. He listened patiently without making any countercomplaints or excuses, but, although sympathetic, for a while afterwards he seemed slightly morose. The enthusiasm had been prodded out of him.

Like all firsts—a first swim, a first beer, a first friend—Charlie was the manager to whom subsequent managers were compared. The ones who followed him were less expert in certain areas, excelled him in others. Judy Daykin was more organized, more thorough and attentive to details, and prettier; Neil Fleckman, more tactful in handling difficult sponsors, more supportive to my sometimes unreasonable demands, and, in personal appearance, less razor-knicked and more fastidious. Bob Yesselman was to be more of a buffer between me and the day-to-day business operations, more able to improve our New York seasons and the dancers' working conditions. Like Charlie, each manager was devoted to the company. Their wholehearted efforts went far beyond the call of duty and nine-to-five hours.

Yet for many years after Charlie left, his presence lingered. An indelible residue of him remained, a sort of birthmark. It was Charlie who practically invented the company; Charlie whom I had the pleasure of griping to, chewing out, threatening, and hardly ever giving in to; Charlie whose pride prevented him from stooping to excuses whenever accused of slip-ups; Charlie who took us to the ends of the earth and who on all our travels together was never heard to complain. In secret he collected the foreign reviews, had them translated, and stapled them to press releases without letting me read them lest they go to my head. And it was Charlie, faithful Charlie, who gave me my most meaningful compliment: he named his son Taylor.

The diagram of the Guthrie ignited a tingle of recognition that started in my head, then worked its way down my spine, spread as I remembered other aggravating theaters, and finally, as Charlie entered the picture, settled into a knot in the nether regions. With the memories came an alarming realization that I was not and never have been a lone rock. The company and I were a house of cards, each trouper delicately balanced, simultaneously leaning on and propping up the other. At any given moment an unseasonable breeze could have toppled us flat. But with Charlie as a windbreak, the company somehow continued.

And the tingle resulted in an alarming realization. It was flabbergasting that I had never properly expressed my appreciation to Charlie. And it was positively shameful, really appalling, that whenever I had turned my thoughts back to him, instead of visualizing a man of importance and generous influence, the first thing that always jumped to mind was a rain-drenched comedian high up in the Alps, shuffling off to seek benzine, accidentally stubbing his toe, and causing general laughter.

Paris and London

In early November '64, following the eccentric American stages, we continue to commute transatlantically—open in Paris at the Champs-Elyseés for a short run as part of the Theatre of Nations Festival. We've been selected as the United States's representative at the five-country festival; others here are the Kiev Opera Ballet, the Royal Swedish Ballet, the London Festival Ballet, and the Ballet de France. Prizes are awarded for best company, best dancers, best decor, etc. I'm awarded a gold star for choreography. The dances are *Aureole*, *3 Epitaphs*, *Piece Period*, and *Scudorama*. Unable to stay for the award ceremonies, we hurry off to London.

By now, Margot Fonteyn's gala matinee at the Theatre Royal, Drury Lane, in aid of the Royal Academy of Dancing has become a permanent part of London's ballet life. Britain is engaged in catching up with movements in American dance, and, likely due to our country's growing prestige abroad, we've been invited by Dame Margot to be in the gala, the first American modern dancers so honored. It's to be a sneak preview of our two-and-a-half-week run at the "downtown" Shaftesbury Theater.

Backstage after the gala, we're presented to Princess Marina, having been rehearsed by a gentleman who showed us the correct way to curtsey or bow and instructed us to address the princess as "ma'am," which, by the way, is what I was brought up to call all women. Besides being the first American moderns in the gala, we are the first of any nation to meet the princess in bare feet.

Martha and her company have danced in London twice, the second time a tremendous success, and her visits have paved the way for other American moderns. London has seen Cunningham and Ailey just prior to us. After our Shaftesbury engagement, Clive Barnes writes the following:

> Some of the adulation accorded Graham was that which Britain traditionally offers distinguished veterans of the theatre. Merce Cunningham had the news value of being wild and way-out, and also had John Cage to interest music students and Robert Rauschenberg to bring in the art students. Alvin Ailey attracted some of his audience by the magic combination of jazz and negroes. Indeed the only modern dance visitor not to have special circumstances surrounding him was Paul Taylor. And although Taylor received rapturous press reception,

his audiences, while highly enthusiastic, were markedly sparser than those of his colleagues.

They certainly were. The Shaftesbury contained numerous seats, vastly empty, and reading about how terrific we were only to go onstage and dance for almost nobody was puzzling. Dan explained that all our viewers had been deeply moved—into a basement down the block. Nevertheless, we were wined and dined and treated royally by Mary, duchess of Roxburgh, and especially by Robin Howard, who was responsible for bringing both Martha and us to London. On blind faith he had hired my troupe sight unseen. We were what he called his "second attack." He had intended to shake up the London dance scene, in spite of, or perhaps because of, his prime minister grandfather, his baron-and-lady family, and his Rudyard Kipling godfather. Intent on presenting modern dance, Robin thought it worthwhile to tweak the establishment, but his primary aim was to transfuse new blood into British dance, a goal that he was to soon achieve by forming the London Contemporary Dance Theatre and its school.

Someone, probably his business advisor, thought it a good idea, maybe even a matter of life and death, for us to give a lecture-demonstration at the theater. A few well-chosen words about my dances, and whatever theories I might have, would bring in the crowds, he thought. I quickly made up some combinations of steps lifted from our dances and tried to think up and memorize different names for them.

"This here's the piddledepoop step from *Aureole*. And you're going to like this one—it's called a whatsis. Now Miss Walton will demonstrate one of her favorites, which looks a little like a changement, but we call it an egg beater. Put them all together and you have here a piddledepoop–whatsis– egg beater.

"And now, ladies and gentlemen, please observe Miss Walton . . . and . . .

"Thank you, Miss Walton; thank you, ladies and gentlemen. . . . Thank you, thank you. . . . Really, it was nothing."

I might have developed some theories to impart had there been time. Trip and Recovery would have been a good one, or Manifest Balance. And I might have snuck in a little of Delsarte's metaphysic Law of Consequences for good measure, but it was too emotional, even if it did have evangelistic overtones which encouraged Victorian women to throw off their corsets. I was also familiar with his Eurythmic Way of Thinking, but it seemed too mental to bring up. Maybe I could have told everybody about the time I did a Dalcroze music visualization to a Delibes suite for harp played underwater. Translated into human terms, the harpist's bubbles, rising and breaking at the surface, would have been a charming compositional detail.

The von Laban Directional Decahedron had been patiently explained to me, but not well enough—something about the dancer imagining himself within a large geometric shape; presumably, the bigger the dancer, the bigger the shape.

And Tacet, full of inspiration and owlish esoterics, had once tried out an original theory on me. He called it Streamlining Your Steps. To begin with, you were supposed to get into the Tulip Position. My legs were not made for the Tulip Position. "No one ever said that Art would not hurt," he chided. "Meditation is all; it is our guiding force. Inspiration and exploration are all there in the breathing. First we inhale the wonders of a fresh new day, then we exhale all worldly travail . . . inhale . . . exhale . . ."

"When do we get to move?" I inquired.

"Patience, Sonny, all will be revealed in due course." Then he left me to practice by myself, but when I woke up my steps were as unstreamlined as ever.

Even with Tacet's help I could not lecture on dance theory. Instead, I simply asked the audience if they had any questions. They not only had many questions but gave most of the answers. After a while, leaning dangerously from her box, a smallish lady said, "Young man, would you please speak up?" This did not surprise me at all, because I had not said anything. The smallish woman said she was Madame Marie Rambert. "Speak up, speak up!" she said. I did not want to, but I lay down on my stomach, where I could get closer to a floor microphone.

I had read of her views on the dependence of choreography on music, so, having been asked, I told her that, on the whole, I agreed with her that a dance should be able to stand on its own two feet, and that I would have made more dances of that type but had found that audiences tended to get jittery in silence and, anyway, added disturbing noises of their own. This was asking for trouble, and, sure enough, it led to someone's asking about which comes first, the music or the dance. I avoided the question by replying that I believed that if a dance and its music were intertwined right, the question should not even come up, and that my highest goal was to dissolve into an absolute and utter chiropody of tonal and pladsome spatial linkages, whatever that meant. Folks always like it when you talk over their heads.

Well, then they asked me to explain the humor of my dances. To that I answered, "Humor? What humor?" (What I thought funny was hardly ever what audiences laughed at, and then only because they were reading something into it, so there was no use getting off on a wild goose chase.)

Several people started criticizing Martha, and then Merce, and baited me to join in, but I was onto them. They wanted to see me do my famous Merce and Martha imitations. But I didn't come to London to publicly expose my relatives, even though within the family I had once heard the words "naughty boy" being bandied about.

After our return to New York, London's leading dance magazine named me "dancer of the year." I was very proud of the citation and hung it in the studio where it could be easily noticed. Perhaps no one will mind if I include parts of it here:

In any year Paul Taylor's London debut would have been an event. . . .
And yet it might easily not have been Taylor whom we have singled out here. It might have been Merce Cunningham, whom we also first saw, by coincidence, standing motionless as he waited to dance a piece almost classical in mood although again in a very idiosyncratic manner; or perhaps Alvin Ailey. . . . Or again it might have been one of the many other fine dancers in the companies of these three American men whose chief point of similarity is that each is unique, pursuing his own lively way through the varied avenues of the dance. . . .
So Paul Taylor stands here partly as a symbol of some thirty dancers and about two dozen choreographers, musicians and lighting artists who both entertained and enlightened us this year. And at the same time we honor him in his own right as an original, subtle and surprising artist. . . . In 1964, his London debut was a part of a great awakening. In any year it would have been an event.

From Sea to Shining Sea

"Trouping, trouping, and more trouping, wearisome times on the road. Perchance might we not pause and settle into some other subject?"

"Sure, Pops, but what?"

"Some topic of pith, a subjective subject with humanistic import. Why not chronicalize your personal relationships, explaining how present ones have been affected by those of the past? Twould be within the classical tradition to begin with family background."

"You mean about you?"

"Precisely. And kindly include the consummatory bliss of our multifold marriages."

Once, long ago in the primeval ooze, my forefather was a lonely trailblazer, a single cell that developed the odd habit of splitting in two. He then split himself into four, the four became eight, and so forth and so on, even though halving was difficult, and hurt. He then developed an even odder habit: the hankering to reunite—that is, each to form himself back into one, a feat accomplished after obtaining foremothers. Though the pressing and pushing was enjoyable, it didn't quite work. I mean, it only resulted in producing offspring that weren't exactly the same as the original. This hankering, right or wrong, is something that's been passed along up to the present.

Now then, since this is supposed to be an autobio, not a treatise on biological mysteries, I should mention that, unlike my forefather, I've found it painless to separate my various personas one from the other and, having done so, easy to keep them apart. For instance, PT the choreographer never confuses himself with Boss the expert on studio trash removal, or PT the objet d'art loather with PT the insect enthusiast, and all that. And it has always been particularly easy to disconnect myself from others of the species.

"True, true, my boy. That you do quite well, and justly so. Most of the species is not worth diddlyspit. Should not we soon be chronicling my multifold marriages?"

As for reuniting, that's something else again. Though it's my own business, I'll say that it's a feat that has brought many happy hours but, so far, hasn't worked itself into a procedure acceptable to concert audiences. In addition, there's been the confusing matter of whom to reunite with. Whenever oneness with someone is attempted, more often than not it somehow turns out to be imperfect and not what you'd call a reproductive relationship. It's real sad.

Now for the matter of marriage. As an institution, I mean. Frankly, I've been unable to understand it as a sensible way of life. Seems too locked in, and like a fad that'll be passé in a few years. If necessary, instead of obtaining wives I'd be glad to settle for a couple of hired flunkies.

"Son, I do wish you had not said that."

Even more than flunkies, I'd like several children—that is, if there don't have to be mothers. And no babies. Definitely not babies. The only thing babies are good for is crawling away.

But as to forming other types of relationships, I'm not against it, have had many, although a large proportion have been unintentional and dearly paid for, such as the ones I'm forced into with the IRS and various traffic violation departments. Still others, ones somewhat similar to the relationship with my company, have grown like monstrous hothouse weeds that now and then seem to twine about my neck, demanding much more attention than I would ever have dreamed possible. And then there have been the undemanding ones. Gone are the days when I was casting around for those. (Found some that seemed okay for a while, but they didn't lead anywhere.) As Tacet says, those kind are not worth diddlyspit.

"*Au contraire,* sonny—unworked-for relationships involving easy persons are *less* than diddlyspit."

Yep, and that they never panned out was keen-o-peachy.

On looking back, I see unworthy relationships, yet also worthy ones. Some relationships went somewhere and some didn't. I see many relationships, many faces, people whose lives crossed mine, faces I loved and faces I only looked at, nice people, nerdy people, some once dear and now permanently gone somewhere. Yes sir, there've been oodles of relationships. There must've been. Why, for example, a big one has been with John Rawlings, who's seven feet tall. Although we never see eye to eye, never get close in physical ways, our relationship is one that's productive and—

"Dear boy, that one is an unpithful matter, and you keep straying far from what we had in mind. Best move on to Art."

"Right. What about my new dance?"

"I suppose that will have to do. Proceed."

The nicest thing about my new dance is working out its costumes with designer John Rawlings. Unlike some designers I've tried to collaborate with, John is unassuming and not only out for himself. His credits in the programs are always an understatement, because he always contributes many other things besides the costume designs—intangible things that rub off, such as his enthusiasm for music and make-believe. And there's a citrus twinkle in his eye, a knack for spotting human absurdities. Just like he is, his designs are bold and magnanimous.

Before deciding what the costumes will be, like a fast game of Ping-Pong, we bat ideas back and forth, many spinning out of bounds and ending up so dented and changed that we're no longer able to tell which of us first served them.

He's one of the few people I've ever really collaborated with. He has an uncanny grasp of what the emerging dance is trying to be, of its possible strengths, but has an untactful way of pointing out the flaws. Even so, these criticisms—acid on a griddle—are beyond price. He's an architect by profession and brings his sense of space, form, and color to each dance. His costumes are better than beautiful; they're fiercely right.

One time when working on *Piece Period*, I showed him the dance and asked what he thought we should wear. "Bananas. I see bunches of large bananas," he murmured, shielding his eyes. After discarding all notions of fruit, we tossed other ideas around; but whenever we start working on a new dance he always begins by describing the same old vision. That's why the dancers and I call him Bananas.

"Sonny, shall we not get to the creative role that we ourselves played in your new dance?"

"Patience, Pops, it's right around the corner."

In '65, while sitting on a battered costume trunk at the Sixth Avenue studio, I'm waiting for the dancers to come rehearse. Thin March sun is piercing the skylight and forming a rectangular shape of glare where it hits the floor. The floor is burnished from being rubbed by so many bare feet, and I'm wishing that it was bigger so that the new piece could be of a scale suitable to a huge opera house; but until a larger studio can be found we'll have to make do.

Because of the perpetual touring it's been difficult to find time to concentrate on new stuff. And the road is beginning to take a toll on everyone's energy and health. Bet's knee keeps acting up, and a resprained left ankle often causes me to be unable to get through a performance without falling. As a part of my preperformance warm-up, however, I practice various ways to get up quick.

The decision to show the new dance in New York without first trying it out on the road—was it a good idea? No, sure wasn't, but too late to change now—theater's already booked, and—good grief, crawling along there on the floor—a dear little cucaracha, followed by dear little bambinos. It's a reminder to hide my box of Indonesian butterflies before Twyla decides to borrow that, too.

Tharp, you are to return my lovely ancient skull found in Israel. Twerp, you are a moocher. Thwat, you are to die very soon. And not from the painful things that I'll choreograph for you today, not from the piercing slivers of glass that I'll strew on the floor tomorrow, but in a couple of days when you least expect it, just when you are again indulging in that awful habit of yours which started in London. You've already forgotten? I mean the one where you go around downing my dances to credulous London critics. And so now, just as you're feeling secure in your errands of sin, just when you're flashing your beady dark eyes in avidity, flailing your fingers and hopping up and down, right there in midair you are to contract a petrification of your little hind legs and a fatal swelling and stiffening of your little barking tongue. But first your body will be subjected to elephantine ticks. I think what I dislike most about you are your strong ankles.

How could you besmirch me, Twyla? I can forgive anything, anything save treason. We returned from London. I told you it seemed as if you didn't want to be in the company, but you hotly denied it, remember? And then together we decided for you to take a six-month leave of absence anyway—you'd have time to know for sure. And then after a shorter time (maybe when you heard of this New York season?), you said you were quite sure you wanted to come back, and I agreed. Really didn't want to lose you, Twyla honey, but why can't you be less abrasive, less watch-spring tense? Because you're talented and insecure and driven, that's why. Like me. And in spite of how it seems, I know you like my work, in the way that I covet Merce's beautiful *Summerspace,* and I know that you're critical, the way I've been of Martha. These things are canonic; there's a pattern somewhere. . . .

"Hi, Sharon. You surprised me. How's the old married lady? Glad you've come early. After you've gotten into your practice duds we'll set some combinations and teach them to the others when they come."

Now married, Sharon has given notice, a long, considerate one. She plans to have a home life and children and is making sure that the troupe won't be inconvenienced. She'll be teaching her parts to the other dancers before she goes. Because of the long, close work together, her departure won't be easy for any of us. Thinking of our loss is a stabbing thing.

My eyes are beginning to well—the glare from the floor, no doubt. Sharon disappears behind the dressing area's tattered burlap curtains.

John Binder had come to tell me of their marriage and to ask me what would be a convenient time for her to leave. Knowing that trying to hold on to her would only delay the inevitable, I'd suppressed an urge to catapult him through the ceiling, and we'd then worked out the date.

Getting off the trunk and dragging over to the tape machine, I'm trying to focus on the new dance. While Sharon dresses I listen to the Ives score. The notes sound doleful and boring and remind me of a door swinging back and forth on rusty hinges. A discordant voice is saying, "Son, great good as well as great evil can come from boredom."

The old geezer always gives advice about how to start making a dance. Inspiration is all, says he, and it is best to begin by revving up your muse. He referred to his as Our Lady of Perpetual Impetus. Mine's too fat and won't rev, is almost always out to lunch, and there's never any time to sit around waiting for her to float back. Worry is my muse. I work myself into a panic, imagine a ferocious clock breathing down my neck, or that the world is expecting a lot. Instead of reading van Loon's *Cosmology of Ce-*

lestial Bodies, Black Holes, and *Human Ids,* as Dr. T recommends, I study the worst of my reviews and let unopened bills accumulate.

"Well! Son, if you are so foolish as to reject inspiration, then the least you can do is align yourself with Truth, Sincerity, and Pretension."

"Doc, I've found that all three, separately or combined, prove to be a terrible experience. Instead, I go for untruths. By that I mean stylized realities."

"Oh, bother and breadsticks, we can do naught with you. We had hoped to secure for you a throne in the Dance Pantheon alongside of Nirska the Butterfly Lady, of whom there is none greater, but no, you have to have your own ideas. Son, if you persist in these flagrant vagabond thoughts . . ."

Turning my attention back to the tape machine, I focus on the work at hand. The new piece is being started not only without inspiration but without any ideas at all. I'm just going to throw some moves together and trust that eventually a dance will begin to emerge that'll be making its own rules and telling me what's needed. Certain gestures have seemed vaguely interesting of late, so when Sharon is dressed, I toss a long string of them at her. She absorbs them quickly with her usual gusto while I struggle to think up enough to keep pace with her.

"Okay, Tweetie, let's see them all again. But this time would you please face the side wall?"

I don't really want to see the gestures again—this is only a way to stall for time. She reperforms the sequence, and, to my surprise, a curious thing happens. The linear shape of the gestures, because they've been designed to be seen from the front, kind of erase themselves, some becoming blurred, others completely undecipherable. It's fascinating, but just as I'm about at the peak of my pique, on the brink of some remarkable disclosure, Niagara-like splashing sounds come from the bathroom.

"Oh, nuts, not again. Be right back, Tweets."

As usual, the sink has been left running. Spillage to cause banging at door to studio in exactly three minutes. Tenants downstairs should be getting used to their ceiling coming down by now. Must be patient with Babe— deaf folks can't hear that they've left water running. No good with taps, but Babe's tops at turning lights off—enjoys the smooth comfort of dimness, bright light often uncomfortable to his acute visual sense. While shutting off the tap I notice my toothbrush on the sink, then return.

"Sharon, where were we?"

"I was being sideways."

"That was very interesting. I've forgotten why. Never mind, let's . . . well, let's practice some tooth-brushing motions."

The usual motions of brushing are enlarged so that they'll project from a stage, and gum display exaggerated. As we're deep into the best way to brush, Dan arrives. Stopped short in his tracks, he seems dumbfounded, then exchanges glances with Babe, who contributes a favorite gesture of his own—the sign for insanity. Ignoring it, Sharon and I go on practicing.

It's strange to see her without her sidekick, Renee, who after four years with the company has just left. Wish I'd been able to understand her better. Had I given her one role, one challenge, one compliment too few? She's now also married—left me a note that said she hoped to dance with some other company, that she didn't need to cling to mine, then at the end added, "Their fear of no other dancing and no other life holds your dancers to you, rather than respect."

I'm trying to focus on Sharon, but Renee keeps glaring through. Could her last words have been valid? True or not, they were an effective parting shot. Missile accomplished, beautiful Renee.

Liz arrives. "Hi, Big Cheese! Hi, everybody!"

At least she's still here. Sure surprised me yesterday—no temper. Was nice of her to let me kick her new boyfriend out of the studio. That had been good for him, might make him less loathsome.

Bet beelines in determinedly. She has no artifice, no nonsense, and, fortunately, no boyfriend. If its den mother should ever leave, the troupe might collapse.

"Hey there, dear Bet!"

She isn't seeming to hear me, is continuing to talk to one of the new girls whom she has in tow. The girl's name momentarily escapes me. Dolly? No, Molly, Molly Moore. Nickname Moo. Bet's known her from Martha's and brought her to our audition. She and Laura Dean, the other new girl, are to replace Renee and Sharon.

Now the studio, indeed the whole of midtown, is being filled by a tiny presence.

"Hiya, Twyla. How's the cold?"

"Excellent, excellent! Actually, it's bloody hell. But what's it to you, Big Cheese?"

The granny glasses, floor-length scarf, and far-out hat are doing nothing for my munchkin's appearance, but her dancing still looks great, and I've never lost my fondness for her.

"Hello, Laura." Her lashes are like a shy llama's.

"Heyya, Danny." His splay like a galloping colt's.

Troupe now a big ten instead of eight—two more than payroll can bear. Karen, sloe-eyed Karen who followed us to Spoleto, is late. Thinking of her gives me a boding of some sort. Both she and Sharon have been looking a little big in the bread basket lately, and you know what that means. Don't know what's worse—satisfied pregnancy or edgy frustration. Speak of the devil . . .

" 'Lo, Karen. Any morning sickness today?"

"Paul! You know I'm not married."

Better be thinking up steps to teach everybody. Rats, now there's the phone. "Hello, Taylor's Meat Market here. Quality hams. Busy now, call you back? Hello? Hello?"

The Babe chortles, slaps my back, then takes the receiver and places the correct end at my ear.

"Who's this? Oh, howdy, Charlie."

After peppering me with pleasantries, Charlie says that he's sorry to have to break the news, but that we're not going to be able to dance in New York after all, that there's no backing for our City Center season. When I'm through moaning, I suggest asking Dick Barr if he'll help, but Charlie says Dick's tied up in other productions, that even if he could, we wouldn't be able to raise the needed ten thousand, and that lighter Tommy is also unavailable. And would I please hurry up and send the girls up to his office (still Isadora Bennett's closet) with their photos and resumés.

"Yeah, yeah, Charlie. You want to look the new girls over, right? Well, I've got good news—you're gonna go for one of them for sure. Her name's Moo."

To lose the season was as incomprehensible as it was depressing. After all the miserable miles on the road, and the endless time, to perform in the dance capital of the world would've meant a lot. Now maybe more of the gang will quit. Will have to think of a way to break this to them gently. But later.

"Okay, everybody. You all here? Startin' time! Sharon, you show the others how we do teeth while I work with Dan and Molly.

"Let's see . . . what we need are some pugnacious-type gestures. [My disappointment over the season speaking:] Dan, how 'bout if you punch Molly in the belly? [Abortion speaking:] Do like this . . . Moo, don't run away, come back here."

I pretend to punch and Molly moos loudly, but when gentle Dan copies, she doesn't react painfully enough. I go find Babe's toy horn and hand it to her. "Now, honey, when Dan socks, you toot. Very good, now that looks like you mean it." I'm not understanding this bit of business, it just seems that maybe it'll fit in somewhere. Maybe if we make up a whole collection of random gestures there'll be some way to use them, and maybe I'll even run across a point of view to work from.

"Dan, now something for you and me. By the way, for months I've been seeing this dance crystal clear, already have it all worked out in detail. This is going to be the conversational sequence. You stand right here and we'll face each other like this . . . no, you should be two inches more off to the left. You know me, I always know exactly how things have to be. Now I'll do this talking stuff with my hands, and you just stand there and look like you're listening intently."

Offstage it's always the other way round. When Dan prattles, I listen, sometimes. As I'm wiggling my hands at Dan's face, Babe comes over and signs, "Is that a dance? Why you not make good dances like on TV?"

"Come on, can't you see I'm busy?"

"Today I buy fish for dinner. I see poor woman in street. I give her money."

"That's nice, Babe. Why not go home and cook the fish?"

"You talk to Dan. Why not talk with me? We not talk today. Terrible. I like big talks."

He was right. His was another kind of punch. Slightly offended, Babe leaves for the plastic bag factory.

Echoing his words, I sign to Dan, "Over there. Big fish. And over there. Terrible. Terrible! Look there. Poor woman," then add a crude sign of my own devising and some flowery ones followed by Italianesque flops of both hands, giving all a pleasing pulse for the sake of rhythmic interest. As a logical statement, it doesn't carry much weight, but the audience wouldn't get it anyway, right? (Wrong. I'd underrated at least one viewer. In '81 in *The Atlantic* writer Holly Brubach is to interpret the signs as "starting out something like 'Fish gotta swim, birds gotta fly . . .' and in no time progressing to a curvaceous woman and a four-letter verb, in Italian.")

"Okay, Bet, let's work out something for you."

She sails over, or "shovels" in de Jongese, snapping her leotard down in back on the way, a motion more decorative than functional, seeing as she's flat as an ironing board in back and the leotard would only creep up again. She's been filling in the new girls on company dos and don'ts, or maybe showering them with eccentric versions of past tours. Am almost sure that she hasn't been mentioning whatever it is that's making her seem so distant ever since our return from London, and am wondering if the older girls have had something to do with it. According to them, Bet's been carrying a torch.

I show her some more of Babe's signs, giving them exact counts and going over their shape and dynamics carefully because, though our Dutch Treat's a fairly fast learner, she's superthorough and prefers an orderly presentation of material. The more demanding the moves, the better she likes them. But her fingers aren't too coordinated, become disoriented. The signs don't fit her tiny hands, and wouldn't project far if they did. She's struggling gallantly to cross her fingers, but they keep popping apart, yet she's not about to give up her notion that she can do anything given her.

"Let's just forget the signing, okay?" I say, which doesn't go down too well.

"Oh, Paul," she says impatiently, "don't be so dispatient!"

Though her words are sometimes off, both her tone and dancing are, if anything, self-assured. To take full advantage of this, I convince her to move on to a series of declamatory gestures.

Dynamo Danny has now run out of things to learn and if not given something soon, is apt to have a meltdown right before our eyes. I motion him over and show him how to huddle interestingly on the floor so that Bet can be all stiff-spined authority while sitting on his back. She will be enjoying it more than he will, but that's all right. Danny being a relative newcomer, it's only fair that he not be given too much of too much importance to do too soon—not that there's anything fair about dancing—and the pedestal that he's making will point up the star presence which Bet's aficionados always approve of most wholeheartedly.

Settling back against the mirrors and yawning from the repetition that Bet thinks is necessary to perfect her moves, I'm drifting back a year or so to when I was sick and she came calling. Can't remember what was wrong with me, but whatever, it had locked me in bed. Babe had been playing part-time intern/dietician by serving beans—can and all—and Ritz crackers. He would arrange them on an atlas, lovingly add a spray of broom straws in a milk of magnesia bottle, set it all down at the bedside just out of reach, then disappear proudly. There's nothing in the whole world quite so frustrating as deaf people when you're immobilized, hungry, and yelling for dinner. Bet knew that I'm not an ideal patient and that I don't accept illness gracefully, so she'd dropped by to cheer me up, maybe say something nutritional to Babe. Smiling a firm smile, she smoothed out the wrinkles at the foot of my bed, then perched there supremely, the way she's perching now. (The bed in the narrow, cardboarded-off area at the back of the studio consists of a lumpy mat on a platform that I'd created of diagonally striped police barricade boards, then painted baby blue. Since it's illegal to live at the loft, the mat is rolled up and hidden during the day in case building inspectors come to call. My bed—not all that important in itself—should be considered in relationship to other environmental details, in order to build up a composite picture so mixed up that it's almost magnificent.)

Bet, after treating me to a detailed update on the weather, then offered to play any game of my choice. This was a generous gesture—she hates all types of games, and they hate her back. I picked the latest craze, Botticelli. After carefully reviewing its rules, we started to play. She, of course, insisted on adding her own rules and inserting her own nonwords. The game got hopelessly ensnarled, then soon died of strangulation. Undaunted, Bet—

glowingly triumphant—reverted to the weather. I tried to respond with
unhearing "um"s and "aw"s, but when she started hitting me with the
whole week's forecast I wasn't able to stand one more humidity index.
Unable to control my own saturation point, and there being no escape, I
burst out, "Get *out* of here! You're driving me up the wall!"

I regretted it the minute I said it. (I am a nice person.)

Unruffled, she went on sitting there, reaching out to lay her hand lightly
on top of mine. I turned my palm to hers and we stayed several minutes like
that, not looking at each other. Then our gazes met, asking unsaid things:

Paul, don't you care?

Sure, dear Bet. Haven't I ever mentioned that I love you? I shouldn't
marry, but I love you hopelessly.

Nothing was out in the open, nothing resolved, nothing is changed.

"All right, dear Bet, we can't go on practicing these gestures forever.
Come on everybody, let's work on some new stuff."

Each dancer is given a different combination of steps, and a tricky arrangement of crisscrossing paths is set. There is one spot that causes Bet
and Karen to swoop dangerously close to each other, so I suggest a slight
spatial adjustment, but when the pattern is repeated, the two girls crash
into each other.

"Bet, I thought you were going to move upstage so Karen could get by."

"I can't, there's no room."

"You can. There is."

"I can't."

"Can. Okay, why not?"

"The floor's too slippery. It's the humidity."

"*Aaaggghhh!!!* Excuses, excuses! Just do like I say."

"But it won't work. That one doesn't solve nothin'."

"Come on, I'm not asking for anything unreasonable."

As I explain the spacing again, I can see her mind spinning off in a million
unrelated directions, and all my demands would be met with "can't"s and
"but"s. My stomach has begun to feel queasy, and the other dancers are
waiting uncomfortably for us to finish our spat and pretending they're somewhere else. Mercifully, things come to a halt when Bet locks herself onto
the barre and declares, "Isn't no good to try it anymore."

I look towards the others to detect some sympathy for my predicament,
but there is none. "Quittin' time," I say with mock cheer.

The rehearsal over, and none too soon, I rush to the bathroom, close the
door quietly, pull the chain, and try to regulate my gagging to the sound of
the flush. When I return, the studio is already empty. They arrived one by
one but sure did leave as a unit. No "so long"s, nothing. Slumping down on

the costume trunk, I notice three things: my toenails need clipping, the glare on the floor has moved three yards towards the trunk, and, close by my elbow, someone's waist elastic has been left draped over the barre like a long, sad, passive worm.

The New York performances off. So what?—new piece never would've been any good anyway. Damn new dance—no point of view, no form, no nothin'. And those gestures were a hopeless mistake. The dancers sense it too. Balky jerks, absolutely no cooperation. How can I kill with the fewest stains? Maybe we should disband. Why, oh why, can't they be buckets of paint, or Silly Putty? I should've stuck to art, wouldn't need people. Will apply for another Guggenheim and go live in Tahiti forever.

That settled, I take some antacid for my stomach and fill the fire bucket with ice water for my swollen ankle. The aching is nothing compared to the ongoing funk. Why is Bet so rebellious? So stubborn? So dead right? And where, *where*, are her haunches? And why are the other dancers always on her side? But they're a family, my family, my dear family. Are they a family? They are, also a collection of unrelated maniacs. If our relationship isn't fully personal, which it isn't, and at the same time not strictly business, which it isn't either, then what the heck is it?

What we all need is someone to organize, finance, and package us, someone who'll have the faith to invest himself in our work. Mr. B had Lincoln; Martha, Bethsabee; Merce, John Cage.

Forget it. There's never going to be anyone like them.

Despair presses closer and comes crashing down. I glance fondly, even hotly, up to the ceiling, picturing myself at the shadowy void at the ledge of the roof. Though the drop seems tempting, less awful than the void of solitude that'll be hounding me through the years, the ledge isn't quite the solution. But I rise from the costume trunk and go there anyway. The air might clear deadly cobwebs of gloom from my head.

The wind up there is blowing humid and chilly. Aren't any butterflies this time—isn't the season. Spotting a comic book (Babe's?) lying embedded in the gooey roofing tar, I pull it free. Things are sticking to its front cover— a hairpin, a bitten bagel, a hollow remnant of an unfortunate water bug. In primary colors, shining through the bits of debris, is Richie Rich, Babe's favorite cartoon character. Little boy Rich is loaded. The Babe, George Wilson. And George Tacet, too—my friends, sure, but neither is exactly a de Rothschild. Well, better learn to be content with folks as they are and with things as they come. I'm already rich, already have investors in me: yes, the troupe. And you, my boy, are a brace of bees. You are Castor and Pollux, David and Goliath, Merrill, Lynch, Fenner, and Smith, and, last but not least, if he doesn't get the upper hand or become the dead-end mirror that I break my nose against, there's Taylor and Tacet—me and my old Pleistocene shadow. Watch out, world—what a team we'll be!

Though we've lost our season, work on the new dance continues (also on 9 *Dances with Music by Corelli*—another new piece—*Duet* to music by Haydn, and *Post Meridian—The Red Room* sans set and with a new, commissioned score by Evelyn Lohoeffer). Even though I've no idea what I've wrought, or the slightest of costume concepts to suggest, we show the gestural stuff to Bananas. Afterwards I ask if he's seeing fruit again.

Unhesitatingly, he answers, "I see red, white, and blue."

"No stars?"

"Stars, yes, and stripes. Get it?"

"Hey, that's terrific!"

Then I give the seven-footer a smooch on the nearest thing I can reach— the knot of his necktie. "I must've been blind. The dance has been trying to tell me all along. Everything's there—all we have to do is revise. Bet will be the Statue of Liberty sitting on her rock, which will then sink her slowly into the bay. Dan and some other pilgrims will disembark from the *Mayflower* and be met by an Indian who'll welcome them with sign language, then get trampled by them. The static poses can be changed into living pictures—you know, Iwo Jima flag raising, Betsy Ross sewing, minutemen limping. All-American corn. Beautiful! The toothbrushing will represent American consumer goods. We'll have a Supermouse, a motorcycle antihero, a whatever. Okay, John, they won't like it down south, but since you insist, we can have the Ku Klux Klan. The dance is old Miss America's wrinkles, patriotism past its prime.

"The sideways gestures, they can be seen as if off in the wings. A seedy-looking troupe will have been performing the whole shebang. It's us, U.S. The crisscrossing patterns—we'll slow them down to aimless wanderings done after a final curtain—one solitary clap of applause—and we'll be wearing our own ratty bathrobes. That'll make a swell contrast to the troupe's glitzy spangles."

Some irrelevant gestures are turned into salutes, Sharon's vaguely flat-footed solo into a clattery tap dance. We go from generalizations to specifics. The dance, thanks to citrusy Bananas, has at last shown its true colors, and a point of view's been found. The title, *From Sea to Shining Sea*, is another of his contributions. A scaffold is shaped to support all the bits and pieces, which fall naturally into three main categories. The three sections are subtitled (1) "Send Me the Wretched Refuse of Your Teeming Shore," (2) "Us," and (3) "Living Pictures."

What had started out as a random collection of gestures has metamorphosed into what some might call social satire. Others might be content to call it funny business.

"John, just one little thing—I don't think we can afford all these costumes."

"Not to worry, cheapskate. You can sort through your dead ones—they're probably grungy enough. And I'll get others ready made on Fourteenth Street. We'll both scavenge sidewalks around here in the garment district for remnants to make other costumes out of."

Just then the phone interrupts us with its jangly fit.

"Yo! Taylor's Cants Dumpany here, Taylor himself speaking. You shake 'em, we break 'em. . . . Oh, it's you, Charlie. What's the news this time?"

This is the morning that birds sing, and when the rectangle of glare under the skylight is a softly glowing pool of pink. Charlie is saying that Dick and Clinton are to present us on Broadway after all. The Ambassador is available, and Billy Ritman, filling in for Tommy, will be doing our lights. Even raising the necessary ten thousand isn't out of the question. Dick and Clinton will be helping, and Charlie has been passing the hat. Other contributors are to be the Blankman Foundation, Lincoln Kirstein, Sam and Judy Peabody, the Jerry Robbins Foundation, Carroll Russell, and Nancy Lassalle.

After the season ends, rights for the Ives music become too costly, and so *Sea* is revised to a new and more fitting score written by John Herbert McDowell. The dance is then often performed at home and abroad. Eventually, a dance panel in Washington decides that *Sea* is anti-American and recommends to the State Department that it be dropped from our repertoire on future goodwill tours abroad. Since there have been no complaints from audiences abroad, however, we are allowed to keep it in. The State Department concludes that *Sea*'s critical view of our country is an affectionate one and that its slings and arrows are outweighed by its being a worthy example of artistic freedom here, something that oppressed countries might very well envy.

Nevertheless, in '81, a number of classic ballet lovers at a benefit performance are unhappy with *Sea* as a vehicle for stars Mikhail Baryshnikov, Rudolf Nureyev, Gwen Verdon, Hermione Gingold, and wordsmiths Betty Comden and Adolph Green. Evidently, flashier steps are desired by dissenting ballet lovers, who hoot a bit—something I hope isn't upsetting to the stars, as they've been generous to perform with us and wonderful to work with. I vaguely agree with the vocalizing out front, but can't get too miffed, since the benefit generates enough income for my company, without guest stars, to cover expenses for the following three-week City Center season.

Back at its premiere in '65, *Sea* came off much better, even though Twyla, unfortunately, withdrew just before opening night. It seemed an unstylish exit at the time, but the other dancers were able to cover for her, and there was a good side to it. She left to eventually start a company of her own, which, with her formidable talent, is to be an important addition to the New York dance scene, then America's, and next no doubt the whole universe's. Perhaps whenever she looked at the skull that I'd found in Israel, the wisecracking little mole-twerp would have fond thoughts of our past times together. As for me, I fully expected someday, whenever our paths crossed, to lunge forth with huge slurps and bear hugs.

Well, Sharon left to raise her family, and Karen soon did likewise. Laura Dean left to begin a brilliant career as an original and highly talented choreographer, also to raise a family—a dance one. Though they gave considerably timed notices, these dancers might have preferred to make the break abruptly if they had known the usual consequences. Past patterns had proved that the span of time from notice to actual departure could be an uneasy period. We were all tempted to collect a few injustices—"This touring life's for the birds," Sharon had probably said to herself; that tweety Sharon, she ruffles her feathers too much, I'd groused inwardly. This was a way to ease the parting: negative novocaine for the heart.

And so it goes. Faces come, people depart, most of them beloved but one or two only looked at, all passing through, leaving indelible footprints on each other's pasts, and followed by others who are followed in turn—cellular generations of dancers, each of the same approximate age while together, each generation growing younger as I grow older. And they look to me for direction—want tugs from their puppeteer boss—and then snip the strings and set up their own shops, not only becoming puppeteers or parents themselves but competing with the great guy who first hired them. The nerve of it!

South America

Due to the company's endurance and to its previous seven foreign tours, but probably more due to Charlie's efforts in Washington, we've become connected with our government's Cultural Exchange Program. The '65 South American tour is to be the first to come under the auspices of the

Department of State, and we're now to be sponsored as official goodwill ambassadors. This tour makes us the second American modern-dance troupe to be sent to South America, the first being the Limón troupe. During the twenty years from '60 to '81 we are to complete twenty-three foreign tours, ten of which receive varying degrees of governmental support, the others being financed on our own.

Usually, the State Department tours come about by Charlie first lining up bookings with foreign impresarios. If our projected itinerary includes countries where U.S. goodwill is needed, the department then sometimes agrees to be responsible for part or all of our transportation costs and often adds engagements in other countries, but only ones preferred for diplomatic reasons. For instance, aid for London or Paris is never given, but it is for Seoul and Istanbul. Before '65 a few dance companies were sent abroad with full financial support; our South American tour is the first that has only partial support. All the performing artists that the department sends are commercially viable, and so Charlie, by presenting to Washington the advantages of a cost-sharing arrangement, has started a trend based on government subsidy of those artists who help themselves.

There are many results of our new affiliation. We begin to be presented on a bigger scale. We're able to perform more often and in larger theaters, many of them the equivalent of the Met Opera House. We're able to have live music instead of our usual taped kind. Resident orchestras in major cities are rehearsed and conducted by Simon Sadoff, our first music director. Some of the world's most sumptuous and respected theaters make a stark contrast to most of those that we perform in at home. For reasons both artistic and practical, however, our minimal stage sets and small number of dancers (between ten and twelve) are not reinforced to fill the larger stages. We've retained more or less the same sparseness over the years, and we're still portable.

On these government-supported tours the company is required to do certain things that ordinarily we do not do as much of, the object being to put us in direct contact with as many people as possible. The United States Information Service (USIS) arranges press conferences in each city and frequent TV appearances, radio interviews (often Radio Free Europe), lecture/demonstrations, and seminars. Informal discussions are arranged for students and people connected with the arts. Receptions and dinner parties are added whenever possible to our already bulging schedules. At each city we are welcomed by members of the diplomatic corps and transported by them to and from our various offstage activities. Though often exhausted by all this, the dancers and I feel lucky to have official connections, and we're determined to live up to our cultural tasks.

The tours offer opportunities to meet and talk with interesting people of all countries as well as our own foreign service. Admittedly, we absorb little of the surrounding politics, but we do meet a lot of American ambassadors. In comparison with other ambassadors met since, the Kennedy appointees in South America were noticeably younger, more often able to speak the language of their post fluently, and, curiously, taller.

Our audiences vary greatly. Perhaps because of our official status, those abroad approach our work differently from those in the States. They have fewer misgivings. In South America, where there is an unusually large gap between the very rich and the very poor, we sometimes give low-priced stadium or outdoor performances as well as the more expensive ones in national theaters and opera houses. A few free performances are given to aid victims of earthquakes and other calamities, and these concerts are attended by a mixture of all types. American modern dance being a rare commodity abroad, we probably benefit from audiences that see our dances through untrained and unprejudiced eyes.

With or without State Department backing, wherever these tours take us, we're always on a cultural errand rather than a political one, and I like to think that we're accepted everywhere not as propagandists, or even as Americans, but as artists. In terms of long-range aftereffects in the visited countries, it's probably too soon to know what we're accomplishing for contemporary dance by undertaking these long tours. It is very clear, however, how the tours affect us. The two things that they most engender are, first, an awe for the communicatability of dance and, second, a certain gratitude for our own nationality.

Here in Brazil the seasons are running backwards. June is cold, and in damp, hazy Pôrto Alegre's Salão de Atos da Urgs Theater everything is sticking to itself. The cabana-style dressing room needs a more powerful electric heater. Hanging over it to dry, my half-red, half-blue Katz costume—the only two primary colors in the room—looks very pretty as it drips against the pale turquoise wall. To delay putting on the icy, wet thing, I'm squatting on a chair and keeping my feet off the recently swabbed cement floor while deciphering a *Diário de Notícias*. The limp pages show a U.S. astronaut floating outside his space capsule. A neighboring article says that Johnson has withdrawn our marines from Santo Domingo but has left our soldiers there. Another article describes an attempt to assassinate our consul in Córdoba, also the riots and breaking of embassy windows in Buenos Aires. This last news is familiar, as we have just come from there. The ambassador's reception scheduled for us had been abruptly cancelled due to him being caught up in the Wanamaker affair—whatever that was.

It was a shame about the current events, but not about the reception; to get to miss one of those is ecstasy. I put down the paper, practice my cultural-ambassador smile in the mirror, and, toying with the next reception's guest list, halfheartedly try to memorize it.

In São Paulo a flame-colored neon sign outside the window of the Excelsior Hotel is flashing on and off—NOVO MUNDO, NOVO MUNDO, NOVO MUNDO. A full moon hangs low beside the sign, and the cold old satellite looks downright ironic next to those new hopeful red words. As it was supposed to do, the moon urges forth aspirations, and since it's a Brazilian moon, my aspirations are hitting their apogee. The repetitious wear and tear of our daily schedules has been exhausting, and I'm already aspiring to be something other than a bringer of American goodwill. Coming from a room next door is the sound of a weary old geezer's Demerol-flavored burp.

A few miles outside Cali, beside the road to the airport, an ancient euca-lyptus towers over a small night spot. The tree seems imaginary—the twist-ing pattern of its white-and-tan bark, its peculiar odor, its droop—a look that's just right for story books. Some of the bark has fallen onto the grass thatched hut below, where a few of us have come to watch some native dancing and copy it if we can. However, before we arrive, a bunch of city folk from Cali have already crowded out the natives. Danny and Karen begin to dance. There isn't room inside, so they go outside to dance and everyone follows to watch. The city folk mistake the couple's original im-provisation for the latest craze from New York, struggle to copy it, and, for all we know, are to go on doing their own watered-down version indefi-nitely. Never wild about public display—"public" is when you can see who is watching—I'm too inhibited to dance, and so, hiding my envy for Danny and Karen with a careless "See ya," I find a cab and return to my single room at the Aristi Hotel.

In Santiago we have a very elegant evening, but afterwards, when I think back, the whole thing seems pretty primitive. After a banshee assortment of noisy TV, newspaper, and magazine photographers interrupted our re-hearsal, and after the performance, at which Simon in tailcoat conducted an orchestra of eighty-four neolithic musicians while standing on two podiums, one on top of the other, and after an audience of several thousand rose and whooped their approval for nearly fifteen minutes, and after a tribe of notables trampled through a jungle of basketed flowers to get a close-up view of us on our cagelike stage, and after being delayed at the stage door to appease a pack of autograph hounds, we were sped to a tribal feast where an ambassador and his mate told me, as Americans, how proud they were of me and my herd. After all that, I returned to my hotel feeling that the evening had been quite primal, and the way sex usually is—that is, when you think about it afterwards, you know that it should have been better.

On the day that a man from the State Department was coming to give us a pretour briefing, life seemed too good for me—South America, the exotic itinerary, the fabulous theaters, our new officialdom. I'm inspired to look my best, so, since there's no hot water at the studio, I go to the Met Opera House and, after Miss Craske's class there, take a shower. There's a long line waiting for it, and by the time I'm done it's gotten late. I rush back to the studio to find the company already gathered but, as yet, no State Department man. Some of the dancers shift uncomfortably; Danny daydreams out the window. Bet fools around in her purse, switching its contents from one side to the other, then back. Sharon looks preoccupied with her new married life and is probably weighing the wisdom of another tour.

Finally the State Department man arrives, and the studio grows brighter and bigger. The dancers begin to come alive. Even the avocado perks up.

The briefing gives us useful information on what to expect in South America—weather, currencies, duty regulations, and so forth. Souvenir items that will be particularly good buys are mentioned. We also get a rundown on what will be acceptable conduct for those representing our country abroad, and what each country's codes of dress and manners are as compared with those at home.

Personally, I'm relieved at having someone other than myself bring up that last subject. After London I had the dancers on the mat about their conduct, and I'm now hoping that coming officially, the request will carry more weight. And I'm hoping to be a good leader and remembering our first trip to Mexico, when I determined to lead the company rather than push. Though there are occasional setbacks, I'm still trying to trust each dancer's maturity and commitment as a way for us to work smoothly together. Once or twice I've toyed with the idea of becoming a more effective leader by standing a little back and keeping out of everyone's way; but, instead, I'm now thinking to set them an example. Monkey see, monkey do.

At some later time I learn that the backgrounds of all, or most, of us have been checked by the State Department. Any records of political cross-purposes, drugs, or other unwelcome histories probably would have spoiled our chances for this tour. I also learn that José Limón has recommended me highly.

*   *   *

We're off. Nothing dampens our excitement about our destination, Lima, except Sharon's tears of outrage at the airport when a Tacet-like person drools on her new white leather boots. Also dampening is when our plane develops mechanical difficulties and has to land in Miami, where, while waiting for the plane to be repaired, Bet, Jenny, and I kill several hours with the usual mixed-up card game of hearts.

We reboard, and about six hours later, flying at 580 mph, we pass over the Andes, then soon see a vast brown desert crisscrossed with man-made shapes—the mysterious Nazca lines. On deplaning in foggy Lima (said to get one month of sun per year), we are introduced to diplomat Gaylord Caldwell and his wife and a Señor Vargas, who is known as the Sol Hurok of the Incas, and a wilderness of other welcomers whose names I don't catch. For the next three evenings we dance for Lima's sweet audiences and after each performance introduce ourselves to Lima's favorite drink, the *pisca* sour.

The tour continues smoothly, bounding through Santiago's Municipal Theater, the Avenida in Mendoza, Rosario's El Circulo, and the San Martín in Buenos Aires.

Good readers, we now come to Pôrto Alegre in Brazil, where we should pause at the Salão de Atos da Urgs, a name worth scrutinizing. This is where the aforementioned walls made such a pretty background for my half-red, half-blue Katz costume.

Since the front and back are different colors, getting into it is not a big problem. The costume is notable in that it is thought by some to represent the duplex nature of its wearer. "How dualistic he is," some said, or, as others said, "How schizoid." Folks, this is unfair, simplistic, and not at all the whole picture. Like most, I'm a rainbow mix. Pure hues, true silences, perfect vacuums, unadulterated people are rare, if existing at all. As in nature, I'm as varied and as right as rain, maybe righter. However, being true to my multiness, I can see that there is some point in unipeople and their clear-cut views, and even admire many definite and unequivocal types. Take Katharine Hepburn, for instance, or Joan of Arc, or my mother's favorite, Norman Vincent Peale. Or Mary Wigman—do you remember the shaded eyes and firm handclasp I was telling you about? She, I'm sure—I *think* I'm sure—was committed to her choreographic views and quite right when she wrote that "genuine art is a product of growth, not of manufacture." Let's think about that. Genuine art is a product of growth, not of manufacture. It seems all right, wouldn't you say? Yet, if we were Mary Wigman, with a little reshuffling of words, couldn't we also say that genuine growth is a product of art? Isn't it just as true? Yes. And it's just as false. I wouldn't say that Mary Wigman was full of hot air—no sir. Perhaps the very next day she changed her mind, but her book had already gone to press. You see, single views, like pipe dreams, simplify and filter the harshness out of reality. Of course it's possible that I've got it wrong. Perhaps we should also believe that harsh views of single pipe filters are like really dreamy. This, of course, may be harder to believe. Or should it be—filters and harsh dreamlike pipes are real singular views? We, for one, feel this speculation is not leading much of anywhere. We, for another, always trust our old Tacet bones about these things and feel that it is.

But back to the Salão de Atos da Urgs, this time to the cultural-ambassador smile in the dressing-room mirror. That smile is only one of a number of manufactured faces of mine. There's the humble inclination of the brow—handy for accepting compliments—and the prissing of the lips—for indicating high moral standards—and so forth. We have a whole bunch up our sleeve. They are the face cards I play in the game of manners—umbrellas to fend off emotional splash, oil for ordinary friction, a stylization of what is called "consideration for others." At other times they can be used for revenge, such as when I want to get even with a rude person. The tour faces effectively mask fear, boredom, and despair and are stand-ins for other emotional responses. There are enough close company members around to show my real responses to without getting involved with the many strangers I meet along the way who aren't likely to be seen again. Naturally, there are side effects to wearing masks. The crafty things are stultifying and can turn unhealthy. Some say they bring about internal burning and that it's better to be caught with your masks and manners hanging down.

The pale dressing room, the vague warmth from its heater, the limp newspaper, the haze outside—taken all together, Pôrto Alegre may seem to be vague and tentative. Yet the place is real enough, just as tangible as the tour journal that lies on my dressing table. My graffiti collection proves that the walls are as real as the names lettered on them. Roland Petit's is there by Leslie Caron's, also those of some fabled American Ballet Theatre stars. Other names have been superimposed on those of older stars. (If they knew, the Ballet Russe's scribbled-on Tiven sisters might be a little disgruntled.) The names on the wall seem to say, "We were here, we exist," and the layering is an emblem that tells of a dance family tree. The names are smiling a benediction and saying, "Our far-from-home feet were freezing, but we *did* it—you too can dance here. *Merde!*"

And the cracks of the walls are as real—almost as real—as the lunar cracks and chasms of Dr. T's face, or the bumps on that old phrenologist's head. The guest list that I'm halfheartedly memorizing would be more appetizing to him. Charlie would have an easy time getting him to receptions, as he was nothing if not single-minded about showing off his savoir faire. If he were at the tour's formal dinners, he could prevent silence from crashing into the chatter and, much better than me, could tell the difference between a hostess gown and the maid's, or even the hostess from her chief. To the discussions of local weather, he could add a more powerful statement than that it made all us dancers sweat like pigs. And when speaking across the table to ambassadors, he would find an elegant way to say, "Hey, pal, any seconds on dessert?" Pop's exits from parties would be less premature, and, though he, like me, is prone to alcoholic overstimulation, he could manage to trip into less furniture. He also would thank the hostess for her hospitality, not the cloakroom girl. This does not mean that he is better mannered than me. Although I have the jump on him when it comes to saying the right thing to the wrong person, tact, not Tacet, tells me what to say.

In Pôrto Alegre, after many lecture/demonstrations, parties, and other nuisances, something happens that at first seems to provide a reason for my mixing-up of people; but later, when examining the problem further, reviewing what happened—in fact, when being confronted with the whole of my past—I grow more duplicitous than ever. By revealing this curious occurrence I may be called a liar, or perhaps only an inventor of riddles; yet, after all, an artist is supposed to make riddles out of answers.

Among interesting people met at State Department functions have been U.S. Secret Service personnel. One of them has told me that Nazis are still nesting there in Argentina, and this leads me to dream of serving my country in another less public and more adventurous way. So I cable the CIA in Washington, pointing out the ideal cover that my position as cultural ambassador could provide, but, though I fill out the formal application that they then send and mail it back in an improvised diplomatic pouch marked Do Not Bend, they reject me due to, of all things, a past history of traffic violations. This is hard to accept. Greenwich Village has been rigidly enforcing a code against jaywalking, but I've hardly ever been caught. It seems more likely that the rejection is due to some type of psychiatric disorder that mistakenly got into my dossier. Subsequently, after obtaining a clean bill of health from a gentleman I mistake for a Peruvian Zen master (he turned out to be a teacher of the tea ceremony) and digesting several books on weaponry, since my knowledge of missiles has been limited to the pea shooters and spitballs of boyhood, I reapply. Nevertheless, I am again rejected.

My interest in spying, incidentally, has led to a passion for mechanical things—hand-held heaters in particular. By '66 I amassed a collection that included two loud Colts with doodads that spun. I called these Lovey and Dovey, my twin birds of doom. They were excellent for scaring off studio intruders, and once I shot up a nest of roaches that had settled behind the studio's toilet tank, nearly drowning myself.

Well, you can imagine my excitement when, in answer to a third application, my diplomatic pouch is returned all starched and ironed. Although there is no communication inside, this is obviously Washington's way of telling me that they accept me as being straight and that I shall soon be given an assignment. At last I am to start a new double life which will change me into a secret agent!

My first brush with Intelligence occurs on the evening of June 10, 1965, at approximately 22 hours, and coincides with a devastating hurricane which whips all the way up from Cape Horn to semitropical Pôrto Alegre, bringing monstrous icebergs that squeeze the bejesus out of that port's tankers, sloops, and children's inflatable rafts. The company and I have just finished our first and only performance at the Teatro Salão de Atos da Urgs (pronounced "Urghzz," with a soft lisp of the Portuguese rolled R), and rain, ruin, and loud pops are reigning outside.

While I am greeting a shivering throng of after-performance admirers, warming them with my smile, our ambassador arrives. As usual, he is tall and wholesome looking. I crouch in politeness to allow his head to be at the preferred level and present my palm after demoisturizing it on the back of my tights. But just as we are sharing the familiar knuckle-shattering scrunch, he is hustled away by several armed backstage guards.

Evidently, he was not who he seemed.

Persevering, I start over with the true ambassador, who has been waiting directly behind the other. This man is unusually short for an ambassador and is displaying a tight, many-buttoned puce uniform which he certainly never could have put on by himself. He arches his back and glides forward, hugs affectionately at my waist, and then, with an air of secrecy, slips me an envelope sealed with a waxen crest.

The angels have chosen to net for me my rapturous dreams of Central Intelligence!

I can barely wait to run to the men's room, memorize my instructions, then destroy them—can already hear the merry sound of flushing. But the hair net he is wearing *would* get caught in the front zipper of my Katz costume, and until some guards can unmesh us, I while away a considerable amount of time by dreaming of Col. Adjutant Pawl Tälürr, aerial double agent to outer space, who at ninety-three is to be one of the solar system's greatest narcs ever. Photographers flash away, their used bulbs bouncing

onto the stage and mingling there with other discards—the broken bouquets, crinkled tubes of liniment, and what may have been the prone body
of an exhausted curtain puller with the cord of one of Bet's dehumidifiers
snaking out from beneath.

Suddenly the tall, wholesome man strides back, leading a battalion of
plainclothesmen who carelessly yank the little ambassador from my zipper,
doing in the hair net forever. What seems a heartless act then turns into
something else. A chloroformed cloth is produced and clamped over the
little man's unprotesting mouth, and as he is being bound and borne away—
to a torture cell, a moonlit wall, who knew where—I am able to assure him
with a wink that his directives will be obeyed.

When I sneak a look inside the envelope, however, it contains only a
disappointing invitation to another reception. The tall man then whacks at
my back, introduces himself with a foreign-sounding name that I am unable
to catch, and congratulates me for the entrapment tactics that he thinks I
have used. He says that he is the CIA's slipperiest customer, the last living
descendant of Brazil's second-oldest family, a Soviet multiple agent, and
none other than the very rich as well as childless and totally insane Senhor
Salão de Atos da Urgs himself. Does he mean the other man or himself, or
whom?

Although the real ambassador has never come backstage at all, having
been screened as a common autograph hound, and although I ponder the
matter of identities for years, it is still unclear as to which man, the tall or
the short, was Senhor Urgs. It is depressing. Was I responsible for the
incarceration of one of my own government's agents?

The glossy prints of the enlarged photos depicting the entire entrapment
are discovered one day by my company archivist in a trunk where they have
been lying among the tatters of a faded red-and-blue costume. Eventually
I find the pictures so unsettling that I destroy them. In some I was able to
make out the shoulders of the three of us, but our faces were a white blur.
The reflection of my smile had overexposed things. But in the penultimate
one of the series, taken just as the short man was being bound and borne
away, I could distinctly see his arm being raised toward me in triumph and
reassurance.

So much for masks and mixups. Possibly, some of you good readers are
ready to leave that fantasy and return to less piquant reality. My spy riddle
limps poorly behind the realities of the tour, and I'm now thinking that, in
general, people are much more fantastic than I had supposed, but dully so,
and there are far too many of us. But let me first confess that the following

facts have not been easy to dig up. For reference there is only a tattered journal, almost a symbol of my past, and it relates more to graffiti and indigenous gestures of the different countries—you know, below-belt scratching by male peasants, and so forth—than to a true itinerary. Nevertheless . . .

After the first stop, in Trenton, New Jersey, a performance that probably shouldn't count, our tour continued with a series of slashes across Peru that rivaled the Nazca lines for impenetrability. We then dipped deep into Chile and veered northeast across Argentina to Mendoza. By the way, Mendoza was founded by "the Good Viceroy" Pedro de Mendoza, who brought America its first printing press, quelled numerous riots, surmounted all efforts to discredit and oust him, and at last, when his city, one that is now known euphemistically as "the Eden of the Andes," proved untenable, died at sea. After crisscrossing Argentina, we slipped south, up and down, east and west, to and fro, leaving the whole continent all but gridlocked with our trail. The entire trip was to last from April 9 (Tacet insists on counting Trenton) through July 15, which is exactly one hundred days, or roughly fourteen weeks, or more than one fourth of a year, or whatever exact fraction of a century some finicky fact checker cares to figure.

And then when the tour was almost over we came to Cali, Colombia. But wait—before going into a precise accounting of that place, there's something more about Pôrto Alegre—

Just as we were about to depart from the airport there I said, "Charlie, old bean, don't you think that someone in Washington made a mistake when they selected this seedy city?"

"What do you mean? It's been beautiful—the gang danced fantastic, we were all sold out. Remember the pretty bouquets with the nifty doilies? You're just tired—you'll see things differently when we get some rest."

"Yeah, I guess. But I wish they liked us at home as well as they do here. Trenton couldn't have cared less about us being official ambassadors of goodwill. Hey, Charles, you notice how I'm always wearing this dignified tie everywhere?"

"It's got a soup stain and you both look beat."

"Well, where's yours? What's with that crappy turtleneck? We're representing American culture, you know. Why can't you at least keep the linings of your pockets from hanging out?"

Charlie doesn't answer, turns himself in one piece without twisting his head, and gazes stoically into the distance. He's not letting either me or the big boil on the back of his neck get the better of him.

"Look over there on that bench," I continue. "Bet and Sharon, flat on their backs. Please go tell them it's unladylike."

"Paul, they've got the flu and fever. Don't worry, I'll find them some chicken soup in São Paulo."

"São Paulo? Isn't Rio next?"

"We've gotta stay loose. I meant to tell you—the São Paulo performances have been cancelled, but not all, only some. Since we'll have some free time, the USIS has added more receptions and free lectures for you to do. We can make up the lost income with the extra performances that I've added in Rio. Each night we'll have one at eight and another at eleven. By the way, Jenny says that our music tapes have gotten erased. Easy there!— it's okay—Simon will try to sneak a recording of our orchestra someplace to use later where we have no live music."

"More places without orchestra?"

"Yes, like when we dance outdoors on the side of a mountain in Cali. It'll be a little steeper than our usual raked stages, but think of the view!"

"Reinhart, have you ever thought of seeking employment elsewhere?"

A loudspeaker announces that our flight is delayed due to fog, so I pass the time by writing three letters, starting with one to my mother.

Pôrto Alegre, Brazil
11 July

Dearest Mammy,

The tour is going fine and lots of fun. Charlie is a great manager, real thoughtful of the dancers and always bringing us refreshments and good news. He has even arranged for us to dance—you'll never guess where—on a beautiful mountainside in Cali. And he has been able to get us some extra performances in Rio.

We are all at the airport and just about to fly to São Paulo. Bet and Sharon are having a little beauty nap. Charlie is saying so long to Mr. and Mrs. Bernhart. Mr. Bernhart, a diplomat with the State Department, just told me that he has never seen such relaxed artists before. He means how untemperamental.

There have been many lovely receptions given for us and you would be proud, I hope, of your son's manners. You are always with me. I can hear you saying, "Keep on keepin' on." Living up to what I imagine you would want me to be is a pretty big order, but I try, and think you would be proud of the dancers, too.

I wish I lived nearer by and could visit you as often as Soph, Tom, and Bettie. I will rush right there soon as this tour is over. This time I expect to be richer than after the last tour. You will like the Brazilian emerald brooch that I've found for you.

In the meantime, these weekly notes. Glad you are enjoying the bird feeder and binoculars. Just watch out that your neighbors don't get the idea that you are spying on them.

I kiss this page and send it with all my love.

Your own,
Pete

This one is to George, who is staying at the studio while I'm away.

Dear Babe,

Got your 12th letter here in Pôrto Alegre. Good! Keep it up. Poor Sharon hasn't had any yet. I'm lucky to get so many from you.

Yesterday I walked around the docks here like we do there and wished you could see these South American ships and speed boats.

Sorry to hear Tabby is sick. Happy to know your finger is healing well. The new decorations that you have added to the studio sound OK, but PLEASE do not add any more. There's no use. I hope to find a new studio soon.

Men here wear lots of pink. Bought you a pink shirt, a new ring, and some more dolls for your sister's collection.

The tour is getting mixed up. Our dates keep changing. Charlie is terrible. He makes me do too many lectures and receptions. So much talk talk talk. After one of them I felt dazed, and even wished to be deaf like you.

Take good care of yourself. I think of you. Miss you.

Lots of love,
Pete

And since the plane still isn't leaving, I amuse myself by entering this in my tour journal—

Eleventh of July, Nineteen hundred and sixty five
Pôrto Alegre Airdrome

Dear Pop T,

Your fine influence is beginning to bear fruit. As I compose this, whilst waiting to be whisked away, a humble urchin of lesser caste is kneeling afore me, his chamois cloth a concertino of flicks and flacks as he transforms the surface of my shoes into mirrors. Sitting here partaking of a halved mangosteen, I feel great sympathy for this poor lad. It is a mark of my own station in life not to believe in stations, and as I gaze down upon him I long for men to be discovered on the moon so that I can show that I am unprejudiced against moonmen, too. I wonder, when he is done will he expect a tip? Like you, I shall draw myself up as if a Roman emperor, chastize this peon for making so much racket at his job, then shout, "Begone!"

You would approve the present apparel of my troupe—the natty gentlemen, proud in their three-piece suits; the ladies shivering in their chiffon frocks of stunning Empire squeeze; Charles in flowing ascot. We are a reflowering of the classic mode, a veritable fin de siècle reborn. Two of our ladies are reclining seductively in positions you would eat up, Sharon pining for John (*sustra niña povre*), her whimsical shape a bit long-waisted, but brave and lovely all the same, and becoming thinner and thinner every day. Her breasts resemble two pommes thrown there that stuck. Alongside of them, Bet's resemble two grapes that missed. (Please bear with my crudities in an area of which you are past master. Yet I try. I try.)

The tour goes splendidly and our public is not as jaded as you might expect, at least about dinner parties. Charles has consented to allow Colombia additional concerts which will include one to be given for rarely seen Incas who are expected to extract themselves from their mountain aeries in droves.

Pôrto Alegre, I must say, has turned out to be under par as a cultural metropolis. Sleaze is the word for it. No matter, São Paulo and Rio are awaiting even more expectantly than my dancers are now awaiting me. We were to play a game of hearts, but hearts, I lately find, is called "the poor man's bridge," and so I shall decline. Instead, I shall finish the archaeological book that you recommended. So far, I have been deeply moved by the Rosetta Stone, by the decoding of linear A and B, and by how all those Babylonian languages got smashed asunder.

Last evening at a formal dinner party I met some local artists. One was an old timer with something celestial about him that reminded me of you. On his arrival the other guests drew together, forming a semicircular mass in front of him, whereupon he began to speak. He described in detail his great passion for stained-glass windows—the manifestation of divine light, oxides fused into scintillating scrollwork, Chartres quatrefoils, Ste Chapelle grisailles. At last, having reached his apotheosis, he positively glowed as doth an opal within a rippleringed pool, and then he daubed a last bit of color, throbbed, sighed a last sigh, and ejaculated a sepulchral cough. In and out of our hearts flowed rainbow-colored blood. His oration had been very uplifting and his voice had been a pleasurable antiphony in terms of spinal music. Of course very few, if any, of us knew what he was talking about. Yet that was just as well—was it not R. P. Blackmur, or possibly Ringo Starr, who said that all knowledge is but a fall from the paradise of undifferentiated sensation?

One surmised that the old gentleman had taken up stained-glass windows before losing his mind completely, as he now seemed to believe himself to be a cathedral. Just after he struck twelve his keeper came to remove him. Nevertheless, the guests remained highly exhilarated. One bass-voiced lady, said to be a painter of kidneys in love with wombs, compared her present state to the luminous globules of glow that travel up the sides of jukeboxes. Coming after his, her words seemed impoverished. Therefore, dazed and dizzy, I paid my compliments and left. You will be delighted to know that I had impressed everyone by getting the correct chronology into my silverware.

Standing outside on marble steps, I wondered where on earth my chauffeur had got to. Hundreds of powdered bugs all full of flap and flit were wheeling around a lamp in the night. It was the party all over again, but much better without sound, and the more I watched the bugs, the less I thought of human beings.

Adieu, mon Padre. Canst thou patiently await my recursion? (Paraphrase: Can you keep your shirt on till I get back?) Tacet/Taylor—a confederation of two. This doesn't sound right. We are a confederation of one and a half.

> Your half, your smaller half,
> Sonny

I don't mind airing these three letters, as none can blame me for the slightly differing viewpoints. As all know, good manners require the shaping of what we say to whom we say it to. If the realities don't agree, so much the worse for them.

Though the fog hasn't lifted, we take off for São Paulo anyway. In fact, we leave three times, each takeoff ending back on the runway, and each time the dancers get slower and slower about reboarding. One of our dancers has developed a fear of flying, and, like a contagious disease, her fear has spread. It isn't unusual to see the dancers holding hands, clamping on to each other and quaking. "We are a closely knit family," I usually had to explain to hosts come to see us off.

On the fourth boarding I urge the dancers up the stairway to the plane, then have to unply their resisting fingers from the hatch. This time the plane does not turn back, and, just as I have assured everyone, the flight is perfectly safe, except for one brief turbulence which causes the stickier parts of our luncheons to be scraped off the ceiling—but that was nothing much.

After a while some of the dancers poke around in their airline bags for the bon-voyage gifts given them on leaving New York. As well as the Spanish- and Portuguese-into-English dictionaries from me ($1.75 ea.), they received small pads in which to keep track of their expenses. Changing currencies of quickly passing countries can get puzzling, so it's helpful to have something handy to record purchases and figure exchange rates on.

The sol, legal tender of Peru, came early in the tour when our minds were open to new concepts, but later in Argentina we refused to understand our leftover pesos and Chilean escudos. Then, just when we'd gotten used to the cruzeiros in Brazil, back came the sol all over again. In Guatemala, though we never converted or even saw any, it was said that quetzals were all the rage. In some country or other you could convert a single American buck into a large wad of whatevers. It was there that Molly said, "Let's give up and call it all cabbage." Later, in Asia, expert numismatists Dan and Liz had worked out a way to comprehend the Burmese kyat and the Mongolian tugrik and their worths in real money. They said that about eighteen hundred of one or the other of them equaled four bits, or maybe that seventy-five hundred equaled one hundred sixty bits; but that didn't do us much good in South America. (The worst rate of exchange was at a hotel in Spain where Charlie was once billed for bottled water that cost 3,750 habitaciónes and 438 lavados!!!)

At dusk, as the plane begins its tipping spiral down to São Paulo's pinpoint pattern of lights, I remember that we are to be met by photographers. As an example to the company, I tuck in my shirt tail, tighten my tie, put my shoes back on, and, as a hint to the girls, pretend to add lipstick to my ambassador smile. Looking swell, I spring from the hatch and onto the high steps. Blinding flashes from cameras cause me to stumble, miss most of the steps, and make a four-point landing at the photographers' feet. The ankle that I resprain is one thing—I'd almost come to expect the waywardness of human flesh—but the loss of balance and ungraceful flapping arms on the way down are something worse. At the photographers' request, I climb back and make a slower descent; and then, at the following press conference, I boast of modern dance—our strong technique, our weighted grace, our thrilling descents to the floor.

The conference continues in a typical way. Many questions come from Communist reporters who ask if my government is financing our tour and if so, how will I spend all the capitalistic dollars that I'm earning? Are we giving benefit performances to aid earthquake victims in Guatemala the way the Polish folk-dance company did? Did we have any ballets on the subject of Kennedy's death? When the questioning gets too sticky, I fall back on the old standby—that we are on a cultural errand, not a political one, or, as I sometimes put it, that we are on a political errand, not a cultural one.

At last we're free to check in at our hotel, La Pignolia—the pine nut. We separate our luggage, go to our rooms, and in no time flat everyone is back in the lobby.

"Charles Reinhart, this hotel you booked us is horrible! Now you're really going to get it," says Liz, her flared nostrils at their widest.

"Someone's been in my bed and broken it," chirps Sharon.

"Someone's been in mine and pissed in it," Danny says.

"Our faucets won't go and the plumbing's upclogged," says Bet, pinching her nose.

A tense moment of silence passes as we all glare at Charlie. "Complaints, complaints," he says. "I'm tired of it—this is the last straw. I'm quitting!"

He means it. "Oh no you aren't," I say, then steer him out onto the street and toward a nearby bar. "Wait there," I call back to the dancers. "We're having a drink, and then good ol' Charlie will find us another hotel—right, Charlie?"

Over other kinds of tourist attractions, one side of me has grown to appreciate the functional hotel—prison cells of paradise, neat, clean, safe retreats. A yellowing window shade can be lowered to create an illusion of North American sunshine when it's actually South America and rain. I used to pay for a double bed to sleep diagonally across, making it seem less vacant, but by now I prefer twins, one of which can be upended against the wall so as to be almost unnoticeable. All the showers have an inclination to turn hurtfully hot or cold without warning, depending on the showering next-door neighbor's whim, to deprive you of the temperature you've so carefully blended. The troupe came to know (*quien sabe,* to use Cervantes's talk) the questionable luxuries of middle-priced hotels—Gran Hotels, Gran Hotel Italianos (lots of Italians in Argentina), Emperadors, Continentals (their ad boasted expert gastronome), Palaces, Bolívars. To me, all the hotels and their repetitive names were variants of Acapulco's Hotel Vacancy.

We speculated on the different sorts of fellow clientele. *Ustedes quien sabe?* (this is fun!): the reformed mafioso, the touring tennis champ, the retired business flop among men; among the women, the incognito whore, the pseudoprincess, the watchful, bearlike mother. We tried to avoid and held in contempt hotels of a faint spermy smell, no shower, and nothing to recommend them except their unsmiling desk clerks.

At the Excelsior, the new one Charlie's found for us, nothing seems particularly South American. In my room, after bouting with key and keyhole, I knee my suitcase past the door and locate a wall switch. A merciless light fills the room, and I note that the lamps, all unmatched, have slightly exotic switches which are at some distance down their electric cords. However, such switches as these, and the oversized round prongs of the plugs, can be found in all foreign-volted countries. The room holds a profusion of furnishings, can hardly contain them, seems about to burst. What's in it could have filled five rooms of the same size. I'm reminded of the maze below my first New York loft where Babe, like a Minotaur, inhabited a maze of secondhand furniture. This other stuff is just as used, just as unmatched. It's as though someone has included each piece to please every possible taste—end tables of spindly, rococo, and heavy Victorian ilk, chairs to accommodate sitters of all beams. When I bump my foot on it, a coffeetable mutation of strident avant-garde and twittering nostalgia loses its marbleized top satisfyingly.

"*Silêncio, por favor!*" cries some senhor down the hall.

The two doors of a dangerously tilting wardrobe are faced with distorting mirrors, and a bulging red bureau stands blushing about its pairs of ill-matched knobs. As I'm transferring my things into it, one of its drawers slips all the way out and bangs onto the floor.

"*Silêncio!*"

I start to restore it, then leave everything lying. The double bed creaks and complains as I lie listening to the pulsing sound of an approaching siren. Making my face do one of its comical masks, I stare at the floor. The worn carpet of floral eddies and crosscurrents is a background to my strewn belongings, curlicue stamens of bright colors edged in black complementing my pale practice clothes, grayed underwear, a dingy packet of moleskin, a warped circle of elastic adhesive tape, a tarnished silver pill box. I reach down for an old snapshot of Mother, one of Bet and me in London, one of Babe, and place them on the bedside table. My swollen ankle throbs in counterrhythm to the loudly pulsing siren, and I try to think about which of my steps will have to be changed, give up, and close my eyes. Part of me fitfully dreams slow twilight dreams; another part, alert and edgy, absorbs the hotel's noise.

To the hum of the air conditioner my mother crawls out from under the bed. "My darlin'," she says, "your room is too bleak and empty. You need some furniture in your life and a wife to keep it all shiny." Then, as she is to do much of in her later years, she begins to count things—the squares of the afghan that I once made her, the buttons on her bed jacket, the toes of one of her visiting great-grandchildren—"This little piggy went to market, this little . . ." A car squeals to a stop outside.

The wardrobe's doors open and Bet steps out wearing a white wedding dress. I'm wearing white tails, and we're leading an endless line of past, present, and future dancers, all dwarfs with pacifiers sticking out of their mouths. In the hall a long, loud laugh echoes off the walls and tapers into silence.

As Bet lifts her bridal veil I see that her chin has grown craggy and nearly all of her fingers are missing. Outside, the elevator's gate clangs shut.

"Talk to me—you never talk to me!" Bet struggles to sign. From the next room comes a sepulchral cough and a gassy disturbance.

"I myself shall speak to Babe," chimes Tacet as he materializes in an art deco chair. I try to sit on his knee but miss and start to fall—slowly at first, soaring in half-spirals toward a city bright with pinpoint lights, then, with frightening momentum, plummet straight down. A train cries in the night with ominous chill, mingling power and hysteria in one desperate scream.

Heart vibrating and totally alert, I clutch the mattress to keep from hitting the floor. Is this place Syracuse? Schenectady? St. Louis? I know it starts with an S. Even with all its furniture, the room seems empty and very bleak indeed. The silence is deadly; real sleep is impossible. I kick off my shoes and reach for the pill box, chew a couple of Demerols, and switch off the lamp.

As I've said—through the hotel window shone a neon sign: NOVO MUNDO, NOVO MUNDO. Hanging there beside it, the big Brazilian moon seemed agonizingly mismatched.

Journal excerpts:

14 June

Again last night, that recurring dream about falling. And something about fingers. The remaining part of Babe's finger was wiggling away from his temple—the sign for dream. Tacet and my real father (both Dr. Ts) have at least one characteristic in common—the peculiar way that they use one of their fingers: when grasping a light object, or when manipulating something, such as when knotting a string, instead of the index finger pressing against the thumb, as most people do, they both use their second finger from the thumb, leaving the index finger and pinkie sticking straight out. I sometimes catch myself doing this. Possibly, my two fathers and I are related.

15 June

My father writes that my great-half-uncle Andrew Barnaby, who was a sea captain, had no children of his own, but made a good deal of (Father's term) his sister's children. On a return voyage from China he brought home three bolts of Chinese silk to be made into his three nieces' wedding dresses. This was perhaps 1880. Georgia, my grandmother, went out to Los Angeles to marry Albert Edward Taylor on December 25 or 26, 1890, and her dress was made in Delaware before she left. Lucie, her sister, had worn a dress made of her bolt at her wedding. Sadie, the third sister, never married. Father writes that he has saved Sadie's bolt for my wife, should I ever have one. He has also saved Uncle Barnaby's watch, or, more accurately, its replaced face, casing, *and* inner works, a tintype of his mother, and several other heirlooms, all of which he thinks of donating to the Delaware Historical Society.

Look, Father, I don't mind that you haven't put anything about me in the genealogy that you wrote on the Belvilles; I don't really mind being only number A113161 in there; and I don't even mind if the long Belville history comes to a final halt with me—but may I not inherit Uncle Barnaby's silver bos'n's whistle? Please, it would mean a lot.

16 June

Though I have no children of my own, still, I've birthed a lot of dances—forget how many. Could look them up, but prefer to forget. In fact, I train myself to forget—not only the titles but especially the steps—and have been pretty successful. I do this so as to start each new dance from scratch. Repeating steps from dance to dance would be boring to audiences and to me. By training myself to forget, I maintain a tremendous edge over less forgetful dance makers.

In São Paulo the full houses and scalpers are gratifying, yet nothing dispels a feeling that's beginning to shade my offstage life. Being familiar with fatherlessness since an early age, I've sometimes thought of myself as some kind of overage foundling in search of a foster home. But today I wake from another dream, look out the window to see that there's a pigeon, a homing pigeon, perched in profile on the sign, and am caught by a notion that instead of finding a home, I've become one. That is, without me noticing when it happened, and without the benefit of a rehearsal, to some of my dancers I've become a father image. Good grief!

My role as surrogate father, as I begin to see it, is to help dancers through the company, molding them, not only to a special stage style but to an offstage one. (In the eyes of the world at large we sometimes sense a strike against us for being dancers of any style.) This role, one that's being played out in reverse between mentor Tacet and me, is forcing me to accept unforeseen responsibilities. That of love, for one. Not only is each dancer an investment of time, energy, and money, but each is bringing a current of emotional feeling. The investment of love is very demanding.

I've met plenty of people I haven't liked, but I've never chosen a dancer for the company who didn't appeal to something warm inside me. I've expected to be proud of them both onstage and off-, and I have been. To prove my pride, and to assume the mantle of fatherhood, I now form certain plans. I'll let them know how engrossing their performances are by hanging my blue bathrobe in the shadowy wings so that they will think that it's me watching. To show how much I care about their good conduct, I'll leave the doors of my dressing room ajar so that they can see me adding their names to my journal's black list. To broaden them culturally, I'll offer architectural information—tell them that São Paulo's Needle changes color at the top because of the monthly flooding of the Rio Frito. To set an example, I'll start warming up before performances.

Danny Williams Grossman is to be the first of a series of professional sons to reap the benefits of new parental attempts to keep him in line. He'd come into the company more or less untrained. Clearly, his raw talent and love of moving for the sheer joy of it needed a bridle, his explosive energy a tether. I determine to pass on to him whatever tricks of the trade I can, as well as commitment to dance, something that had been passed on to me. In his case, the difference in our ages, heights, and weights would likely strengthen my role of father figure. However, the difference in our backgrounds would not. That his parents were California liberals and my mother a staunchly conservative easterner may be a reason for our differing outlooks. For instance, what I think is decorous, he usually considers ridiculous. Yet maybe this type of thing is only a surface matter of style which belies a mutual agreement on basics.

Based on journal excerpts:

Lima Airport
May 25
   Customs officials mistake shaggy Danny for a hippie, strong-arm him into a back room where they search for a dope-filled pouch or pocket within his attire and anatomy. Danny confides to me that they now have to marry him.

Santiago Airport
May 28

To avoid another delay at customs, I canter Danny into a men's room to trim his mane. A news photographer follows, hoping for some candid shots of us, and the crowded urinals are speedily vacated.

Hotel Cervantes, Mendoza
June 2

Tieless Danny barred from this hotel's fancy restaurant. He retreats to his room, returning in hat, jacket, bow tie, and no shirt.

Hotel Ambassador, Rio
June 18

Sporty Danny sits in lobby wearing his crummy peon hat again. I walk over, remove it, and treat the top of his head to a swat.

Municipal Theater, São Paulo
July 16

I show foot-damaged Danny how to bind the splits on his soles so that the outer edges of adhesive tape won't roll into a lump that would be painful to prance on, and point out some other tricks of the trade. "And Pony," I say, "that wild shaking of your head whenever you dance isn't in the choreography."

"I do it so's everyone will think I'm a blur."

"Forget it. And another thing—you better start thinking of theaters as sacred places. After dancing in them we leave the boards and dressing rooms beautified, sanctified—not strewn with your used Kleenexes and other crap. And furthermore, if you think that dancing until the wee hours in nightclubs is going to help your next night's performance, you're nuts."

A roadside nightspot near Cali
June 22

An ancient eucalyptus towers over this steamy spot's grass roof. Danny, Karen, my date (a girl lately met at a reception), and I move outside to get away from a group of Colombian dolce vitas who've been using dance as a pretext to press front-to-front. To a deep-rutted record by the country's latest heartthrob, Danny and Karen begin to dance, a dance related to the pony (what else?), a hydraulic bounce with alternately bobbing knees interspersed with random flourishes of the ulnae and a special play of the abdomen.

I stand there under that odoriferous tree admiring—no, envying—
no, *hating* Danny's dance, his youth, his easy nonchalance, the singsong cadences of his voice, the perpetual puzzlement in his eyes, and
the slight edge of mockery. For a moment I feel that I am in love with
him—not difficult when your emotions are inconsistent. Romance between trainer and colt? Not possible. Not good.

Saying my most careless "See ya," I leave Danny and the others to
dance as long as they want, returning to my single room at the Aristi
Hotel and its nice clean white towels.

It has been almost four months since we left New York. According to a
USIS brochure that I read on the plane, Cali is in west-central Colombia.
It is having a population explosion and has become a tourist center with an
arts festival, at which we are to perform. It is also the headquarters of the
Cauca Valley development project, supposedly modeled after the Tennes-
see Valley Authority.

As we deplane, Danny remarks, "It's nice to be back in Tijuana."

"Quiet, creep," I tell him. "Here comes the dictator."

As things develop, the man is only a tawdry customs official. I'm not
mentioning it to the dancers, but to me the place smells of imminent
revolution.

One of my usual activities on arrival is to check out our stage, but in Cali,
since my stomach is acting up, Charlie and Jenny go to check for me. I
manage a press bout, feed my ulcers a couple of bananas, then go to bed.
Charlie and Jenny return to tell me about the three places where we are to
perform. They say that our first stage, the Municipal Theater, is the size of
a postage stamp and that all of our dances will have to be entirely respaced
to fit it. Our second performances will be at an Olympic gym which seats
about four thousand. Some sort of platform is being built there for us which
will have no drapes, no entrances or exits, and will feature a dangerous
five-foot drop at its edges. Jenny says that we'd better watch out, as it won't
be possible for her to light the edges.

My beloved cohorts are making my stomach worse, and for the time
being I'm loving them a little less. They notice me squirming, so mercifully
say very little about the third place, only that it's on a mountainside, not too
near, but here in Colombia someplace. Jenny's eyes roll and roll. Charlie
offers to bring me some chicken soup.

After a while he comes back with several soups. "Try to get some rest,"
he tells me (if only he'd quit saying that!). "I'm taking these other soups to
Liz and Sharon. They don't feel too hot either."

On the second view of my soup, a clear broth that hasn't stayed down, I notice that my ulcers have colored it pink. It's inconceivable that I might not be able to dance. The troupe must not lose its engagements. I *will* dance. Being just as human as the next ape, and needing bananas more, or as human as any other creature that covers his eyes so as to believe himself invisible, during hourly regurgitations throughout the night I keep all the lights in my room turned off. In the morning Charlie asks how I liked the soup, and I truthfully say that it was out of sight.

That evening at the Municipal I keep throwing up during *Aureole*—once just before going on, once in the wings before Liz's solo, and again in another wing during Dan's solo. The small offstage area is packed with festival people who shouldn't be there. Between one of my exits and the next entrance I go over to one of them who has a camera dangling from his neck and ask him to leave. He says that he is a *Life* magazine photographer and, to prove it, tries to show me what looks like a phony identity card.

"No photos, *no me gusto*," I tell him and, leading him by his camera strap, show him to a hallway, then return to go onstage. He follows me back to wait in the middle of one of the wings which is the place where I have to make my next exit, and just as I leap into the dark there, he flashes off his camera. I come down on top of him, he falls and rolls, and I ricochet back onto the stage. I'm not hurt, only mad. (What I next did to him is unrecorded in my journal.)

The next day he limps to my hotel where he asks to take a portrait of me. I'm so astounded by his persistence that I give in and let him. He says his name is Hernan Díaz and turns out to actually work for *Life*. On future tours to Colombia I see him several more times and we become friends.

Journal excerpt:

Olympic Gym, Cali
June 23

Jenny just called half-hour. This may be an unusual evening. Audience started coming in twenty minutes ago and already the seats are filled. Standees blacken the back of the house. Menacing noise is coming from the direction of the ticket windows. Last week an unruly mob at an Argentine soccer match stomped a stadium like this one to bits, causing numerous deaths and injury to hundreds.

A giant gnat has gotten stuck in my eye. Why aren't our sponsors and State Department people here? No guards, either. Everybody's vanished, leaving only Charlie to handle things. Gnat now leaving a scribble of blue eye shadow across my cheek. Through the wall I can hear

Jenny and some of the dancers. How can they joke and laugh and eat at a time like this? Our platform is as slick as ice, with nail heads sticking up all over. When we fall off we will have already been lacerated. Sharon's laugh sounds desperate. She's trying to keep her spirits up. I wish I hadn't told her and the other girls that if they didn't want to wash their own costumes, to give them to me to do. To say that was not gentlemanly. And I should've thanked, not sworn at, Chas for having soups sent up three times today when I was trying to sleep. Got to be more patient with everybody.

I hear Bet urging Chas to bring me my red-and-blue costume. They're all afraid to bring it because it is wet. They don't know how afraid I am myself, scared of a lot of things—the stage, the audience (it's clapping and stamping for us to start), afraid of not dancing well enough, of this tour not paying for itself, of being a bad-will ambassador. If ulcers don't soon leave me alone, my dancing days will be numbered.

Jen just called us onstage. I've lost my legs somewhere. If I can get myself scared enough, maybe legs will come back. That mob out there— I'm scared, I'm scared. It's no use, I'm not scared. I'm only scared that I'm not going to be scared. Stomach hurts. I feel contempt for the audience. Am supposed to feel lucky to be here. Will work on it.

After the first dance:

The audience clapped louder before it had seen us. At least the ice is broken. Also a lot of pop bottles. Someone should ask refreshment vendors to hawk only at intermissions. One of them dropped his whole tray during Sharon's bird dance. Maybe the noise wasn't noticeable, as it sounded exactly like the taped sounds of her music. My solo's music would have sounded better if the tape had been audible. All I could hear was pop bottles and belching.

After the second dance:

I've had it with this performance, with this damn city, with this life. Have now danced my worst, if not anybody's worst. Would feel ashamed if not so tired. The idiots out front seemed to like me. I must try to remember never to please idiots again. Forgot about there being noplace to exit. Improvised till time for what would have been my next entrance. The improvised steps were better than the right ones.

We perform a third dance and the ordeal is over. Charlie steers me to a room where a doctor gives me some belladonna. The stomach spasms slow down, and after lying down for a while, I get up and Charlie helps me dress.

He asks if I feel like attending a dinner party that has been planned for us at the consul general's residence, and I tell him that I do, but only if they will give me bananas and not make me stand in a receiving line.

As we get into a limousine, a group of strangers who have been waiting at the stage door crowd around. They've seen the performance and want to express their enjoyment. Among the things that they hand me is a Cali travel poster, some books with photos of Colombian architecture, and, my favorite, a small clay head which is a rare Indian artifact from the little-known Tumaco culture. Other people give me the names and addresses of friends and relatives of theirs living in New York whom they think I might like to look up. One excited lady says she is going to write Columbia Concerts Management in New York to tell them to start booking us. And they all want to know the same thing—how do I like their city? They say "*ciudad*," but I know they mean how do I like themselves. I'm swamped with remorse, and for so recently hating them, their city, and my life, Lord, I'm ashamed. There's only one thing to answer, and I mean every word— "Your city is beautiful. I'm having a marvelous time here. Thanks!"

At about eight the next morning the troupe piles into a vehicle that's to take us to Los Cristales, the place on the mountainside. I remember the vehicle as being an old, beat-up army truck, but Liz remembers it as a limo. The limotruck, or camouflaged Honda, or whatever it was, is very crowded, and everyone's legs are overlapping as we slump down trying to get back to sleep. The driver, by the way, has fabulously large teeth. Liz says that he grins a lot; I say his dentures click. She was always finding the bright side of things. For instance, once when we were returning from a visit to a convent in Cuernavaca, somebody said that the nuns stank, and then Liz replied, "Yes, but they make interesting jam." That's Liz for you.

Anyway, after four or five hours we get to the mountain. It steepens, and we turn onto a narrow dirt road that bumps us awake. Bet reorders her long legs and remarks, "Was dumb, that dinner party last night." Though her words also need reordering, our Bet is always right—that is, whenever she says things that I agree with.

In lieu of a front lawn, the consul general's residence had a large, pretentious swimming pool. The U.S. tax dollars that it must have cost could have kept several modern-dance companies in business for years. Having had a cocktail or two, a welcoming lady in ruffled chintz gown fluttered unsteadily at the pool's edge, attacking the water with her laugh. After waiting for us to come greet her, she said, "What fun hors d'oeuvres we'll all have," then teetered over the edge and into the pool. The dinner part of the dinner party never came, but after a proper amount of time we were allowed to leave. Two days later a Communist paper was to report that we had left because of the "capitalistic" richness of the food.

"That dinner wasn't nothin'," Bet continues.

"Right," Liz adds. "But the peanut butter hors d'oeuvres were real yummy, real American."

On arrival at Los Cristales's outdoor performing area, we find another platform, this time a safer one. At its "upstage" edge is a small one-room shack for us to dress in, the only structure for miles around. Its floor is packed earth, and its two back windows look out over a steep slope that plunges to the Cauca Valley below. The boards of the shack look hand-hewn—hand-bitten, we almost feel. Inside the shack, as seen through the cracks of the boards in front, our view of the rising mountain is cut off by a low, tar-papered roof. The thick door has a plank attached to the inside of it that can be swiveled to fit into strong wooden fixtures. Such security seems strange for so insubstantial a shack. The total primitiveness is marred only by the toilet—a shiny new bucket in the corner—the drape that hides it, and some newspaper torn into small squares.

For all of us to share the same dressing room isn't unusual. Like most dance troupes, we've grown used to that. However, there have been times when the oldest member of our group did not take such arrangements for granted and derived immense pleasure from sneaking a glimpse of people's posteriors. He liked to compare the girls' soft ones to the guys' pairs of hard bubbles, and as we change into practice clothes I twist around to see if my own are still there. There seems to be a slight slackening of tone. Late youth is creeping up like a thief in the night.

I then open a costume case and, after shooing away a six-inch cockroach which Sharon mistakes for a bird, hand Bet our damp, mildewy costumes to hang out, and go outside with the others to warm up.

Distant heat lightning twitches around in an overcast sky. Nobody speaks, and I'm thinking that I'm not the only one to sense the oppressive weight of the weather. We're all tired and edgy.

Charlie comes over doing his comical toed-in ballerina walk and feigning cheer. Before he can speak, I say, "That's cute, sweetums. Hold it—don't bother telling me again that I look like I need some rest. How come you're working so hard at being cheerful? And another thing, why are we giving this performance for free? It's not as if we're rolling in dough."

"Take it easy," he says. "Our money problems will work out okay."

"Yeah, sure. Uh, look over there. Who's that seedy-looking bunch coming down the mountain?"

"They're probably the first of our audience. Kind of early, aren't they?"

I turn, notice Danny stretched out on the ground, and call, "Hey, Pony—
yeah, you with the stupid little bow legs—quit goofing off and warm up!"

Danny winces and mutters something I would've preferred not to hear.
I make a mental note to try to speak more gently to him, have to remind
myself that no one, not dancers, not ponies, not trained fleas, likes the reins
to jangle at the bit. He spreads a towel on the platform to keep his tights
clean, sits down with a sigh, and busies himself with some floor exercises.
Looking up, he tosses me a resigned smile.

Though he possesses a dancer's strength and lithe grace, there's something about him both fragile and gauche, and as he twists and turns there
beneath a sky now filled with billowing thunderheads, he looks young and
tiny. My Pony so tiny. The close clouds are heaving themselves up in
heaps, miniaturizing him and the rest, and I'm thinking how vulnerable we
all are. Ridiculously, humiliatingly, an inexcusable tear hits the top of my
foot. Surely, there must be some value to this touring life? I'm confused and
look up at the formations above that are so different from things here below,
as if *they* would be able to tell me of some threat, some omen that I've
chosen to ignore during the course of the day, or some miraculous cure for
days to come. We wouldn't be on the road forever; a new day was coming—
wasn't it?

All during the rehearsal, silhouettes rise at the crest of the mountain—the
Incas of the area. The tops of distant trees nod to each other as if conspiring,
and heads of savage bushes huddle and whisper together. Dreamlike, the silhouettes continue to rise at the ridge and turn into long black fingers trickling
down silently. The Bach piece that we're rehearsing to begins to sound like
tom-toms in a grade B movie, seems to be warning us that, far, far from home,
all because of our devotion to dance and a ruthless State Department, we're
about to be the victims of a horrible massacre.

After the runthrough we go into the shack to put on our costumes. The
mountainside is now coated with a dense layer of squatting humanity—
mostly Incas but also tourists. The official USIS estimate is thirty thousand.

As we take our opening positions, the horde quiets and stays that way for
the first minute of the dance, then erupts into howls of hearty laughter. It's
not the timid laughter of aesthetes, or the nervous laugh of insecurity, but
the delighted explosions of children—the way straightforward people whose
views are uncluttered with preconceptions react to some curious new discovery. We're caught in a cleansing shower of kisses. The Indians perhaps
are amused by *Junction*'s bright, bicolored tights, or Bach's singsong cello
music, or Bet's blond hair, which this afternoon was fingered surreptitiously
by an Indian tot, or, more likely, the unexpectedness of our movements.
Whatever it is, most of the audience has probably never seen its likes

before. Like Orientals, the Incas are unused to seeing men and women dancers touch and are finding our lifts particularly hilarious. At the end of the dance, when my back becomes a dais for Bet to stand and be raised on, the horde outdoes itself.

Back in the shack at intermission, Liz says that she knew all along that they'd like us. I'm relieved that we haven't been attacked and am coming around to her sunny way of thinking. Like the *Life* photographer and the friendly people who waited at the stage door, maybe these Incas weren't so bad.

Bet, Danny, and three of the others put on their hoods and go back out to perform 3 *Epitaphs*. Liz, Dan, and I are changing. Suddenly, our ears are split by the sound of a lightning bolt and thunder to end all thunder. Wind of hurricane force smashes open the door and scatters our containers of makeup in all directions. Giant raindrops begin battering the roof. Through the open door we see the audience rising and looking around desperately. Caught naked, Liz tries to hide behind Dan. Everyone except us knows that Los Cristales is notorious for mud slides. The folks out front have just one thing on their minds—quick shelter. As Dan and I struggle to push the door closed, part of the crowd is already up on the platform, mixing there with the dancers. The *Epitaphs* dancers, unable to see well because of their hoods, at first think that a few enthusiastic Indians have joined them in their dance onstage, but soon realize that the whole audience has gone berserk. I'm picturing the thirty thousand trying to cram into our shack.

"Keep this door shut tight," I tell Dan. "I'll go get the others."

A couple of strangers slip in as I squeeze out. I push through the mob, single out the dancers, then tug them by the arms back into the shack. Danny is still missing, so I batter back. When I spot him, he's been knocked down but is still doing a sort of horizontal version of *Epitaphs*. I shout, "Get up, clown, before you get trampled to death! *Get up!*" A driving mixture of rain, mud, and skidding bodies pushes us toward the shack, then right past. After being sledgehammered and knocked down several times, each time able to help each other up, we eventually turn back, press our way through the mass of bodies that is hurtling down the steep slope, and manage to scramble into the shack's back windows.

The rain has splashed between the cracks of the walls, turning the earthen floor to mud. Danny slips one last time and sits there, his nose bleeding. But we're safe, and the worst of the storm is over.

I say, "Get up, hotshot—you're ruining the costume."

Indignant, Liz cuts in—"Paul, what a mean thing to say! Can't you see the mud's red with his blood?"

Something is happening to her sunny side. If I were thinking quickly enough, I might say, "Yes, but it makes interesting jam."

When we go outside, the air smells fresh, a sliver of a moon smiles down, the Incas have retreated over the ridge, and our driver is waiting. The downhill trip back to Cali would be better if getting stuck in the mud didn't force us to spend most of the night in what I could swear is a limo.

Three weeks after we leave Cali, an expected revolution hits. Colombia is going through another unstable period, both political and financial.

The tour continues, plane flights alternating with danced flights of fancy, and the more the days are crammed with on- and offstage doings, the less sprightly we become. We begin to think that Simon is speeding up our tempos, and by the time we get to our last stop, Mexico City—an engagement that has been added at the last minute—all of us can barely drag our feet to any tempo. Even so, the last performances are received well, and then we pack for one last time and board the plane for New York.

Journal excerpt:

Late, Chas has just huffed and puffed into the plane, buckled his seat belt, and leaned over the aisle to thank me for holding the plane. One thing that I've learned on this tour is that when the head count is too few and the hatch is about to be shut, rather than pull the dancers off, it's best to go stick your foot in the door and, no matter what anyone says, keep it planted there till the missing person has shown up.

By Sharon's count, we have done thirty-eight performances in twelve weeks and fifteen letters from her hubby. She has let down her tray and, as I asked, is writing thank-you notes to the hosts I haven't already written. Chas is working on the tour's final accounting. Jenny is showing the passenger next to her a gold Aztec calendar trinket that the dancers have given her for stage managing so well. Bet is sitting here beside me and rubbing her knee (trouble there). Her face is drawn. Tired Bet, good Bet, my Bet. Even so, she says her face is a heyday for photographers. Sharon has come over, cocking her head like an interested wren and allowing Bet to reiterate the sinus condition. Liz has come over, too, but doesn't seem to agree when Sharon says that it's been a nice tour. A hunch tells me that Liz is also planning to leave before long to marry and have kids. Pony has just passed by with no tie and that crummy peon hat on again. I give up. Anyway, he is a bridle-broken performer now, a tour veteran. Karen, Dan, Molly—they and the others have danced beautifully and done us proud. Most are injured—strains, split soles, stone bruises—but, luckily, nothing drastic.

Lima, Santiago, Mendoza, Rosario, Buenos Aires, Pôrto Alegre, São Paulo, Rio, Cali, Mexico City. Phew!

Things to remember:

(1) Cali—its three stages, its three types of audiences—the three I was sure not to like, but then did.

(2) Hold on to some of Liz's contagious sunny side.

(3) The neon Novo Mundo sign and its message of new fatherly responsibilities.

(4) Tell Chas not to book any more gyms or mountain slopes.

(5) Get a company wardrobe mistress—a rich one like Bethsabee.

Right now I'm feeling strongly that what the company does is worthwhile. Some good things on this tour:

(1) High recommendations of us sent to Washington.

(2) Packed houses and scalpers.

(3) Job offers (good, but unacceptable) to make dances for National Ballet of Chile and Paris Opéra.

(4) Director of Ukrainian Ballet who saw us in Cali is trying to get us invited to dance in Russia.

(5) The TV taping of us in São Paulo, though not so hot because of dim lighting, made up for money lost when some of our performances there were cancelled.

(6) Earnings—?

Had to ask Charlie about that one. He tells me that the total income from fees, before expenses are deducted, is $40,773.77. Dancers' earnings were $1,800 each, plus per diem. My personal earnings are $7,362, before paying N.Y. studio rent, new costumes needed for the tour, sheet music, etc.—which leaves me approximately $300.

(7) A diploma awarded to me from Santiago dance and art critics (last on list, but OK even so).

I'm feeling that gradually we're accomplishing something, and that being cultural ambassadors means something more than scattering a luxury commodity abroad. We bring imaginings, which are perhaps just as important as monetary aid and practical gifts. Without imaginings, where would politicians be? Even scientific discovery begins with dreams. Yet having imagination is both a blessing and a curse—a blessing from above and a curse from below, or just as true in reverse—a curse from above and a blessing from below.

Here in the plane above the clouds it seems as if the plane is around us rather than us being in it, but when I'm down on the ground working, striving, fantasizing, there's rarely time to think the matter out or take time to decide if isolation is a lonesome thing or lucky.

After entering the list and random notions, as I lean over to tell Charlie something, a letter from Babe falls out of my jacket's inside pocket and into the aisle. The letter includes an interview that Babe had made up—some imaginary questions from an imaginary dance critic and my answers. I pick up the letter and reread.

Why did your studio so plain with nothing on walls?
So I will know where doors and windows are.
Why did you dance barefoot?
So my socks would not get dirty.
Did you work with Martha Graham?
Yes at least till I found out how old she is.
Will you marry soon?
Depend if she agree to let me have naps.
What you do if you become famous someday?
I will rule the world.
Why do you like bugs?
They got these skinny legs that make me laugh.

The interview is typical of Babe's attitude towards me and my work. I fold the pages and, with them still in my hand, settle into the semiconscious state that precedes sleep.

As our plane circles, the pilot waiting for the go-ahead to land, New York's skyscrapers poke up through smog like fists through an orange pizza. Nothing anywhere beats the view of Manhattan from a distance, not even Rio and Sugarloaf. The back edges of our wings extend, break our speed, and we land. Passing through customs is smooth but slow. Charlie gets us a Brown's limousine and the driver wants to know if we are go-go dancers. In the Midtown Tunnel, as a reminder that there's no place like home, he runs into the wall and loses his muffler. While we wait for him to tie it back on, I'm reminded of the awful sound of our canned music and can't help wishing that we didn't have to return to it. No more orchestras, large audiences, or sumptuous theaters. Charlie notices my glumness, I guess, and says, "Cheer up—we've done great."

At the studio, while the dancers grab cabs and head to their places, Charlie and I unload the costume cases and drag them up the four flights, taking plenty of rest breaks on the landings. Babe has been waiting, lets us in and points out his new decor, pats Charlie's stomach and compares it to Tabby's, who's gotten fat. Then he puts a TV dinner on the hot plate for me and hangs out the wet costumes. On his way out, Charlie reminds me of the Radio Free Europe interview that I promised to do later that evening. There goes my one free night. The next day we're to leave for Europe—Amsterdam, The Hague, Rotterdam, Cologne, Middlekirk, and Ostend—after which we'll be rushing back for a tour of the States.

"See you bright and early in the morning," Charlie says. "We're meeting down on the sidewalk at six for an eight a.m. flight. And, sport, you'd better try and get some rest."

Orbs

No longer under State Department auspices with goodwill obligations, all we need to do in Europe is dance. This eastern leg of the South American tour runs without major snags, and the theaters are first-rate, except for two. On arrival at a gambling casino's dining room in Middlekirk, Belgium, we find that tables have been loosely connected to form a raised surface just large enough for a dwarf to tap-dance on. Danny tells the girls that they'd better go put on some pasties, and Jenny, throwing down her headset and gazing dejectedly at the single wall switch that's supposed to be her lighting board, says, "I came to Brussels, or Ostend, or wherever we are, for *this*?"

The other less-than-first-rate place is a drive-in movie theater in Ostend. Wearing practice clothes in order to keep our costumes from being shredded by a rough stage, we amuse a small audience—our jumping having aroused a pack of stray dogs that appears from under the stage and nips at our heels.

Charlie explains that he's booked Belgium as our last stop in Europe so as to lessen our culture shock on returning to the States, where we are to begin a tour of similar places.

After several months of Midwest, including basketball courts at Culver Military Academy and Iowa State U., we think Belgium was not all that bad. Midwestern sponsors apologize for their facilities and tell us that should we return in several years, perhaps there'll be a regular stage for us.

We long for an Act of God to cancel our nine-a.m. performances at elementary schools, for a konk-out-proof tape machine, and to be able to back up our U-Haul without harming anything. Sponsors seem more interested in "education" than in performances, so we do scores of lecture/demonstrations and master classes. Sometimes the classes are crammed with as many as three hundred eager but inert girls in hot pants, and there's an occasional bashful guy in jeans. At a few places, people station themselves around the room to pick up and carry away all injured students. When we ask why they think there'll be injuries, we're told that's what always happens. On giving a fairly hard class to see if this is true, I find that it is, and afterwards limit the classes to a few slow exercises; but once in a while I slip in a leap or a run so that the company and I can stand back and enjoy watching the wreckage.

In February '66 Charlie helps me look for a new loft to rehearse and live in. We find one on Broadway between Spring and Prince, practically in the Bowery. Once used as a sweatshop for the manufacture of wallets, it's larger than the Sixth Avenue studio but has less heat. It's not exactly a prissy place; in fact, it's crummy. For one thing, there's a derelict living in the hallway, and for another, there's no shower or bathtub. (As of '86, it's still the company studio; but instead of costing eighty a month, as it did before the area was legalized for artists to live in and became SoHo, the rent is now two thousand a month.)

Dozens of mismade wallets have been left by the manufacturer. After scooping them up, intending to put the dancers' next paychecks in them, I then resurface the floor, buy a fancy new double-burner hot plate, make stew in a fire bucket, and throw the dancers a studio-warming party.

The next day we begin work on a new dance. The two-and-two-thirds of Beethoven's last quartets that I pick might have been less intimidating had I realized how revered they are. It's to be a large-scale dance, its subject no less than the solar system, the seasons, and Man in general. (Dr. Tacet would've been more excited if it had been Woman in general.) Some of the dancers are to represent moons; others, planets. Since I'm biggest and boss, I cast myself as the sun, a two-faced sun wearing a Janus mask on the back of my head. When the piece is finished, I call it *Orbs*.

As much as we all want to show it in New York, we can't find backing for a season, so we first perform it abroad: Holland, Belgium, Tunisia, Germany, Scotland. Nowhere do we experience outrage from music lovers, not even— much later—when we dance it at the Beethoven bicentennial in Vienna.

Later that year Charlie and I are able to raise funds to show *Orbs* in New York. The season is to be our fourth on Broadway.

The night before we open I can't sleep. Huge rats are rumbling around like nocturnal elephants in the studio's tin ceiling. When cornered, they rear back on their hind legs and scream, and Tabby has learned to leave them alone. Concerned that they might sneak down and chew my face, I'm trying to sleep with my *Orbs* mask on backwards.

Today's been Christmas. To take my mind off ticket sales being low, I'm contemplating the Christmas tree that's standing nearby, attempting to associate myself with its shiny star. The tree has only a few, grayish needles left but is draped with angel hair so you can't tell. It's Babe's tree. He wanted it here instead of at his flat on Spring Street. He and his co-workers on the night shift at Poly Print have been given free Christmas turkeys, and he wanted to share his with me, but I didn't need it, since I already had the one used for making a mold for the rubber turkey that is a prop in *Orbs*. Still, Babe hacked up both turkeys and crammed them into the fire bucket on the hot plate, also cooked up a huge mess of macaroni, powdered potatoes, and Wonder Bread. Quantity, not quality, is his idea of Christmas.

His gifts to me included a stack of comic books, some deodorant, a whole carton of toothpaste (each tube individually wrapped), a dozen pairs of underpants, and a back scratcher. Tabby's gotten a box of chocolate mice. Thinking it over later, I realize that the gifts involve all the senses but hearing. As usual, we went through the long, careful unwrapping ritual, saving the paper for next year. I pretended to go nuts over his gifts while he proudly pointed at the price tags. The Babe's great; but I don't know— sometimes I wish deaf-mutes were more subtle and less refreshing.

At about three a.m., still unable to sleep or to keep my mind away from the opening, I get up to take some aspirin. Like most of the other dancers, I've a cold. And Bet's done something to her knee: it's very swollen, and although she's assured us that she'll be okay, it's doubtful. Dear Bet, she's a trouper.

I return the mask to the costume trunk, crawl back in bed, and bury my face in the pillow. One or more of the elephants in the ceiling have died; the stench is unbearable. The loft's freezing, well below zero. I get up again, pull on two sweaters, and place Tabby under the covers down by my feet. After gnawing at my socks for a while he quiets down.

Next morning I'm groggy and dizzy from the endless circling of planets and moons that have spun me through the night in an endless downward spiral. I make instant coffee, scald my tongue, and drop the cup. The splash shorts out the hot plate. The cup, its handle broken, turns in slow circles around itself. Asking for breakfast, Tabby heaves himself against my shins, and when I step for a chocolate mouse, I tangle him in my feet, trip, and sprain my ankle.

At noon the BMT rattles me up to the ANTA Theater. It's warm there and pretty posh. In dressing room number one is a half-full jar of honey left by some previous performer. After gulping down most of it, I unpack my practice clothes and Ace bandages and set up my makeup, then find that I've forgotten to bring the rubber turkey, so I lend Bev Emmons, our new assistant stage manager, the studio keys so she can go and get it. Shortly before the dress rehearsal Bet and I limp onstage to find out which of our steps will have to be changed. She's able to partially bend her knee, and my grapefruit ankle seems strong enough. We can manage most of our steps, although it will be a challenge to perform without wincing.

The others are in high spirits and laughing, glad and grateful to be here. They're warming up furiously. The season means a lot. Our past year on the road suddenly makes some sense. Instead of warming up in a dark corner as usual, I take center stage, certain that Broadway is the core of the universe.

Back in the dressing room I find that someone's set out my mask. An unsigned note attached to the nose with a clothespin says, "Merde, Big Cheese." There's also a pile of telegrams, one that says, "Darling to you and your company glory love. I shall be with you tonight." It's from Martha.

Just then Olive Adams arrives with a Christmas dinner for the whole gang. She's the mother of Carolyn Adams, our newest dancer, has heard that most of us haven't gotten around to having much of one, and somehow has been able to keep it piping hot—turkey, cranberries, the works. Munchkin Janet Aaron asks if it's wise to eat before a performance, but everyone's mouth is too full to answer. I dole out my gifts to the dancers, each with a limerick. The one on the bottle of vodka for Jenny Tipton goes:

> For beautiful Jennifer Tip
> To pack in her dainty tool kit.
> All know beyond doubt
> That when touring about
> She loves to both light and get lit.

The dancers toss me a bright blue velour bathrobe. Bet has embroidered a monogram on the pocket. Feeling like a personage, I slip it on; we all kiss hard and go reapply lip rouge. Charlie rushes in off the street to tell us that a TV news crew is catching Tennessee Williams, Lincoln Kirstein, Balanchine, and other notables as they enter our packed house.

At eight on the dot the curtain lifts, and a warm puff of expensive per-fumes from first-nighters fills the stage. The dancers and I depart from this world. Moving within their slowly swirling orbits and feeling encouraged by a happy response from out front, I'm plugged in on both burners. It seems that two thousand friends are patting me all at once and gently, and the electricity is making me powerful; I even have the impression that I'm directing attention away from the grapefruit ankle.

Later, in the second act, when Sun transforms into a tipsy preacher staggering around with his Thanksgiving Day turkey, I'm higher than on an earthly bender. In the coda we all outsizzle ourselves and afterwards receive a standing ovation.

Backstage there are smiles from friends and strangers. Like a phoenix's ash, I'm still coiling down from outer space, shrunken and nicely used up, but too beat to fully enjoy the attention. John, the hard-to-impress stage doorman, bows me out as I leave, and I make a mental note to borrow ten bucks off Charlie to tip him later.

Over frozen slush and leaning into a piercing wind, I skid down to Times Square, intending to wait for the reviews. A cluster of bums is huddling around a burning trash can, the rising heat quivering their outlines.

There's nothing in the *Daily News*, but *Newsday* carries a short notice— says I've been too frequently mysterious. On the other hand, Clive Barnes of the *Times* says that *Orbs* is an epic masterpiece. Taken together, the reviews just about cancel each other out; but when I reread, my head tells me they're both right, my bones tell me they're both wrong. Like the hoboes around the trash can, critics are quivery and undependable.

The underground platform of the BMT is colder than outside. My nylon jacket isn't lined. I'm still damp from dancing, and it seems risky to sit on a bench—legs might stick to it like fingers to an ice tray. I check out gum and candy machines for unclaimed coins, avoiding the mirrors in case leftover eye makeup may look weird, and breathing shallowly because of the cold. A wave of insecurity travels down my spine, and I have to remind myself that I'm the Sun, a hero, a big Broadway star. Backstage, someone has told me that I danced magnificently—like an anaconda, he said. Before you knew it, everybody'd be saying that. Maybe I'm to be a legend in my own lifetime—or, better yet, a legend in my own bathtub.

Finally a train screeches in, and, getting on, I tread on the toe of a spike-heel prostitute, but it turns out that she's a forgiving type. Seeing her leads me to think that with *Orbs*, I may've done a little compromising myself. The dance could be better, is my forty-third or so and still not the unanimously acclaimed success that I know I can—must—come up with before it's too late. Being thirty-six, there's not much dancing time left to me. Exhaustion suddenly catches up; I drift off and miss my stop.

I limp the sixteen blocks back to the studio, where I find that I've forgotten to get my keys back from Bev. It's after two, but I can still call Charlie for help—if there were a pay phone and a dime, which there aren't. Nothing's open, and there's nobody on the streets of this strictly commercial neighborhood. Crossing the street, I lean in a doorway where the wind isn't so strong. Babe's the only other person with a key, but he's at work. The Babe—how often he's reminded me not to go off without keys! "Sure, sure," I'd tell him. "Quit pestering me. I've got dances to make."

Leaning in the doorway becomes uncomfortable, and as I let myself slide down the wall into a squat, I feel a crinkling sensation on my back. The shirt's frozen. I should get up and go somewhere, but it can't be all that cold. Anyway, I'm too sleepy. Anyway, what's it matter?

Hunched here, I'm kind of willing my door across the street to open. It looks centuries away. I take a piece of frozen slush from the pavement and rub it across my face. It's numb. Fuzzily, a broken-handled coffee cup begins to circle itself, then gets bigger and whiter until it's all around, and inside there's no wind, no noise, no cold, nothing, just a golden honey of sleep.

Two hours later Babe gets to his place and for some reason decides to come check on me at the studio. He's surprised not to find me there and goes to the front windows, where he notices a sleeping form in the shadows below. He races down and, taking me under the arms, steers me up to bed. I sign for him to heat water in the fire bucket and to find my electric pad. Whimpering, realizing that I might never have woken, he rushes around like a lunatic, knocking over the Christmas tree and scaring the pants off Tabby. After prolonged rubbing, welcome stabs of pain indicate the return of circulation.

By dawn I'm thawed. No frostbite. Even my nose is operating—to test it, I'm whiffing the odor of dead rat. Babe signs a piece of good advice: "In wintertime, is best to stay indoors." Then he wants to know about the opening. I spell the word "glamorous," and add that he should have been there, because he would have been proud.

Paris, Copenhagen, and Liverpool

The spring of '68 is different. Not like Botticelli buds bursting or his modest Venus posing on her half-shell. It's more like the sacrificial maiden in Stravinsky's *Rite of Spring*, and what's bursting are bombs. May is mad, all craziness and rioting. Our country has been split by growing objections to Vietnam, and there are demonstrations in Central Park—chaos not only at home but in Stockholm, Belgrade, and, of course, here in Paris.

Ah, Paree, citadel of drippy chestnuts (I refer to the springtime weather, the people, and their art, all three at once). Our income is again fizzling out, spirits plummeting, and because of a recent injury, the dancers are having to perform without me. However, the tour has begun with a brief span of satisfaction, a momentary islet of solace, not an actual occurrence but only a sensual something that's happened in another dream of mine, yet something that, if these hectic times of joylessness reverse—who knows?—might one day be coming true.

I was ravenous, and if the Frenchie would permit, if my hunch was right, I was about to experience the loveliest of sensations—tête-à-têteing. We had first glimpsed each other from separate tables at Les Deux Magots, across the crowded room on one enchanted evening, and knew only then. As steam from bouillabaisse rose between us, I waved and she noticed, but she then continued to nibble at her picturesque poisson. She soon waved back, however, having choked and become desperate for attention. I rushed over to apply the latest method of tracheal treatment, after which she mouthed appreciative words breathlessly, indicating that she had had a close call but was now feeling exquisitely alive. I then obtained her address and later that evening entered her apartment through a back door and traversed a hallway, at the end of which I found her parting velvet drapes to let me pass. What black, bottomless eyes she had! And oblong, both of them!! She was Odéona, Odéona of France, France's Odéona. Yet she said that she was to be *my* Odéona. And then her black, bottomless, oblong eyes became two blissful, half-lidded circlets of whiteness.

In all conscience, I suppose that I should now present this nocturnal adventure in another way, a less fantasized way, the right-side-of-a-mirror-image way. This, then, is the same thing again, but in reverse chronology, and factually:

Sensual satisfaction almost occurred, not at Mlle Odéona's but at the Théâtre Odéon, where, waving my crutch and angry, I passed through a silent mob of insurgents who were coming down the aisle to take over my theater. True, it was the theater of France, yet it was *my* Odéon. And as I went up the aisle toward the front doors (damn if I'd leave by the back!), the scruffy mob parted to let me pass, each Frog having grasped the fact that if they stood in my way, said a word, even dared to cough, they would be made totally, exquisitely dead. My anger was marvelous, and if they had given me an excuse to tête-à-tête them with my crutch, I would have been able to experience that loveliest of all sensations—killing.

*   *   *

It's too bad that the teacher whose writing class I have lately attended has given me only a D-minus for this chapter's twin beginnings. I guess he missed the point. Was hoping he would go for the analogy of sex and death, or the inference of surrogated sex (pacifying dreams are indispensable to me and will be related to the deprivations to come). He might have at least appreciated my backwards transformation of fantasy into truth. Anyway, I'm pleased to be switching over to reportage, since recollections of Paris are already bringing back pains in my ankle, not to mention the very hurtful thing that happened to my heart, or as Tacet calls it, "the extraordinarily injurious extrapolation which rent my interpersonal connection bondings."

Saved in a shoebox by Mother and found among other clippings having to do with her garden club and grandchildren's weddings is this one from the *Washington Star*. She had not heard from me and was probably worried about me and the company after reading it.

PARIS—While American and North Vietnamese peace negotiators huff and puff at each other from across the Seine, the rebellious students and workers of France are threatening to blow down the walls of Charles de Gaulle's Fifth Republic.

Students have been on the rampage for the past two weeks and the red flags of the Communists and the black banners of the anarchists flutter today over most of the country's 18 universities.

Union leaders said they feared this might be considered provocative. But red flags flew from half a dozen other Renault plants occupied by workers.

Producers and directors of ORTF, France's national radio-television network, struck and radio-television newsmen said they would no longer accept government orders on how the news should be presented. . . .

COMMUNISTS URGE CAUTION

Strikes by newspaper deliverers have shut down most Paris newspapers and airline schedules are fouled up by walkouts of ground technicians at this city's Orly Airport. Even France's Communist party, which late last week reversed an earlier stand and came out in favor of the students, is showing signs of concern about the direction events are taking.

While the party's politburo yesterday forecast that "the conditions are rapidly ripening to end Gaullist power," it warned workers not to participate in an "adventure" which would lack the muscle to topple the regime.

Around this time I'd gotten hold of an international edition of the *Herald Tribune*. Politics usually didn't interest me, but the cobblestones of the streets around our hotel were being torn up and formed into crescent-shaped barricades, so I wanted to know more about what was happening. The headline ran POMPIDOU READY TO USE FORCE TO STEM STUDENT REBELLION.

> Prime Minister Georges Pompidou made clear tonight that his government is prepared to use force to prevent the French student revolt from spreading beyond the universities.
>
> In a dramatic three-minute television appeal, he accused the students of trying to spread "disorders with the avowed purpose of destroying the nation and the very foundation of our free society."
>
> Some 10,000 gendarme reservists were called up throughout France. Police were stationed around all the main public buildings, including the Eiffel Tower and the Opéra, to prevent their being taken over by the students.
>
> Mr. Pompidou's stern warning came after the student leaders announced plans to demonstrate in front of the state television studios tomorrow.

As seen from my hotel window, the guys who are rearranging the streets aren't seeming like students or gendarmes. Most are like Con Ed workers, look kind of covert and seem to know exactly what they are up to. When I go out for a closer look, parked cars start exploding, so I hustle back in and find that one of the explosions has blown a head-sized hole in a wall of my room.

Who made the hole? An anarchist? One of de Gaulle's henchmen? A labor unionist? Nobody knows, and I don't much care, the main point being that our Left Bank hotel, the Michelet, is right on the Place de l'Odéon, an area that is fast becoming the eye of the storm.

Squatting in splendor on the square, our theater looks romanesque or Naziish and has a large André Masson mural on its ceiling. It is France's most progressive state theater, having introduced the works of Ionesco, Albee, and others. Only two blocks from the Sorbonne, it's also a sitting duck. When the students decided to have a cultural revolution, instead of choosing a more bourgeois place in which to shout their protests, they have settled for the conveniently nearby Odéon. Besides, the police probably would have prevented them from crossing the Seine to revolutionize the Opéra or other truly decadent theaters. Unhappy with the world in general and the French educational system in particular, the students are in a state of turmoil which everyone calls "the Manifestation."

After examining the hole in my room—a room that, by the way, is at the front of an old hotel already pitted and tilted enough, as are its beds and bidets—I go to make sure that all the dancers have been given safer rooms at the back. I warn each of them to stay off the streets, and we all agree that it would be foolish to leave the hotel just now.

However, the urge to rubberneck being great—what can compare to a stroll among guns?—out in the plaza we soon run into one another. Of us all, accident-prone Eileen Cropley would be the most apt to be blasted to bits. Sure enough, there she is, dithering halfway between one of the rebel-infested barricades and an advancing squad of gas-masked cops. Blithely unaware of her predicament, she sees me and waves.

"I just couldn't stay inside," she calls happily. "Isn't this exciting?"

"More than you realize," I reply, and escort her back to the hotel.

Anxious about the others, I return to look for them. They've disappeared, but must be within walking distance, as public transportation has been discontinued.

Bet isn't a worry. Her good sense would keep her safe.

Danny and Carolyn can also be counted on to take care of themselves.

Molly is Charlie's responsibility now that they're married.

Janet Aaron and Jane Kosminsky I can also forget. For the rest of the day they'd be in their room, meticulous Janet unpacking, and patient Jane waiting for her chum to get done.

It's the newer dancers—Cliff, Karla, Senta, Jack—who need to be corralled. If I know Senta Driver, she'll likely be up front leading one of the student skirmishes. And if I can spot Cliff Keuter, Karla Wolfangle will be trailing close behind.

Dan might be by himself.

Dapper Dan the dancing man. It takes only a moment to realize that he isn't around, or with us anywhere. It isn't easy to accept. Right after our around-the-world trek, after more than ten productive years of working together, he left the company. Someday it might make sense; right now I'm still feeling glum. When he shyly told me that he wanted to make up dances and form a company of his own, it was hard to believe. He hadn't seemed interested in that kind of thing before, and he didn't possess the magnificent ambition of, let's say, Twyla. Why leave, Dan, why? He thought it would be fun. I could think of no way to dissuade him, nothing to say; I could only wish him well and say so long.

That he would be adding something of his own to the dance sphere is consolation, but now there's no one left whose forked jokes can rile me like his, no one with such bright flea eyes, no one to compete with onstage, no more healthy sandpaper between us. Senta has turned out to be as big a yammerer—maybe more so—but it isn't the same. I wish I could be looking for Dan.

Searching for the new dancers, I cross the plaza and investigate side streets. That Union Jack Nightingale, where was he? Like Dan's, his jokes were hard to bear—not as needly, but quite-British-you-know. A hunch tells me that it will be only a matter of months before he, too, will leave. He seems to have no huge commitment to dance. Am not sure why I'm bothering to look for him. Maybe a good scare from a grenade would do him wonders.

I wave to a passing group of rebels out for a fine march. They wave back.

Where's Jack, that hale fellow well met? And what's that sparseness on his upper lip supposed to be? If he didn't take his mustache so seriously, he might compare it to a soccer team—eleven on each side. His humor is so clearly delineated, its limits so narrowly set, that it makes me aware in a way that I seldom am of my own limits, and I often say to myself, "To someone he is funny; to someone else I'm funny." Evidently, Janet is his someone. They are to be married soon (and later on, to go to a Guatemalan jungle, join a commune, build a thatched hut, dance for the natives, and survive on breadfruit—proof positive that my company is an excellent preparation for that kind of life).

Unable to find anybody, I return to the hotel, where Madame the concierge advises me to keep my dancers indoors. She advises this in English, I think. She's given up on my ever learning French. At each of my stays at the Michelet she's made me promise that by my next visit I'll speak the world's most beautiful language. I haven't wanted to. French makes your mouth look ridiculous—that prissy persimmon look. Parisians really lap at their own tongue and, from foreigners, won't stand for anything short of perfection. Later on, when their tourist trade drops off, maybe they'll be more lenient. And another thing—their impresarios, or empressarios, don't always pay up. And most of them smell bad.

I go up to my room, lie down on the bed, and mull over the current events, or maybe daydream of Odéona, but probably I go to sleep, which is what I usually do in times of stress. It isn't quite time to pick up Charlie and have dinner with Jean-Louis Barrault.

Good reader, due to certain expectations that I should write something insightful about my work, the forward momentum of this narrative's surge toward Jean-Louis Barrault must be delayed. Not that dance is to make much difference in how events turn out, but, after all, one should rise to the task of including somewhere in here some of the progress, forward or backward, of artistic endeavors.

With us is the ever-present *Aureole*, still hovering like an incubus and daring me to top it. *Post Meridian* is plodding along, liked by Bet but aware of its own shortcomings. *Lento* and *Agathe's Tale* are the new pieces. *Lento* consists of several long sections of slow importance relieved only by a little zipping around at the end—very avant-garde in a molasses sort of way—and seems likely to flop even though Paris has always gone gaga over pretension. *Agathe's Tale*, a manifestation of my own, is an out-and-out narrative with dancing characters and a plot, something that in New York has been out of fashion for years. I guess my yen for nonconformity has gotten the better of me. The plot concerns a virgin (Eileen, who is both inhibited and wanton), and her machinations with a lecherous Satan (me in the disguise of a monk), with the angel Raphael (Cliff in the disguise of a unicorn), and with an undisciplined sprite called Orphan Pan (Danny in no disguise and little else). Carlos Surinach has written the medievalish music for peanuts. The costumes might have been richer looking if there had been a budget for them. To me, the interesting thing about this dance isn't that it mirrors the personalities of its performers, which it does, or how we bring our own personalities to its roles, which I haven't encouraged; it's how my role of a lecherous Satan bent on seduction is affecting my own personality. I swear this isn't another dream. Lately I've not only become fascinated with palindromes and retrograded dance sequences but also become aware of certain other changes in me. For instance, old lech Tacet seems to be shrinking—a serious problem when you're already as wizened as he is—and at the same time I'm having an opposite problem with below-belt bulgings. It seems our roles are reversing.

But as to background on the changes brought about by *Agathe's Tale:* At the beginning, it may have been because of Antony Tudor's influence. He once told his other students and me that to achieve a position—an arabesque, an attitude, etc.—we should become more aware of the specific feeling that each position gives us, get to know each linear shape's sensation. Ever since, especially whenever working on dramatic roles, I've tried to follow Tudor's advice. But when making *Agathe's Tale* I've realized that Satan's shapes need not be the kind that are ordinarily used to communicate feelings of lechery to an audience. For instance, the ones used in his seduction of Agathe could just as easily suit the angel Raphael, whose character is supposed to be antithetical to his. It occurred to me that, in addition to a linear shape being a sensation, the shape gains a large part of its meaning from context—something, I guess, that Tudor thought too obvious to mention. But I've also found that shapes—gestural ones such as those implying romantic love, lust, tenderness, anger—are easily interchangeable. (Am unsure whether Tudor would go along with this last.) And so, recognizing the multiplicity and many uses of a single linear shape or gesture, I've dug up any old feelings from within myself and applied them to lecherous Satan's various shapes.

But why should this be affecting my own nature? Who knows? Maybe I've been inversely affected in the way that therapists use dancing as a means of improving their insane patients' mental outlook. Maybe by overfamiliarizing myself with how lechery feels I've caused an imbalance between opposing natures, or maybe I've activated something in me that's best left dormant. Anyway, before the role spilled off the stage and into my personal life I'd been fairly able to keep my lechery to myself; yet I'm now sensing animal changes that, if I can't find a way to stifle them, will surely bring increased frustration during solitary nights as the tour continues through Stockholm, Copenhagen, Yugoslavia, and—the last stop, which somehow I dread most—St. Helen's, a small village that lies just outside Liverpool.

Folks, at times such as when thoughts of lust and disorder upset me and keep me awake, I play this game—just a game—that's almost a twin to the one about oblong-eyed Odéona, but in this one there's no Paris and no St. Helen's and for sure no Liverpool:

You're airborne, sailing effortlessly, gliding in an upward arc, then riding the crest of the world's greatest leap. There are trees below, Norway spruce at first, then honey locusts blending into mimosas, eucalyptus, and then royal palms; and way down there, gathered in glades, too far away to hear but near enough to see, are clusters of people waving welcome banners, and their upturned lips shape into pretty little smiles; and in the long length of that leap you pass over more such clusters, sometimes rosy people, sometimes shining black, and further on, people of varied pigmentations, all with smiles of welcome; and you wonder how many more miles, and the soft air presses on your face. And you think—lucky, lucky to be welcome, and that it would be nice to rest your head on one of their shoulders or sleep with an arm around you. Yet there's no pause to that arc, no break at the crest of that neural glide which is taking you to some unnamed place.

Maybe there have been no trees, no people—never mind, it doesn't matter much. Maybe an unpopulated countryside is stretching out below, a peaceful, starlit plain, and you're the one to see it first.

And so you sail and glide on and on.

And the plain slopes gradually up to a mountain chain, and the mountains slope gradually down to a sandy stretch, and the stretch slopes up, and you think you're getting the idea as to where you're headed. And then, sure enough, beyond some dunes is the turquoise sea, and you know that at last you're coming home, floating gently downward, breathing sighs at the beauty of the place. Starlit wavelets lap a gleaming shore. It's midsummer. It's dawn, the beginnings of a sunset in reverse. The night sky lightens, the sun peeps up. Suddenly everything's all-over pink.

Leaving their nestless eggs lying unprotected on the sand, snowy terns run their beaks along the surface of the sea. Below, waving blades of eel grass shelter multicolored minnows and—oh, why not?—an admirable, large blue shark.

And now it's exactly noon. The moment has come to unwind your Ace bandage or throw off your clothes or donate your old truss to a museum, and the salty sea is just great for whatever ails you and you're about to have your lovely noontime dip.

You drop right in. A light caress. The water's deep, but not so deep that you can't see bands of sandy furrows far below, dappled by dancing lights, and you let yourself sink down and down, and there you are on the bottom, stretched out comfortably, arms crossed at your chest.

Ah, that's better. The day was getting glary. From far above, the sun's now cooler light shines in long shafts through the sea.

No, this mustn't be. No, it's not time yet. Dear God of All Order, please delay this leap.

Well now, that game was supposed to be without lust, but an awful lot of suggestiveness kept creeping in—upturned lips, rising and falling motions, taking off clothes and all that—and some might say that this could be what's called lust-related doodling and may be glad for all that suggestiveness. But I didn't mean it, for when it comes to dreams I never promise how they're going to end up, I mean bottom out, I mean come—nuts, more suggestiveness. Forget it.

You see, when you try to clarify your thoughts so that you can get rid of them, or maybe put them into a dance, they won't always go in the right direction. Ideas sprout minds of their own and trail off over here, head off over there, and then you have to back up because you've been taken on the wrong route. Not just a route but also a root. A bunch of them, mostly growing in the dark where you didn't want to go. These dreams and dark places don't come at you in a big flash. They're gradual and insidious and tedious, and you have to show patience and leniency towards your dreams and your darkness. It's as if you're tugging up a tree so that you can see how all its roots keep branching into the next and the next. There're a lot of ways to go, and it would be nice if the tree had only one root, not all those confusing side issues. So you can't help but look at things from different angles, even backwards, and it's easy to get mixed up about which is the tap route. So if that one's the tap, which one is the trunk? You've gone and up-treed the wrong bark. So, to get it right, you have to take the tree and turn it upside down with its trunk in the soil and its roots all exposed, and by doing this you not only lose sight of the trunk but the leaves that it breathes by, and you're apt to kill the tree. Sometimes when you dig into your dreams, try to order your thoughts—look out! That's a perilous time, and profoundly frightening.

Well, to continue the surge toward Jean-Louis Barrault—the actor/director Barrault who's famous for roles such as Hamlet and the mime in the film *Children of Paradise* and at whose feet everyone fawns. Occupying a high position in the French Ministry of Culture, he has invited us to participate in the Festival of Nations, offering us the gate receipts minus eighteen percent. If our performances sell out, we stand to earn about ten thousand dollars for the one-week run—an amount that after company expenses and payroll are met, will enable me to pay off some music, costume, and studio costs.

Jean-Louis and his wife, the actress Madeleine Renaud, are giving Charlie and me a big welcome at the Restaurant Mediterranée, and we're sitting there soaking up the Barrault graciousness and charm, thinking how nice it is that they will be picking up the tab, and that they hardly seem Parisian at all. But they've got charm bad and that ain't good, but, even so, they're very very good, and anyway if they aren't good they're less than half-bad.

My high evaluation of Barrault proves true later through a magnanimous deed of his. What is soon to occur to the company clearly comes under what is referred to in a clause in our contract with the festival as a "case of tumult," but when we are prevented by the revolutionaries from latching onto our gate receipts (which turn out to be nothing minus eighteen percent), Jean-Louis offers us his personal check, which, though it's generous of him, I refuse. After all, the revolution wasn't *his* fault. He then comes up with a cash amount from someplace (cloud of mystery here) which enables us to go on with the rest of our tour. He is not only more than fair but enormously courageous when he stands by and for the students who take over our theater, knowing that to do so will endanger his high position with the Ministry of Culture, a position that the distinguished achievements of his career have earned him. Of course, the State then dumps him and his life is ruined, but he surfaces later to continue where he left off. There are other good things to say of him, but nothing that hasn't been said before.

I've been skipping ahead, though—gunning the jump, as it were. Best go back to my disastrous leap at the dress rehearsal, the "small death," old Martha would've called it. No, let's go to my room at the Michelet after that leap so as to get a backwards look at it.

All over. Lavender and red, lavender and red. Over and over and over.

Put lavender and red together and what've you got? Stupidity, that's what you've got. Stupid wallpaper. Fruity French shapes. Stupid fruity Parisian room. Shoving my plaster-encased leg further down the bed, I cross my arms and switch my attention to the ceiling. Prissy little cracks.

The omens—I should've recognized them. When unpacking—the exploded can of shaving cream. And before that—my Valpak's busted zipper (a Freudian zip?). And at Easter—the lunar eclipse on the night before we left New York.

Fateful omens? Let's face it, the fact is that I shouldn't have gotten so excited about our opening. After all, there have been openings before. But the stage was uneven, and if only the stagehands hadn't gone on strike and our floor covering could have been laid, and if only things hadn't felt so urgent and rushed due to short rehearsal time . . . If only the opening hadn't been postponed because of the theater's electricity being cut off. And if only I hadn't been so eager to finally get to dance, maybe the accident wouldn't have happened.

And now the ankle has swollen into a huge, lopsided *pamplemousse*, its splintered bones condemned to a plaster coffin. One can forgive one's ankle almost anything—anything save treason. It deserved what it got. Good riddance.

The rehearsal was going great. But no, like an excited kid on Christmas morning, I had to get carried away. Instead of trying to finish the dance I should've stopped and applied ice. What about the other dancers? How are they supposed to get along without me? Now you've done it, buster. Put excitement together with carelessness and what've you got? Guilt, that's what. Big guilty American jerk.

But what a great leap it had been! Not *the* greatest, yet one of the longest. Time seemed to stop midair. But instead of landing properly, my foot had come down with too much weight on the outside. As with most drastic displacements, the pain wasn't much—only a split instant of overall flash and a deafening little pop, and then a vague sense of something having shifted the wrong way. I could stand up and smile, but the surroundings were out of focus. Gathered close, the fuzzily formed company looked almost near enough to touch, almost real. Bet and Charlie were too sympathetic, and I'd tried to ignore their supporting arms, had said, "I'm fine, just fine, don't bother."

Good reader, how I long to reverse that leap. Let's run it backwards slowly as if on film. There's nothing like a long backwards leap for leaving the tribulations of real life in front.

To begin, we sink upwards, then tell our thighs, "Stop that bunching—no need to prepare for a takeoff that's already happened." We then notice that leading our leap and fluttering are the loose edges of our practice clothes, also that eternal unravelment, the Ace bandage.

Gravity, too, has gone into reverse. Head in tow, our hair has unsettled and is standing on end—maybe in delayed reaction to the scary fall we've left behind. Time halts as we creep in reverse along the path of a backward arc. How splendid to be floor-free, with so much time to savor the scenery below! Though never tired of it, perhaps we should stop trying to identify the genders of the people down there. Top views of bottoms can be confusing, so we direct our gaze outward and up, this bit of theatrical know-how to reassure the audience that we have no fear of falling.

And we sail and glide on and on.

And scent from a stagehand's cigar wafts up to merge with that of our feet, and the top of the pinrail and upper part of the proscenium slide past, and we're getting the idea as to where we've been backing up to, and high in the flies there's no confusing puzzles of gender, no yearning, no solitary wandering. A rat is backtracking along the catwalk, and so we know that at last we've come home. That is, since everything is in reverse, we know that we've escaped from home.

Yes, this must be. Yep, God of All Disorder, now we can see—within every home lover is a home hater struggling to escape.

And it's true.

As I lie here in bed caged by stupid wallpaper, I remember how before the leap, I told myself that all our French troubles were over. But they'd just begun, and the dream digging, this backwards leap, has revealed that I both want and don't want a home, and has now branched into a worse revelation—that as well as loving to dance, I despise it. Maybe the injury had been in some way self-induced. Guilt, what impounded guilt!

Before I know it, a doctor has slapped a cast on me which, according to him, will have to stay on for two months. Ridiculous. By that time the tour will be over. I curse my ankle for allowing itself to be encased in plaster and wonder where to find a saw. An ankle hasn't ever prevented me from performing before, no matter how swollen, and it isn't about to start now. Inactivity would be very bad for it; it would heal much quicker without the cast. Obviously, the doctor hadn't any idea of the recuperative powers of a dancer. But the saw would be a last resort. Though a long shot, there seems to be a better solution.

My old friend Mark Rudkin, who lives here, knows many interesting people, among them a group said to be witches or faith healers or, as Mark calls them, "doctors of unnatural practices." They're Lapps, I think, but look to be masquerading as Californians who've rejected their guitars in hopes of seeming East Coasty, and they have no amulets, runes, dishes of guacamole, herb-filled skulls, or other trappings; but it isn't the lack of those, it's the Mafia in their manicured nails and the strange glint in their eyes that are making me suspicious, and especially their favorable remarks about my room's wallpaper.

After some disorganized milling at the foot of my bed they perform a ritual consisting of a moment of silent concentration aimed at the cast, and when nothing happens they tell me that unless all of us can maintain focus, their efforts won't work. I want very much to cooperate, and so, during our repeated attempts, I tell myself that I do believe in quacks, I *do* believe in quacks. But it's no go. Ankle refuses to be taken in, and Mark and his friends leave under a cloud of resignation. Added to my guilt over the fall is the disquieting admission that I lack the ability to have faith, not only in quack Lapps but in my old friend Mark.

And I can't push away accumulating omens—that the troupe numbers eleven dancers plus Charlie and stage manager Judy Daykin, making us a total of thirteen, the same as a witch's coven. And that our opening, before being postponed, was scheduled for May 13. And though I thought the tour was our fourteenth foreign one, am now wondering if it's our thirteenth. Am doubting facts, doubting my friends, even doubting my doubts. The room's little purple shapes are wallpapering my mind and sapping my will to dance. But the body is supposed to do as I tell it; I will and it obeys. Ulcers, disease, torn tendons have never stopped me; never before has there been a doubt in my mind that I can get up and dance. But now . . .

Charlie has found a medical supply store and brought back some crutches, which I refuse to touch, telling him that they are the wrong size. He then returns to exchange them for larger ones, which are now lying across the foot of my bed. It's the day of the opening, and the shiny new crutches are exuding something terrible and tempting, something soft like a flying dream. I smell acceptance in the air, a giving-in-to-fate odor, and the more the crutches exude their opium, the less I think that I can dance tonight.

Doubt weakened, I don't try to saw free. Instead, I take the crutches and hobble to the theater to work out a temporary emergency program. I'd let myself miss the opening but not the rest of the engagement. *Lento* and *3 Epitaphs* are substituted for *Agathe's Tale*, my solo in *Post Meridian* eliminated, and Cliff, who has been understudying, goes into my part in *Aureole*. Our French orchestra isn't available for the rehearsal, but our conductor, John Perras, assures us that it will show up for the performance—not that the dancers will necessarily recognize the music.

The opening has been sold out, and the rest of the week looks so good that an extra Saturday matinee is being planned. If this keeps up, our income will be twice as much as what we expected.

After the rehearsal I return to the hotel to put on a suit and tie. Just at the dot of seven, the time when I usually warm up, the old nerves begin to jangle and adrenaline flows. To my surprise I find it impossible to resist doing a small one-legged warm-up.

The Barraults have invited me to sit in their box with them. It's the first time that I'll be seeing the troupe from out front, my own performances having allowed only short glimpses from onstage or in the wings. Sitting in the box during the performance, I can barely look, am too concerned with the audience's reaction. At its slightest stirring I want to demand that everybody be still. Whenever they're still I want to tell them to react. The dances stretch out interminably, and it seems as if the curtain puller has gone off duty. I'm embarrassed for the choreographer, who thinks such a boring display can possibly keep anyone from rushing to the nearest exit, and sink further and further down in my chair until I'm below the box's railing, keeping my eyes closed like at the dentist's.

At intermission I pretend to be doing something down near the floor so as not to be spotted by anyone who might recognize me. When the Barraults express curiosity, I explain that I'm having an itch, and then Madame Renaud bends over to see if she can help by running her spindled program up and down inside my cast.

As the program continues, whenever I hear music that I would have, should have, been dancing to, I react with small involuntary twitches that correspond to my steps, and it's all I can do to keep myself from waltzing around in the box.

After the last dance I open my eyes and look around. The audience is clapping and stamping, then rises to its feet and settles into a rhythmic pulse that threatens to flake the André Masson mural from the ceiling. Though impressive, I can't help feeling that the ovation is for the dancers, not me, and so when Jean-Louis suggests that I go onstage for a bow I try to beg off. Being seen onstage with crutches would be embarrassing, but Jean-Louis insists, so I leave the box and go through a side hall, taking my time and hoping that before I get to the stage the audience will have quieted. After several minutes I arrive in the wings, but the audience is still at it, so I crutch out onto the stage, where the dancers seem glad to find me with them. Their welcoming smiles are touching, and suddenly I regret not having watched them.

The Barraults then escort me to a party for the company at the Mediterranée, where I'm seated at a center table between a countess and the American ambassador. Champagne and an all-white meal is served—

endive salad, poached flounder, cauliflower with white sauce, and little pale
peas. The guests, dancers, even the restaurant staff seem delighted with the
opening. The more elated they grow, the more morose I become. I join the
conversation as best I can and try to pull off a proud air while surveying my
laughing coven, but when my eyes fall on Cliff I quickly redirect them. In
all the years of dancing *Aureole*, I can't recall it ever having had such a
response, and this even though Danny was dancing Dan's part and Cliff
mine. I'm thinking Cliff hasn't been quite up to the part. The white meal
starts lacking flavor, tastes very gray, and, although not the best thing for
ulcers, I pepper my plate black.

The next night's performance goes even better, and then—

PARIS STUDENTS CAPTURE THEATER

Paris, Thursday, May 15 (AP)—Insurgent French students swarmed
out of their bastion in the Sorbonne early today to take over the Odéon,
majestic left bank branch of the French National Theater.

The single night watchman said he was overwhelmed by the crowd
that swept out of the liberal arts school as the last of the audience at an
American ballet performance was leaving the theater.

The theater seats 1,200. Police said the students filled the seats and
occupied the premises from the basement to attic.

Other student groups in a dozen cities also were occupying university buildings and trying to set up committees that they hoped would
be allowed to participate in school administration.

STRIKING FOR WEEKS

The Sorbonne students have been striking and demonstrating for
weeks in support of demands for education reform and modernization.

Premier Georges Pompidou told the National Assembly Tuesday
that he would appoint a committee of interested parties to study the
problem and make suggestions.

The students have paid little attention, apparently feeling that they
have the upper hand after the government offered concessions in the
wake of street battles on the left bank. They seemed in no mood to start
classes until they have something positive in hand.

Well, that's all, folks, this is where we came in. Do you notice how things
have circled back like a snake eating its own tail? And isn't it ironic that such
a far-out dance troupe was forced outside, is now right where it started, and
that those who forced us there were doing so in the name of antiestablishment beliefs? Isn't it paradoxical that we who at home have been judged to

be relentlessly adventurous were now being called a representation of the *théâtre bourgeois*? Not that it mattered how anyone categorized us—what's in a name? The point was not to get stuck in any slots at all, to keep circling.

In real life, not dreams, there's hardly anything when you're up (or down) a tree that's easier to hate than a right-about retrograde movement, a systematic going-over of already climbed branches, especially if you've got a yen for adventure. Such a course seems distasteful so long as there remains hope for trying out new difficulties. It is with such a hope that, instead of hightailing it out of Paris, which is impossible since all transportation has ceased due to strikes, I attempt to get us back into the theater.

We'll be without funds if someone doesn't do something. Pleas and sympathy from Jean-Louis fail to dislodge the twenty-five hundred squatters, so I decide to go speak to them myself. Accompanied by friend Mark, who has agreed to go along as translator, and armed with the crutches with which I so successfully cowed the rebels at the conclusion of our second performance, we bang on the stage door and, after some wheedling, are allowed inside, then escorted to the stage by two burly gents who are pushy but not vicious, one of them with welts and slashes on his face and hands that strongly suggest the impacts of barbed wire. Gendarmes have been stationed at trouble spots, crowded and confined for hours in their own paddy wagons, and then, their antagonism for student upstarts heightened by discomfort and seclusion, have been let out to attack. This is before the government sends in its Tactical Patrol Force, a group that knows how to beat up people without it showing.

Our receptionists lead Mark and me to a rostrum that has been placed downstage center. Since my recent passage up the center aisle, the Odéon's newly refurbished interior has gone downhill. Any lover of beautiful theaters would be shocked. Through layers of smoke coming from small fires to cook by, we can see political graffiti being smeared all over the walls. Whatever could be split into firewood—railings, moldings, seats, and so forth—has been, and is being used to prepare concoctions that are bubbling in the campers' caldrons. The place smells like a gastronomic mistake and looks like a hobo-town dump. The Odéon's expensive new grand drape has been pulled down and torn into blanket-sized pieces. Protruding from under one of them can be seen two pairs of rendezvousing feet, and, good grief, I shouldn't try to describe the type of movement that is shaking that poor piece of drape.

Others who are not occupied with goatishness or housekeeping swarm everywhere. Two groups of students have taken sides against each other, and when I ask Mark what they are yelling about, he tells me that they are debating the pros and cons of existentialism and other refined philosophies.

In the orchestra pit a tight-sweatered coed with artistic tendencies is pounding the hell out of a spindly harpsichord. (Eventual renovation of the Odéon is to cost the government two hundred thousand dollars.)

Mark and I are having trouble getting everyone's attention. Waving and calling and thumping my crutch on the floor doesn't work, so I draw back the heavier of my legs and use it on the rostrum, causing a sizable crack in my cast which leaves it looking like a cloven hoof. The noise attracts attention and I greet the revelers in my best French. "Bone sewer, masseurs!" I say. "Sono Masseur Paul Taylor san, lay ballerino—"

A derisive roar cuts me off. They think crippled dancers are funny. One of them calls out, "Talk French, you joker!"

So Mark takes over, saying something like "Mr. Taylor bids you good evening and wishes to thank you for allowing him a moment of your time." Then, turning to me, he says, "What shall I say now?"

"I'm not sure. You have any suggestions?"

"How should I know? This whole thing was your idea. Let's just say good luck and that it's been nice meeting them."

"Old pal," I say, "I'll tell you what—tell them that my group and I are all for art and education, that we're real avant-garde and are an unsubsidized commune just like them, but smaller and not so noble, of course, and that we really depend on our box office, and that by preventing us from working—we're only workers, too, see?—they're taking the bread right out of our mouths, and I hope they'll never know what a hard thing hunger is, hard as all getout, and though the festival is trying to find us another theater, we need the Odéon's stagehands, but those guys are loyal to Barrault and won't leave here since they refuse to be ousted by students, and will everyone please give us our theater back?"

Gripping his head, Mark replies, "You expect me to remember all that?"

But he does the best he can, and whatever he says is interrupted by hecklers' hoots and flutter-lipped sounds. The students are being very unsympathetic, very disgusting; but us, we're being very patient and polite. Our leniency, however, is tempered by fear. I tell Mark that I'll try some flattery on them. "Volly voo, lay miserables," I say. "Lay amour too jour. Lay jeté tray amours. Lay bone revolutionaries. Bone bone, lay lay!"

When that proves to have the wrong effect, I suggest that Mark tell them how poor and hungry I've always been. "Tell them about the canned dog food," I tell him. (For reference, please turn to the back or the front of this book, according to how you may be reading it.) But nothing works.

We observe their unfriendly gestures for a time, and then I remember what old Tacet always says—that when one's goals are blocked by primitives, people who are argumentative and reluctant to recede from what they erroneously recognize as the correct course, it is de rigueur to enlighten them by pointing out the fallaciousness of their argument, and that when this proves futile, one has to move forward firmly, reminding them of how their uncooperativeness may be a disadvantage to them, thusly and thereby presenting them, and others like unto them, with an indisputable reason to acquiesce. Translated, this means that when dealing with deadheads, blackmail's the thing.

So I ask Mark to say that we don't like their squat-in and if they don't get out, I'm going to tell a bunch of TV, radio, and press people who are waiting for me back at the hotel that their dumb revolution stinks.

"But there are no reporters there," Mark whispers.

"So what. Charlie said there might be at least one—sooner or later, maybe. Go on, build it up, pile on colorful details, describe the thick black TV cables, the ones known in the profession as horse cock—that ought to be something they can relate to—which are being strung up between my window and a dozen or so trucks parked outside. Say that these cables are going to have to transmit very antirevolutionary words to the entire news-hungry world. Say that if they don't scram, their image and their cause ain't going to be worth diddlyspit. If you want, you can put a tear in your voice."

"But they're in an awful mood. They'll kill us."

"No they won't, and anyway we can always bash our way out of here with these crutches."

Mark starts translating but is interrupted by an ear-splitting roar, and when the burly gents come at us threateningly, we have to slip quickly out of the theater.

On the way back to my hotel we pass a street entertainer who has set up shop under the front portico of the theater—a smarmy gypsy with sharp ears poking through a tangle of black hair, and he's wearing a monkish robe that reminds me of the one I wear in *Agathe's Tale*. He has a poor pet goat that's teetering precariously at the top of a tall ladder as it performs a little tap dance with its cloven hoofs.

After we pass I'm tossing the gypsy around in my mind, wondering if I could work his kind of icy grotesquery into my role of Satan, and I'm almost admiring the seeming lack of concern for his endangered goat. How he looks reminds me of a talisman that I've been carrying around in my makeup kit.

This good-luck charm, given to me in Iran, is an ancient Persian statuette of a goateed and handlebar-mustached king—exactly four inches tall, with knobby arms and a crown with three blunt points. When dressing-room tables were perfectly level, he could be balanced upright on little flat feet. His nose, a large Persian one flanked by crossed eyes, looks as if it's been worn down by kisses, but before I leave him to go onstage it's always the butt that I give a big ceremonial kiss. The king seems tremendously heavy for his size, despite being made of bronze or iron which the centuries have coated with a dark patina. In fact, whenever toppling off tables, he's apt to dent the floor rather than himself. His vintage is uncertain. He could be a son of the aboriginal potato-shaped Venuses that were made in caveman days when extreme chunkiness and pendulous sag was the ideal of feminine charm, or the fact, or both. Whoever sculpted these Venuses, and whoever forged my king, must have agreed that royalty should be depicted in a perfectly symmetrical way with left and right sides matching. But if my king sounds nice, then I've left something out.

This part should be whispered: His dark shape, his unnatural geometry, his unreasonable weight, each matching stub of his crown erected to the same height, the equally spread stance of his legs, the mirror-image crossed eyes, all gather into a single hiss of unworldly power, an excessive power that might easily be misused. He's charming, see, but not nice. And perhaps most disquieting and fearsome of all are the ridges that run across his chest and icy thighs, which hint of leather straps and leggings of a sadistic— yes, gentlefolks, a definitely sadistic—nature.

Now Mark and I are going into the hotel lobby, and the powerful king and gypsy are crowding my mind. As for myself, I'm having trouble maneuvering the crutches and feeling pretty powerless over recent events, stewing over being unable to get the company out of such a fix, and dreaming up torturous things to do to the revolutionaries. Then Mark says, "I don't believe this! How did you know?"

I say, "What're you talking about?"

"Didn't you see the TV truck we just passed and the cable running up to your window? What are you, a warlock or something?"

"Sure, sure, and you're a big black cat."

"I'm not kidding. Go on, look back outside and see for yourself."

And there it was, a trumped-up truck come true.

Have you ever seen Nemesis on wheels? She looks mighty tasty, right? By wicked king, by fatso queen, by gosh, *now* those rebels would get it!

The hotel's self-service elevator is an open-shaft kind and slow, allowing time for me to plot out a proper crucifixion. On reaching my floor I clang open the cage's accordion gate and leave it open behind me.

The news crew filling my room isn't quite ready for me; the director's still planning shots to be aired on local and foreign stations. At the window a camera is being jockeyed to get an exterior view of the two flags that are flapping over the Odéon—one red for revolution, one black for anarchy. A telescopic shot is being worked out of a banner that has been placed across the theater's front doors which says CLOSED TO BOURGEOIS AUDIENCES. IMAGINATION HAS TAKEN OVER AT THE THEATER OF FRANCE. The students haven't seemed to remember that imagination, as Broadway's George Kaufman once said, is what closes on Saturday night.

After a makeup lady sponges some base on me and spritzes my hair, I flop down on the bed to wait.

I'm nursing my resentment, firing up my outrage, savoring sweet revenge, and reviewing every time we'd ever come to Paris. Always there'd been unpleasantness. Our sponsors had wanted to worm their way into artistic matters; they made it hard to collect fees, were always starting fights, loved to. How often I'd had to threaten to cancel, but we'd always gone on, then gotten invited back the next year. There's a public for us here, but this time things have gone too far. Mobs aren't logical. The rebels haven't known exactly what they've been doing, or why, or what to do next. Poor lambs, scared goats. Hold it—don't forget their mutilation of the theater. Yet their need for political reform isn't so off-base. Charlie has said that what they are saying is that if there's a cancer you've got to cut it out, and you don't have to make plans for what's next. That barbed wire. Youch! Unforgivably cruel. My anger's slipping away. Mustn't let it. They've trod on my territory, and here's a chance to blast back.

"Mr. Taylor," says the director, "stay right where you are, but lift your cast two inches up off the bed and to the right so that it will show in the foreground with that pretty wallpaper behind. Start talking on cue, and while we're angling back and forth at the window keep holding your leg up and talking for exactly six and a half minutes. Watch my signals for when to talk faster, and no mumbling, if you please."

When the makeup lady has finished fiddling with my collar and patting all over my face with a Kleenex, she gets out of range, and the director says, "Get ready, get set . . . go, guy, you're on. Give those troublemakers hell!"

Well, I would have, and could have; I want to; but when it comes right down to it, all I can say is about how we've been caught in the middle, that Jean-Louis has done all he could, that I don't feel bitter, but hope not to come back here for a while. I don't know, I just can't blast the students. It wouldn't seem right somehow.

The plot now thickens, or I should say thins, since it's reedy Bet who's about to enter. Starting with the news crew, there has been a steady stream of visitors through my room—the Becks, Danny the Red, some others, and then one of the company girls, who didn't leave till dawn and who for tactful reasons I'd better call Fred. No, that's misleading. Better call her Lucy.

Lucy Night. But she comes later. To keep up retrograding, I'm starting with the last visitor, dear Bet.

It's about ten in the morning and I've been awake all night. Lucy's been gone a short while. Bet hasn't come in yet, but she's been on my mind. Have I ever mentioned that I love Bet? Always have. I've loved that weird two-tone-eyed Dutch Treat since the day we met in Martha's kitchen. Don't know why I love her like I do, I just do. And as years pass, I've had reasons to think that in her way she loves me back. But though we are close in many ways, there is one way in which our relationship (awful word) has been limited ("limited" is less awful than "consummated," "consummated" being something that happens to soup). But maybe I'd better leave our limitation to an analyst and the romantic stuff to songsmiths.

Anyway, I'm lying alone on the bed feeling burnt out from something that's been a lot like—oh, what the heck—a lot like soup. And I'm mixed up about it, and, well, I'm feeling how I always felt about Bet and dreading to face her. Within small dance troupes like ours, everyone's private life is an open book, and news of the latest bedroom romp travels double quick. I can almost see Bet coming down the hall and so am not at all surprised to hear familiar raps at the door. They sound gentler, more hesitant, than her usual ones. My Bet was never a scratcher or fingernail drummer. When she raps, you always know right away who it is, and it's good to see her. This time I'm not wanting her to see me, but she knows I'm here, so I do a fast job on the messed-up bedclothes and let her in.

She goes to sit by the window by the bombed-out place. Her posture is worse than usual, and red rims clash with the bicolor eye. Without fooling around she comes right to the point.

"Paul, I know about last night."

"Bet, I don't know how it happened. I . . ."

"No need to say."

"Bet, aw, Bet . . ."

She sags, straightens up, and folds her hands in her lap (a gesture she is one day to repeat in *Esplanade*). "We should face facts. It's over between us."

"Don't say that, Bet. This won't make any difference."

"It's okay, I understand. You prefer her, she's your type. I know you can't help it."

"Bet, you're the loveliest, the best, the most . . ."

She rises to leave. "Really, it's all right. I just wanted to tell you not to feel bad."

"How's about having breakfast together?"

"Thanks," she says, smoothing out her skirt and smiling crookedly. "I'm having room service—costumes to wash, post cards to write. Another time."

Before Bet, halfway through the night, almost at the witching hour, Lucy hasn't come in yet but she's been flitting around in my mind. I like Lucy and sometimes fantasize about her. Her appeal could tug at anyone with an affinity for waifs. There's something vulnerable about her—poignant shoulders, heartbreaking dimples here and there, the hint of a knock to her knees. But she's not in the least weak; she's spunky, and with stamina that sails her through rigorous dances all but unstumblingly. Minor slipups onstage are less serious to the audience than to her because of the vulnerability. Possibly, she knows that her appeal makes up for the slips; in fact, some would question who is in control—fate or Lucy.

Among imagined others, she waits in a line that forms at the foot of my fleece-covered casting couch, a couch that, strictly speaking, has never existed. Nevertheless, the drabber the reality, the more color I like to daub on, and I muse of gaudy silk sheets and the choreographer's rights and power—forces comparable to those of a doctor, an attorney, or an uptown plumber. As the bills and questionable services of professionals such as these are condoned by their clients, so should a dance maker's slightest whim be taken seriously by his dancers. Indeed, I've noticed that my every mood affects my flock. I laugh, they laugh; I get tough, they get tough; I cry, they pretend to cry. There are possibilities here, and I sometimes dream of seducing Lucy.

So, as I said, it's about midnight, and my fantasy is heightened by footfalls in the hall. I sense that I'm about to be visited by . . . at the sound of her soft breathing at the door, I sit up in bed and call, "Come, Lucy!"

The door is kicked open; a wheezy old waiter teeters in and plops a heavy tray onto my lap. What a way to have your bubble popped! To express its regrets about our cancelled performances, the management of the Mediterranée is treating me to one of its all-white meals. "Where's the pepper?" I ask. He doesn't understand English, so I make some brisk up-and-down motions with my loosely curled fist. Misreading the gesture, the old coot frowns disdainfully and hurries out.

Then, just when I'm debating the pros and cons of a certain backward belief championed by Tacet which views all human coupling as being merely a sublimated form of masturbation, who should come in but Lucy, and she's gazing at my cast, looking very sympathetic, very morbid about my lameness and all. I guess she sees in me a fallen angel or plucked Icarus or someone. "Dear PT," she says. "Your foot hurts, doesn't it?"

"Not exactly. It's my ankle, and it only hurts when I kick something."

"You must feel just dreadful not to dance."

"Yeah, I do. Just dreadful. And tired of lying around doing nothing at night, and this bed is always so empty with me in it. I haven't had any fun for a long time, and now this terrible itch."

"Oh?" she says innocently, completely missing the point. Then she goes to the wardrobe for a coat hanger, unbends it, and starts poking it down inside my cast. This isn't my idea of total satisfaction, but her sympathy is nice, and her scratching is downright uplifting—you know, very expansive. I lie back and command her to scratch harder.

"PT, your foot is—"

"Ankle."

"Sorry. Ankle. All this trouble—the revolution, you've been so . . ."

She can't quite express what she means, just sits there on the bed with her lips moving silently and her eyes beginning to brim.

Like me, but more so, when Lucy tries to say heartfelt things, sometimes there is communication and sometimes not, and there's an incompleteness to it, a restraint. It's like tentative probings from outer space. For people like us, maybe for many dancers, maybe for nearly the whole world, communication with words is unreliable.

This night Lucy needs meaningful communication. After all, we've been caught in a revolution which, if not a full-out war, seems like one. We're disoriented and not even sure if we'll be able to get out of Paris in one piece. We both need to share uncertainties, fears; we both want to escape to a realm of solace. Our bodies are used to doing the talking, and so we dispense with words, also the coat hanger, and this night communicate in a more trustworthy way.

And afterwards she nestles her head at my chin. Perhaps she's fulfilled, perhaps not. It's hard to know. Her breathing evens out and she sleeps, her lips shaped into a small, quixotic smile. I'm unable to sleep; her head has gotten heavy on my shoulder. I'd like to wash up but don't want to disturb her. I'm trying to match the rising-falling motion of my chest beside hers. Still, sleep won't come.

Something is wrong. There's been excitement and release, and no question of morality—our bodies couldn't be wrong in answering a natural call. Even so, I feel—well, okay, so I'm ashamed. Though I've only done what's been expected of me, somehow, even at the helm, somehow I feel I've taken a passive role. It's me who's been seduced, not by waiflike master-of-her-fate Lucy but by my own weakness for fantasy. I've used her as a dream goddess, an object—may just as well have been alone. And I'm thinking it's been a lot like work, sort of pounding the wrong street with pneumatic drill work. Also that I've misused my company boss power, and

I've broken a longer and stronger tie with Bet. Maybe most upsetting, I've given in to a Satanic side, in a way answered a call from my Persian king.

I'm Agathe's Satan. I'm Tacet's lie. I'm nothing.

Thoughts are all fighting with each other and mixing me up. It's impossible to sleep, and now it's me who's brimming, and I shift my head away from Lucy Night's so as not to dampen her smiling face.

"We do not like the world and we are going to change it." Speaking was Daniel Cohn-Bendit, otherwise known as Danny the Red, leader of the student rebellion. That's what he said. That's what he always says. And now he's saying it in my room, him with his three tough-looking chums.

It's the same night, but before Lucy.

"We are changing the world," he tells me. "We do not like things, not a bit. We do not like things at all." He means that they don't like things. He says so, and means it.

Cohn-Bendit is about five years younger than me, and shorter, about five foot ten. He and his chums look scruffy, like they've been up Manifesting for several nights, and they're armed. It's best to be affable. "Yessir, you're right," I say. "Everything's awful, very, very awful. Things these days just aren't worth it." Then I ask if they would like to put their satchel of fire bombs or whatever over on a side table and sit down. Three of them sprawl out on the floor, yawning and looking sleepy, as if maybe they're going to stay there all night. Cohn-Bandit pulls up a chair.

"Ahem," he says. He says it as if he's getting ready for one of his rebel-rousing orations, and he's running a bandaged palm over his carrot-colored hair. He's just one big gleaming stigmatum all over—extremely serious. "The world calls for a theater of combat against bourgeois Gaullist culture," he tells me, then gives a rundown on Marxist theory and one about how money, as we know it, is to be a thing of the past—that we're all soon to be on the barter system.

"I know, I know," I say. "The Becks were just here telling me the same thing."

Julian Beck and Judith Malina and their Living Theater from New York have been playing Paris. They're in favor of the revolution and have been trying to do what they can to tip the scales of political justice. They came to invite me to join up with the students, to which I'd said thanks anyway. I once auditioned for them in their Upper East Side apartment at a time when I needed any kind of work. When they offered me the job, I turned it down, because I wasn't so sure about them—Judith reminded me of a Charles Addams lady, and Julian's neck was long and skinny like a turtle's—but mostly because it wasn't going to pay anything.

Now Danny the Bandit's being fervent about the Masson "graffiti" at the Odéon, blasting it and cracking his knuckles. "Anachronistic [*pop*], right wing [*pop*], we do not like it [*pop pop pop*]." He sure was sure of his taste and allegiances, probably even heard of Leonardo and Picasso, and you can tell he's able to toss them into the right slot. He's a definite sort of person who sees things as if they were labeled, and he goes on stating his preferences, separating the grain from the chaff, and I may as well not be here. You'd think he always kept his back so straight and his face so in profile, and his focus is shifting way off in some other direction, all of which are the signs of a very definite person. He might be admired for being a man of taste and conviction, a guy who is suffering for his opinions, but if you are like me when confronted by a certain sort of crudeness, you are feeling like a Tasmanian devil dog, a black cat, or an instrument of God, and ready to return his type of crudeness in kind, scorch him to ashes.

But people like him are all around everywhere—I mean, not just in my chair and on my floor—and you can't slip them a KO, and it's not okay that you have to suffer in silence. It makes you cold and hot, and you get your quota of angst by being unable to forget that they are all around and about everywhere.

But let's look not only on the dark side. At this same time I'm admiring Daniel-Bandit and want to pat his carrot top and tell him what a nice definite man he is. I don't know about you, I'm not sure if other folks swim in such alternating currents as mine; but that is how I feel when meeting this sort of person.

Now he's moved on to corruption in the Department of Justice, and pops are punctuating his serious stigmatum. I say, "Excuse me, but is there any particular reason that you gents have come to see me?"

This is what he says: "Taylor, we know that you are not a dancer. You are a hoax, an agent working for the Gaullists, and you were sent to the Odéon to talk us into a retreat. You are nothing but a capitalist hoax, are you not? Yes, at the very least you are working for the Establishment. We know about you. But something puzzles us: Why didn't you attack our cause on TV?"

Evidently, when his gang took over the Odéon they didn't know that there was an international arts festival going on, so I try to explain that my company is one of several foreign ones being sponsored by the festival, not by de Gaulle. "Believe you me," I tell him, "I'm no spy," and he finally believes me.

Do you believe me? Do you believe that I wasn't one of de Gaulle's spies? The heck you do. But my mother up in heaven believes me.

Well now, he's not in profile anymore. He's looking straight at me and not so rampant. Now he's thoughtful, and the flesh of his face drooping, looking flabby as if he's losing some of that hard kind of inflorescence that rebels and Robespierres have. I don't tell him how he's looking because I'm being as mild as Marie Antoinette and would never be so unkind as to say, "Danny boy, your inflorescence is getting flabby." No sir, I don't say that.

"Well," he thoughtfully says, "Mr. Taylor, if you are not on de Gaulle's side, then we would be glad for your help. Will you give us free performances at the Odéon?"

I tell him thanks, but the dancers and I have to move on to our next city.

Then he wakes up his pals with some kicks to the soles of their serious brown boots and they get up, retrieve their satchel of stuff from the table, and clear on out.

By the next day a notice has been posted on the front of the theater that says ticket holders can ultimately obtain refunds, but that anything left over will go to the American visitors, who have been the unfortunate victims of events. And you know what? These Parisians don't all smell bad. They aren't all completely neurotic. And there are even a few of them that are all right.

Good folks, maybe there has been too much incongruity piling up, much too much conflict and seesawing feelings. What's needed here is something consistent, something in life that is as ever present as death:

There was nobility to the final flight of Michael, a medium-sized bee. Having been sucked through the front grid of a speeding truck, then through its glove compartment, carburetor, differential, and other mysterious places, Michael was miraculously expelled from the tail pipe and thrown onto one of the piles of trash which so often border the Long Island Expressway at Sunnyside Boulevard at exit number 46.

After floating round and round in a rain-filled Dixie cup, he was lifted out and subjected to the indignities of artificial respiration. Yes, folks, a little kid pumped Michael's legs and poked on Michael's chest, and such a crying shame, you'll say, but better him than me, better Mike who's born self-sufficient and can't understand that sort of stuff.

Well, back came Michael's strength!

And after shaking dry his wings, he spread them giddily, flew up a ways, then fell. On his back, and sensing some last undefined, not wholly understood final outrage, Mike jabbed his stinger every which way in vain, uncoiled his long lip at the world, doubled up, and died.

Although due at our next engagement in Stockholm and eager to leave Paris, we are trapped, since all commercial transportation in and out of

Paris has been discontinued. Fortunately, our conductor, John Perras, knows someone with a bus, and thanks to Jean-Louis we have enough money for the trip. At dawn we pile into the bus and drive to Brussels, where we wait six or seven hours for a plane to Copenhagen. The airport is jammed. We're all sitting around on our luggage, some of us coughing and feverish. Bet and I haven't much to say to each other, and Lucy's being overly attentive—offering to sew buttons on my coat and such—and I'm wishing she wouldn't. Am picturing how it might be to have a real family, then trying to push away the words of an old song that goes "and at the end of the plot a wedding knot, but not, not for me." Aw, Bet, dear Bet, never will we marry. Although I'm convinced that I'll be able to dance soon, throbbing inside its coffin the ankle is telling me that it has gotten worse.

On arrival in Stockholm, we're relieved to learn that there are no riots or strikes here, but John is concerned about our orchestra—a local pickup one—since he's heard that it's second-rate and that he'll have only two hours of rehearsal to pull it together. (We later get a chuckle out of reading a music critic's high opinion of our "fine orchestra brought from New York.") John and I go to our theater, the Strads-something, where we run into quite a sight—another mob of protestors, a line of them bobbing placards and circling the theater. At the main entrance, instead of a dancing goat, is a cluster of coeds leaping up and down in place. It's as if they thought they were nuns and had taken up the trampoline in order to get closer to God. An infuriating sight, and me with no crutches.* The strikers won't let us through, so we return to our hotel.

I find Charlie and say, "Guess what?"

"I can see you're in a bad mood," he says. "You're feeling like punching out our sponsor or someone?"

"Nope, but you're close. Again, just like in Paris, there's a turd in the punch bowl."

"Oh no, you don't mean that there's something wrong at the theater?"

"And how. Charlie, you go over and get us in. This whole tour was your idea, so get us in there and then get us *out!*"

He ducks down his chin and starts off. "Hey, Charlie," I call, "how come you never say anything back?"

And so Charlie, long-suffering true-blue Charlie, wades to the theater to see what can be done.

I guess I could've been happier about him being able to get the company past the marchers, and more grateful for the following performances, if I

---

* Because of blistered armpits, Mr. Taylor left his crutches leaning in a corner of his room at the Michelet. When the company returned two years later, he found them still there. They had been saved by Madame the concierge and repositioned in the same spot.

wasn't being beset by waves of doom and envy. Evidence continues to prove that my presence onstage isn't as indispensable as I'd like.

Then we fly back to Copenhagen, where we'd been for a while just before Paris. With the rest of the itinerary looming ahead, I'm making a big effort to look forward to better times and, simultaneously, trying to flee backwards from some sort of vaguely defined degradation that I fear will trap me forever in St. Helen's.

Sunny, cool Copenhagen with its royal botanical garden just beginning to sprout, its lovely palaces and parks—if not for its lack of canals and tulips, it might be mistaken for Amsterdam. You don't see a truly grotesque person or building along its clean streets, except perhaps at the Nye Scene, where we are to perform. Horses hitched to ale wagons clop between toy cars, shiny bikes, and neat pedestrians. Some of the street signs depict walking green or red stick figures, and at construction sites, ones of little men digging, which symbolize little men digging. Growing in planters along "the walking street" are jonquils, as most say, or "buttercups," says Danny.

Our small hotel, the Codan, is right up the block from the harbor where the statue of Andersen's Little Mermaid sits on her rock, tail folded, ladylike and dreaming at her reflection in the water. She has no need for splay-kneed positions. Each of the hotel's rooms has a tub, deep but short, and when they're filled, then unplugged, water bubbles up from drains under the sinks, flooding the floors and causing urgent calls to the front desk. Small trundle beds for one have three high sides and force tall sleepers to fold themselves into uncomfortable positions, but, even so, some part of you has to hang out. And each bed has a huge tubular bolster to hug. Presumably, the management is encouraging sublimative person-pillow interrelationship bonding.

Our pre-Paris trip to Copenhagen was to teach *Aureole* to the Royal Danish Ballet and tape *Agathe's Tale* and a lecture/dem for TV. These two sources of income are making the whole tour possible. Charlie, having lived several years in Copenhagen, considers it his second home and is glad and proud to be bringing us here. However, when hearing of the plans in New York, I wasn't overjoyed. I felt that since our dances are made for proscenium stages, the TV would be unlikely to turn out well, there being little time to adapt for the camera. And I was also unhappy about selling *Aureole*. It was a piece that I'd always valued as if it were a mild and sunny child. In a way, it was a better part of me, and I hadn't wanted to release it to dancers trained only in classic technique who might not be able to bring it off. Selling *Aureole* meant risking child abuse. But the Danish Ballet wasn't to get exclusive rights and, with luck, might keep it in its rep for only one

season. And the TV was to be aired only once. So, since we needed the
income, I'd reluctantly gone along with the plan.

According to Inge Sand, assistant artistic director, her Royal Danes can
dance anything perfectly, if not better. Because royal rules and regulations
prevent Bet and me from giving an audition, we watch them taking their
classes. One of the best is young Peter Martins, later to be co-director of the
New York City Ballet. I don't pick him for *Aureole*, because a hunch tells
me he wouldn't be interested in barefoot dancing. (As it turns out later, he
wanted very much to dance *Aureole*, and in '84 asks me to create a new
dance for him and his partner Suzanne Farrell, which I do, and which they
generously perform at a benefit for my company. However, there is a slight
misunderstanding—what I intend as a classic pas de deux, they perform in
a modernistic way—not that they aren't wonderful and brave.)

Rules also forbid Bet and me to line up our choices from the classes in
order to see their relative heights, and we're told that once the dancers
have been chosen, there will be no exchanging them for others. Dancing
without ballet shoes is also verboten.

Ten ballerinas, seventeen soloist men, and about thirty corps members
later, we've made our selections. Without knowing their names or status
beforehand, we've picked Anne Sonnerup, the wife of our TV director; Vivi
Gelker, ballerina wife of the Danish Ballet's new artistic director, Flemming
Flindt; Henning Kronstam, leading male dancer; Aage Poulsen, the whiz
kid of all Northumberland; and Sorella Englund, a nobody, but for my
money best of all.

At the first rehearsal I show *Aureole*'s basic steps and tell the cast that the
five roles will be allotted according to whoever learns the steps the fastest—
not an ideal way to do things, but necessary in the short eight-day rehearsal
period given us. As aped by the great Danes, the steps come out looking
like those of an ostrich with lumbago. My insides are turning over, and
when I glance at Bet, she's not holding her head, only diddling with the
stray wisps at the back of her neck and pretending to be calm.

The second rehearsal is cut from two hours to one because of the Danes'
heavy schedule. The third is cut entirely. At the fourth only one dancer shows
up, the others having to be at someone else's rehearsal. Time continues to
be lost in this way. To make up for it, I call in my company's *Aureole* cast
to help teach, assigning each dancer to his counterpart while I concentrate
on Henning. He's musical, or at least able to count, and a speedy learner,
but his dancing looks like a series of still pictures rather than a flow of movement. Vivi, coached by Eileen, does fairly well, but Anne seems to be in-
timidated by the strangeness of her steps. My favorite, Sorella, would do very
well if she too could get over her tentativeness. Aage, anything but intim-

idated, is a bantam-weight pug with a devilish glint in his eye—the reason
I picked him—and whenever the girls get in his way, he gives them light
swats on their derrieres. All of them are trying to break second-nature ballet
habits and are floundering in a sea of ballet don'ts.

Surprisingly, their landings from leaps are very heavy, and so a lot of valuable time has to be spent on that. "Try to land like molasses," I tell them.

"Excuse me, but what are molasses?" Sorella wants to know.

"Honey, it's honey. You know—goo, gunk, rubber, thick air."

"Oh?"

At one rehearsal a linoleum floor covering arrives, and when I ask about
it, the Danes tell me that they've gotten permission to dance barefoot. They
want to do *Aureole* just like we do. I warn them that their feet aren't
callused like ours and that they may rue the day. They insist, and it takes
about a half-hour before the undersides of their big toes are puffed with
blisters the size of quarters. But they persevere. They're interested in
Aureole and determined to conquer its style; and eventually their toes firm
up and their fears drop away, replaced by shining assurance—an assurance
that would be nicer to watch if the steps were being done right, not embellished with extra tosses of the head and dainty flourishes of the wrists.
Bet and I could go after them with a cleaver. The rigidity of their knees,
backs, and pinkies, and the sniffy tilt to their noses! But their good intentions, as Mother would've said, would warm the coddles of your heart. Bet
and I feel like tossing in the towel.

By the last rehearsal, however, their dance looks somewhat related to the
original, and we leave the studio to go space it on the opera house stage.
Though exhausted from being up since dawn to prepare for a performance
of Bournonville's *Sylfiden*, they're eager to get their strange new American
dance right. But just as our rehearsal has gotten started, along comes Inge
and takes her charges away to some other rehearsal. As they leave, Sorella,
Vivi, and tough guy Aage look back at me with expressions of futility, as if
maybe they're going to break down and bawl.

A month later, my company having returned to Copenhagen from
Stockholm and the mess in Paris, and the Danes having practiced *Aureole*
while we were gone, the time has come for me to decide if the dance looks
good enough to be performed in public. I see a dress rehearsal; it looks
paler than ours, but not bad, and at least is a showcase for the sweet-
natured Danes. I've gotten used to their not-quite-accurate steps, have
even gotten fond of them; so I give permission for them to dance it.

So the last rehearsal is off and there won't be anymore. Sunny child *Aureole*
is adopted and the rest of the day is free, so I take my cast—I mean the

plaster one—for a walk along "the walking street." Protruding from the cuff below, the white foot is looking like a dirty snowman's, making one leg too long and giving a hobble to our walk. Placing it just below the curb with the other foot on the sidewalk only makes us dip the opposite way, but down the streets we go, any streets, chilly streets, streets from noon to dusk, rocking past gateposts that resemble totem poles or tribal demons, past tubs filled with Danny's buttercups, past stop and go signs—icon men of red and green—our walk a dance of wanting, wanting. Yes, to dance onstage again; but something more . . . what is it? Exactly what?

Let's forget that and enjoy the cityscape. Lighted windows, lace curtains, warm home life inside and, above, a slightly surrealistic sky—blue innocence fading into green (my favorite colors, you know). Those are pretty childhood colors, the same as were once on a choice piece of jigsaw puzzle, also the ones of Teddy Bear's pearly-buttoned jacket, my good-listening chew-eared bear, dirty, eyeless, offensive to half-sister Bettie. But that's long past. We mustn't trail bright colors in the mud.

Here, the streets of Copenhagen, dusk, warm windows, rows of totems too easy to relate to. How different is life nowadays! And here's one of those faceless little men digging, and there's another, and here's a sign that says Tuborg Beer with a nice-looking neighborhood bar attached—the Pink Club. Think I'll have some Tuborg for that undefined road I'm wanting, always wanting, dreading, and lately seems I'm needing so.

Loud jukebox music. Dim boy-and-girl-crammed cave. Barkeep says, "What will you have?"

"Pardon?"

"Will you have a drink?"

"What?—This music—"

"Can you speak up? Do you want a beer?"

"Yes. A hot Tuborg, please."

"You want a hot tuba?"

"Please, with a double scotch on the side."

"We have no hot tubas. Are you sober?"

"Okay, a triple scotch then. Two of them."

Now the light seems not so dim, and I can see there's dancing. So this here's a dancing bar. Couples frontally oriented, arms clasping, thighs brushing, left-right, left-right. Revolving in slow, slow circles and getting nowhere fast. But, hot dog, some are kissing to a music other than the jukebox's, and over in a corner two girls together, one young and attractive, her moves innocent, her pelvic thrusts curiously chaste. But her partner, who's older and trying to look sexy, is only managing to be crude. And over in another corner, two paired-off men swaying in the shadows, and two others in the blare, one with a toothbrush mustache, and on his arm a tattoo, a permanent installation of his own pierced heart—which signifies affection for his mother?

"Barkeep, more scotch, please."

"Sir?"

"Vodka, please."

It isn't a matter of not speaking up; it's more a matter of being unsure of what I want. Anyway, alcohol's not exactly what. Who wants a drug that deadens while it stimulates, who needs such—well, whatcha know? Here's some dexies in my pocket. One should do, maybe two.

And now I'm all set to dance. Am going to ask someone. I will.

I can't. Somebody'd see. But maybe they won't mind if I dance by myself.

I can't. Somebody'd see. And now I'm tapping the cast on the floor below the stool—an unseen solo turn—and looking "with it," as they say back home, all set for social dancing, but there's nobody asking so I'd better be breaking the ice. First a little small talk is what you do, how you do to be nice. You're supposed to say, "Hey, you—yeah, *you*, way over there by my elbow—what's your age, occupation, annual income, and [*nudge*] sexual preference?" That's how to break the ice.

I'm not speaking—some things are too dark to utter. Not looking anywhere, getting swallowed in a vacuum. So, so long everybody, and so what? I've gotta get going, guys and girls, and it's your tough luck. You're too late now, because I'm about to be sick, and it's too bad because I'd have been great for you, any of you.

And in a swaying men's room far out at sea where I've come to feed cookies to the fish, and looking down through the cracks of the boards of the dilapidated craft that good old Charlie has booked for an unlimited engagement, I can see slurping water swirling and, very unlike our swell new stage manager, Judy's forgotten to mark the boards with an arrow, and I can't tell which way is supposed to be frage stunt—stage front. And I'd give anything to know the direction that folks are watching me from—but wherever it is, they'll have to be watching through high-powered binoculars.

Letter written to Edwin Denby:

Codan Hotel, Copenhagen
30 May '68

Dear Edwin,

Thanks for the long-distance phone call. I'm OK, really. Sorry you heard about the Paris mishap and that it's caused you concern.

As you've probably guessed, the Danes don't do *Aureole* as badly as I'd expected. There are differences between their version and ours, but minor ones. More important, their own sweetness of nature comes across—something I'm sure you'd enjoy. Though they don't move as fluidly as we do, and could move with more weight, Aage (Dan's part) prances feistily and the girls' smiles are so pretty that nobody could mind anything they do.

At the Danes' first performance of *Aureole* the audience broke Royal tradition by giving several, instead of the traditional single, curtain calls. You would've laughed to see me trying to keep my balance without crutches, hold hands with the dancers, and keep from dropping a bunch of red roses, all at once. Best of all was a single yellow rose from Sorella with a note thanking me for my "beautiful ballet."

Director Flemming Flindt asked me to replace *Aureole* on my company's coming programs at the Nye Scene with a lecture/demonstration. As we're to perform *Aureole* at the same time his company is dancing it at the opera house, I suspect that he's concerned over comparisons in the press. I tried to tell him that the comparisons might be to his dancers' benefit, and that our L/D isn't anything much. He seemed unconvinced, but anyway I refused to change our program.

I've seen the doctor here who you recommended. He says that, as far as he can tell without X-rays, the ankle is still inside the cast, but now atrophied, and that the cast should stay on for a couple more weeks. The thirteenth is the day we're to arrive in England. I'll be able to dance before then for sure.

It's a shame that the dancers are having the extra burden of dancing my parts, especially in Yugoslavia where we're to have six performances in four different cities in four days. I'm not sure what kind of miraculous transportation will get us around in time. I've the feeling that Yugo. will be something like Timbuktu and have been storing up canned food to take.

Our opening here came off OK—had to miss seeing most of it, but won't bore you with details as to why. The dancers have been taking turns having a stomach virus, but they don't complain, in fact it's been hard to find out that they're sick because they instinctually keep away from me when I'm nursing an ailment of my own. Everything will be back to normal soon.

Thanks again for the call, and for the card.

Fond regards,
Paul

An effort was made to mention things about the Danes that I thought Edwin might like to hear, but, though true enough, it wasn't the whole picture. To my taste their performance was sweet—too sweet. A frivolous pastry, the Danes' *Aureole* was *Aureole* as a danish. That criticism, however, was mild as compared with an underlying attitude that I might've expressed in a letter to the ballet world at large:

Hotel Everywhere, Planet Earth
Days of Past, Present, and To Come

Classic Ballet,
   Keep away, keep building your creaky fairy castles, keep cloning clones and meaningless manners, hang on to your beanstalk ballerinas and their midget male shadows, run yourself out of business with your tons of froufrou and costly clattery toe shoes that ruin all chances for illusions of lightness, keep on crowding the minds of blind balletomanes who prefer dainty poses to the eloquent strength of momentum, who have forgotten or never known the meanings of gesture, who would nod their noses to barefoot embargos ("so grab me" spelt backwards). Continue to repolish your stiff technique and to ignore a public that hungers for something other than a bag of tricks and the empty-headedness of surface patterns.
   Just keep it up, keep imitating yourself, and, *please*, go grow your own dance makers. Come on, don't keep trying to filter modern ones through your so-safe establishment. We're to be seen undiluted, undistorted, not absorbed by your hollow world like blood into a sponge.

                              Yours truly,
                              A Different Leaf on Our Family Tree

And then Bet and I are sitting in the darkened Nye Scene watching our company's runthrough of tonight's opening program. The cast, which I've propped on the back of the seat in front of me, is looking like the rear view of a skull. At either side I see that the dancers are doing their steps better than the Danes but, to me, not juicily enough. The stomach is yearning, trying to burn itself into the dancers, and by the time I've had them run *Aureole* for a third time they're nearly dead.
   "Oh, Paul," says Bet, "just leave them alone. They do it fine."
   "Well, they don't. They should be gooier—and why don't they look happy? The lighting is awful, too." Then I call for Judy to set the lights at the highest reading and to leave them there, and I tell the dancers to smile, smile, keep on smiling—"just like the Danes do. More flashy white teeth!

And why can't your feet be pointed like theirs? And, damn it, your hands are so untrilly and drab."

I go on to make last-minute changes in *Lento*, erasing steps and inserting unlikely new ones, patching and picking the dance apart, and, after making dancers apprehensive as to my sanity, I threaten to fire everyone on the spot, but in the end leave them to finish the rehearsal by themselves and return to the Codan to dress for the opening.

It's to be a formal affair. I'm squirting the boardlike armpits of a T-shirt with deodorant and have decided not to bother with a shave and am debating whether to wear my loudest sweater with my baggiest pants or with a goatskin rug that Lucy's lately given me.

When the phone rings, I'm hoping it's not Edwin wasting his money on another transatlantic call, but it's only Charlie reminding me to bring my ticket. I ask if he's gotten me an aisle seat, and he says no. I blast off, accusing him of messing up my appointment with the doctor Edwin had recommended, and then, getting no response and gaining steam, I top things off by accusing him of only caring about his twenty-percent cut. At the other end of the line Charlie's no doubt looking like a tight-lipped long-nosed Persian, not grinning his usual Alfalfa grin, and I'm raking through the past for pent-up slights from him, exaggerating, uncorking resentments and shooting them at Charlie as if he were at the root of every unlucky thing that's ever happened.

Then we take a cab to the theater, and he says he's noticed a change in me, that he believes me to be sad, and that the sadness is about being unable to dance, but that it'll pass. He sees something stormy in me, feels anxious. How gentle and therapeutic Charlie's being, so I'm not affronted and begin to feel that indeed my life is sad and that we're looking at me from a great distance, and there's this curious little piece of matter down there in me being sad and, *tsk tsk*, very wacko. So we're on the outside looking down at a devilish bee buzzing around and around down there inside Paul, and I'm looking down on Charlie, looking back and forth from him to me, and seeing that as for himself, he's found a peaceful place in there, a starlit plain where he's put up shelter against the kind of disquiet that drives other folks wild. But there's no shelter inside Paul, and he's running swiftly in the wilderness, reaching out for who knows what, and much too far because he's gotten to a dark and gloomy place indeed. There's a middle-sized bee in the trash and he's feeling undone and cheapened, and there's nothing noble in defeat, no rewards from blasting, nothing sweet about desire.

Now I'll tell a secret, something real and comical, and at the end you'll see that it has something to do with bees and deviltry but even so will be understandable.

"Go to your seat," I tell Charlie, "I'll join you there in a minute."

The lobby lights are dipping, the ushers are interrupting animated conversations, then urging stragglers inside. The last go traipsing in like so many rats dancing along after the Pied Piper, and on the bar they've left their glasses, some half-empty, but others half-full, and haste makes waste, I'm thinking, just as Mother would've said; and impartially, democratic to the differences in color, I'm picking up and tossing down the leftovers, accompanying them with an occasional green tablet or two.

"And what are you taking with those drinks?" Charlie might have asked. "What're you popping there?"

"Well, Charlie old boy, these are only what my New York doctor gave me, guaranteed to be non–habit forming—just Dexamyl you take every night to make you talk in your sleep, and just the thing when you've got to give a lecture/dem, and they also give energy to stay awake or whatever."

Charlie, maybe you'd be getting slightly pop-eyed. Charlie, what a lovely vision you'd be seeing of your drug-fiend friend for you to rescue with nobility and quiet patience.

"But, Paul, you want to be very careful. Now what's in them pills?"

"Well, what's in is part stimulant, part deadener. A mix of chloroform and airplane glue."

And to think of Charlie is to admire his peace, the place where there's no great big burden inside. But now, with pretty green pellets comes peace, softly, drop by drop. So softly that you barely notice. It ain't exactly gushing out. And you sure don't need no rubbers and a raincoat, for there's hardly a drop of peace there on the cloven cast, hardly a mist on the sweater— loud-patterned sweater echoing the stress and strain inside—very little peace on the goat-hair rug that's wrapping hotly round the thighs.

So now I'm feeling pretty nauseous and have to pay a visit to the men's, and now the overture has started. I must be going to my seat, but it seems my ticket has gotten lost, and so it's a relief not to have to watch—better to be out here in the lobby with my droplets of peace and my smokes and my buzz.

Out here I'm forming pity for all those saps who've gone inside, and by the time they're coming out for intermission I've gotten greatly concerned, thinking only to protect them from themselves. "Hey, you all, it's risky to go back. The next dance is deadly, you won't like it. Better leave now while you can!"

But they draw back, sort of red faced, and one of them slips over to the head usher, who comes and says, "Here now, do not go bothering people," and so I have to block the door, keep all these poor ignorant souls from returning to their seats. Then the house manager comes, but I tell him it's okay, that I'm Paul Taylor himself.

"An unlikely story," says he. "You are intoxicated and disorderly, sir. You must leave at once or we shall summon our security guard."

So Tacet's done all he could for our big formal opening, and there's nothing left but for him to take himself out the front doors, slamming them once or twice just to let everybody know that their ingratitude has not been taken lightly, and nowhere is there a taxi brave enough to stop and take this wild person back to his hotel.

In a Royal Danish office, soon after the company's three performances at the Nye Scene, even though against doctor's orders, I enlarge the split of my cast, tear the hateful thing off, and, as a parting gift, leave the odoriferous pieces lying in Inge Sand's wastepaper basket. It's not meant as a vendetta against Inge personally, just against ballet in general. Those in the psychiatric profession might call the act a sublime example of subliminal sublimation. Or maybe antisocial antidotalism. Others, outside the profession, who prefer less lopsided terms might call it plain stupid. Anyway, whatever the term, it was a relief.

And so we leave trundle beds, cold Tuborgs, hot actions, Danny's buttercups, the whole quaint city, and we're on our way, getting closer, ever closer to the town at the edge of black-holed Liverpool.

Well, I was really hoping to spare myself the trouble of bringing up another Danish downer, but now see that a brief mention is needed in order to make what happened later even faintly intelligible.

So now we'll not be leaving, we'll have to be dragging our feet back to when we first came to Copenhagen, into some bar where I met someone whom, to put it as quickly and simply as possible, I fell in love with. Well, you say, well, love is not a simple matter, and you can't just meet over a drink somewhere and the next thing be in love and so soon be leaving and going off to somewhere else. But I was still youngish, see, and didn't know it was unlikely. Two weeks and a million marvels later I realized how unlikely it was. Unlikely and hopeless, because my life was the road, and this other person's was Copenhagen, and that was that. And that was a klunky bit of realization, and you'll have to pardon me for rushing past the who-what-why-how, and just take my word that the parting was not so sweet, not so Shakespearean, and nothing grand or noble to that little pop inside, which was a devastating, most deathlike thing.

Now, *now* we're leaving. The others and I have crowded into taxis that will take us to the airport—Molly nestling on Charlie, Karla staring starry-eyed at Cliff, Janet at Jack more so, Carolyn and Danny pressed side to side, the rest exchanging small talk, and Bet on my knees, her bones weighing sharply. Bet, my long de Young who's kind and has her own troubles and is a stranger, heavy on my knees in an outward semblance of earlier, closer times. Dear Bet, now so bored.

The close, dark cab starts off, pressing one of the butter-bean bumps at the top of her spine into my chin. Aw, she's so quiet—no fret and fume up there, no mind sickness and delinquency and thoughts upon death. The window by us is closed tight to the dawn sky; outside are wet pavements with a suggestion of steam—enervating to the body, overstimulating to the mind and to uncontrollable thoughts that rush pell-mell, scattering the peace that might have been. How deathly cold in this taxi, but everybody's remarking on the heat. Senta's voice is droning on and on, and it's almost pleasant to be far away and listen and not listen. Fetid is this bursting place that never had an open window and reeks of cigs dropped and ground into the floor long ago, and no derelict would smoke these butts. No, thanks kindly, we'll be passing up the discards this time.

And then my thoughts are breaking ranks and rushing to love left at the Codan just an eon of a moment ago, undisciplined, tearful thoughts reaching back, and in my hand dangles something cold and metallic—this key that I've forgotten to turn, to turn in at the desk.

The key. It's hard to explain the vividness of small sights and occurrences, some of which, if I let them, circle like loops of magnetic tape just as if they were parts of the future run backwards. For instance, take that hotel key, one of a hundred others unwittingly stolen, then sometimes mailed back, that seemingly trivial key which goes on opening up torrents of hopelessness, and isn't it amazing? As to any lesson learned . . . what lesson? You'd think I'd be more careful about which key I let spring from the past; yet, though time brings more than aging, and though I can see the Codan key as being connected with crisis, I've never known why I must keep going from key to key as if there were hope in each of them. But there is: hope and dreams. Golden dreams hovering like honey bees, passing and repassing, dreams like jonquils covering the pages of each year's seed catalogues, dreams thick as thieves, thick with pollen. Yep, many are down there inside—light ones, dark ones, long-loved dreams vibrating the surface of a turquoise sea into waves that crest and wash distant shores, drowning out all hopelessness.

We fly to Yugoslavia. Ljubljana for two performances, Belgrade for one, catch an overbooked night train and arrive in Skopje, a wrecked city that is just recovering from a disastrous earthquake. The dancers do a performance during a thunderstorm that blows out all electricity; the roof leaks and everybody gets soaked. A large lady with a small flashlight brings a bouquet onstage, then, undecided as to which dancer to give it to, exits with it.

Next day we rise early to catch a bus which is too small to hold all of us, and so we lose half a day while Charlie finds us a larger one. Our fee has been paid to him in single bills, so more time is spent while he counts them out to pay for our hotel and bus.

Barely in time for a performance in Opatia, and wearing practice clothes because of a rough concrete stage that would have shredded their costumes, the dancers attempt to entertain an audience of twenty-three implacable women who've brought their romping children and yowling babies.

From there we plane to Zagreb, and the next day fly to Manchester, England, stopping in London, where we're rejoined by conductor John Perras. A bus from Manchester then takes us through June countryside to St. Helen's, home of the Pilkington Glass Works, where we're to perform for the next eight nights.

Ever since Paris the ankle has remained stubbornly inoperative, and now, even here at our last stop, I still can't dance. It's been too long to be a limping pedestrian. As far as I can see, the whole tour is a bust. I've become certain that without my presence onstage the troupe is only so-so, and that being unable to be up there with them makes me nobody. Taylor the dancer is gone, evaporated. Nothing but the bare outlines of my dances remain—an unsatisfactory legacy at best. Though I'd expected that the gang would fall flat without me onstage, this hadn't happened, and there have been moments when even I can see that they aren't bad without me. Still, this is no compensation. It's invalidation. Watching them night after night and craving to be up there with them is firing up the stomach and building panic. Multi-guilts munch on. I've become a self-consuming cannibal. I dream of going to sleep and waking up dead.

Perhaps all this isn't sincere. It's hard to tell. Maybe I've manufactured these feelings in order to indulge in a catharsis, hit bottom in order to bounce back. After all, there will be other tours someday. But right now I'm longing for lost strength, lechery and/or death. Am doom-eager, old Martha would've called it.

The minute we walk into the oak-beamed room I know the reception is going to be unbearable. Another duty to perform, another mask to don, the old tedious ritual. We're here by invitation from tall Lord and short Lady Pilkington. His phallic gold scepter is unimpressive; her lewd tiara must be some kind of joke. There's a consistency of logic to the shapes of their two trappings, but the difference between his height and hers is causing me to be unable to understand how his lordship and her ladyship can kiss and copulate at the same time.

Watercress sandwiches are trotted out, powerful drinks served. The hosts, guests, and servants begin moving in fuzzy slow motion and seem to be entangled in some sort of humpy scrunch. Unaccountable details of gesture appear in muddled sequence, the meanings elusive at best. Being here intensifies a sense of remoteness, brings back feelings of loss, encourages lust—cold lust. There's something forlorn in these English, even tragic, and I'm all set to fool around with any or all of them.

Charlie, more concerned about my stumbles to the floor than my salacious winks, steers me back to our hotel, where he's unable to explain why, of all cheap places, he's picked one with the name Hotel Fleece.

I may as well have stayed in my room that night. By morning it's clear that finding fun in St. Helen's is hopeless. Lucifer himself wouldn't have stayed long in such a shamefully stodgy place. Before escaping to somewhere else for a respectable binge, however, there's one last duty to perform. I attend our dress rehearsal, wish the dancers luck, then get some petty cash from Charlie, stock up at a liquor store, and board a train for Liverpool.

Forward, you son of Persia, crouched in hope at the brink of chaos and sprinkled with railroad dust. Tinkling bottles of booze, smut thick on both the window and the brain, fumes of sulfur—an aroma suggesting depravity, malice, and suicide. In such a setting there can be no high-mindedness about underhand types of intercourse.

So I'm searching out faces of strangers, these British strangers, some with honest-to-goodness stiff upper lips and their other features looking resolute, too. And I'm noting which might be a primal-type face to go with primal activity, and, last of all, I'm checking out the guy in the aisle seat next to me.

Well, his face isn't so primal. It's Fred Astaire–ish, somewhat long in the chin, and the lips are fairly thin but at the same time not so thin for such a fairly long chin, and his eyes are neutral colored. He would have been hard to caricature, and it's too bad that the fingers are clean, delicate worms. Too immaculate, not primal at all. He sure has a neatness dementia, probably thinks that everything everywhere has to be, *has* to be, just so. And there's something around the nostrils there somewhere that tells me he's the sort that's easily pissed.

But his expression as he adds almost imperceptible pressure at my knee is very ordinary, very much no particular way of looking.

Something is telling me that he's saying to himself, "Why is this chap next to me not getting the hint? I wonder, is it a hint? It *is* a hint. He has absolutely no reason not to take the hint. Perhaps he is taking it, but is a bit exasperated. I have pressed so many times. Is he exasperated? But no, I, *I* will not be looking exasperated, although over and over I am showing him how my knee presses there, so it is not he who has anything to be exasperated about."

Another passenger—a mighty ship of state just risen from the seat behind and towing a little girl in her wake—in her passage toward the loo brushes against Fred Astaire, who quickly disengages his knee, swats at the shoulder of his jacket as if it's been exposed to germs, and exchanges clipped civilities with the woman. Then, as she and her little pink dinghy continue their zigzag course down the aisle, he's promptly back to business, placing the knee just so.

I hold out one of my bottles, but he squeezes his eyes, so it's just as well to be tanking up alone.

And I'm thinking ahead, facing up to the fact that this train lacks intimacy, sure was out in broad daylight. It's puzzling what he's planning. Exactly what kind of thing might the other passengers find acceptable? Maybe he's heard of something I haven't.

Anyway, he certainly has a bookish hand. And the outer edge of his pinky is tracing a series of circlets on the side of my knee, just perfect except that they're a creeping spiral, and very slow progress there, him being intent on precision and all, and taking his own sweet time. Am wondering if the arrival will be worth the wait.

So far, this hasn't been much to write home about, and this spiral stuff is taking up a lot of time that could be better spent by getting to the good part.

But now I'll tell you that always in the past, for all of my life, there has been a good deal of emotional sparsity. There has been affection and kindness and sometimes warmth, but not so much emotional-type love. Love as most folks understand it, or don't understand it. And always love has been making a great deal of trouble for me. You see, by the time I boarded that train, love was a four-letter word. Desperate characters are glad to settle for less, see? Settle for something not as engaging, but related; and right then, right there, if the guy would hurry up, I wasn't going to be picky.

Well, just about the time he's finally located the tab of my zipper, there's a delay due to the conductor's parading to and fro, and at each passing the guy's hand draws back. There's impatience there in those sharp movements, also unruliness—I mean how the hand clenches and drops heavily to the top of his leg, the fingers uncurling and drumming—un-British fingers, not stiff lipped at all. And this is disappointing, because if there is one thing to dislike in an Englishman it's emotional tension.

And now he's pondering, as in the devious ways of a crossword puzzler, and after a while it turns out that his solution to the privacy problem is to remove his jacket, fold it neatly, and lay it across my lap. But of course he's not satisfied until he's picked it up again, smoothed out the folds just so, and returned it. A sense of order has been achieved.

His hand is now invisible, but at no particular place, and his expression, to all intents and purposes, at no particular place either. In fact, you might say that both the expression and the hand are under wraps. But the tab is hard to locate, his bewildered fingers going off course, and for me to help with the search would spoil half the fun and be in poor taste. After all, there should be rules and regulations in games with strangers: no talking, no laughing, no peeping and so forth, and unzipping yourself is unmannerly and no, not nice. And who cares? So I speed everything up by getting the zipper started, then he takes over.

The teeth are unlocking. Two teeth part. The next pair, the next—a pause for the conductor to pass—and now slowly the next. At this rate we'll be too old.

And then the conductor shouts, *"Liverpool! Everybody off!"*

Sorry about this, folks, I really am, but sticking to the facts requires it. Sadly, my stories have to be true. The zipper never gets any farther than halfway down and therefore doesn't count.

We detrain, the guy says that he has to be somewhere, says, "Cheers, chap," and disappears to phone his wife.

So the binge has begun—disappointing as sensation, yet at least fairly covert. A step in the right direction. And once I'm off the train, there's lots of promising directions, though it's unclear as to which leads to the most evil part of town. All the streets are looking equally sordid.

Walking one, whiffing out wickedness, I turn off course to follow some windblown trash. Newspapers, cigarette butts, Dixie cups whirling, scooting, skidding. And I follow them through a pack of rogue dogs, one a serious male in middle life with an upward rake to his tail and a twisted smile, very tense, and such a wicked animal. Probably the kind who goes around sticking his head through housewives' lace-curtained windows, and so quiet. Quiet the way animals are quiet.

The trash is blowing every which way, and I pass a church photographed in sepia, its windows broken and front columns all scrawled with obscenity. I'm following along and swigging, popping pills, searching for blocks and blocks, maybe thirteen or more, and after a while there seems to be no method to my walking, no sense in the direction of the trash, so I go back to where there's traffic lights and, according to their color, turn off or reel straight ahead. But after a time this also seems senseless—too systematic, too orderly a plan for storm and tumult as a goal.

And so the sky is growing dark and resentful, my last bottle empty, the street corners getting round, and the lamps casting multiple shadows, maverick shadows angling out from the feet of the son of the mother who always said he was such a good little boy and that he had such well-shaped ears and I forget the poem she read to him from *A Child's Garden of Verses*. One of the shadows is shooting out free, free to wander up foreign alleys. Another one's isolated as it passes upright and lonely along a wall. Another's forced to conduct some sort of survey into cracks and crannies. Each grotesque, each freakish in its own way. Freak shadows cast by a freak.

And now I'm stopping off in an empty liquor store, standing there at the counter with my eyes closed and praying out loud for life, liberty, and the pursuit of sappiness. Then I call, "Hey, anybody in here? Doesn't anyone want to service me, or vice versa? For Christ's sake, let's get hopping!" Then a man comes up from behind a cash register, goes upstairs, and comes back with his wife, and she says, "Here now, you—there will be none of that blasphemy talk," and they get behind and shove me out a side door and onto the pavement, where I fall against some dust bins, I believe they call them.

Further on, after more pills and a couple more propositions, I begin to wonder where it was that I lost my tooth. But maybe that happened later. Am sure I still had my shoes, so it must be that I lost it before waking up on the park bench at the same time when I first noticed my wallet gone. Or maybe it was after the tussle with sailors and the cops and the handcuffs.

Folks, I've just decided to generalize parts of Liverpool, and I hope you'll understand if there's only a brief outline here and there. This to retain some glamour and marvelous mystery in my past.

And one morning the liverish Liverpool night sky lightens and all around is funk. Somewhere there in the slums on a flophouse bed I'm noticing the dawn excite a roach that goes skittering across my pillow, and I'm thinking that if I could figure out sex I could figure out life.

It's which is the active and which is the passive role that's got me. Take blowing, for instance. No, take something in general. Take gender in the abstract. By and large, people are supposed to think that it's masculine to fill up empty spaces. Well, what about when the spaces are doing most of the action? Does masculinity depend on being the activator of whatever on whomever? What's a gender to do? There's no clear-cut definition, see? This thing needs to be firmed up. That is, activeness needs redefining. And I'm lying here and I can't get it straight—my *thoughts* straight—and thinking of the variety of possibilities open to each gender brings on an awful throbbing. A *headache*. And the answer to this condom—*conundrum*—to do or be done to—becomes extremely important, because if these nuts can't be cracked, how am I to know exactly what is what?

So the roach is gone wherever roaches go for the day, and I'm listening to this person here next to me laughing in his sleep and covered all over with oozing sores. He's got something like acne gone berserk, and I'm thinking that maybe I needn't make any decisions about preferred roles after all, that maybe I don't prefer any of it. That night in the dark I wondered why there seemed to be so much goo everywhere. In general.

The headache intensifies. Going against one's own nature, whatever that was, was very, very dangerous. I should run to a VD clinic, except that I can't much care.

While getting my clothes on, it occurs to me that maybe a lack of romance might've had something to do with the evening's low priorities, but I doubt it. I tried to love this person. The closest I could come was to feel a bit of sympathy, which didn't help me to have all that much fun. I should've known that when people meet, if one of them's a derelict, there can be limitations. Mostly it was fun to pick up the tab for our meals and bed. He was grateful.

So I'm looking at this sleep-laugher, and for some reason that childhood verse that I couldn't remember before comes rushing back.

> I have a little shadow
> That goes in and out with me,
> And what can be the use of him
> Is more than I can see.
> He sometimes shoots up tall
> Like an India rubber ball
> And he sometimes gets so little
> That there's none of him at all.

Leaving some of the sores covered with bills, I tiptoe out.

Then I'm out walking again. It seems I've failed everybody—the dancers, Mother, Bet, Charlie, myself. But possibly I've done some atoning, atoning by piling new guilt upon old. It's as if I'm trying to leave Sodom by traveling to Gomorrah—taking the concept of Christian brotherhood and extending it beyond town limits.

And as I walk there's a calm, cool distance growing between me and the pavement. It seems as if I've been pretending everything—the train, the streets, the trash, and before them the pops of ankle and heart in Paris and

Copenhagen. The pill popping, too. That had been going on—weeks? Months? My whole life? Anyway, a long time. Dexies do that—time takes quite a while. It's the same kind of time as when you're dancing. What you notice most is strength and bravery and an extraordinarily relaxed control and the perfect manipulation of destiny. With dexies, all becomes feasible. It's only too true what they say—the more you have, the more you need.

Focus is a little off. That amoeba over there in the shadows—it's Charlie? Maybe Bet? No, certainly not Bet. She's never in shadows, ever. And there's an odor pounding me. Heavy, sickly sweet. And a foghorn's braying at a buzz saw, and as the clouds part I can make out two whores talking. They're too ladylike and well dressed and genteel to be ones I could ever dream up. There in the distance they're just out of reach, but I'm reaching anyway, coming at them like a black cat prancing forth light and malicious, but an inner mechanism in my head falters, disrupts my balance, and gravity floats me to the floor or the sidewalk or some lower surface, where, mouth open, barking, screaming, the severed head of a dog rolls over me. Inside, everything's chaos and false imagining. Outside, the branches of a snow-laden tree seem to bend down and snap.

At another unspecific place I find myself with a new person. As usual, a stranger. Yet her strawberry hair, perpendicular breasts, and horizontal hips are familiar. Her body's plump, translucent, and can turn radiantly pink when stroked—looks that recall a college sweetheart, except older. But her high-pitched voice frazzles, grates girlishly, and there's this practiced quality to the small, false gestures of joy that she keeps arresting midair, as if she's deep-freezing them for all time. Her glitter's as hard and as hollow as the ancient Vesuvian lava that reformed Pompeiian victims into sad, empty molds.

Personality going full tilt, she's requesting a novel, rubber-jointed speciality of hers, making it sound like a game of tiddlywinks. I'm barely understanding what she means, not quite getting the mechanics of it, and though I'm being impartial to roles played, and though upset and dippy, still, in the back of one of my minds it seems logical to be conducting a sort of scientific exploration into the meaning of gender, maybe discover my true calling.

It's a lot of work. And Liverpool's a dance—a hard day's night, but I'll get the hang of it yet.

And then I feel a third presence at the foot of the bed. "Someone's watching?" I ask.

"Only my husband, ducks," she pipes. "Don't pay him any attention."

"Don't pay attention?"

"No. Just go on as if he isn't here."

"He'd care to join us?"

"No, no, you silly, just go on."

"But I think he's got my big toe in his mouth."

"Oh, isn't that smashing! It means improvement. He usually only likes to watch."

The situation's impossible. I start to get up. Her voice lowers and she says, "Wait. Don't go. Please. He'll be terribly disappointed. You see, I love him so much."

Sometime afterwards, or maybe before, I'm unable to locate my shoes and wallet, so I'm looking for bricks to throw through windows, but can't find any, and then, with the assistance of a couple of house flies, I'm checking inside my pants to see if at least there's still something left with which to piss on the whole planet. And I'm noticing that my shirt's on inside out and torn. There's caked blood on knees and elbow, and purple places at both nipples. And I'm smelling several smells at once—my own and several other people's. From out of the generalized past, only these grubbinesses are specific. If my survey is to continue successfully, I could certainly stand some sprucing up.

So I go down underground to a public rest room and splash tap water on my face. The water doesn't do too much for me, but the stench from the urinals is wildly sobering, and it occurs to me that I may have overstayed myself in Liverpool. Can't figure out how many days I've been here and am suddenly anxious to return to St. Helen's. If they haven't already, I don't want the dancers to take off for New York without me.

After getting directions from a newspaper vendor who expresses interest in my bare socks, I drag to the outskirts of town and pick a spot by a highway where weeds are tall enough to hide the socks, then start hitch-hiking.

The spot is similar to the edge of the Edgewater Beach road where as a tot I'd waited with a bunch of locust clusters in one hand and a For Sale sign in the other. It also reminds me of when I used to thumb from Syracuse University to Cambridge for weekend visits to my girlfriend. On the last of these I'd gotten to her place to find a message from her. She'd asked her roomie to say that I was no longer welcome. I hadn't gotten it—our weekends had been great, and a recent letter from her gave reasons to expect that this one would be, too. If she'd wanted to end things, it wasn't like her not to tell me herself. I'd hitched back to Syracuse, sure I'd get an explanatory note, but none came. Years later, I learned that she'd had an excuse—

a lame one, it seemed—but by then the disappointment, the wrench really, was pretty much gone.

Anyway, I'm hitching again and also remembering a truck driver who had given me a lift back to college. He picked up people, he'd said, so that by talking to them he could stay awake at the wheel. He'd sketched out his life—his not-so-hot marriage, the loneliness of the road, the unfortunate condition of his sex life—and had ended up by aiming some obvious hints in my direction. I'd gotten uncomfortable and pretended not to understand, so when we stopped at a diner and he said that it was the end of his run, I knew it wasn't but was relieved to get away and thumb another ride.

And here by another highway I'm thinking how, ever since I started to dance, some of my off time's been spent wandering in many different directions, none all that enlightening, and that this dip into the lowlife of Liverpool, though more elaborate than anything before, as usual hasn't taught much. It's dawning on me that maybe there's been no salvation in the recent survey, that there's no moral to immorality. I've been wrong in thinking that the point to sex is solace. There's no point at all, and I'm out of pills and sober and there's no point to anything.

As to preferred partners, with men if they were passive, I usually preferred more action. If they were active, it brought out overactiveness in me. It was like faulty electronics, like two positive terminals that can't close a circuit. Yet this didn't keep me from trying. The men's original attraction—their strength—on contact seemed to disperse and leave behind some kind of soft but unconvincing femininity. And when I was with a woman, though the softness was convincing, and the convenience, I tended to look for familiar traits in her that might make me feel more comfortable with our differences. I guess most times I preferred whomever I wasn't with.

Yet to pick partners of a consistent gender would've run against an arbitrary streak. Perhaps my partialities for one gender or the other alternated because of genes or surroundings or some type of aging process. Actually, I don't know what to think. All of it shouldn't have been a big deal, but it was.

At times I can accept alternating currents in other people but am not sure about mine. Yet at other times I feel sure about mine but am suspicious of them in others. Sure, to most folks this would be ridiculous, but then so's having unnecessary limits.

And I have to admit that since I hadn't cared much about the Liverpool partners, showing that I did by cooking up whatever they wanted had been a strain. That cold kind of lovemaking was dishonest as well as dehumanizing. It rubbed the romantic side of me the wrong way, ran against a preference for fidelity which ran strong. But understanding even this much isn't making the guilt or the pain go away.

I hadn't been expecting love in Liverpool; still, those playmates would probably haunt me. Will attempt to exorcise them with a dance. I've a source to draw on, perhaps something not uncommon to all people everywhere—the icy heat. But it will have to be abstracted, put into formal terms, and the audience could be turned into a bunch of voyeurs. (This was to be the dance *Private Domain* in '69.)

Cars whiz past, and I'm thinking that even if I'd wanted I couldn't have sustained many more days in Liverpool. Clearly, the relationship between the dancers and me comes a lot closer to love. Even though we aren't all that passionate toward each other, at least the work we do together is an act of commitment, a symbol of love. I'm itching to get back to them as quickly as possible. As near as I can guess, it's been about a week since I left St. Helen's, and they may be at the airport right now.

A car stops. I run to get in but the driver, getting a closer look, takes off without me. The same thing happens again. Finally, just when I'm beginning to panic, a van stops. The driver stares, shrugs, and jerks his chin, indicating that I should get in. When I ask if he's headed to St. Helen's, he turns away, mumbles inaudibly at the sky, then spits out the window. I ask again and he doesn't answer. I decide to watch the road signs, get in and settle back. Clearly, I won't have to listen to his life story or explain about the shoes.

A couple of glances tell me that he's about forty-five, six feet or so, has a crew cut and a goony face. It's like Kilroy's—as if the little eyes and bulbous nose were drawn the way servicemen did, a single-lined peeping head with nose drooping over a wall. Only this guy's eyes are sunken within brown circles. He has balloon forearms, the barbell kind more often seen on younger men. His open jacket is fake leather with a lot of pockets and fancy hardware, too much of it. And hanging from a thong around his thick neck is a five-inch cartridge which, like him, looks World War II–ish. He keeps diddling it, testing the point with the tip of his finger, jiggling one knee incessantly, and rotating a cigar on his tongue. There's something ominous—his silence maybe, maybe the troubling little Kewpie doll that's hanging upside down from his rearview mirror.

After twenty miles or so he pulls up at the side of the highway, gets out, goes around to the back of the van, seemingly to check something, then saunters past my door to the front, where he deliberately angles himself so that I can't miss seeing him take a leak. In contrast to the overdeveloped forearms, his dick's conspicuous by its near absence.

A few more miles and we stop again, this time at a roadside restaurant.

After the days of Dexamyl-induced fasting, my appetite's returned full force, but since I'm broke, I wait in the van while he goes in. He comes back with a British version of a hero sandwich, eats it slowly, and then, after grating me with a blank stare and swallowing the canary smile, pokes a leftover piece of uneaten roll at my face, then tosses it on the ground. If he's trying to make me edgy, he's succeeded. I'm not absolutely sure that we're on the way to St. Helen's, and am thinking of getting another lift.

A few more miles and he has another rest stop. The waits are a pain in the neck, and our slow progress is making me frantic to get back to the company.

It's beginning to get dark when we turn onto a country road and stop by a wooded area. That does it. I thank him, say that I'm in a hurry and that I'll be getting another lift. It's as if he hasn't heard. I get out. He gets out, too, and goes to the rear of the van. I start walking back toward the highway.

By now my kidneys are making urgent demands. I look back to see him checking his tail lights, and step a few yards into the shadowy woods. I've been standing there for a minute or so when I hear some twigs snapping behind me. Even before turning around I know what to expect—he's there, and unzipping with one hand. What I didn't expect was for him to be holding a knife in the other. His feet are spread too far apart and his pelvis thrust too far forward for him to be in anything but a pseudomasculine stance. I'm not sure he's serious. When I look straight into his eyes, they shift away nervously. Finally, he speaks. It's a one-word command telling me what he wants me to do for him. He says it peeved, as if whining about something. Even at some other time and coming from a nicer type, the word would've been unforgivable. I can't stand the idea of a jerk bossing me around. He's made a big mistake.

I put on a light air and comment on the smaller of the two things he's holding. And that's where I make *my* big mistake.

He's very sensitive about his size, starts yelling about what he's going to do to me, and before I know what's happening, he has the point of the knife at my stomach and is trying to shove me to my knees.

That, nobody does. Nothing would have made me madder, except having to kiss him on his mouth. More than anything, more than my life, I'm crazy to hurt him, along with all the rest of the world's sadists. My knee shoots up into his groin. The knife flies out of his hand. He sinks to the ground, and while he agonizes there, I get him under me and sit on his chest. To keep from getting socked, I manage to get a grip on his wrists. While we're struggling his eyes go from wild to teary and then seem to go soft. It's weird, but I could swear they're saying something like, "Please, I like you."

It's hard to know. Possibly, I'm seeing the reflection of my own eyes there. But then his eyes glaze over, roll back, and his whole body turns limp. I can feel the life in him fade and flicker, taper right out.

He's not dead, couldn't be. There's no blood, no rock under his head. I couldn't have hurt him that much, but he's completely still. He must have fainted. But there's no pulse, no sign of breathing. My God, he *is* dead. He must've had some kind of seizure.

My mind's racing ahead. Unintentionally or not, I've been the cause. I'll be blamed, brought to trial, and there would be only my word as defense. It takes about two seconds to decide what to do. I'm going to zip him up, put him back into the van, ram it into a tree, and hope that when he's found, it'll look as if he was alone when he died.

I'm so intent on the plan that I almost don't notice when he begins to come around. His eyes flutter and he tries to say something but can't. With effort he gropes toward one of his jacket pockets. I reach in to find a bottle and put two prescription pills in his mouth.

While waiting to see if they work, I'm stunned, shocked by what only a moment ago I was planning. I'm unsure, don't know if I would've, am hoping that I'd have gone to the police. Am also amazed at what I'd seen in the guy's eyes—that almost loving look. It seemed to be saying that he'd needed pain and had been grateful for it. And worse, most upsetting of all, is the realization that my knee going into his groin had given me a lovely sensation. Yes, like him I was duplecast, maybe triple. There'd been at least four of us involved, and all of us had wanted to harm, all of us were capable, all of us savage and hungry.

So I'm juggling around this idea of pleasurable pain when he tells me that he's just had one of his attacks. It's my turn to clam up. I don't ask what kind, or if there's anything more that he needs. He smiles a faint version of that canary smile again and gets to his feet—seems too soon—saying that he's able to drive.

Watching the van ease back onto the road as I stand at the edge of the woods, I'm wondering if he might've been faking everything. In the distance his tail lights blink back at me as if laughing.

That's Liverpool for you. Bars, bushes, boudoirs, rides both free and paid for, dark streets of windblown trash. Liverpool, where I'd been heading all along. It's been more than I intended to tell, but less than I remember. The rest will have to stay with me, and we'll let it go at that.

I'm soon able to thumb another ride to within a few blocks of Hotel Fleece. Since I don't care for anyone to see me, I avoid the front entrance and go in through the back, then hurry to a room used for storing our stage stuff. The cases aren't there, so I assume that the troupe's already left. Being without an airline ticket isn't as grim as realizing that everyone's gone off without me.

In my room I find that at least my passport and belongings have been left. I shave, have a good scrub, and put on clean clothes, hoping to find some cash and a message at the front desk.

In the hall, on my way downstairs, I run into Charlie. To see him and know that he and the others are still around would bring more relief if I weren't feeling so sheepish. The bath hasn't washed away a feeling of trash. Before leaving I'd told him only that I was going to Liverpool. If I knew Charlie, he'd have gotten the general picture, and now he's probably wanting to hear any details that I care to tell, but I don't. And even if I did, he wouldn't have batted an eye. There are times when he seems to be a whole group of fans cheering on not only my own exploits but those of the entire global population, including the verbose and mental Parisians who, as I often tell him, will never be anything but lousy in bed.

He's as warm as ever, gives me a big hug, and says a few gentle and understanding words to let me know that he's been worried. Suddenly, I'm not just nobody anymore. With what's supposed to pass as a star dancer's authority, I ask if he's made proper travel arrangements for the trip home. After all, though I've had a hard day's night, now I'm back as the leader of the pack.

"Charlie, when do we leave for the airport?"

"You don't know? Tomorrow, early at seven. When you came in, didn't you see the schedule I posted in the lobby?"

"Nope."

"You came in through the back door?"

"Course not. I never sneak in back doors."

"Sure you don't. Well, anyway—I told everybody, 'All bags down on time, and—' "

"Yeah, yeah, I know—'and bring your luggage,' right?"

"Right!"

An airport is an airport is an airport, and the Manchester waiting room is like all the rest, except that it's a reprise—both the end of the trip and its beginning. Starting in Paris, things had turned from what was expected to be a joyous journey into a dirge.

Considering what has happened along the way, I'm not at all sure that I feel up to resuming my role as ringleader. A lone desperado galloping off to nowhere would be more in order. But the waiting room's a place to mark time, means no decisions to make and no authority figure to be. For now the company's future rests in the hands of the pilot and the weather. A good thing, too.

As I sit here, inventing reasons to justify my binge, it seems easy to align my recent fall from grace with the state of the world. It's a time when governments seem to be falling like snowstorms of dandruff. So why not me? That I was caught in riots and turned to chaos was only a microcosm of things that were happening all over.

As for others around me, they seem to be in the best of spirits. Bustling strangers, some who've perhaps never flown before, all seem glad to be going someplace, and the dancers are excited over returning to familiar patterns and the relative comforts of home. For them the mishaps in Copenhagen, Paris, Stockholm, and Yugoslavia have already become ritualized anecdotes that grow more hilarious with each telling. Carolyn and her luggage-laden pack mule, Danny, are singing to Cliff and Karla a made-up song—"You go Yugoslavia, I'll go . . ." Danny, though weighed down, is jumping around like a Watusi. Senta, who was happy to do a lengthy St. Helen's press interview in my stead, is regaling Jane with more dance talk. Others are grouped in twos and threes, more or less oblivious to space and time, little Janet and her hubby-to-be sitting cheek by jowl within a pink bubble. Married several years, Molly and Charlie are looking nearly as happy, but somewhat sated. Dear Bet and Lucy are sitting on a bench together, both diligently scribbling last-minute postcards home. Each seems amused about something; each is smiling at her own private joke.

I'm on a different bench and sinking into a sea of everyone else's good cheer. As far as romance goes, I can forget it. Probably the closest I'll ever come to making human contact will be when correcting the position of someone's hand in rehearsal. Well, anyway, the hands would be "family." Maybe that wouldn't be so bad.

Some of the company come over to inspect my ankle. They've been aware of my week-long absence but are being tactful not to ask questions. We all agree for one last time that the ankle will be all well soon.

Then Charlie comes over to say that airplanes might not be taking off.

"Reinhart, you're the limit! Didn't I tell you that these airlines, or the weather, or whatever the problem is, all have to be checked out ahead of time?"

"Sure you did," he says, knowing full well I hadn't, and, as usual, not feeling it necessary to explain that he's already checked everything. Pointing outside to the sidewalk, he says, "See that picket line beginning to form? All the airline employees are going on strike."

"You mean we can't leave? *Crap!* Now you'll have to book us a hotel where we can put up till the strike's over."

"Paul, you'd better get ready for a surprise. I hate to tell you, but we're broke. Sorry, but I forgot and left our St. Helen's fee in an envelope back at the Fleece. But don't worry—I've already sent a taxi, and maybe the money will be here soon."

"*Maybe?* Charles, please. I'm very beat. Just get us out of here, or else bring blankets so that we can spend the night on these benches. You'll have to stay up guarding our shoes."

The next day, the cab comes with the cash, and just before the airport shuts down, we luckily board the last flight out.

Auditions

Whenever dancers were needed, they were taken from classes or from seeing them perform or, as Danny Williams was, spotted somewhere such as a backstage beer party. This still happens today, except that due to the growing number of fine and accomplished dancers available, we have open auditions every two years or so, which are mobbed by hundreds. For them all to be seen it takes between three days and a week, and the one or two finalists sifted out are usually asked to attend company rehearsals, understudy, and hang around in general in order for us to get to know them and vice versa before they are asked to join. The new company member is then assigned roles, usually three or four lesser ones, but sometimes, depending on the dancer and the situation, larger ones, regardless of past experience or training. It usually takes about three years before a new dancer is able to completely master the style and be fully integrated into the repertoire.

Besides looking for the obvious requirements of technique, coordination, stamina, and learning speed, I pay attention in auditions to their body language. This gives telling hints that sometimes speak louder than resumés. It's important that the new dancer be the type of person who can fit well into an already existing group. Strong mutual trust will have to be established, and relationships that can weather the closeness of a life spent on the road for twenty-five or thirty weeks of the year. If not naturally good at it, new dancers need to learn to play their part in a life that involves a lot of mutual leaning.

Naturally, looks count. I like to have a variety of types—tall, short, dark, light, etc. Any kind of attractiveness is in. Since I prefer not to have a pack of Chiclets, I'm careful to select dancers who don't resemble existing members too closely. However, I prefer the men to be larger than the women, to have one woman noticeably taller than the other women, and one shortie of either gender. I'm not particularly attracted to men who resemble women, but if a woman resembles a boy, that's okay. And if any of them have looks so perfect that they resemble mannequins, that's not. To me, attractiveness has more to do with interestingly flawed beauty. But there are limits to how flawed they can be. Fatties are out.

For most dancers, the word "audition" is slightly apoplectic. Auditions are scary games to see who can best fake assurance; audition halls are places of hard-to-control terror. There's usually an obnoxious air of business, and the whole thing can be like a meat rack. Numbers are assigned to nameless bodies, and practical assets are tallied. Not only livelihoods and futures but breakable hearts are on the line.

If there's something worse than taking an audition, however, it's giving one. Who on earth has the authority to say who is best? It usually all boils down to a matter of personal taste and instinct (my track record isn't bad—most of my dancers stay for eight years or longer). The fairest I can be before eliminating the first batch of dancers at an audition is to give everyone equal time. I do this mostly not to offend anyone, as it's fairly simple for me to make quick eliminations after seeing only one plié at the barre. And I try to remember to warn everybody not to expect me to be fair—discrimination, taste, art, maybe even life itself, have little to do with justice. Nobody likes to be rejected, but, personally, I'd far prefer to be rejected myself than to be rejecting a whole roomful of others.

When Laura Dean and Molly Moore auditioned, their insecurities hadn't been hidden very well. It didn't matter, as I was impressed with their eyes. Laura's soft velvet ones with llama lashes spoke of a dreamer, wistful, but not the wishy-washy time-killer type. She seemed to be a young visionary, and though her technique wasn't great at the time, the person behind the eyes was of a caliber not easy to come by. Since then she's formed her own company and invented a way of making dances which, to my way of thinking, amounts to a choreographic church, a cleansing of dance cobwebs which is perhaps the beginning of a whole new tradition of deceptively simple yet theatrical dance. After Laura had been in the troupe for only a year, one of my best contributions to the dance world was in letting her leave.

Molly's eyes were glazed with terror, one which alternated between regulation fear and sheer panic. She seemed to be someone who had a bubbly enthusiasm for fun in a great big way; however, she turned out to be more or less innocent. Her strong technique carried her through the audition. Besides the eyes, I was impressed by Moo's torso and two of its structural details.

At the same audition Carolyn Adams was obviously a sure bet, a gold mine, but it was best that she join us the following year after studying with Bessie Schönberg and graduating from Sarah Lawrence.

During the seventeen years that Carolyn stayed with the company I tossed quite a few dance gauntlets at her feet. Most she picked up, but a couple may have seemed to her to be the wrong size or repellent. Even so, she wouldn't leave these lying. She'd gather them up and, holding them at a safe distance, scamper back to the lovelinesses so natural to her dancing and for which everybody adored her. It was okay—more than okay. When you're able to get dancers, even ones as fine as Carolyn, to do a third of what you see in your head, that's a very good average. Whatever the role, her dancing was unmannered and wondrous. To put it poetically, she was an elegant nectar laced with warm delicacy, easy and effortless. To put it less poetically, she never heaved, let her tongue hang out, or even sweated. Her neck was without noticeable tendons, as was the rest of her, and she was one of those dancers who jump from the small bones of the foot without any understandable preparation. Seen up close, these feet—a little larger than life—resembled lightly fried pancakes, and, as if it mattered to anyone else, she was always darkening their pale edges with—you guessed it— pancake makeup. Having very little turnout, she knew how to make it appear that she did, which, after all, is what counts. There was a seamlessness to her dancing, and within her phrases there never seemed to be any noticeable attack. Whenever I thought some accents were needed to vary the continual evenness, I'd sprinkle in some stops so that she'd be forced to begin again, something that I expected would separate one phrase from another. Somehow my solution was never very effective. Not particularly interested in stillness, she'd take a zigzag series of steps, minimize my pauses, and turn the whole thing into a hummingbird's path. Her dancing, like her voice, tended to climb upwards, then slide into falsetto bubbles. A charmer that no one, *no one*, could resist, and we always let her have her way with anything she fancied.

Both on- and offstage she gave the impression of being about the size and weight of something you could lift with one finger and drop into an eggshell. She was able to pack more steps into a second than most dancers could execute in a full minute, and she made this seem as if nothing much had happened. The other dancers and I were always shaking our heads in disbelief. An extremely fast learner, with a single glance she'd absorb long intricacies into her body.

Besides golden talent, her sensibilities as a person were impressive. To me, most impressive was the sense of family. The Adamses are a giant, continent-straddling clan, and I think it must've been her Harlem parents who passed on to her their civic pride as well as the spirit of togetherness, a knack for self-fulfillment, and the art of organizing her ambitions into a career. These attributes she brought into the company and generously applied to our work. On tour or at home, whenever the road took a bumpy turn, especially when predicaments looked hopeless, she'd be the dancer best able to reassure the rest, leveling things to human proportions with a burst of ridiculous patter or a cheery song. Carolyn's offstage eyes were by turns joyful, frightened, triumphant, and, once in a long while, indignant, but never were they bleak.

Nicholas Gunn, although he was eliminated at his audition, was permitted to hang around the studio. For several months he patiently tried to pick up whatever steps he could until one afternoon, just before the company's umpteenth South American tour, one starting in Lima, I asked him to go out and buy a suitcase. Returning, he held it out and said, "Your new satchel, sir."

"What? Oh, that's not for me," I said. "I guess it must be for Bet."

Bet, in on a prearranged plan, said, "That's not mine. Try Carolyn."

Carolyn sent him to Danny, and so forth and so on, until the last dancer sent him back to me. "Nicholas, I thought I told you it's not mine. I guess you'd better keep it."

"Me? What d'ya mean?"

"You want me to draw you a picture? Get out of here and go pack. You're leaving for Lima."

Another dancer, a large guy, David Parsons, had also been allowed to hang around the studio. One day, to pass the time, I asked him what he did for a living. He said that he pumped gas and repaired cars. "Great," I said. "I'm discouraged with mine. It keeps getting lost, and there's been something funny going on down under the hood. Could you find it and take a look in there?" He said that he would, so I told him he could go on hanging around.

Much later, when my car was seriously bent by a truck, I remembered that there was a mechanic somewhere and when I asked for repairs, he again agreed. And then, more than a year later, right after a final rehearsal before the start of another tour, as I was hurrying out of the studio, my way was blocked by a large person who was looking shy and harried. "Who are you?" I asked politely. He said his name was still David and asked what I wanted him to do next.

"What do you mean what do I want you to do next? Are you a dancer?"

"Mr. Taylor, don't you remember? Two years ago you chose me from three hundred men at an open audition and told me to hang around."

"In that case, it's time for you to learn all the men's parts in all the dances. The videotapes are in the closet. There's the machine over there. I'll take a look at whatever you've been able to learn when the company and I get back." This was a difficult assignment, as the closet was kept locked and the key hidden.

Then one winter, right before another tour, Tom Evert injured himself. "David," I said, "let's see you do Tom's part in *Esplanade*." David had somehow managed to get to the tapes and, after a single rehearsal, was able to dance it without bumping into or hurting anyone. I then sent him out to buy some extra large long johns, and when he returned with them, said, "They're yours, big trouper. You're coming with us to Russia."

"Gee, boss," he replied. "You mean it?"

Those of us who saw his face will never forget the astonished eyes, the gleeful Puck grin, and the dimples at their deepest and very best.

After really remarkable Ruth Andrien was picked from an audition, the tables were turned. As I'd strung David along by pretending that I thought him only an auto mechanic, Ruthie went on fooling me. It took a long time before she'd admit she knew I wasn't just a truck driver who'd wandered in off the street to watch the girls.

Brooklyn

Have I ever mentioned my death in Brooklyn? I doubt it. Brooklyn was where I knew my life as a dancer was over.

Now and then acquaintances ask me what stopping was like. That's some question—you know, sort of personal. Like asking what it's like to stop breathing. They say, "It was hard, wasn't it?" and I say, "No, it was easy." Or others ask, "Was it easy?" so I say, "No, real hard," then make a quick switch to something else. The question's a stumper, makes me apprehensive, is something to enjoy being shifty about.

Truth is, it was both.

By the time the house lights came up, I was flat on my back stage center and already dead. Doesn't seem right that I never got to hear the thump of that final curtain. However, for years I've heard it. That is, I sometimes dream of hearing this profound sound that echoes through the night. *Thawmpth . . . awmph . . . wmph.*

Folks, I'll tell you what stopping was like. But first, so you'll understand what Brooklyn meant, I should try to say what it meant to dance at all. Anywhere.

Dancing was It. Dancing was what life was all about. If you wanted to be a dancer, you didn't just want it, you felt *chosen* to be one. You see, dancing was more of an obligation than a whim. It's a religion, a monstrous itch, a huge and illogical church. In my case, even before learning to dance, I was positive I'd been ordained to it. (Didn't intend to be a choreographer. That came later and, even then, only served to scratch my itch. I made them to dance them.)

At the late age of twenty-two, after several false starts, I was given that work scholarship at the American Dance Festival, where Martha had treated us students to a talk. She spoke of the dancer's foot, and of what she claimed was the oldest profession, and then, sweeping a pointed finger across us, prophetically cooed, "*One* of you is chosen." There was no need to jump up and down, pound my chest, and yell, "Me, *me!*" You see, I already knew. Later on, when she took me into her fold, it seemed a perfectly natural occurrence. I suppose that my being the youngest child and my mother's Darlin' had given me a feeling of being special.

As a professional dancer, I found social dancing slightly sacrilegious. Dancing with your date at a party was something to avoid, and I was inhibited to begin with. I also didn't care to dance in natural settings. Moving for its own sake was sheer joy, but dancing wasn't dancing unless you could do it on a stage and in front of an audience. The same thing was true in college days, when I'd enjoyed moving through water while coaches checked stopwatches and crowds cheered.

However, in exchange for the privilege of being onstage, you had to offer an enormous part of yourself, a blow-up of what you were in real life. Your strengths were supposed to be trotted out and magnified. But what if your weaknesses showed—what about that? Well, it was just too bad. Vulnerability had to be laid on the line. Audiences, if not able to spot flaws precisely, can sense them, just as they can perceive a performer's virtuoso niceties without knowing exactly what they are. As a dancer you have to open up and take the consequences, and this is the humbling part—it forces you to earn the right to be chosen.

For a dancer to be able to perform well, most of his waking hours must be devoted to preparing for the holy white instant of performance. Preparing your body comes first, your soul second, and your brain a relatively unimportant third. A proper preperformance psych-up enables you to get yourself onstage without fainting from fear, but once the curtain lifts, there's security and power of a kind totally absent in everyday life. To perform is something that nothing in the whole world even faintly resembles.

Today I'd say that dancers are still pretty much what they used to be—though better technicians, and perhaps not as evangelistic. Offstage they're still permitted to be soft-spoken, inarticulate, even tongue-tied. Offstage they can think of matters other than dance, but always their minds must return, must be inundated by words to do with dance, for without a thought on dance and a dance to dance they're left with nothing but a lot of talk. A dancer's true voice is his body. At a call from it audiences look, listen, and understand—all types of audiences, everywhere. Dance, truly an international language, from prehistory on, has always been one of the most direct means of communication. And so I guess that's what wise old Martha meant when she said it was the oldest profession—yet maybe not the *single* oldest.

As to death in Brooklyn, I'm still not quite sure how to approach it. Dr. Tacet—whose head, by the way, becomes too large for his body every time there's a full moon—would have had a very definite slant. Distinguishing between internal and external treatments of death, he has said that in Renaissance plays subordinate characters were allowed to succumb to external forces but tragic heroes died from within, and he's always urging everybody, especially lowly subordinates, to take death in, make it a member of the family, even learn to love it as the final reward for all their striving toward completeness.

"Succumb to internal forces" indeed! (Have begun to see my approach.) Soon after the big thump, when the old geezer stated his view, I didn't much care for the implication. After all, I was neither hero nor lowly subordinate, and I hadn't been the one who'd decided to drop the curtain. And then he'd gone on to say that it's an artist's duty never to give up his Magic Invisible, and . . . what baloney! What would a hack phrenologist/costume designer know?

Brooklyn wasn't such a bad place to bow out. It might've been worse—Pôrto Alegre or Perth Amboy, for instance. Brooklyn's beautiful old opera house was good enough for Caruso's last high note and was plenty good enough for mine.

Year '74—six years after Liverpool. By then there had been a lot more new dances and we'd toured nearly every corner of the globe. I was forty-four and had been on the stage for twenty-two years—a fairly long run, as dance lives go. Even so, I felt there was more dancing in me and hadn't intended to retire. The end was premature, yet not so sad. Once in a while it seems sad, but most times it seems comical. Our dance god, the Great Puppeteer up there in the flies, that ineffable string snipper, turned out to be an old-time prankster.

The big thump came during the premiere of *American Genesis*, a dance that we'd tried out in Philly, where the size of the audience had caused Carolyn to quip the old quip, "You can fill a cup and you can fill a glass, but you can never Philadelphia." The mixed notices had been somewhat surprising, as by then I'd gotten fairly used to untarnished laurels. However, I was still optimistic that Madhatters back home would probably be brave enough to risk the wilds of Flatbush Avenue and would recognize quality when they saw it.

Being someone with a very American background and proud of it, even though patriotism in general had gone downhill due to the unpopular Vietnam War, one of my itches had required that I make a dance full of American history. It didn't bother me that Americana-type dances had gone out with the forties. However, if I'd known that our country's bicentennial was coming up, I probably would've been able to wait for a less obvious time.

It was to be a long affair, my first full-evening work, and in modern dance that's a rarity. Other than Martha's *Clytemnestra* there'd been few, if any. I'd no illusions that my piece would compare with hers. After all, *Clytemnestra* had come as the summation of that great woman's lifetime work, and, by comparison, it was easy to see myself as a babe in the woods. Greatness and relative experience aside, the way I felt about America's past didn't match her rosier view, at least if the upbeat *Appalachian Spring* was any example, or her tendency to turn caves of despair into phalluses of renewal. This may have been because I'd absorbed some of the disillusionment typical of my generation. I was seeing my dance-to-be as an offshoot of *From Sea to Shining Sea*, the one made nine years earlier in which I viewed the USA backwards, sideways, and askance. A part of America's history that particularly appealed to me was the combination of puritanism and free spirit, a paradox that, by the way, was a large part of Martha's own character and a warring part of mine.

As if the subject of paradoxical America throughout the ages wasn't epical enough for one dance, I was attacked by a simultaneous impulse to bring the Bible into the picture. I hadn't paid much attention in Sunday school, so had to dig into the Old Testament, where I was surprised to discover myself in the grip of enchantment. The first few stories, in their stirrings of what was tempting to think of as racial memory, hit home, and it somehow seemed imperative to connect those ancient stories to the American heritage. I'd relocate different eras—colonial strife, the revolution, western

plowmen versus cowboys, plus the years just prior to the Civil War—
transplant and try to braid them into corresponding biblical days of Creation, Fall, Fratricide, and Flood. All was to be presented as one eternal
single-stranded conflict and shown in dance images that made double, even
triple, cross-references.

What an idea, I thought. I was going to hit an all-time high in paradox-
icalness. The concept seemed simple at first but soon became troublesome.
The trick was to build the dance's scaffolding so that each thematic part
could click neatly into place. By the time we got to Brooklyn, though the
scaffolding was still a little shaky, I was fairly certain that magical fizz was
about to be uncorked.

From the beginning the music had been a nuisance. I'd hoped to com-
mission an original score but couldn't afford one. Although grants from the
Ford and Mellon Foundations had recently come through, these grants
weren't to be spent on production costs. It was necessary to use music old
enough to be in the public domain, but I couldn't find any one piece
suitable or long enough, so settled for an assortment of Bach, Haydn,
Martinů, Gottschalk, and some bluegrass folk music. In the past I'd sometimes preferred to use musical patchworks, but this score imposed a set of
demands that I really could have done without.

Putting the dance together was like a blind arthritic teaching himself the
art of juggling, or a miserable speller attempting an acrostic. The ideas were
too few or too many to fit the allotted sections of music, and at first the
grammar wouldn't come, and later it seemed that I'd used the wrong vocabulary. After six weeks of rehearsals I was tempted to blame things on a
new opaque period that I imagined myself to be entering. Actually, my epic
was in danger of becoming a comic strip. I rationalized that a comic strip
would make things all the more American and that if anyone should ask
what it meant, I'd tell them *American Genesis* was about apple-pie warfare.

There was one rehearsal when, preferring to put the blame for my difficulties on the dancers, I called their breakneck cavorting stupid and told
them they should take up taxi driving. "Get out of here," I growled. To get
even they stood around looking broad-minded and too lenient—a Christian
revenge if ever there was one. I began to think that there were nastier
things in the world than open hostility. They then drew back to the far end
of the studio where they silently ate their yogurts. My remorseful stomach
ate itself, but in a few minutes they came back and the rehearsal continued
as usual.

Genesis required a minimum of thirty different roles. Since we were only
a company of ten, this meant triple casting. There was to be a consistency
of type within each triple role. Costumes, music, and most artistic decisions

were based on the necessity of a small budget. Tacet took the prize for frugality with a truly protean set piece—a semicircular object representing altar, Noah's ark, spoked paddleboat helm, Eve's giant womb, planet Earth, gray rainbow, dawning sun, Plymouth Rock, and Lucifer's go-go platform.

When I'd been in Martha's company she'd usually cast me in bad-guy roles. Since then I'd choreographed several more for myself, including a Hell's Angel in *Sea*, the destructive side of the sun in *Orbs*, *Agathe*'s Satan, a warped warlock in *Churchyard*, an all-American rapist in *Big Bertha*, and now, Lucifer. Even in my good-guy roles there was usually a demonic element. To me, antiheroes were an old sweet song. Triple-threat Lucifer (Angel of Light/Puritan Father/Captain Noah) wasn't all bad. That God had cast him, the former king of Babylon, into the pit—had literally fired him—seemed unjust and made him only a mistreated underdog. Lucifer's arch-enemy, the defending angel Michael, was danced by Bet. The announcing angel, Gabriel, was Eileen (both women being transformed in gender without help from Copenhagen).

This is the plot:

(1) The Creation. Dressed as a pair of Pilgrims at Plymouth Rock and surrounded by Mayflower cherubim and seraphim, Michael and Lucifer engage in their Eternal Battle. An olive branch grows from the top of an altar and is stolen by Lucifer in vengeance for having been thrust from heaven.

(2) Before Eden. The battle continues in the form of colonial minuets during which Lucifer introduces his cohort Lilith to Adam, whom she seduces.

(3) So Long Eden. A shift of locale finds hillbillies Adam, Eve, and slithery Jake dancing a ménage-à-trois hoedown. Their loss of innocence is less important to them than their regrets at having to separate at the end of their dance.

(4) West of Eden. In a Gomorrah-like saloon infested with pimps and floozies, the angels, now town elders, vie for possession of two locals—cowboy Cain (who was Jake) and farmer Abel (who was Adam). These rivaling brothers are used as pawns in the angels' ongoing battle. In a flashback, Eve gives birth to the brothers as Gabriel acts as midwife and announces the event. Cain, seeing that his mother prefers Abel, is jealous and turns to Lucifer for approval. Aided by the saloon denizens, Lucifer then indoctrinates Cain with lessons on sex and violence. Cain slays Abel and lays the corpse at Lucifer's feet. Abel's offering is ignored, however, as Lucifer and Michael continue their battle.

(5) The Flood. The Reverend and Mrs. Noah—an evangelistic bigot and his equally rigid wife (Lucifer and Michael)—with growing disapproval watch

their fun-loving children perform animalistic antics in a riverboat minstrel show emceed by interlocutor Gabriel. The Eternal Battle has diminished to farcical family bickering. On instructions from above, Gabriel instructs Noah to turn his paddleboat into the Ark, and he eventually succeeds in herding his reluctant family aboard. Beneath the rainbow sign of the Covenant, the Noahs are led up to heaven by a black child (Lilith's daughter) who had made a pest of herself during the minstrel show by stealing the males away from their mates, was ejected from the Ark by the Reverend Noah, and drowned, but whose spirit is now reunited with the Noah family by Gabriel.

Throughout, Gabriel has been heralding, consoling, reconciling, and representing the American conscience. As the curtain falls, Gabriel kneels at the altar while Lucifer follows along menacingly after the Noahs.

The triple role of Lilith went to Carolyn Adams. I often said to her, "Carolyn, honey, you're a gold mine, a *gold* mine." According to the Talmud, Lilith was Adam's first wife. She was a very bad girl and fooled around right under God's throne, shaking the bejesus out of Him, and things like that. She later appears in the fratricide section leading a bevy of hookers, then pops back for the Flood as Lilith's flirty, cakewalking child. (When, as Captain Noah, I unintentionally died, one of my parting thoughts was that I should've heeded the warning early in the Bible that says that anyone who fiddles with its stories will come to no good.) Rather than take advantage of the airiness to which her dancing was more naturally suited, I gave the role to Carolyn as a challenge. The part was supposed to add a certain weighted demonism to her range. As Lilith she brought a curiously weightless dignity to all three roles: colonial wench, western harlot, and paddleboat Lolita.

Inevitably, during the nine years that separated Liverpool from Brooklyn, dancers had left the company and were replaced by others. Besides Carolyn, the only remaining troupers were Bet and Eileen. Newcomers were the gifted but relatively inexperienced Elie Chaib, Ruby Shang, Lila York, Monica Morris, Nicholas Gunn, and Greg Reynolds. Those who'd left had stayed with the company for at least six years each. Danny had left to choreograph and dance in Canada; Jane, to co-found 5 × 2, a chamber-sized repertoire company; Senta, to choreograph for a company that she inexplicably named Harry; Molly, to become a full-time mother, rightly preferring the company of her two small sons. Charlie still booked us, but had stopped touring in order to tend the growing stable of other dance attractions he'd taken on. (Have I ever said that his and Molly's older son, Taylor Reinhart, was conceived in Calcutta and named after me? If so, I don't mind saying so again.)

Fortunately, these departures hadn't all come at once, and each dancer, after giving notice, stayed on long enough to teach his roles to the newcomers. Still, I hadn't become so used to dancers leaving that each separation wasn't an emotional jolt. Our work together, the peaks and dips, always formed strong bonds, and those of us who remained usually went through a sort of mopey mourning period, as if we'd never see our dear departeds again.

For instance, take Danny's departure. Since I first spotted him as a footloose kid at a New London beer party, watching him grow into an artist had brought me much joy. If the reins I'd sometimes used on him had been held too tightly, his will to improve had bridged over what less devoted dancers might have shied away from. As if overnight, he'd now become a highly educated thoroughbred. It was at rehearsal, while working with him on his part of Adam in "So Long Eden," that we first learned of his plans to leave.

The rehearsal had been going smoothly—no friction, no hostility, no need for the dancers to get back at me with Christian revenge. Out of the blue Danny retreated to the far end of the studio, where he dropped down onto a costume case, sobbing uncontrollably. In all the years he'd been with us nobody'd ever heard him cry. I went to turn off the tape machine. The others were shifting uncomfortably from foot to foot, undecided as to what to do. He hadn't hurt himself, and nobody knew what was the matter, and all were looking to me to make the first move. I didn't know if I should go console him or just tell him to stop it. (Now, thinking back, I see that everyone's dependence on me to make decisions made the situation strangely like the one soon to happen in Brooklyn where it took forever for anyone to decide to bring down the curtain.)

Danny cried on and on. Obviously his heart was breaking, and if someone didn't do something soon he was apt to drown in his own tears. Since he and Carolyn were close, I asked her to go over. She replied, "All right, but I think it's you he's going to have to talk to." It turned out that Danny was being torn, ripped apart by his devotion to the company on one hand, his need for independence on the other. East Coast discipline was warring with California free spirit—that old American paradox again. Carolyn quieted him, and I finally went over to say, "What is it, my Pony?"

His explanation didn't take very long. He answered simply, "I'm my own man."

I could still recall my own feelings on leaving Martha and well knew what he meant. Other pastures had beckoned; he was a colt no more. The time had come to part, to say a triple farewell. So long, Eden. So long, Adam. So long, my Pony.

And then, after booking us for a total of eight years, good old true blue Charlie left, too. The dancers hadn't been easy to replace, but finding a new manager seemed unthinkable. Managers were a much rarer breed. Who'd find us work? Bring us good news, bad news, and chicken soup? Whom could I lay out now? This was very, very serious.

Merce Cunningham's manager had been the catalyst in Charlie's departure. When Charlie, besides booking dance companies, began serving as coordinator for the National Endowment for the Arts dance touring program, Merce's manager accused him of having a conflict of interest, and with the help of others in the field whose companies weren't yet included in the government's newly formed program, he demanded that Charlie choose between his position with the NEA and his booking business. As Endowment tour coordinator, Charlie was completely innocent of favoritism to my company—if anything, he'd overcompensated. Nevertheless, he went along with the manager's demands. Charlie felt that he could be more helpful to the dance world in general by staying with the Endowment, and so he discontinued his booking business and, with regret, told me that I'd have to find a new manager. My first reaction was one of tragic proportions; then I got mad; and then, in about six years or so, after Charlie had indeed accomplished much of value for the field, I was able to make some sense out of his departure.

Our stage manager, Judy Daykin, had become exhausted by the road, and so, since she was extremely capable, and since she preferred to stay in our New York office, she agreed to take over for Charlie. Both were always fond of the troupe and deeply committed to our work together in an extraordinarily unselfish way. I'd have trusted my life to either, and sometimes had to. Charlie had arranged escapes from riots in more than one country, and in Brooklyn it was Judy who rushed to call the police who called the ambulance.

Just before dawn on the day of our premiere at the Brooklyn Academy of Music—called BAM because of its carefree curtain puller—in bed and dreaming, I'm revolted to see a whole troupe, or whatever they're called, of swollen gray ticks detaching themselves from my dog Deedee and falling one by one to the floor. There's something familiar about those bugs— reminding me of someone, Dr. T maybe. At the sound of my own snores I wake. I think I've heard someone calling my name. I answer and hear a voice saying, "My boy, we suspect that you are up to your old shenanigans again. Don't you dare remove a single one of those round gray rosettes from my gorgeous Puritan Frocks!"

"Easy, Pops, things'll be fine." (I'd waited until he was safely out of town before ripping them all off.) "Where are you now? Your voice sounds far away."

"Venezia, dear boy, glorious Venezia, final resting place of Diaghilev—my soul mate, you know."

"Hey, Pops, I meant to tell you—you know your Pilgrim bonnets? Well, the dancers want them different. The veils are too long and everybody keeps tripping on them."

"Mercy, darst not touch a thread!"

"But you know how much leeway we need when we get going good. Those veils fly all around and tangle us up."

"Precisely. Our intent was to blend the Arts of Decor and Choreography. Just as in Yeats's immortal phrase, one should not be able to tell the dance from the decor. We shan't compromise our original concept, and that is final."

I'm picturing Dr. T's lopsided smile and remember how long it's been since I began to call him Pops. I'd fantasized a father or trainer or someone and had tried to think of him along these lines, but it wasn't quite working out anymore. He wasn't much, was only a half-baked designer, and now had turned into a shadowy parasite. There'd been times when I was able to summon up feelings for him. "He gave me everything," an acquaintance once said of his father. I'd say that Tacet gave me not much, and feel something for him that, through love or hate, other people hardly ever feel for their real fathers. I'm feeling . . . apathy. Yet I'm nervous about Brooklyn, and my mind is full of the kind of things you don't inflict on dancers or managers. An ear is needed, and Tacet's would have to do.

"Pops, let's leave Yeats for a minute. To tell the truth, I'm scared about the week in Brooklyn. I've tried to get in shape—daily classes, swims, runs up and down stairs. Even so, I get winded easily. And I'm overweight, though the dexies that I've taken ever since Liverpool completely take my appetite away. And they keep me awake, so then I need sleeping pills. Both kinds have turned out to be addictive. Wish someone had warned me. I try to quit, but then the ulcers hurt and I have to force-feed them every hour or so. I've thought about going somewhere for a cure, but our touring schedule never ends, and whenever we're not on the road I've got new dancers to break in and new dances to make."

"My poor boy, surely tablets of such lovely hues cannot be harmful. The weight problem is an aberration of a confused mind. You have simply thought yourself fat; now reverse the process. And *do* forsake all those overly strenuous exercises. Focus on your interpretive powers. Fear not—if all else fails, my costume will carry your role, and the evening will go splendidly."

Well, he was right about my interpretive powers. I was sure that my

Lucifer would be the bees' knees. In fact, after we'd performed in Philly a Catholic priest had come backstage and offered to exorcise me.

"You're right, Pops, we both love performing. I'll concentrate on my dramatic presence. Really, there's nothing in life, I mean real life, as real as realizing the life that we live in unreality, if you know what I mean." (Even if he didn't, he'd go for the word play.)

The fears that I'm confiding to him are ones I've never told anyone. I could barely believe the facts myself at first, then have been slow to accept them. It was hard to admit that for years I've been hooked on uppers and downers. The accompanying guilt has been overshadowed by a fear of being found out; but even more disturbing is the possibility that my source might be cut off. Since I've gotten the prescriptions from several different doctors, each doctor has been unaware of the full extent of my habit; had they known, they would have stopped writing them. I also feared that the company would find out. So far, nobody has. Bet knows that I always kept a silver pillbox in my makeup kit, but she assumes that, like herself, I'm given to vitamins and desiccated liver pills. The nervousness and depressions that occur every time I've attempted a withdrawal have been attributed by everyone to overwork and emotional stress.

Half a Dexamyl would be potent enough for most people, but after six years of consuming bottles of them regularly, my body has built resistance, and to produce much result, I now take as many as ten or twelve tablets at a time. My physical and mental health have been undermined, but not my dance technique. If anything, control, flexibility, line, and ballon are improved. It's just that I have absolutely no endurance. The pills give energy for only a few minutes of full-out dancing; then the body cranks down and the heart practically pumps itself through my chest.

On travel days during tours, usually after only three hours of drugged sleep, I'll rise to find it impossible to carry my luggage toward the next point of departure, and, for the first time in my life, I begin to splurge on porters. The girls have discovered wheeled luggage, but pride has kept me from resorting to such cream-puff contrivances.

The frequent eating to relieve the ulcers is soothingly therapeutic but makes it necessary to keep punching new holes in my belts. And foxy old Tacet should be credited for the way in which my paunch is more or less hidden by a costume jacket of kindly length.

Just before Brooklyn I sprain my ankle again. This time the good one. After X-raying it, a doctor tells me that I'm "feathered." Not understanding, I ask what he means, and he explains that my tendons have been pulling too hard on the ankle bones, causing them to splinter and giving their outlines a feathered appearance. He warns me that there is some danger of the "feathers" piercing the flesh, and when he offers to show me the X-rays, I refuse to look, and tell him that, no matter what, I've no intention of missing a performance. "Perform?" he responds. "I'm amazed you can stand up, much less dance."

And then there are the increasingly frequent bouts of nausea and the ulcer-related losses of blood. The face that stares back from dressing-room mirrors looks crazed, the skin yellow, the eyes discolored, with bags underneath dark enough to be noticeable through the thickest of makeup. What I am noticing are the symptoms of a specific disease. Not knowing, I've thought that the signs indicate poor health in general, and somehow I've managed to get through the tour that precedes Brooklyn. It isn't until some weeks after the opening that the cause of the symptoms is discovered. In addition to the other maladies, I've contracted a deadly form of hepatitis.

BAM is packed. There was to have been an eight o'clock curtain, but because of waiting for ushers to finish seating everyone, we're to start a half-hour late. It's as if the audience has heard and is out to prove that dance goers in this country have grown from a million to fifteen million during the last ten years. The majority here are those already believing in the magic of dance, many secretly wishing they were dancers themselves, some traveling long distances to search out that special dance, or bright cluster of dancers, or chosen one. The audience is here to have its belief in the art reconfirmed and hoping that at the curtain's close it will leave the theater feeling bathed and purified. There's a large proportion of professionals present—established dance makers, new ones, dancers of all ranks, agents, publicists, writers, others crucial to the field. Backstage the word is that, among other notables, Martha is out front.

All this doesn't soothe any of our nerves.

Anxious at the dress rehearsal, Bet and I have squabbled about a certain balance in one of our mirror-image duets which requires careful cooperation. The spat, our usual kind, has gone unresolved (perhaps by coincidence, perhaps not, the made-up relationships in *Genesis* aren't so far removed from real ones), but we always get over our differences. Besides, stage time is too precious to spend smoothing her ruffled feathers. And if she needs soothing, Carolyn's bubbly humor and Eileen's consideration will do the job better than I can.

In my dressing room I can sense the murmuring rumble of faceless forms beyond the pit as they fill a house that soon will be turning into a great black void. After trying a few pliés I become dizzy and, too depleted to warm up, I lie on a cot, terrified of the battle ahead—the one with my own body. Am counting on the dexies to furnish strength. It's imperative to earn the right to be seen. My thoughts fasten briefly on atonement, then swim away. Am filled with dread, false dreams, and at least thirteen amphetamines.

After what is probably only a few minutes but seems to be a much longer series of blurred imaginings, I hear a gentle knock at the door. Automatically my hand locates the pillbox and shoves it out of sight. I rise unsteadily as Gabriel steps in. She tells me that the audience isn't quite seated and, with genuine concern, asks how I feel. Only half-lying, I reply that I'm as high as a kite, then wonder if she's on to me.

In the adjacent dressing room Michael is having an attack of jitters and is downing a handful of last-minute vitamins and desiccated liver pills, an act that seems sanctimonious to her mirror-image Lucifer. Good Bet—if she had to, she could, she would, forgive a bad partner.

Of all cardinal sins, for a dancer to miss the mark is the worst.

Gabriel now announces that it's time to take our places. She wishes me "toi"—her British version of the American "Get out there and knock 'em dead."

Onstage I find some frazzled-looking cherubim and seraphim scattered around in twos and threes and whispering together. Carolyn's going from one to the other, dropping smiles and mildly risqué jokes in an effort to make everyone less tense. When I greet them, they seem reluctant to respond. They're keeping to themselves, and if they're concerned about me, they aren't showing it.

Eileen walks over to a table offstage where Vinnie, the Academy's prop man, hands her three stylized objects—an olive branch, a clarion, and a sword. "Have a ball, hon," he says, winking brightly. Eileen gives the sword to Bet, and the two women drift to stage center, where the overhead work light shoots down its glare. Their brows crease, converge, and there occurs a conference of angels.

I've stationed myself as far offstage left as possible, the murky wings there being a place of last refuge from the unprotected stage space. As I ease myself down onto the pinrail and lean back against its parallel ropes, they remind me of the front of a cage that's barred with hemp. Noticing that our set piece has been placed slightly off its mark, I return to the stage to reposition it but find that it's become too heavy for me to budge. Beckoning to one of the new dancers, I ask him to move Plymouth Rock half an inch. Glad to do whatever he can to help, Elie prepares to shove, but Bet sails over and says, "Wait. We shouldn't touch anything—stagehands' union rules, remember?" She then asks one of the crew to shift the set piece to its correct spot, and, a little annoyed with her self-righteousness, I return to the wings.

The overture is about to start. It's aggravating that the dancers are still milling around instead of getting into their starting positions. Even though they're at a good distance and speaking in hushed voices, I'm able to overhear most of what they're saying.

Nick says, "Wow, if PT can't move the set himself he must be really beat."

Simultaneously I hear another dancer at the opposite corner of the stage mutter, "Sure is picky."

"He must be feeling better," Carolyn answers.

I'm able to hear them clearly and am tempted to go at them with sharp little precisely placed bites. Sometimes it's as if I have the equipment and instincts of a bat. I suspect that my heightened hearing might have been due to adrenaline, or, more likely, the Dexamyl. It's the same kind of hearing that I have when my dentist, Joe Towbin, anesthetizes me with nitrous oxide. Softly blended background sounds become amplified and, even though concurrent, are simple to isolate. I'm almost painfully aware of small overlapped sounds such as Joe's humming as he dials a number in the next room, also from an air conditioner there, and the seemingly drastic change coming from rubber-heeled shoes as the nurse steps from carpet to linoleum. And when someone is talking on the phone, strangest of all is to be able to pick up nearly every word that's coming from the other end of the line.

So it's big bat Lucifer there in Brooklyn with dark wings around him, watching and able to hear everything.

Lilith has joined Michael and Gabriel under the work light and the conference continues. As it usually does at stressful times, a tic is attacking Gabriel's right cheek, and, as she picks distractedly at the collar of her gray jersey Pilgrim dress, she says that she doesn't think I've warmed up, and that I've been looking just awful, and she tells the others that as I was coming from my dressing room, I'd swayed and had to catch my balance on the wall. She's worried and wants to know what they should do.

For a moment Bet stops smoothing the strayed wisps at the back of her long neck and says, "Oh, he's sick?" (With the same dawning enlightenment, she once said of *From Sea to Shining Sea*, "Oh, I see—the title's from a song?")

Grasping the olive branch that Eileen's given her, Carolyn drops her eyes and says, "You're right, Crops. He's sick—but can we do the season without him?"

Bet suggests that she might try to dance the duets alone and improvise my solos. "How about that one? In New London I—"

Carolyn flashes her eyes straight up and exclaims, "Bettie! *That* one's no good."

Clutching at straws, Eileen suggests that if they tell me how concerned they all are, maybe I'll cancel the performance. But Bet doesn't agree, says I'm stubborn.

They're burning me up. Gabriel is being her overly concerned self; Lilith seems like an unconcerned New Yorker who won't notice when someone else is being mugged; Michael is really only thinking of those damned wisps of hair. I swoop out of the wings and say, "So you're trying to gang up to make your own decisions, right? Well, if I'm too sick to dance, I'll be the one to decide! You just worry about your own dancing."

Bet shrugs one shoulder and takes on the air of a martyr. The other two turn away sheepishly. As I stomp back to the wings, I hear one of them say, "You see? When he's sick he's like an animal that'll bite anyone who comes near."

Over at stage right Vinnie notices that a pitchfork's been left lying on his prop table. Knowing that Lucifer will soon need it, he picks it up and hurries over. Vinnie was once on the crew of some past theater where I'd briefly danced and lately has been treating me as if I were a long-lost brother. He was quick to recognize the pitchfork as a not-so-abstruse phallic symbol, and, holding it out to me, he says, "Hey, pal, forgotten something? Here y'go—jeeze, but ain't *we* got a big one!" Priding himself on being a vital part of each and every performance, Vinnie always says "we."

I start to lift the pitchfork, meaning to demonstrate how it'll look when angled out at crotch level, but have to stop with it only halfway up, since, like Plymouth Rock, it's gotten too heavy. Suddenly I'm attacked by stomach cramps and a wave of nausea. Putting the prop down and settling an arm between its prongs, I use it as a crutch to steady myself on.

"What's the fuckin' matter?" Vinnie asks. "You can't get it up, huh?"

"Don't be too sure. Maybe you'd like me to show you how it works later when I feel more in the mood."

"Shit, man, I mean it. Youse don't look too red hot."

"Don't worry about it. I'm okay—just saving myself for the big push."

"Yeah? Well, we'd better be good. There's a terrific house tonight."

Harsh stage light is now softened by Jenny's gels and shutters. The floor's a glowing field of bluish ice. I hear a cue that's followed by the soft rush of the curtain as it gapes upward and disappears into the flies, leaving the stage peeled and virginal. Skidding to a stop, time changes into something unearthly and newly meaningful. Distant noises filter through the music that's coming over the loudspeakers—a jet's whine, the BMT's rumble, the harsh rustling of playbills, the piercing snap of a woman's purse—all causing my pulse to go berserk. Vinnie's gravelly "Let's go get 'em, tiger!" is all but inaudible.

I aim the pitchfork upwards and look across the stage to Michael, who's waiting in the wings directly opposite. In mirror unison we gulp air, take that one huge and ever scary step from sheltering wings to open space, then stride purposefully toward each other across our boarded battlefield. My Pilgrim hat's strangling the throbbing veins at my temple, and my feet feel inexcusably distant, as though trapped in ten-ton coffins. Icy trickles of sweat run down my made-up neck, staining my pointed white collar. All at once there's an encouraging warm clamor from the audience. It nearly knocks me over. What more could an ex-swimmer want than for them to do something like that? (For one thing, to be able to crawl out of the pool at the end of the race.)

After only about ten seconds, when Bet and I converge at stage center, I feel practically used up. The short trek has been a long, slow wade through frozen mud. I'm thinking that if the dexies don't start working better, I'll have to give up all hope for a decent performance, maybe have to settle for plain survival. An ignominious drowning in Brooklyn would be too shameful to contemplate, even when doped up.

The music races ahead, leaving me four or five beats behind. I urge myself on, but the body won't listen. Jumps come out in miniature and other moves degenerate into pallid mutations. Then, to catch up with the music, I leave some steps out altogether.

In our duet, Bet's slowing down to match my tempo and diligently omitting the same steps that I do. As I try to partner her, she's doing everything by herself, supporting her own weight, and whenever my balance goes off, she's trying to prop me up. There's frenzy in her face. Her eyes won't meet mine. For bungling our duet I've no remorse—am only intent on remaining upright till after my first exit, when the pinrail would offer support and relief from the shooting pains that are coming every time I put weight on the feathered ankle.

When the duet's over, I aim myself toward the nearest wing, am blinded by the sidelights there, run into a drape, and strike the ankle on an iron stage weight. All Hades erupts, and I find myself flat on my back just inside the wings. I sit up to see that the ankle's been torn open. Numbed by shock, there's no pain or feeling of any kind.

As I'm trying to stanch the flow of blood that's forming a puddle on the floor, Vinnie rushes over—"Christ, what a mess! I'll be right back—just keep grabbin' your foot." He goes to find something to mop with and, returning, holds out one of the dancers' towels. "Youse better take care of it yourself," he says. Then, gravel voice going dog-whistle high: "I'm about to fuckin' faint."

No bones are showing through, and I'm still able to move my foot, so I get up to prepare for my next entrance. "Hold it, pal," Vinnie says. "There's still some more of that stuff on your hand."

I look down to see that a palm's been scraped. I tell him, "No time to wipe now—there's my music."

Back onstage, the Eternal Battle's being turned all around—instead of fighting me, Michael's trying to help me overcome my difficulties with steps, space, and tempo. She's not seeing my gleaming red foot or the smeary handprints that I'm leaving all over the waist of her dress. The palm and ankle are burning like hell and making it nearly impossible to focus on anything else. Vinnie's "Christ!" echoes in my ears, and what was meant as an expression of concern takes on a paradoxical twist. I can't help thinking, now that I've slipped out of character, that perhaps as a token to remember Lucifer by, I've been left with only some kind of messy and not very ecstatic stigmata.

My second exit goes smoother than the first. At last I'm free from the eyes of the audience, and the wings offer temporary haven. For this I would have gladly sold my soul. It's tempting to collapse onto the floor, but I know that if I do, I won't be able to get up, so I settle onto the pinrail and let my chest rest on my knees. Dazed, I'm studying a small area of the floor where a mixture of blood and sweat has dripped from my clasped hands.

Eileen's feet pad into view, and her voice drifts down from above. "Paul, don't you think you should go to your dressing room?"

Without looking up I say, "Can't—still got more to dance before inter-mission."

"No you don't. It's the trio now—you're not in *Eden*."

I sure wasn't.

"You better go rest," she says, helping me to my feet.

The walls are rippling and tilting in and out, and the dressing room at the other end of the hall looks as if I'm seeing it from the wrong end of a telescope. I'm moving as fast as I can, because if I can get the door closed behind me in time, I'll be able to throw up into the sink there without anyone watching. After a short skirmish with some stagehands who're blocking the way, I find another one of them stretched out in my room. He rises from the cot and leaves without having to be asked. Then I hear Judy outside the door saying, "Paul, will your ankle be okay? Do you need anything?"

There's a strong taste left in my mouth from what I've just left in the sink, so I ask her to find me some breath freshener.

My paunch is rock hard from cramps, and bloated. I've never been a sylph, but this is ridiculous. If I'm going back onstage, I'd better try to forget the cramps and get into a more positive frame of mind. Eden's country music is coming over the room's intercom, and I'm picturing a quiet, restful place of my own somewhere off in the sticks, and dreaming up a newspaper strike that will cancel out the next day's reviews, and envisioning some sex soon—anything for incentive to get myself through the rest of the dance. And I'm practicing mind control—you know, being levelheaded and broad-minded. To Dance was to Live. Nobody asks you to do either, and you have to expect long tricky combinations of one obstacle after another. Then I'm feeling better, but still dopey. Some of the bile that's missed the sink has splattered onto the ankle, and it seems mildly funny that just as the gash was coagulating, along comes this acidy stuff to dilute the clot.

Soon Judy returns and, handing me a stick of gum, notices something on the floor by my chair. She says she's happy to see that at last I've come to my senses and that she'll go make an announcement that the performance is off.

"What do you mean 'off'?" Following her gaze downward, I see that my body's been trying to tell me something. Automatically, my hands have removed my costume and my legs are halfway into my street pants.

"Got mixed up," I explain, kicking the pants away. "These look a lot like my Act II ones. Nothing's off—I'm coming right back onstage. But I need a couple of extra minutes. Tell the house manager that intermission will be a little longer."

"Whatever you say, PT, but I think you're bonkers."

So I'm putting my costume back on, and, though it's unlucky to whistle in dressing rooms, I'm whistling "Go Tell Aunt Nancy" and "When I Grow Too Old to Dream," two of my mother's favorites. Mother has become the strongest incentive to get myself through.

A heart attack during the past year has confined her to her bed. She'll be waiting in the nursing home and thinking of me—perhaps this very minute. She'll want to know how the performance went and be expecting her bedside phone to ring.

Not long ago a wire saying that Mother was dying was handed to me at intermission during one of the West Coast dates. I finished the program, rushed to catch the first flight out, and when I came into the intensive care ward, Mother's other children had already gathered at her bedside, where she was giving a farewell address—something that she'd done twice before, perhaps as an intentional dry run to prepare us for the real one. She stressed that the four of us should not drift apart, then embraced each, starting with Soph, the oldest, then Tom and Bettie, and, saving me for last, she held me extralong. Even through her advanced cataracts she was able to see the desolation in my eyes, and she said, "There, there, my darlin'. It's all right—I'm ready to go."

"Well, you may be, but *I'm* not ready for it," I replied.

Perhaps it was then that she decided to live a while longer.

And tonight, in a tilted-up bed with oxygen nearby and tiny pills of digitalis handy in a small bag suspended from a string around her frail neck, she's still prolonging her departure to suit me. There isn't a doubt in my mind that the least I can do is earn her continuing esteem. So far, my performance is nothing to phone home about. I pop the fourteenth dexie of the day, wash it down with Mylanta, slap two new globs of blue makeup on my eyelids, and make some quick, broken beelines to the stage for Act II.

Entrenched on Lucifer's platform, I'm waiting for my cue to move and trying to build up steam. The shriek of strings, the flutter of a tongued trumpet, and something that sounds like a death rattle are fighting with each other. A florid haze is permeating the stage, hanging there heavy and obscene. My raised pitchfork feels hot to the touch, its prongs indistinct as they blend upwards into thick air.

Though it's hard to make out the fragmented patterns that the others are dancing in front of me, I've the impression that, in place of the order that I usually aim for in my dances, there now seems to be a masterpiece of disorder. In making it, I must have drawn on chaos as a guiding force, and told myself that I should trust all those chaotic fiascos of actual experience that won't give in to my creative disciplines.

Gasps and loud crashes of bodies against bodies aren't bothering me a bit. It doesn't matter to me that Abel is being throttled too roughly by the Gunn family's hedonistic son Nick, or that Carolyn, the pride of Harlem parents, is whoring it up—moving like a beautiful comet, and at last achieving some of that demonic dancing that I'd so long urged on her.

Mechanically, I'm presenting my pitchfork to Cain, and the choir of red floozies is celebrating the joys of lust and murder, streaking by with wild steps and orgiastic gestures. And now, carried high, Lilith is riding triumphantly on the corpse of Abel, and dropping a silken red scarf which flutters down to my feet, settling softly there like a widening stain of gore.

At the sight, my mouth again fills with bile. My mind recoils, shrinks backwards. Suddenly, I'm in Berlin where that awful acid taste started, and I'm underneath a pile of corpses at *Scud*'s premiere. And I'm crying at Mother's bedside. And I'm back in the slums of Liverpool—me, Mother's pride and joy—alone on squeaking beds in the company of strangers, heart gone cold, soul given to Gomorrah—no, not given—it was just a loan, a lark. By God, I wouldn't be caught in a lifelong rut! That was all in the fuzzy past, barely real now, only an unimportant source of my devil dance to come. Today I'm out of fleabag beds, back on my feet in Brooklyn, and Jenny's stage lights are the reality—beacons guiding me through the hell at hand. Tonight will be what counts.

But when my cue comes, what was intended to be a solo filled with jubilant spasms of evil fades into something like feeble hiccups. Frequent distractions and memory lapses cause me to fill in missing steps with ones from other dances. Running out of even these, and desperate, I let my body fall into a frenzy of improvised vagaries. When it's over, I drop behind the platform feeling that somehow, in some pathetically weak way, both my solo and I have been raped.

And now Eve's giving birth to twin brothers. They roll forth to opposite sides of the stage, Cain coming to rest at my feet. Taking him under the arms, I guide him up and, as I've done ever since his audition, introduce him to steps of a strange and turgid dance, and I'm thinking, "Cain, baby, I've shown you Lima and Rio and Istanbul, and you've known me well. I'm sensing the care and concern that you're radiating at me. Nicholas, fresh young Gunn, transfer your pep, lend me your youth, give me a helping hand."

Later on, I can't keep my thoughts from straying back to the intensive care ward. I'm hearing Mother say, "Darlin', who's that?"

"He's the cardiologist, Mother."

"Who?"

"You know—for your aorta—the vein man."

Feigning a deep sigh, but more than half-serious, she'd replied, "Aren't they all."

Yes, maybe we were. It had been selfish to say that I wasn't ready for her to die, and now it was taking enormous effort and costing her much pain to postpone what was inevitable. Her courage! It would've been better for me to have said nothing as she gave me that farewell embrace, better to have been silent and given back a smile.

While I wait for my next cue I'm watching Elie. Big, gentlemanly horse is flinging some of the women up into the air as if they're nothing but hay, then catching and guiding each down to a noiseless landing, then exhaling little snorts of happiness. Clearly, he's loving every lift, each stage minute.

His dancing is better than graceful. Besides assurance and a certain something that might be called droll serenity, there's a health, a summer glow, an inner strength like the force in a seed about to burst. As an emblem he's very powerful. And when dancing or not, his graciousness is genuine—not some phony-baloney storybook prince. A combination of genuine gent and classy Hermes. We never talk much, and when we do it's the kind of conversation where you talk to hear the other person's voice, only neither of us can think of much to say. Right now I'd like to go over and muss up his hair so that he'll know how great I think he's doing, and how grateful I am that it's his turn to dance.

But then it's mine.

And when Act II is nearly over, a violin is creaking down to a last long scrape. Bet and I have been making more travesties, skirmishing back and forth, or, as she'd say, schlaging, and finally we've gotten into our last pose. Arms raised with palms pressing into each other's palms, we're tilted precariously toward each other and balanced in the shape of a steeple. Eileen's sitting between us and directly below. She's gathered the corpses of Cain and Abel into her lap and is rocking them to and fro. Having been used as mere tools in the Eternal Battle, the brothers are looking as cast out as a pair of old tennis shoes. Eileen's doing her best to look heroically compassionate. Bet's full of stoic courage. More dead than alive, I'm having doubts about the effectiveness of this final tableau. Dramatically and architecturally, it stinks, but at least it's sapping little of the energy that I'll be needing for Act III.

The violin scrapes on and on. Bet's weight becomes too much for me, and our point of balance begins to shift. Just as we're about to break and topple, I sputter to the wings, "Hey, curtain man, let's get that thing down quick."

Missing us by a hair, the grand drape hits thunderously, sending up a volley of dust. Bet flinches, and, like a misstacked castle of cards, we plummet to the floor, landing with the back of her head in my crotch, my face in her fanny, and the other three tangled somewhere underneath.

Elie's been watching from offstage and darts out to help us up, but I motion him away, both Bet and I too stiff-necked to be pampered.

By the time I'm able to get myself onto my feet it's a relief to find that the others have already gone to their dressing rooms, leaving only the crew to see how long it's taken for me to get up.

"Aha," says Vinnie. "Been muff diving, huh?"

I go to change for Act III. Outside my room I'm having a problem with the door knob when someone else opens it from the inside. This time, Judy, Harvey Lichtenstein, and two or three others are in my room. Harvey's who hired us. Once a classmate of mine at Juilliard, he'd soon decided to give up dancing and has now found his true talent as head administrator at the Brooklyn Academy. He's wearing one of his swell suits and isn't smiling his usual big smile. Judy's looking even glummer. Evidently, she's told him that I'm not well, and he and some of his staff are there to try to get me to call off the performance.

Sure enough, after some very kind words about how I've been dancing, Harvey comes around to telling me that he's worried about my health and that they all think that I should stop.

Some nerve, I'm thinking. He and his cohorts should get back out front and count heads or whatever they do. It wouldn't surprise me if they've hidden my Act III costume.

I ask Harvey what stopping would mean financially. He says that's not the point, so I ask Judy. She tells me that by cancelling, our company would lose six thousand per performance, forty-two thousand for the whole week. I tell Harvey that there's no understudy for me and that I'll be deeply in debt if I don't dance. He and the others go on trying to talk me out of it, but I'm not listening. My mind's programmed to finish. Louder than anyone's voice, ticks from the clock on my dressing table are telling me that intermission is almost over. I say that *The Flood* is going to be the best part, that they have to get out and let me change. They leave reluctantly.

At first my black coat and minister's collar are nowhere in sight, but then I spot them on the back of the door exactly where I've hung them. I try to put on a dry pair of tights backwards, then get them right. I'm having serious doubts about lasting much longer and frantically trying to get my thumbnail between the tiny clasps of my pillbox. The lid pops open. The damned box is empty.

Fetuslike I curl up on the cot with a vague hope of becoming catatonically locked there. Nothing happens. Maybe if I could take a short snooze . . . but there's no sleep. The present is claiming me, and there's only unrelieved fear and nothing happening except the intercom blaring, "Dancers onstage—places, please."

The guillotine curtain lifts and Eileen begins to dance. As I watch from behind Noah's helm, I have no idea how I'm going to be able to hold it over my head, turn it upside down, and convert it into the Ark. Merely thinking about the effort brings on a muscle spasm in my back, and the cramps grow. Knowing that an audience is listening helps to stifle a scream that rises in my throat. Gradually the tension dissolves, and I'm aware, almost gratefully, of lesser discomforts—the clammy, wet costume, the blurred vision, the shortness of breath.

I begin to dance with Mrs. Noah, then Noah's three children. For me there's such noise and such confusion that it seems a miracle I'm still on my feet.

My pulse is racing faster than the music's tempo. Indiscriminately, musical accents fall on or between the intolerable pains shooting up from my stomach and ankle. It doesn't enter my head to pray. My mind's washed vacant by fear, and long fits of trembling run through my body as I stumble through mangled patterns. Enough presence of mind remains for me to face upstage each time I need to wipe away blinding tears.

While dancing a sermon to erring son Shem, my tongue's gotten caught between my teeth, and I'm not sure that I haven't lost the tip of it. My breath comes chokingly and my lungs are unable to absorb enough oxygen, the air itself too thick to breathe. Blood from my ulcers rises to join the blood that already fills my mouth. There's no discreet way to get rid of it, so I close my eyes, swallow, and continue to dance.

An accidental fall sends me to the floor, where the impact erupts in a geyser of flame and sound. When I struggle to my feet, my ears are as though packed with cotton and the boards are left smeared with sweat.

The frequency of continual accidents is appalling. One moment a step is almost right, and the next it's snuffed out like an insect. No courage, no skill, no strength could make an iota of difference. I pin my faith on the clock's slow progress toward the final curtain and endure, inept and insignificant.

Finally the solo's over and I'm back behind Noah's helm. Slowly, internally, I prevent my muscles from locking by alternately flexing and relaxing them. At the brink of unconsciousness I'm thinking that if I'm going to faint, it'll be now. By contrast the pain is more noticeable than when I was moving, the sources easier to locate, and it's arrowing straight ahead like an endless highway.

Tightening my grip on the helm to keep from falling, I notice that my scraped palm has again opened and is leaving the white-enameled spokes streaked with red.

As Eileen dances by, she whispers, "Shall I go tell them to bring in the curtain?" I don't answer—to let her know that I've even heard the question would be demeaning, an admission of defeat. I increase my efforts to dance and then, with surprising detachment, find myself suddenly able to look down on the dance as if I were no longer involved in it. On one side of the stage I see the gaping faces of the semicircularly grouped Noah children, each horrified at my state but not knowing what to do about it. On the other side the two angels stand a little apart from each other, Bet's eyes frozen on me but unseeing. Eileen's are unseeing and hysterical. Sitting in the glow that's spilling from the stage is a front row of gleaming faces—merry folks who are blissfully unaware that things aren't going quite as planned. They and the rest of the audience are out there laughing. *Laughing!*

Never in all the out-of-town performances had Noah been half so funny. For a while it seems that what I'm going through might be worth the effort, but not for long. It soon strikes me that it should be perfectly clear that at any second I'm going to die, die stage center, give up the ghost right in front of everybody. That would be much too public for so private an act. It seems impossible that the audience's reaction is actually occurring. Adult human beings of the civilized world couldn't be so hardhearted. There's been a mistake that should be corrected before it's too late. Possibly, I should gesture for the music to stop, then explain the situation. Even halfwits can be reasoned with.

Suddenly a new type of pain comes from somewhere below. A single blast travels up my spine and explodes in my skull. The type is familiar, and it seems not worth the effort to look down to find out which toe's been stubbed.

I throw back my head and, up in the flies, glimpse the soles of a stage-hand's roughshod feet. He's standing on an overhead grid, and above him spreads what seems to be a dome of unending darkness. Light years beyond that, the cold glint of a solitary star pierces a small, uneven rent at the apex of the opera house roof. The star is impossibly distant, implacable, a wrenchingly immortal star, and the sight of it fills me with envy, resentment; and then I'm hit by an overwhelming tide of hate at the unfairness of things here below, where corruption outwits and topples our temple-bodies, and I'm able to imagine what it might be like to plunge the pitchfork through the twisting torso of my Great Puppeteer.

Little by little, what reason is left forces me to understand that this is as far as I'm to dance. I relay the message to my feet, but they've gone deaf and, out of pure rote, continue their senseless attempts. The drop from the apron to the pit looms dangerously near.

Suspended for a fractional moment at the peak of a minuscule jump where the whole weight of the night seems to be a dam about to burst and drown me, I've become utterly helpless. Once a useful friend, gravity is now the seductive enemy. To object or fight it is like shouting into a storm that tears the words from the corners of your lips before you can hear them. Hanging limply, I'm caught between a tantalizing sensation of weightlessness and gravity's unconquerable pressure.

Events of the past seem to have marched inevitably, tritely, toward this place of suspension. My dancers, me, the audience, everyone everywhere, all of us are nothing but dying leaves cast into rushing currents, drawn ever nearer toward the black vortex of a mysterious whirlpool. Pictures from the past are swirling by. An unforgettable one that Babe had once drawn for me: an icon stick figure representing himself as a singer—voiceless George happily exuding from his mouth a cartoon balloon filled with broken notes. Other images float by, pictures thrown up on a teeming shore. Trash. Wretched refuse.

And while the audience laughs, part of me is laughing too—maybe at comic-strip Babe, my old pal who's always been a heartbreaking comedian, and I'm smiling at folly in general, at everything and everyone, at all that I've ever known and cared about. What I've always held most dear now seems pathetically, hilariously insignificant, yet brilliantly foolish, and all communication through words, dance, pictograms, through any means whatever, is no longer possible. Indeed, seems never to have existed.

Images surfacing, then swirling at the whirlpool's lip, never to be seen again, all vanishing with finality as though being flushed down the drain of a great black toilet.

Clearly, this Noah was never meant to reach Ararat. Instead of earthly Eden, stillness lies ahead, shining there like an ingot of gold. The coming silence will be an angel's song.

Not counting intermissions, I've been trying to dance nonstop for nearly an hour and a half and, with barely more than four minutes of the dance to go, have almost come to the end of a last solo of evangelistic fury over the antics of Noah/Lucifer's animalistic children. Somehow, I've been able to plow through an indeterminate space filled with molten lead, but now my body has itself become a leaden blob. At the edge of unconsciousness I'm hovering there, no longer caring in any way about life, only wanting to witness the curtain's close. Teetering, suspended limply, my arms are lifting high overhead as if death were a voluptuous dive into the depths. Slowly, in a dreamlike trance, so slowly, Lucifer begins his fall from grace. Though the drop takes only a second, the watery walls on the way to Hades seem to inch by.

I know nothing but that the dance is not over and that I should not be falling. All other thoughts and emotions have withered away. Body has lost all power of movement. An inner light board is failing, and sharp, short flickers alternate with total blackouts. The floor is creeping upwards and there is no way to hold it back. I'm locked at last, shackled, caged, am being sucked languidly down. There's nothing left except to wait out the descent.

Like a sleepwalker's, my hand stretches out to touch the hardness of the slowly rising boards, which in turn accept it in the same way that a mushrooming pillow swallows a nodding head. At the end there are no flames, no explosions, only a single distant throb and then the vast comfort of nothingness.

I never heard the curtain's final thump.

Afterwards

As consciousness seeps back, I'm trying to understand what's happened. Am feeling drenched and can vaguely remember sinking through water. Unpleasant jarrings are forcing my breath into a succession of fast gasps—artificial respiration? Have I dived from a starting block, made an imperfect entry, hit my head on the bottom of the pool, and been fished out? If so, someone disrespectful is being too rough. After all, even when champ swimmers lose, they've worked hard and deserve to recuperate gently in their own sweet time. As Coach Webster says, it's not the winning, it's how you swim the race. But he and the team would've been counting on my best. Besides being waterlogged, I'm now shriveling with mortification. I open my eyes and see two policemen, one in front and one in back. They're rushing me off on a stretcher. Too groggy to deal with this unexpected new setup, I lapse back into unconsciousness.

It isn't until after arriving at the emergency ward of a Brooklyn hospital that I completely come to. While Judy, Harvey, and some other friends are waiting with me for a doctor to come, they express their concern and try to ease my embarrassment by telling me that after my blackout Bet had circled me with a frantic but sincere little improvisation.

"Oh no, that must've been awful, too," I say. "But at least she filled out the last of the music?"

"Not quite," Judy replies. "There were about three minutes of it left. I was watching from the wings and worried sick, and then Eileen started waving frantically to me from the opposite side of the stage, so I cued the curtain in. I would've done it sooner, but none of us felt that we should make the decision for you. Afterwards I went out in front of the curtain and announced that due to you being indisposed, the dance's ending was having to be omitted."

"Gee, Judy," I moan, "maybe if you hadn't said anything, the audience would've thought Noah's collapse was part of the plot."

Harvey agrees, reasoning that my untraditional interpretations of Bible stories had prepared everybody for almost anything. "Charlie was the only one I know of who noticed anything unusual," he says. "He at first thought that you looked looser these days, then realized what was really happening and freaked out."

"While I was making the announcement," Judy continues, "Elie was carrying you to your cot. Swooped you up like a feather, according to

Carolyn. Your dressing room was so quickly swamped with people that the dancers and I couldn't get to you. I asked Harvey to phone an ambulance, but I guess they were all busy because, only some cops in a paddy wagon came."

A doctor finally arrives, gives me an EKG, and recommends that I stay in the hospital for several days. I'm worried that more tests might reveal all the Dexamyl that I've been taking, so I insist on going right home.

The next day, since I'm still feeling extremely weak, I phone Judy to tell her that we'll have to cancel that night's performance but that I'm intending to finish up the run and will do the others. She says that everybody thinks I should stay in bed. I tell her I'd like to, but can't because of the financial loss.

Hauling myself back to the opera house, I manage to get through the six remaining performances. They aren't exactly my greatest. Hardly a night goes by when I don't leave out some steps or fall, but I'm able to get up and finish each time.

Passing out has convinced me that continuing to rely on Dexamyl would eventually mean the end of my dancing days or worse. (The medical profession at this time was unaware that the drug is dangerous and highly addictive, but it was soon to be taken off the market.) During the week, although I try, I'm unable to quit cold turkey but am able to taper down to two or three pills a night rather than the usual handfuls. Cold sweats, shakes, and other withdrawal symptoms are thought by the company to be a case of flu—an assumption that I prefer not to contradict. The hepatitis is yet to be diagnosed, and the ulcers continue to bleed.

The reviews are fairly favorable. Before they go on to evaluate *Genesis*, space is devoted to my collapse—much more than I feel comfortable with. Bet, Eileen, Carolyn, Elie, and Nick are singled out for praise, and considering the strain that they've been under due to concern for me, the praise is doubly deserved.

Soon after the season ends, the hepatitis is diagnosed. I go to bed and remain there, or close by it, for nine weeks. During this time I'm able to completely kick the Dexamyl habit. It's a period of extreme jitters, edginess, and deep depression. Small, ordinary routines of daily living are hard to cope with. I'd become dependent on the pills for performing and giving lecture/dems; for other things, hardly ever, and so not having to dance or speak publicly lessens the temptation to backslide. But mostly I'm able to kick the habit by realizing that if I don't, it may kill me. For years after I quit, like a dried-out alcoholic's, occasional cravings suggest that the habit is only sleeping. Ever since then, except for coffee and cigarettes, I haven't dared to go near anything remotely connected with drugs.

After Brooklyn, in June, the company performs at the American Dance Festival in New London, which Charlie is directing. Though back on my feet, I haven't entirely recovered from the hepatitis, and so I transfer the parts that I would've been dancing to Elie and Nick. If I were to dance in New London, it would be on the anniversary of my debut on that same stage as a student twenty-two years before. However, since I'm not intending to stop, such a well-rounded finish isn't to be.

My parts are meant to be only on loan; dancing is still everything. A life without it would leave precious little and is unthinkable. But, even so, I'm beginning to get the idea that my body, this house I live in, this well-oiled machine that's always been quick to carry out my commands—possibly, just possibly, it might be cranking down? Yet even if it is, stopping is a notion to fight off.

When dancing my roles, Elie and Nick aren't able to do them exactly as I did, but their energy and individual traits pretty much make up for the differences. Watching them rehearse, I begin to grasp the fact that if a dance is well crafted, it can withstand a multitude of interpretations. Anyway, the point isn't that my roles be danced the way I dance them but that they be brought to life in a way suitable to Elie or to Nick. Accordingly, I replace a few of the steps with more appropriate ones. Bet, a stickler for maintaining dances in their pristine form, isn't too pleased with the changes at first but eventually comes around.

After New London the troupe goes to Lake Placid in upstate New York, where we're to spend eight weeks giving weekend performances and working on new pieces and revivals.

Since it's expected for the hepatitis to take several months to go away, my doctor's told me not to dance and says that the less I move, the better; but he says it's all right to choreograph—if I can do it while seated in a chair. He's also put me on a strict ulcer diet and told me that if I don't stay on it, he'll have to operate, which is something he'd rather not do. According to X-rays, my duodenum is so layered with scar tissue that he feels an operation would be too risky.

During the summer residency we present eight programs, a different one each weekend. This requires us to have more pieces in the rep than we've ever needed before. Besides transferring my parts, I add ten revivals. The two new pieces are *Sports and Follies* and *Quartet.*

Choreographing from a chair is something completely foreign and at first seems impossible, but then I remember that the crippled Doris Humphrey did it, and so, instead of demonstrating steps as I've usually done, I try teaching them to the dancers by using words, gestures, and expressionistic little noises (*sssst, whumph, tic tic tic,* and so forth), most of which the dancers respond to in short order. Although I don't always come up with the perfect vocalizations, having worked together for so long has made the dancers and me almost able to read each others' minds. In fact, they even seem to know what's going on in mine before I do. They're freed from my sometimes useless efforts to get them to do the steps as I do, less learning time is spent, and the new steps usually look better than ones first made on my own body. After all, I'm not creating vehicles for myself to dance and wouldn't want to disappoint people who keep punning about Taylor-made dances, or as some wise guy once said, Taylor-made dancers.

While the company is working at Lake Placid (placid enough for me, but Lake Beaver to the others), Judy gives notice. She's accepted an offer from Harvey Lichtenstein to be his assistant at BAM. Having been with us for eight years, first as stage manager, then as general manager, and having administered both positions with as much devotion, expertise, and atten-tion to detail as anyone could, she now feels a need for new challenges. Her departure is a serious loss, not to mention being an emotional jolt. How-ever, she's been training Neil Fleckman, her assistant, who's also fond of the company and who now takes over for her. On leaving, she consents to serve on the company's newly formed board of directors as an advisor and also becomes the executor of my will. (Croaking in Brooklyn has impressed me with the possibility of perishability.) But losing Judy is offset by a happier departure—by the end of the summer the hepatitis is gone.

Richard Barr then offers to present the dancers and me in *American Genesis* and another program, featuring *Aureole*, at the Alvin Theater in October. After nearly five months of not dancing, and with only a few weeks to get myself back in shape, it doesn't seem likely that my performances will be up to par. A better plan might be to postpone the season, but the theater isn't available later, and Dick feels that the troupe won't draw well enough at the box office without me onstage. As further insurance against loss, he asks me to invite Rudolf Nureyev to appear with us as guest artist dancing my role in *Aureole*, something that Rudolf has generously done before in London and Mexico City. Though grateful for his past performances, in general I've never been especially enthusiastic about having guest artists, but, seeing the financial advantages, I ask him and he accepts.

Always a fan of Rudolf's, both onstage and off, I've enjoyed working with him. The spunky way he sails into my dances (the first modern ones he tried) is admirable, and he works hard, is brave in the face of adversity, has unquestionable star quality, flamboyance, and magnetism. However, prob-ably because of a basic difference of approach between modern and ballet dancers, so far I haven't been completely successful in getting him to dance my dances in a way that suits both of us. It's my opinion that if he could take about a year off from his grueling performance schedule to study modern techniques, he'd be sure to come a lot closer to the style. But audiences have never complained, so why should I?

The season at the Alvin comes off all right, and Rudolf generates enough income from his two performances there to allow Richard to just about break even.

Rudolf's rendition of *Aureole* has been very popular. I haven't been able to get back in shape, and my dancing has been less than tops, but I've lost weight, haven't fallen even once, and have managed to do it all without dexies. Even so, something has dampened my appetite for dancing. The season has been a chore, mere rote to be gotten through. I've begun to reassess my own abilities, to question the things that I've always aimed for in my dancing—internal concentration, a certain intended distance, various shadings of rhythmic and dynamic texture. Were they what the folks out front really wanted to see? And though my stage presence is still operative, and most of my technique, the inescapable fact is that I'm over the hump. I've seen dancers of a previous generation, even contemporaries, go on performing past their prime, and there's nothing tempting me to do likewise.

And so the season turns out to be my last. Not like in Brooklyn—it's really the last. I haven't made any definite plan to stop, but, somehow or other, something has run its course. I just never get around to getting back on.

Aureole, the dance that caused me to decide to take on the responsibilities of a full-time company, first enabled the dancers and me to visit nearly every corner of the globe, a piece that for quite a while was our bread and butter, has been the last dance on the last program. I couldn't have ended up my dancing days with a better friend.

Two years later, in '76, it's not my dancing but the company that's done for, or nearly so. Bob Yesselman has just become our new business manager. The dancers and I are back for a third summer at Lake Placid, working on a new dance, *Polaris*, with marvelous music by Don York. When Bob calls from New York to tell me that a long South American tour has just been cancelled by our South American booker and that we're left without income, have salaries to pay, absolutely nothing in the kitty and no future income in sight. I pass up seeing the premiere of *Polaris* and hop on the first plane to New York City.

There seems to be no solution to the financial problem and nothing to do except send out a press release announcing that the company is disbanding. John Holmes, a Wall Street investment counselor, reads of it, fortunately, then generously volunteers to reorganize our board and be its president.

Patrick Hayes of the Washington Performing Arts Society, longtime sponsors, arranges for us to give a benefit performance which brings in enough
to put us in the black, and we're back in business.

Since then, the company has had a few similar close calls, but none as
close; yet, like other nonprofit organizations, we still have to depend on
donations, determination, and good luck.

Aureole gave a rounded finish to my dancing, and now, like a revolving door
opening to both the past and the future, it was cueing me about what was
to come. Without realizing it at the time, I'd benefited greatly from transferring that role and others. When seeing the troupe from out front at the
Odéon, although that wasn't a particularly pleasant experience, I eventually
accepted the fact that they could hold the stage without me. I also saw that
parts of my roles hadn't transferred well and so, from the chair in Lake
Placid, began to work within a movement vocabulary that was more easily
transferable, thereby enabling the works to survive the cast changes that
would inevitably occur; and when making up steps, I began to choreograph
directly on the dancers' bodies. The movements were meant to suit them
yet weren't geared to their idiosyncrasies. Within limits, it seemed a good
idea to take advantage of the dancers' individualities by giving steps that
they would naturally excel in, or if their range was to be given a chance to
broaden, by presenting ones unnatural to them but more of a challenge. At
that point both the dancers and the dances began to look better.

After I stopped dancing, the touring was pretty much over for me. There
was no longer any reason for me to be on the road—the dancers needed no
supervising, were disciplined and, with Bet's help, meticulous about keeping their performances fresh and the dances tidy.

Yet in a sense I'd still be traveling. That is, making dances could be a
journey—a studio journey, but adventurous, and one that required just as
much daring and stamina, filled just as much need. No, not need—that was
something I thought had driven me, but somewhere along the line it had
been left behind. Now things were different. Dances were no longer made
out of necessity, or to prove anything, but because that was what was left
that I knew how to do, and because of time, an old adversary. But, still, the
strongest reason was that the act of making dances brought me happiness.
A new life lay ahead, another focus. Now that I wasn't dancing, I'd be able
to channel my energy and concentrate on choreography.

"Right, Doc?"

"One presumes so. Although no longer an aerial agent to outer space, not
to mention being the most bedeviled jumper of all time, it now seems likely
that you will be able to unclog your creative, ahem, juices. If so, your

choreographic conceits should billow and bloom. In each new work no past flaws will arise, all graceless movements eschewed when espied. Brilliant reforms will flower forth flaringly, all as infectious as sweet tsetse flies. Clearly, my boy, we are now free to go from feculence to fecundity. . . ."

For quite a while, to me all else but dancing had been twaddle. Aspects of dancing that enabled me to dance—the booking, the packaging, the ticketing—these were necessary evils, and as unexciting to me then as they are now. Today it's the dance making that brings excitement. The rehearsing in itself is everything and is its own reward. Even seeing the completed dances for the first time onstage isn't as thrilling as working in the studio. Today each dance is a new beginning, a new place to discover; and though each one may be related to a past one, at some point in the making, if I'm lucky, it shows me its own special face, though it's not always in the country that I had expected it to be. Like an unexpected change of itinerary, it takes me over its own particular terrain. Yet what one dance may have pointed out to me is of no help in the making of another. Most begin as a swamp; all pose a danger of slippery footing. The only firm ground seems to be a certain craft that I've learned by trial and error, handy to fall back on—a roller to help squish the path dry. But craft is never the heart of the matter. No craft, however finely honed, can disguise a passionless base—that is, if the dance doesn't come from a particular and vivid place, my craft can't rescue it.

Strangely enough, the best places that new dances take me can usually be traced back to things in the past that have already left an imprint and are being revisited, continuations of paths or patterns that started in childhood, or maybe even much earlier, and which repeat themselves in different forms without me realizing it until later. For when I'm at work nothing else exists. It seems to me that my ability is not one of inspiration but one of focus—a knack for screening out anything that doesn't have to do with the subject at hand. It's something that I've always been able to do for long periods of time, several days and nights if need be. Admittedly, I sometimes have to lie down and take short naps, but then, if I can remember where my half-sleeping mind led me, the naps are often as beneficial as being awake. Phantom passions are the butterflies that are sometimes netted, then released to flit through the work.

Although very little distracts me when at work—not pneumatic hammerings outside, not fire inspections, not frigid radiators—sometimes the dancers can be disruptive. Instead of being passive objects to mold, they have an exasperating habit of making their presences known. I don't really mean "exasperating," for their individualities and strong senses of identity are the very things that bring me much pleasure in doing a job that otherwise

would be a solitary one. But then, on third thoughts, sometimes the dancers are a *bit* distracting—when their birthday parties hold up rehearsals. It's
then that I'm usually reminded by the ancient adversary that hours, years,
life spans, all dancing times, have a way of scooting by.

The company started from nothing and then, like Topsy, it just grew. In '54
(thirty-three years ago), with no vision for the future, and only as a means
to get myself onstage, I corraled a small number of acquaintances and began
to give concerts. Back then there were no grants, no organization, no
packaging, and no one to consult for guidance (in retrospect we can skip old
Doc's questionable advice). Except for a collegiate flash of mine which had
pointed out a direction to take, I had no idea of how to get there and no
inkling as to how to form a company, even if I'd wanted one. There was only
an appetite for dancing, and an attitude that had to do with taking days one
at a time, and a naive belief that there were no obstacles or riddles that
couldn't be solved by ignoring them. Out of that, everything else has come
as a by-product.

As I glance back, it's amazing to me that this company not only has
survived but seems to have arrived at a relatively secure level of existence,
and that a person like me, one with no artistic background to speak of, can
come this far as a dancer and maker of dances. Sure, there have been many
lucky breaks, and the faculty of a trusted eye, but, all in all, the whole
bootstrap operation seems incredibly romantic to me, an American dream,
and not a little corny.

When I think back, most of my past seems unreal, yet even so, it seems
to bring, well, a kind of a benediction. Liverpool, the BAM bummer,
etc.—all those vicissitudes I see as being beneficial. They helped me win a
renunciation of a charismatic view of self, and a redemptive view of my
work, and showed me that a new sense of life could be made on the bodies
of others. The downers helped me to discover the difference between a
need and a calling, and to realize that ongoing changes of communicative
style, continuing utilization of the faculties that have been given me, are
what I'm made for, not impossible, over-the-rainbow consummations.

That this book has dealt mainly with the troupe's beginnings, its early
tours, some of the private and public bumps encountered while I traveled
a many-segmented path, and is now stopping without describing in detail
what has come, is because I feel that beginnings are usually more interesting to read about than the repetitious scenery that usually follows a successful arrival. Not that I've got anything against success, but, as I've said,
being able to work is the largest of my rewards, is still plenty exciting, and
has brought unexpected bonuses. And, since I'm proud of them, and since

mentioning a few may help give an upbeat ending to the preceding chapters, I hope no one will object to a recent list of assorted names:

Master Taylor (honorary degrees from Duke, and Connecticut College, and Syracuse)
Sir Paul (a knighthood from the French Government)
Commandre (also from there, and classier)
Fellow Fellow Fellow (three-time Guggenheim grantee)
Sammy boy (Sam Scripps/American Dance Festival award)
Mr. Smarts (headiest of all—a MacArthur grant).

". . . And, Sonny, speaking of happy endings, as much as it pains me to say so, you have written a Great Book. Just as I have done with my twenty-two-volumed autobiography, it is in the grand tradition of Wordsworth's *Prelude* or Carlyle's *Sartor Resartus*. Alas, would I be as fortunate as you in having a publisher. Might your editor Bob Gottlieb of Knopf, Inc., be interested in my manuscript? I shall reimburse you for the derrick, whatever the costs may be."

"Sure, Pops, I'd be glad to. You know, it takes one to know one, but I guess you aren't such an old jerk after all."

"Precisely. And now would be as good a time as any to reiterate blessings—by not dancing, our position as troupe leader has been strengthened. The relationship between the dancers and us, the one that grew from being pressed together intimately on the road (although often not intimately enough), has always blurred the boundaries between boss, father, disciplinarian, and chum—I mean, how could anyone know where one of us began and the other started? But at present things have gotten clearer, perhaps because of differences in your rapidly changing age, or your increasing bulk, or whatever. Anyway, today the dancers are more responsive than before, since they no longer feel like echoes of us, and now they speak to the audience in their own tongues. But worry not, sonny boy, we shall still be telling them what to say, and should they stutter, they can always seek a therapist. And another blessing is . . . mercy, for Pete's sake, wake up!"

Nobody's home. I'm revisiting the past, floating backwards to a mild afternoon in '74, not all that long after I stopped dancing. The gang and I are beginning a new dance—

"Okay, dancers, you all here? Startin' time! Eileen and Elie, you stand here in front. Ruthie, honey, you go stand between them. Carolyn, you gold mine, go over there by Nick. The rest of you can spread out in another line in back. New sprout, or whatever your name is, stay on the sidelines and follow along as best you can. All right, troops, from where you are let's run the sequence we set yesterday—you know, the tricky part with all those walking patterns. No, not you, Bet—you'll be in a slow section later. Oh, by the way, from now on you're going to double as dancer and rehearsal mistress. Till we get to your section, can you make me some coffee? And then please ask Babe to come here. I meant to tell him that since he's to be our official studio supervisor, he can quit his job at Poly Print. And then you can answer some of those pesty letters that keep coming from misguided souls who're always asking Tacet to design their costumes."

"Oh, Paul, why can't you answer them yourself? I have needlepoint to do, and then I've got to help the dancers clean up all those crazy catch steps you've been making."

"Auntie Bet, dear old dear, let's not start with the excuses. Our scrapping might embarrass the new sprout. Oh yeah, I keep forgetting to tell every-body—hey, you all, the name of this here dance is going to be *Esplanade*. Okay? Now let's get started. Ready, set, *and* . . ."

Index

PHOTOGRAPHIC CREDITS

A NOTE ON THE TYPE

This book was set in Caledonia, a type face designed by William Addison Dwiggins (1880–1956) for the Mergenthaler Linotype Company in 1939. Dwiggins chose to call his new type face Caledonia, the Roman name for Scotland, because it was inspired by the Scottish types cast about 1833 by Alexander Wilson & Son, Glasgow type founders. However, there is a calligraphic quality about Caledonia that is totally lacking in the Wilson types.

Dwiggins referred to an even earlier type face for this "liveliness of action"—one cut around 1790 by William Martin for the printer William Bulmer. Caledonia has more weight than the Martin letters, and the bottom finishing strokes (serifs) of the letters are cut straight across, without brackets, to make sharp angles with the upright stems, thus giving a modern-face appearance.

W. A. Dwiggins began an association with the Mergenthaler Linotype Company in 1929 and over the next twenty-seven years designed a number of book types, the most interesting of which are Metro, Electra, Caledonia, Eldorado, and Falcon.

Composed by American–Stratford Graphic Services, Inc., Brattleboro, Vermont
Printed and bound by The Haddon Craftsmen, Inc., Scranton, Pennsylvania

Designed by Peter A. Andersen